ROCKY MOUNTAIN
ADVENTURES

FRASER BRIDGES

An On-Route Communications Book

PRIMA PUBLISHING

© 1996 by Fraser Bridges

PRIMA PUBLISHING and colophon are trademarks of Prima Communications, Inc.

Library of Congress Cataloging-in-Publication Data

Bridges, Fraser
  Rocky Mountain adventures / Fraser Bridges.
     p.   cm. — (Road trip adventures)
  Includes index.
  ISBN 0-7615-0225-4
    1. Rocky Mountains—Guidebooks.   2. Automobile travel—Rocky Mountains—Guidebooks. I. Title. II. Series: Bridges, Fraser. Road trip adventures.
F721.B76   1996
917.804—dc20   95-43054
                                           CIP

96 97 98 99 00 01 DD 10 9 8 7 6 5 4 3 2 1
Printed in the United States of America

How to Order:
Single copies may be ordered from Prima Publishing, P.O. Box 1260BK, Rocklin, CA 95677; telephone (916) 632-4400. Quantity discounts are also available. On your letterhead, include information concerning the intended use of the books and the number of books you wish to purchase.

Contents

MONTANA

WYOMING

COLORADO

Using This Travelguide

This book is divided into regional chapters, each covering a state, with the exception of the Canadian Rockies, which are described in the first series of drives.

Each chapter begins with our scenic **Drives**, which explore the most exciting scenic highways and byways in the state. Each drive description includes an overview, which leads to the **Strip Map** and **Highway Log** for the drive.

We've tried to include all of the interesting places along the drive, including picnic parks, campgrounds, fishing spots, walking and hiking trails, and water sport locations.

Following the drive descriptions are **Destinations**, covering the major towns and cities in each state (and the Canadian Rockies area), as well as the great national parks of the Rockies. Here are our recommendations on places to eat and things to see and do. These pages are designed to help you in planning your trip and in deciding what to do and how to budget your time after you arrive at your destination.

Finally, each chapter ends with a listing of **Places to Stay**, with short descriptions of motels, hotels, resorts, inns, lodges, campgrounds, and RV parks for many of the destination towns and cities. Cost ranges (**$ to $$$+**) are included for making reservation decisions, as are telephone numbers and locations.

In preparing this book, I drove more than 30,000 miles and—even then—found that it was just impossible to include every worthwhile scenic location or attraction along the routes. For a first-time traveler on any of the drives, this will be a voyage of discovery that will long be remembered.

Recommendations and Price Ranges

Places to Stay

You'll find a broad selection of places to stay in the travel planning pages, whether you're traveling deluxe or on a tight budget. We have included recommended hotels, motels, inns, lodges, guest ranches, and camping places for the cities and towns.

Price ranges for hotel and motel rooms are based on double occupancy and are marked with dollar signs:

- **Inexpensive:**
  40–65 dollars ($)

- **Moderate:**
  66–100 dollars ($$)

- **Deluxe:**
  101–150 dollars ($$$)

- **Super-Deluxe:**
  Over 150 dollars ($$$+)

Deluxe and super-deluxe accommodations are found in the city hotels and in unique, specialized resort hotels, inns, lodges, and guest ranches. We have included these but have also listed budget inns and resorts that feature housekeeping cabins.

Private campgrounds and RV parks are better equipped than public campsites, almost always with sewer hookups, hot water, showers, flush toilets, water piped to sites, and electrical supply. Prices for government campsites range from $4 to $10 per day. Private facilities run from $10 to $20 per day.

Places to Eat

Locations of roadside cafes and taverns are located in the Highway Logs. We have not included fast-food chains, as these places are easy to spot along the way. Other suggestions for dining are found in the Destinations pages, including places for fine dining, plus cheaper places with local and historical atmosphere.

Introduction

W hat started as a simple trip or two to research the Rocky Mountain highways for this book became much more than that. In the end, my tour of the "spine of the continent" became an odyssey through uncharted territory, resulting in a type of book I had not intended writing and a journey through space and time that amazed and confounded me. As a result, what appears here is a series of drives through the heart of the Rocky Mountain ranges, organized as a series of geographical and historical explorations, which—for me—define the nature of the Rockies. More importantly, these journeys recount the incredible saga of the people who first lived here, the others who explored the region, and still others who journeyed to the Rockies to find adventure or riches, or both, or to find a special kind of peace.

The first three books in this series are straightforward guides that provide a lot of information about Alaska, Canada's North, the vast landscape of British Columbia, and the Northwest Pacific Coast. The Rockies proved to be a different challenge. First, as a Canadian, I had spent some time in the Canadian Rockies—from the Arctic Circle to the U.S. border. But the U.S. Rockies were a new experience, one that would put my earlier Rocky Mountain encounters in a new perspective.

As my travels progressed, I found myself looking into a mirror reflecting the historical mileposts marking the cultural heritage of the Rockies:

- The history of the indigenous peoples of the mountain West, the prehistoric cultures including the Fremont and

Anasazi peoples, and more recently the nomadic tribes (Kootenai, Crow, Cheyenne, Sioux, Arapahoe, and others) who sought shelter between the mountain slopes and traveled widely across the mountain passes to find buffalo on the plains for their food supply.

- The heroism of the early explorers sent to the West to chart new paths to the Pacific Coast.
- The saga of western settlement—the inexorable reaching for new frontiers, and the trouble and tragedy that this brought to the Native Americans and to the nation.
- The daring, and often foolhardy, rush of prospectors, miners, and adventurers into this unknown landscape, filled with great hopes, with some riches gained and even more dreams stifled.
- The settlement of the valley towns by the resilient ancestors of many of the people who now live in the Rockies: ranchers, merchants, saloon-keepers, artists, artisans, and many others who came to the mountain regions to escape the harried urban life.

So what follows is the story of an odyssey that began when I crossed the Nevada/Idaho border and entered the Sawtooths, ending—still in awe of the Rockies—with a tour of the Alberta and British Columbia mountains, near the source of the mighty Fraser River. It was an exhausting journey of more than six months (with a week off now and then), and one that I would not recommend for vacationers. That's why this book is structured as it is: as a series of 38 vacation drives allowing for relaxed interaction with the mountains as well as time for savoring the history and the wonderfully independent people of the Rockies.

Threads of History

. . . hearing a tremendious roaring above me I . . . was presented by one of the most beautiful objects in nature, a cascade of about fifty feet perpendicular stretching at rightangles across the river from side to side in the distance of at least a quarter of a mile . . . the water decends in one even and uninterupted sheet to the bottom wher dashing against the rocky bottom [it] rises into foaming billows of great hight and rappidly glides away, hising flashing and sparkling as it departs.

Meriwether Lewis at the Great Falls
of the Missouri, June 14, 1805

There were three historical migrations through the regions of the American Rockies. All were related to treks, journeys, and expeditions, all of them were dangerous, and all tested the personal mettle of those involved.

The first journey was that of Lewis and Clark, who were directed by Thomas Jefferson to find a usable overland passage to the Pacific Ocean in order to open up the fur trade for America and to establish settlements in country that was controlled partly by Mexico and partly by British fur trading enterprises, particularly the Hudson's Bay Company.

Their dream was to find the fabled Northwest Passage to the Pacific. The same quest for Pacific routes took place in Canada at about the same time, and even earlier. Fur trading companies sent explorers and surveyors by canoe down the great rivers and overland, to establish trading routes through the Rockies and on to the Pacific Ocean. Such explorers as Alexander Mackenzie, Simon Fraser, and David Thompson are legendary throughout the Canadian West and North.

The second great trek through the American Rockies was the flight of Chief Joseph and his Nez Perce people in 1877, escaping the intolerable conditions forced upon them by the federal government. This was a humiliating flight from oppression, which became a tragedy for both the Nez Perce and the Union. Through a winding pilgrimage toward the Canadian border, to what Joseph thought would be sanctuary, the Nez Perce and the army clashed on several occasions, with the Nez Perce winning but barely surviving, until the end and their ultimate defeat a few miles from Canada and safety. Chief Joseph proved to be not only a compassionate man of great wisdom but also the final moral victor in what remains a shameful episode in the history of the continent.

The third migration was the stampede—actually many stampedes—of thousands of easterners across the continent on a continuing quest for gold and silver in the Rocky Mountains and beyond. Following the 1848 gold discoveries in California, the search for precious metals took prospectors into every nook and cranny of the Rockies, and in many cases they were successful in their quest. A few fortunes were quickly made; hundreds of instant mining camps sprang up and just as quickly disappeared when the gold and silver ran out. Some of the camps lasted only a few months, with the gold seekers moving on with word of the next strike. Some of the miners stayed and became the first eastern settlers in the Rockies.

All of these travelers helped to define this vast land of the Rocky Mountains, a region steeped in tumultuous passions and personal privation—a land of triumph and, for many, defeat. Today, the communities of the Rockies share this collective ingenuity and the migrant cultures of the searchers for riches. The current residents are in debt to these travelers who came to the Rockies thirsting for adventure and freedom.

Lewis and Clark and the Quest for the West

We arrived . . . at the most distant fountain of the waters of the Mighty Missouri in surch of which we have spent so many toilsome days and wristless nights. Thus far I had accopmplished one of those great objects on which my mind has been unalterably fixed for many years . . .

Meriwether Lewis, August 11, 1804

Beginning their journey in St. Louis on May 14, 1804, Meriwether Lewis and William Clark found themselves to be compatible travelers. Clark had once been Lewis's commanding officer in the army. Lewis was Thomas Jefferson's private secretary and was thought to be a man who would not only provide leadership for the cross-country journey but would also write a complete journal of the expedition. Could Jefferson have known that Lewis's spelling was so atrocious?

The pair set out with a party of 43 men in a keelboat and two pirogues, sailing up the Missouri River from its confluence with the Mississippi. They crossed the Great Plains by boat—and by foot when necessary—across the Dakotas, where they wintered that first year, setting out again in the spring, this time with French fur trader Joseph Charbonneau and his Shoshone wife Sacagawea as guides. Their infant son, who was born during the winter, went along on the trip. Lewis and a smaller party entered what is now Montana in late April 1805 and arrived at the Great Falls of the Missouri on June 13. Clark and the rest arrived on June 16, making a portage of 18 miles around the falls. The delay getting around the falls provided time for the hunters to bag enough game and fish to feed the party for a few weeks. There were warnings that food was scarce in the mountains; a caution that proved to be an understatement.

By July 25, Clark's advance party reached the Three Forks (of the Missouri) near present-day Bozeman, Montana. The East Fork was named the Gallatin, after the Treasury Secretary, and the South Fork was named the Madison, honoring Secretary of State James Madison. The West Fork was named for President Jefferson. Reaching their third range of mountains on July 31, the party ran out of meat. No buffalo had been seen since they entered the mountains a month earlier. Although the party had been searching for guides who might help them find the route across the mountains, no one was in sight.

Dragging their boats overland, they wandered on, and Lewis reached the Big Hole River on August 4. Deciding that this was not the route to be taken, he left a note on a green willow for Clark, but a beaver chewed the willow down before his colleague arrived. Because of the pesky beaver, Clark's party moved up the treacherous rapids of the Big Hole. Boats turned over and others filled with water before Lewis arrived, and then all retreated to the Jefferson.

On the morning of September 4, the travelers came upon a Flathead village of 33 lodges and 440 people. From the village's 400 horses, Lewis and Clark bought 13, and on September 13 they set out for Lolo Pass, over which they crossed the Rockies once again, and moved into what is now Idaho—Nez Perce country. With no food remaining except what they called their "portable soup" (a very thin mixture), they were forced to eat horses and candles as well as the awful soup.

The Nez Perce were friendly and welcomed them to their villages, giving the travelers food and agreeing to keep their horses until the party returned.

The rest of the trip down the Clearwater, Snake, and Columbia Rivers was uneventful, and in November, they reached the Pacific Ocean near the present-day town of Astoria, Oregon, building a winter fort, which they christened Fort Clatsop after the neighboring Clatsop people.

They spent that second winter on the coast, and on March 26, 1806, the expedition began its return up the Columbia. The return trip to St. Louis was far less hazardous, as they largely returned by the route they had charted over the mountains

They had traveled more than 8,000 miles and found a practicable route to the Pacific Ocean. They discovered and made note of many plants and animals and were friendly with most of the tribes they encountered, earning a solid place in American history.

Little did Clark know when he saw the Big Hole for the second time, that his friends the Nez Perce would, one day in the future, face the revenge and power of Union troops at this very site.

Chief Joseph and the Quest for Freedom

The Cho-pun-nish or Pierced nose Indians are Stout likely men,
handsom women, and very dressy in their way, the dress of the
men are a White Buffalowe robe or Elk Skin dressed with beeds
. . . Some fiew were a Shirt of Dressed Skins and long legins &
Mockersons Painted . . .

William Clark, October 10, 1805

It was the most extraordinary of Indian wars.

General William Tecumseh Sherman

The second historical theme running through much of the Rockies region, in present-day Idaho and Montana, is the tragic story of the Nez Perce, the peaceable Native American tribe that was driven to one warlike act, resulting in tragedy for the tribe and the U.S. Army.

Between May and October 1877, the Nez Perce were involved in what is now considered to be one of the most cruel and unnecessary episodes in Native American history.

From the day of their first meeting with Lewis and Clark, the Nez Perce had been friendly to the explorers and travelers as the West was settled. Composed originally of many independent villages and bands that occupied a vast tract of land, mainly in what is now Idaho, they welcomed missionaries, fur trappers, and settlers to their homelands in the western Rockies and along the great rivers of southwestern Washington, northeastern Oregon, and the north-central portion of Idaho.

When settlers came to the wide river valleys in this area, Washington Territorial Governor Isaac Stevens negotiated a treaty with the Nez Perce, which recognized their right to their homelands and set aside a reservation of 5,000 square miles.

Gold was discovered in the area, and prospectors, settlers, and merchants overran much of the reservation, stealing horses and other livestock and perpetrating other acts of injustice. It became a crisis, and the federal government negotiated again with the

Nez Perce, wanting to reduce the reservation to only a small part of what they had.

A large treaty council, held in 1863, had representation from most of the tribal bands, but some of the bands refused to give up their lands and left the council. Among these leaders was Chief Joseph. The bands that signed the new pact were called "treaty Indians." Chief Joseph and his followers were dubbed "nontreaty Nez Perce."

The nontreaty Nez Perce continued to live on their former lands and insisted on staying, but conflicts arose with the settlers, particularly in the area in northeastern Oregon that had been Chief Joseph's homeland. In May 1877, the Army ordered all the nontreaty peoples to move onto a small reservation. Most of the chiefs did so to avoid conflict, moving to the reservation at Lapwai, Idaho.

Emotions became very strained, particularly among the younger warriors in the nontreaty group. For years, the Nez Perce had calmly taken whatever mistreatment the settlers had meted out. The order to leave their homelands was the last straw. A small group of embittered young warriors rode to the Salmon River and killed several people, avenging past murders of tribal members.

The flight of the Nez Perce began on June 15, 1877.

The nontreaty Indians were pursued by the Army. Chief Joseph and his people hoped to find safety with Crow people who lived on the plains across the Rocky Mountains. However, this plan eventually failed, and the group was forced to continue looking for a new homeland. The Canadian prairies became their destination.

There were 750 in the fleeing group. Only 250 of them were warriors; the rest were mostly women and children, leaving with 2,000 horses. They were involved in a conflict that nobody had wanted, but they were forced to flee because of the rash actions of only a few young warriors and an army that would not understand. The group was outmatched by an army force of 2,000 men augmented by volunteers and even other tribes.

The Nez Perce fought a total of 20 defensive battles and skirmishes along a circuitous route taken through mountain valleys, starting in Idaho with a major battle at White Bird on June 17. They crossed over Lolo Pass and then moved south through the Bitterroot Mountains to Montana's Big Hole, where the Nez Perce rested in an encampment.

Chief Joseph and his people were peacefully gathered on the western edge of the Big Hole when they were ambushed by army forces on August 9 and 10. It was a decisive battle, with the army losing many men and the Nez Perce surviving—but barely. While the army troops did not win the encounter, the number of Nez Perce warriors was greatly reduced, and Chief Joseph had to flee even farther south and then east—across the mountains again— where another skirmish took place on the Camas Meadows on August 20. What was amazing and confounding to the army troops was the canny flight strategy of Chief Joseph, who managed to outwit the army, always staying two days ahead of the troops throughout the flight, being ambushed only when the fleeing people (many of them elderly women) were forced to rest.

Retreating once again, they passed eastward through present-day Yellowstone National Park, getting in the way of a party of tourists, and then moved north into Montana, with another major battle at Canyon Creek—near the Crow Reservation—on September 13. The army continued to pursue, and the Nez Perce made their final, desperate push toward the Canadian border. Another skirmish took place at Cow Island Landing on September 23, but the Canadian border was not far away.

From where the sun now stands, I will fight no more, forever.
Chief Joseph, October 5, 1877

Chief Joseph and his tired band made what was to be their last bid for sanctuary. They were now in the Bear's Paw Mountains, southeast of the present-day town of Havre. The Nez Perce were ambushed on September 30 by new, fresh troops. After several days of conflict, Chief Joseph—tired of it all and fearing for the lives of the few who were left—surrendered to the troops just short of the Canadian border.

The whole sorry episode proves to be one of the great ironies in the relationship between the Native Americans and the U.S. Army. The Nez Perce had been friends and allies since the days of Lewis and Clark in 1805 and 1806. For nearly three-quarters of a century, the behavior of the Nez Perce was free of the warlike traits of many of the other western tribes. This was a peaceful tribe. But they wanted to stay on their familiar, traditional homelands, and the settlers got in the way.

After Chief Joseph's defeat, the surviving nontreaty Nez Perce were banished to exile in Oklahoma, before they were permitted to return to a small reservation in the northwest region.

The flight route is now the Nez Perce National Historic Trail: some of it is abandoned, but much of it is walkable and driveable. It stretches for 1,700 miles, from Wallowa Lake, Oregon, to the Bear's Paw Battlefield, near Chinook, Montana. Along the trail are the sites of the battles, some of them National Historic Landmarks, including the battlefield in Big Hole, Montana. The trail was dedicated in 1986.

In northwestern Idaho—in the area east of Livingston—Nez Perce National Historic Park is a collection of 27 separate sites depicting the long history of the Nez Perce, commemorating several of the battle sites including the battlefield at White Bird. These sites—particularly the Big Hole National Battlefield—offer a poignant reminder of the pitfalls of human "progress" and add a special dimension to a tour of the western U.S. Rockies.

Prospectors and the Quest for Gold

. . . a log city of 150 dwellings, not three-fourths completed nor two-thirds inhabited, not one-third fit to be.

Horace Greeley, Denver, 1859

Much of the pleasure of driving in the Rocky Mountains is visiting the ghost and not-so-ghost towns that sprang to life during the gold and silver rushes of the 1800s. They were founded by a collection of people who are best known for their greed—searching for riches to set them up for the rest of their lives. It is my proposition, however, that the gold rush pioneers were more motivated by a search for adventure than an all-encompassing lust for wealth.

Some were restless young men (and women) from the eastern cities of the young America, who journeyed west to savor the wilderness and to earn a living in an unknown occupation. It sounded so good that they had to do it—much as mountain climbers seek their own personal peaks or astronauts seek the darkness of space. The stories of gold-seeking "Argonauts" of the California Gold Rush in 1849 convinced others of the need to leave their homes and venture into the unknown, to an adventure they would never forget. After California, this search for adventure continued until 1898 with the last of the great gold rushes—in the frozen Klondike of the Yukon.

Nine years after gold was found at Sutter's Mill and the stampede to the Sierra Foothills began, a small group of prospectors from Georgia arrived in Colorado territory. At the foot of the Rockies, they too found gold. It was not much, but it proved enough to cause another stampede to the frontier wilderness. Soon, "Pike's Peak or Bust" became the catch phrase for the hundreds of adventurers who came on horseback, in covered (or uncovered) wagons, and even on foot, pushing wheelbarrows or carrying their few possessions on their backs.

This excitement over gold (and also silver) was not unique to Colorado. The same thing was repeated in all of the mountain regions. Montana, Idaho, Utah, and Wyoming all had their gold and silver stampedes, and the lasting evidence of those rough and ready times is stamped on communities throughout the Rockies.

Leadville, Cripple Creek, and Central City were scenes of gold and silver discoveries, and these towns are among the delightful old mining towns that dot the mountain ranges. The mining towns remaining are just a few of the hundreds that sprang up—virtually overnight. Most were abandoned, disappearing from view within five to ten years. Some lasted only a year as the adventurers moved on to richer finds.

Bonanza and Crestone were little mining camps in Colorado's Saguache County that you can visit by driving along Colorado Route 17 and into the mountains on a backroad. Unlike most of the other mining towns, these two were peaceful places, kept in order by the women of the camps. In the 1880s, the matrons of Crestone became angry when the saloon hired "bar girls" to serve their customers. The doughty ladies marched to the bar and tore it down. Neighboring Bonanza, which boomed from 1880 to 1888, was chronicled by author and Bonanza resident Anne Ellis in her book *The Life of an Ordinary Woman*. In its peak, the community boasted a well-educated population of 5,000. Production stopped in 1915, and now about 20 people live in this near-ghost town.

* * *

Central City is a town that has fared better now as a 19th-century museum piece. It was called the Richest Square Mile on Earth in 1859, after John Hamilton Gregory, another Georgian, discovered gold in a gulch near the site of Central City. Only 34 miles from Denver, Central City soon became the center of commerce and culture for the territory. The rich and famous visited the bustling city. President Ulysses S. Grant strolled over a walkway of silver bars (worth $12,000) leading from the street to the new Teller Hotel. The newly built Central City Opera House brought the greats of the operatic world to the Rocky Mountains. On New Year's Eve during those days, the assembled dined on oysters, black bear, buffalo, cream pastries, and cakes— for the sum of $10 per couple. In 1874 a disastrous fire almost wiped out the town. It was speedily rebuilt, this time with solid brick.

Gregory, who was a penniless prospector when he arrived in the gulch, left Central City several years later with a small fortune. Even though it was located deep in the Front Range, transportation to the city was available and cheap. The rocky stage ride on the Oh My God Road from Idaho Springs cost $1. A one-way train trip from Denver cost $2.65.

While Central City faded as a mining center, the town lived on, with a revival in 1933 when Lillian Gish reopened the Opera House in a performance of *Camille*. Today, the Central City Opera is a thriving institution and is largely responsible for the continued good health of the city, even if it is much reduced in size from its heyday of the 1870s. In recent years, gambling has come to Central City, providing a new focus for visitors.

* * *

Situated at 11,000 feet elevation, in Lake County, the two-mile-high town of Leadville provides views of some of the most impressive of Colorado's "fourteeners," those mountain peaks that rise more than 14,000 feet above sea level. Leadville's cemetery tells many stories of another famous and still lively old mining camp. Spread across the 131 acres of graveyard, wooden headboards tell part of the saga of Leadville's incredible days of the 1870s and 1880s, when it was the richest mining region in the world.

Leadville is the town where Molly Tobin, a young woman from Missouri, married James J. Brown, a miner who had been given a part interest in the Little Jonny Mine. The mine proved to be one of the most productive in Colorado. Profits from the mine took "Leadville Johnny" Brown and Molly to Denver, where Mr. Brown built the famed Brown Palace Hotel. His wife became the "Unsinkable" Molly Brown, the heroine of the Titanic disaster celebrated in the Broadway musical and movie.

Oscar Wilde packed Leadville's opera house on April 14, 1882, when he gave a lecture to the assembled miners and other townsfolk, haranguing the crowd on the ethics of art and reciting passages from the autobiography of Benvenuto Cellini. Wilde got away from the unappreciative audience with his skin barely intact. The author had previously been told that, if he went to Leadville, the locals would be sure to shoot him or his traveling manager. Wilde wrote them back: "Nothing that they could do to my manager would intimidate me." Wilde would later speak about Papa Wyman's Saloon in Leadville and a sign over the bar that stated "Please do not shoot the pianist, he is only doing his best." Wilde said, "This is the only rational method of criticism that I have ever seen."

Henry A. W. Tabor and his wife Augusta arrived in California Gulch, near Leadville, in 1860. Tabor opened several stores in the area—at Oro City, Malta, and finally in Leadville. He was known for giving credit and bartering for goods, and when August Risce and George Hook walked into the Tabor store in 1878, and asked to be grubstaked for some prospecting items. Tabor agreed—for a stake in whatever the men found. This was the beginning of Tabor's wealthy career as part owner of the fabulous Matchless Mine, and he gained a fortune that earned him the title "Silver King." Tabor then had an affair with a young woman named Elizabeth "Baby Doe" and subsequently divorced his wife, causing a scandal that occupied newspapers across the country for months. He served a brief stint as a U.S. senator, but ended his life in poverty. The first Mrs. Tabor—Augusta—lived in luxury in Colorado Springs to the end of her days. Baby Doe froze to death in a small cabin next to the Matchless Mine, several years after Tabor's demise.

Such are the stories of Leadville, and they are typical of any of the mining camps of the Rocky Mountains. The ups and downs of these communities make a tour of the Rockies much more than an outdoors experience. The history of the land is here, complete with tales of avarice, hard work, greed, self-denial, double-crossing, and kindness, combined with high culture, low behavior, and extraordinary triumphs and failures.

It's all here for you to see, and to live.

The Ten Best Places

Peak Experiences

It's difficult to rank all these experiences in the Rocky Mountains, but people seem to want to have the destinations put in some sort of pecking order, and it's my duty to oblige. Including five scenic drives and five destinations, here's a personal Top Ten of the Rockies.

Five Superb Drives

1. Glacier National Park and the Going to the Sun Road

This dramatic 41 miles of park road traverses the northern Montana Rockies, climbing above the tree line between St. Mary at the eastern entrance and the entrance near West Glacier. High meadows, waterfalls, pinnacles, deep valleys with rushing streams—they're all here on this impressive drive.

2. Trail Ridge Road, Rocky Mountain National Park

Like the previous route, this is truly an unforgettable experience, crossing the Continental Divide at 12,183 feet. Starting in the resort town of Estes Park, the route speedily climbs to the top of the mountain ridge above the tree line to vast regions of alpine tundra. You'll look down on deep valleys with fast-flowing streams cascading down the mountainsides and across the valleys to mountain meadows. There's a visitor center at the top, with a short trail leading up the fragile tundra to a scenic viewpoint that provides a panoramic view for miles around and across the Colorado River, with much of the park in view. The town of Estes Park offers a pleasant diversion from the park attractions.

3. San Juan Skyway

This loop drive starts in Durango and leads through the San Juan Mountains, through the old mining towns of Silverton, Ouray, and Telluride, and then south to Anasazi country at Cortez. The tour provides high mountain experiences, resort attractions, scenic byways, hot springs, and exceptionally fine views. The Skyway takes up two of our scenic drives in this book. It offers access to several top backcountry byways, including the famous four-wheel-drive Alpine Loop that climbs through Engineer Pass, linking Lake City with Silverton and Ouray. The Ophir Pass route provides another spectacular backroad drive across the San Juans.

4. Grand Teton Park Road

A drive through the length of this national park is secondary in most people's minds to "doing Yellowstone," the park just to the north. Don't be misled. The Tetons are a wonderful sight, with small, reflective lakes, unparalleled canoeing, the winding Snake River, and the civilized joys of Jackson south of the park. Several winding sideroads take you to scenic overlook points for incredibly fine views of the full range and the Snake River winding its way through the valley. The mountains are reflected in the small valley lakes, making the sunset and sunrise hours a magic time. You can raft or canoe down the Snake, stay and eat at rustic but comfortable lodges (Jenny Lake Lodge is a real delight), or camp in some of the most restful and scenic campsites in the country.

5. The Canadian National Parks

The four joined national parks in the southern Canadian Rockies (Banff, Kootenay, Yoho, and Jasper) offer something for everyone: the most dramatic scenery in the Rockies, millions of acres of wild country, glaciers that you can walk on, wildlife galore, great places to stay and camp, and good highways to drive on. The Trans-Canada Highway leads past Banff and Lake Louise. Each town site has its own special attractions. Busy Banff offers gondola rides to the top of Sulphur Mountain and a soak in the hot spring pool at the base of the gondola. Lake Louise is one of the most scenic spots in all of the Rockies and is probably the most photographed view. The Icefield Parkway leads north from Lake Louise to Jasper National Park, passing the Columbia Icefield, the largest in the Canadian Rockies. The Banff-Windermere Parkway leads through the unspoiled Kootenay River Valley, and the Icefield Parkway takes you beside the Columbia Icefield, the largest chunk of moving ice in the Canadian Rockies, as the route leads north from Lake Louise to Jasper National Park—the largest and wildest of the four parks.

Five Great Towns

1. Durango

Our favorite of all the communities of the Rockies, sitting at the bottom of the San Juan Range, Durango is a cowtown and a historic city that reflects the influence of its three founding cultures: Native American, Spanish, and north European miners and railroaders. The Durango and Silverton Narrow Gauge Railway offers one of the finest scenic train rides on the continent, and the antique hotels and inns in Durango provide wonderful historic places to stay. It's hard not to be enchanted by this city.

2. Telluride

This gold mining town turned ski and summer resort is an unlikely combination of chic wealth and laid-back post-hippie ambiance, with a wonderfully historic main street. Telluride's summer festival season includes chamber music, jazz, an internationally renowned film festival, the Wild West Week, and many more. The views from the top of the ski hill are superb, in winter or summer. Two Forest Service recreation sites just south of town offer scenic places to camp—an alternative to the increasingly pricey and super-deluxe resorts that have developed in recent years.

3. Ouray

A perfect little Victorian town in Colorado's San Juan Range, with jeep tours and fine dining (the hot spring pools aren't hard to take, either). The community lies at the northern end of the Million Dollar Highway, part of the San Juan Skyway loop drive. This stretch of road was literally built with gold (low-grade ore) linking the town with neighboring Silverton. The backroads in this area are historic mining trails, and you can rent a jeep or take a jeep tour to the high, alpine gold, and silver ghost towns.

4. Bigfork

A diminutive resort town on Montana's Flathead Lake, Bigfork is close to Glacier National Park and the Bob Marshall Wilderness. Fishing, golfing, a summer arts season, and superlative hiking trails are all available. The Jewel Basin Nature Area provides easy (and more strenuous) walks and hikes, and the town is filled with antique shops, crafts and art galleries, with a summer musical-comedy theater season and good places to stay and eat.

5. Liard Hot Springs

This isn't even a town. It's an Alaska Highway lodge with the finest natural hot spring pools on the continent, in a unique setting at the northern end of the Rockies—just south of the Yukon border, in British Columbia. The two pools are protected in a provincial park, and when you walk to the pools over a boardwalk, you'll see steaming hot water and tiny, transparent fish that thrive in the year-round heat of the marsh. You'll also see and enjoy talking to people who come here from around the world to soak in this superb natural environment. The pools have created a unique ecosystem, which includes plants that shouldn't be growing so far north and several species of orchids. The pools are particularly atmospheric after dark and early in the morning.

Canada

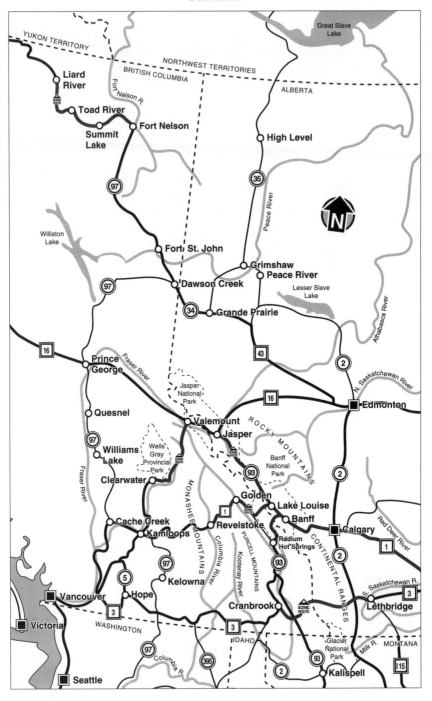

Canada
Drives

They're not the tallest, nor do they cover a wide swath. The Canadian Rockies consist of a narrow stretch of peaks, while the United States ranges spread across more than a hundred miles in Colorado. However, because of the relatively low altitude of the surrounding territory, the Canadian Rockies provide the most impressive scenery of all of the ranges that form the Continental Divide in Canada and the U.S.

Our Canada drives run from just north of the Canadian border through the Elk Valley to the rugged country along the Alaska Highway—as far north as the Yukon boundary.

Along the way, the Rockies offer a backdrop for Canada's best-known national parks, Banff and Jasper. But other nearby parks also deserve attention. The following drives are organized to provide a tour of these relatively unknown parks, including Kootenay National Park (straddling the Alaska/British Columbia border) and Mount Robson Provincial Park in northern B.C. The latter is home to Canada's tallest peak, which towers over a pristine setting that defies description.

As with all 38 scenic drives in this book, the routes in Canada can be driven in one day—most in half a day. But this isn't the point of touring in the Rockies, because these mountain highways offer many diversions to occupy your time and scenic attention. Each drive is the basis for a trip that could last a day or a week. Put several drives together and you have a full vacation of several weeks' duration.

The Canadian Rockies have won a special entry on my list of places to visit, and I hope they will find a similar spot on your list.

Crowsnest Drive

Lethbridge to Cranbrook

This east-west drive leads from the heart of Alberta dinosaur country into the southern Canadian Rockies through the historic Crowsnest Pass, ending in British Columbia's Kootenay Region. The name of the pass comes from the old Cree name *Kab Kacoo-wut-tskis-lun,* the "Raven's Nesting Place."

The route is dotted with coal mining operations that have been here since the early 1900s, when the Canadian Pacific Railway (CPR) constructed its southern track through the mountains to exploit the rich mineral finds near the border in Alberta and B.C.

For thousands of years before European settlers arrived in the region, the nomadic Kootenai Indians used the pass to cross into the Alberta foothills for summer buffalo hunts, taking the food back to their winter villages in the Columbia River Valley, the southern part of the long Rocky Mountain Trench. The first part of the drive passes across the southern Alberta prairie, north of Waterton and Glacier National Parks.

The development of the early coal mines near Crowsnest Pass brought hundreds of miners, and small towns sprang up to service the mines. Two towns—Michel and Natal—are now only memories, as they first burned to the ground and then were replaced by large open-pit mines. Three buildings remain from the Michel townsite, one being the original **Michel Hotel.** Next to the pass, on the B.C. side, is the first of several provincial parks that provide excellent stopping places. **Crowsnest Provincial Park** has a developed campground and a picnic area. Other smaller parks are placed along the Elk River.

On the Alberta side, the town of **Pincher Creek** features a fascinating historical park dedicated to the memory of a famed Canadian mountain man named Kootenay Brown. **Kootenay Brown Historical Park** includes a museum devoted to foothills artifacts. Log cabins in the park include one belonging to Kootenay Brown, going as far back as 1889.

Frank, a coal town near the pass, was mostly decimated in 1903 when 90 million tons of rock slid down from Turtle Mountain and killed nearly 70 people. The **Frank Slide Interpretive Centre** provides an overview of the area's coal mining heritage as well as good views of the slide. It's open daily, year-round. There are tours of present and past coal mining operations along or near the highway, including the old **Leitch Collieries** 15 kilometers (9 miles) east of Blairmore, Alberta. A self-guiding trail passes mining remains, including coke ovens and the mine manager's residence. Guides lead tours during the summer months, and you'll find picnic tables at the site. Other mine tours are available at the functioning **Westar** and **Fording** mines on the B.C. side of the pass. The town of **Elkford** is a good staging place for visits to these mines and exploring outdoor activity in the Rockies.

After descending from the pass through the Elk Valley, the highway leads to the southern part of the Rocky Mountain Trench, a long valley carved by the Columbia River between the Rockies and the Selkirk Mountains. The temperate climate in this valley has resulted in the development of several resort towns including Kimberley, Invermere (Panorama Resort), Fairmont Hot Springs, and Radium Hot Springs. Radium is the gateway to Kootenay National Park, with Highway 93 providing a scenic drive north to **Banff** and **Lake Louise** (see the Banff/Lake Louise Drive on page 28).

HIGHWAY LOG
Lethbridge to Cranbrook
297 KM (184.5 miles)—3 hours, 45 minutes

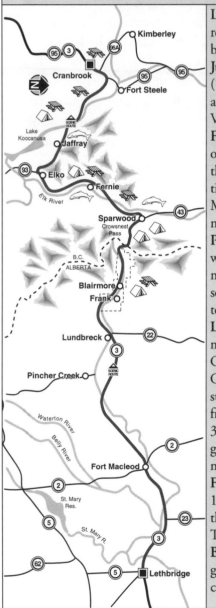

Lethbridge Hotels, motels, stores, restaurants, gas, museum. Near Alberta's dinosaur badlands.

Junction–Highway 23 27.3 KM (17 miles) from Lethbridge. This is a country route, running north to Vulcan and Calgary.

Fort Macleod Town at the junction of Hwy. 2; go south to Cardston, the U.S. border, and Glacier National Park. Restored Northwest Mounted Police fort/museum. Gas, motels, cafes, stores.

Pincher Creek 71 KM (44 miles) west of Fort Macleod. Gas, cafes, motels, stores. Junction–Hwy. 6, south to Twin Butte and Waterton/Glacier National Parks.

Lundbreck Falls 46 KM (28.5 miles) east of the B.C. border. The Crowsnest River plunges 39 feet. Crowsnest Pass (the municipality) stretches 35 KM (22 miles) east from the B.C. border along Hwy. 3. Coal mining established this region. Villages include Frank, Blairmore, and Coleman.

Frank Slide Interpretive Centre, 1 mile north of hwy., where more than 60 lives were lost in the 1903 Turtle Mountain slide.

Blairmore Just off the hwy., with gas, motel, camping, picnicking, cafe, and store.

Volcanic Rocks West of Blairmore (12 KM or 7.5 miles east from B.C. border). One hundred million-year-old volcanic outcrop, viewed from the pulloff, south of hwy.

Alberta/B.C. Border 88 KM (54.7 miles) west from Lethbridge.

Crowsnest Pass (the pass) Ancient mountain route for nomadic Native Americans, traversed by CPR (Canadian Pacific Railway) in the early 1900s.

Crowsnest Provincial Park Just west of the Alberta border, with camping and picnic area.

Westar Mines (former towns of Michel and Natal).

Elk Lakes Provincial Park This subalpine park has hiking trails and walk-in camping.

Junction–Hwy. 43 Elkford is 35 KM (22 miles) north of Hwy. 3, with gas, motel, cafe, store, campground, golf, and skiing. This coal town is home to the Fording and Westar mining operations. Info-centre on Hwy. 43 at Michel Road; call (604) 865-4362.

Sparwood Gas, cafe, campground. This town is 18 KM (11.2 miles) from the Alberta border.

Rest Area Picnic tables 14 KM (8.5 miles) west of Sparwood.

Elk Valley Provincial Park 2.5 KM (1.5 miles) west of rest area, with picnic tables.

Hosmer Village with gas, store, and restaurant.

Fernie 30 KM (18.5 miles) west of Sparwood, with gas, store, motels, golf, campground, and RV park.

Ski Hill Road At south end of Fernie—to **Snow Valley Ski Area** and **Mt. Fernie Provincial Park** (campsites, picnic area, walking trail beside Lizard Creek).

Morrissey Provincial Park 21 KM (13 miles) from Fernie. Picnic area beside the Elk River (fishing).

Elko 81 KM (50.3 miles) from Alberta border. Town with gas, store, cafe.

Junction–Hwy. 3/93 Northwest to cities of Creston and Cranbrook.

Jaffray Hamlet with gas and store.

Kikomun Provincial Park On the Baynes Lake/Jaffray Road, at Jaffray. The park is 11 KM (7 miles) south of Hwy. 3, with camping, dump station, picnic area, swimming, and fishing.

Junction–Wardner/Fort Steele Road A scenic alternate route to Fort Steele, a restored pioneer town and theme park.

Wardner Provincial Park Day-use park with picnic area.

Wardner Village off the hwy. (2 miles past the park).

Rest Area 19.5 KM (12 miles) west of Wardner Road junction.

Junction–Hwy. 95 Take Hwy. 95 north to Fort Steele, Columbia River Valley, Fairmont and Radium Hot Springs, and Kootenay National Park. Take Hwy. 3/95 south to Cranbrook and Creston.

Cranbrook Gas, stores, hotels, motels, museums.

Banff/Lake Louise Drive

Canmore to Revelstoke

Banff National Park is the most popular park in Canada. Some say, for that reason, it's best to avoid the crowded Banff townsite entirely. We wouldn't go quite that far, but there are myriad places to explore in the park without getting caught in the clutches of the chic boutiques, fast food places, and souvenir stores, which seem to be the essence of Banff these days. But maybe that's your cup of tea, as well as millions of other people's. Banff has become a major destination for international vacationers, with stores specifically geared for the many travelers from Japan.

The drive through Banff National Park starts just west of Canmore and continues past the park through Yoho and Glacier National Parks. The route offers the most concentrated mountain scenery in all of the Rockies ranges. You'll find superb visitor facilities along the drive, including a score of picnic areas and campgrounds and trails leading into subalpine meadows beside several waterfalls.

Heading west from Canmore (which is west of Calgary and the gateway to the Kananaskis Country, the east slope recreation area in the Rockies foothills), you're quickly inside the park. Vehicle permits are available at the gatehouse should you wish to stay in the park. Go 3 KM (1.8 miles) east of the gate to find the ghost town of Anthracite, a former coal mining community, located across the mountain from the Cascade electric power plant.

The Banff townsite is 17 KM (10.5 miles) from Canmore. Banff is blessed with excellent accommodations, including the **Banff Springs Hotel,** the first of the famous Canadian Pacific Railway (CPR) "chateau" resorts. There are also many motels in all price ranges and a full selection of restaurants, from continental bistros to just about the best charbroiled hamburgers in the West at Harvey's fast-food joint. Banff is the home of the **Banff Centre for the Performing Arts,** the site of many concerts and drama presentations during summer and a year-round arts school. Downhill skiing is available at Banff and at nearby Sunshine Village (just west of the town). The sulphur springs—the reason for the resort's founding—are still flowing and in operation, with hot pools open daily.

An excellent alternate route, particularly for those driving westward, is the **Bow Valley Parkway**. This scenic road veers off the Trans-Canada just west of Banff, running beside the mountains on the east side of the valley. It rejoins the main highway at Lake Louise, with a one-way sideroad to the Trans-Canada and Kootenay National Park at Castle Junction, about halfway between the towns. The parkway passes Johnston Canyon (with a wonderfully scenic trail) and offers superb views of several peaks, including Eisenhower and the craggy Castle Mountain.

The Trans-Canada leads through the center of the park, providing access to the main recreation areas. The first major campground is at **Tunnel Mountain**, just east of Banff. Five campgrounds located near Banff hold 1,602 campsites.

Two Jack Lake Campgrounds (two separate campgrounds) are 13 KM (8 miles) northeast of the town on Lake Minnewanka Road; from the Trans-Canada junction, go two miles north of town via Banff Avenue, the main street. In all, the national park holds 14 campgrounds with 2,499 sites. The main park Infocentre is downtown, in a former church, at 224 Banff Avenue.

Back on the Trans-Canada Highway, heading west, the **Sawback Range** is seen from a viewpoint. This ridge was tilted almost vertically more than 70 million years ago. Erosion then exposed the sawtooth peaks. The ridge is topped by Mount Isabel (9,540 feet) at the north end of the range.

Near the west end of the park is **Lake Louise** and its eponymous townsite. This is a more relaxed town than Banff, with deluxe resort hotels and several less-expensive motels. There's an excellent new park information building in the town, and the renowned **Chateau Lake Louise** anchors the collection of resorts beside the lake. Farther into the mountains, **Moraine Lake Lodge** offers accommodations, meals, and canoe rentals. The Lodge has undergone extensive renovation and expansion.

HIGHWAY LOG
Canmore to Revelstoke
301 KM (187 miles)—3 hours, 30 minutes

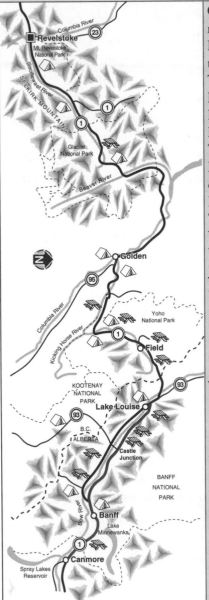

Canmore Gas, stores, motels, restaurants (see page 57). Alberta Infocentre at the north end of town. Hwy. 1 is also called the Trans-Canada Highway.

Rundleview Picnic Area Just inside Banff National Park (eastbound only).

Banff Townsite–East Entrance To Tunnel Mountain Campground.

Buffalo Paddock Home to a herd of wood bison.

Banff Townsite–West Entrance To Mt. Norquay Ski Area.

Viewpoint View of the three Vermilion Lakes (eastbound).

Junction–Bow Valley Parkway Scenic drive on east side of valley.

Riverside Picnic Area On the banks of the Bow River between the Bow Valley Parkway and Trans-Canada Highway.

Junction–Sunshine Road To ski area and village via gondola.

Borgeau Lake Trailhead 7.5-KM (4.6-mile) trail along Wolverine Creek.

Wolverine Creek Picnic Area 0.5 mile past the trailhead.

Viewpoint View of the Sawback Range, 29.4 KM (18 miles) from the park gate.

Redearth Creek Trailhead and Picnic Area Picnic park, 0.5 mile west of trailhead parking.

Viewpoint Castle Mountain.
Copper Picnic Area Beside the Bow River. There's a view of Castle Mountain from the riverside.
Altrude Creek Picnic Area 46.7 KM (28 miles) from the park gate.
Junction–Banff-Windermere Highway (Castle Junction) To Bow Valley Parkway (east) and Kootenay National Park.
Taylor Creek Picnic Area Highest mountain in Lake Louise area (11,626 feet).
Junction–Bow Valley Parkway (at Lake Louise) 72.5 KM (45 miles) from east park gate. To Lake Louise townsite (west).
Junction–Icefields Parkway 2.7 KM (1.6 miles) west of Lake Louise turn-off. To Columbia Icefield and Jasper.
Viewpoint Mt. St. Piran and Mt. Niblock.
Alberta/B.C. Border Change to Pacific time. Gate of Yoho National Park.
Rest Areas A dozen picnic parks are found between the B.C. border and Revelstoke.
Junction–Lake Louise/Great Divide Drive To Lake O'Hara Basin and Lodge. Sideroad to Lake Louise townsite.
Viewpoint Wapta Lake to the south of the hwy.
Viewpoints "Big Hill" and Spiral Tunnel exhibits on CPR construction.
Junction–Yoho Valley Road 13 KM (8 miles) to **Takakkaw Falls.**

Junction–Emerald Lake Road 8.2 KM (5 miles) to blue-green lake at foot of Presidents Range.
Ottertail Valley Trailhead Gravel road to trail to Kootenay Park.
Ottertail Valley Viewpoint 3.5 KM (2.2 miles) west of trailhead road junction.
Viewpoint View of Mt. Hunter, 3 KM (1.9 miles) west of picnic park.
Avalanche Trailhead 1-KM (0.62 mile) nature trail to toe of rock slide.
Hoodoo Creek Campground 3.1-KM trail (1.9 miles) to Leanchoil Hoodoos. Trail to beaver dams.
Chancellor Peak Campground Junction–Wapta Falls Access Road 3 KM (2 miles) off hwy. Views from road of Mt. Vaux and Chancellor Peak.
Golden Town with gas, motels, stores, camping, and cafes.
Junction–Highway 95 (at Golden) To Radium, Invermere, and Cranbrook.
B & J Gasden Provincial Park Picnic area, Moberly Marsh wildlife viewing.
Glacier National Park Highway climbs to Rogers Pass. Motel, cafe, park info, and camping at the summit.
Albert Canyon Hot Springs Camping, hot pools, cafe. 35.5 KM (22 miles) east of Revelstoke.
Mount Revelstoke National Park Wilderness camping, trails, skiing.
Revelstoke Town with all services.

Kootenay Park Drive

Radium Hot Springs to Banff National Park

The highway is formally named the Banff-Windermere Parkway and was constructed for purely commercial purposes during the early 1920s. In 1905, Windermere businessman Randolph Bruce proposed bringing Columbia Valley fruit and produce to the Banff resort by building a road across the Kootenay Valley wilderness. The B.C. government and CPR took up the challenge.

The park, with its magnificent valleys and mountain views, was almost an afterthought, created only after the initial highway builders ran out of money after building 14 miles of road. After several years, Bruce went hat-in-hand to the federal government, which agreed to finish construction only if it included five-mile strips of protected land on both sides of the road. Kootenay National Park was created in 1920, and the highway (a narrow gravel track) was completed in 1923. Randolph Bruce's dream of an orchard industry was not fruitful, but the park remains, providing one of the finest short drives in any of the Rockies regions.

The highway is possibly the best route from which to view the wildlife of the National Parks area that straddles the Alberta/British Columbia border. You may see elk, mountain goats, black bears, and coyotes among the animals and birds that inhabit the park. At the south end of the parkway, Radium Hot Springs (the town) has a number of motels, cabin establishments, restaurants, and stores. It lies at the junction of the parkway and Highway 93/95, the Columbia River Parkway, which runs south to Cranbrook and the U.S. border.

The hot springs lie inside the south boundary of Kootenay National Park, with a fully developed complex of hot and swimming pools, bathhouse, and cafe. The **Aquacourt** is open daily, year-round. You'll find lodging within the park across the road from the Aquacourt. Radium Hot Springs Lodge has a restaurant and its own hot pool. Three cabin operations are near the Lodge.

The 10 KM (6 miles) of road past the Aquacourt lead up Sinclair Canyon, following the path of **Sinclair Creek**, which drops at a fast clip—about 250 feet per mile. The geology of this area of the park is fascinating. Just after entering the park, the highway passes through a very narrow limestone cut. This little canyon and the Iron Gates area just beyond (marked by red cliffs) sit on a major fault that extends for at least 10,000 feet below the earth's surface. It's suitably called the **Redwall Fault**, and it is through this fracture that the hot mineral water rises to the springs. Several picnic areas offer scenic viewpoints, and four trails are available for hikers and walkers. The **Juniper Trail** is near the park entrance: a short hike around the canyon and Aquacourt area. **Redstreak Creek Trail** is 4.5 KM (3 miles) from the park gate, leading up the creek canyon for 2.6 KM (1.6 miles).

At the 7.3-KM (4.5-mile) mark, the **Kimpton Creek Trail** provides 4.8 KM (3 miles) of hiking through the forest, following the creek along the Redstreak Mountain slopes. The **Kimberley Pass Trail**, north of the picnic area, is more arduous. It leads to the watershed divide of the Brisco Range, arriving at high alpine meadows and then crossing the ridge to connect with the **Sinclair Creek Trail**—the trailhead is at the 10.7-KM (6.6-mile) mark.

After crossing Sinclair Pass, the **Kootenay Valley** appears. You'll find magnificent views of the valley as well as the Brisco and Mitchell ranges from the **Valley Viewpoint** pulloff.

After descending to the valley floor, the highway follows the course of the Kootenay River, through forests and across meadows. Frequently spaced picnic spots dot this area. The McLeod Meadows Campground offers tent, trailer, and RV sites (26.8 KM or 16.6 miles from the park gate).

Several trails offer distinctive hikes from the valley floor, particularly the **Paint Pots Trail**, which leads to ochre beds used by Native American tribes for body paint pigments. The drive ends at Castle Junction, intersecting the Trans-Canada Highway midway between Banff and Lake Louise.

HIGHWAY LOG
Radium to Banff National Park
104 KM (64 miles)–1 hour, 45 minutes

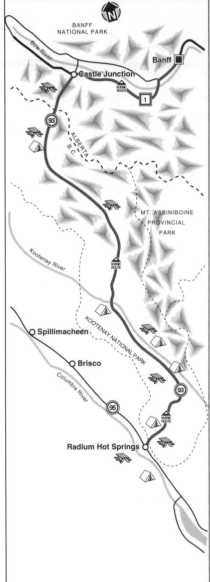

Radium Hot Springs Gas, motels, cafes, store. Town at the junction of Hwys. 95 and 93.

Redstreak Campground Within Kootenay National Park, the campground is reached via Hwy. 95, south of town.

Kootenay National Park Take Hwy. 93. Information center at south gate. Lodge and cabins opposite the hot spring pools complex.

Sinclair Canyon For 10 KM (6 miles), the route passes through this scenic canyon.

Juniper Trail An easy 3.2-KM (2-mile) nature trail, leading to the top of Sinclair Canyon and down to the pools.

Radium Hot Springs Aquacourt Hot pool, swimming pool, cafe, and bathhouse.

Redstreak Creek Trailhead 2.6-KM (1.6-mile) trail up Redstreak Creek Canyon.

Kimpton Creek Trailhead Trail extends 4.8 KM (3 miles).

Sinclair Creek Picnic Area 10 KM (6 miles) from the south park gate.

Kindersley Pass Trailhead Leads to high meadows and connects with Sinclair Creek Trail. Look for mountain sheep.

Sinclair Creek Trailhead 6-KM (4-mile) hike up narrow gorge.

Olive Lake Picnic Area Just east of lake, near the summit.

Sinclair Pass Named for Metis guide James Sinclair.

Cobb Lake Trailhead A 2.7-KM (1.7-mile) walk on Mt. Sinclair.

Viewpoint A wide view of the sumptuous Kootenay Valley, which stretches more than 80 KM (50 miles).

Junction–Settler's Road Gravel road leads 7 KM (4.3 miles) to park border and Canal Flats.

Kootenay River Picnic Area Panoramic views of Mitchell and Brisco ranges.

Nixon Creek Trailhead 1-KM walk through woods to a small lake.

McLeod Meadows Picnic Area Dog Lake Trail, 2.7 KM (1.7 miles).

McLeod Meadows Campground With dump station and RV spaces.

Dolly Varden Picnic Area 34.5 KM (22 miles) from south park gate, with winter campground.

Kootenay Crossing A picnic area is north of the bridge.

Viewpoint–Hector Gorge High pulloff with Vermilion River view.

Mountain Goat Viewing To north of hwy., on slopes of Mt. Wardle, 1 KM beyond viewpoint.

Hector Gorge Picnic Area

Wardle Creek Picnic Area

Animal Lick Moose, elk, and deer often lick the mineral-rich mud along the Vermilion River.

Viewpoint–Mount Assiniboine Matterhorn-like peak is highest mountain in this section of the Rockies 3,620 M (el. 11,870 feet).

Vermilion River Bridge Lodge and picnic area. Gasoline and food during summer months.

Floe Lake Trailhead Parking area to west of hwy. Floe Lake trail is 10.5 KM (6.5 miles) long. A short (1 KM) walk leads to a small canyon.

Numa Creek Picnic Area Trail to Tumbling and Numa Passes.

Paint Pots Trailhead Leads to ochre beds, used by Native Americans for pigment. A spring is at the end of the trail.

Marble Canyon Picnic area, park information center, trailhead for Marble Canyon Trail, and campground.

Stanley Glacier Trailhead and Viewpoint Trail leads to cirque, passing through a 1968 burn area.

Vermilion Pass 1,651 M (5,416 feet) At the Continental Divide, the Fireweed Trail shows how a burned area recovers.

Boom Creek Picnic Area

Castle Junction–Highway 1 (Trans-Canada) Midway between Banff and Lake Louise.

Icefields Parkway Drive

Lake Louise to Jasper

The Columbia Icefield is the largest body of ice in the Rockies. Situated approximately halfway between Lake Louise and Jasper, this 337-square-KM (130-square-mile) body of ice feeds several glaciers, the most accessible of which is the **Athabasca Glacier**. The annual snowfall on the central icefield (the névé) is often more than 7 M (23 feet).

From the "toe" of the Athabasca Glacier, you can look upwards toward the center of the névé, which is beyond the horizon. The ice "flows" downhill from the central icefield, arriving at the toe where the ice melts and, in the case of the Athabasca Glacier, becomes the Sunwapta River, the milky flow containing glacial silt. This glacier has been retreating for more than a hundred years. In the mid-19th century, the ice projected to the location of the present Icefields Parkway; painted rocks show the surprisingly speedy recession since that time.

The maximum depth of the glacier's ice is about 304 M (1,000 feet). The icefield névé itself has a thickness of up to 1,200 feet. Scientists aren't sure when the glacier might begin its next advance. It will take heavier snowfalls and cooler summers to begin the cycle.

Jasper National Park operates a summer information center across the highway from the icefield. The center has information on the icefield, and backcountry camping permits may be obtained here. Next door is the **Icefield Chalet**, where visitors go to and up the glacier on buses with huge wheels that allow driving on the glacial ice. These tours are offered daily during the summer and early fall season. A lodge supplies gas, food, and lodging during summer months.

The impressive drive between Lake Louise and Jasper offers many scenic views, frequent picnic areas, several campgrounds, and trails both short and long. The shorter trails lead to nearby rivers and glacial lakes. The more rugged, longer trails lead up the mountains to alpine meadows and several glacier views. Among them is the **Helen Creek Trail**, 28.6 KM (17.8 miles) from the Highway 1 junction, and **Parker's Ridge Trail** at 118 KM (73.3 miles). An easy half-day round trip, the latter trail climbs above the tree line to alpine tundra and a wildflower display from midsummer into fall. With a frost-free period of not much more than a week, the plants cling to the surface of the tundra. Plant life here includes moss campion (pink flowers), mountain avens with white flowers, and white and red mountain heather. The trail continues above the tundra over Parker's Ridge to a view of the Saskatchewan Glacier at the 2.4-KM (1.5-mile) mark. Hikers on this trail in the early summer may see "red" snow, colored by minute red algae. This phenomenon is common in the high Canadian Rockies snowfields. The tree line along Parker's Ridge Trail is at 2,100 meters (which is slightly more than 7,000 feet).

Three lodges offer accommodations along the parkway. The first, **Num-ti-jah Lodge** (at the 36-KM or 21.4-mile mark), was built around 1920 by pioneer mountain guide Jimmy Simpson. The lodge is close to the Bow Glacier, and a fine 5-KM (3-mile) trail leads to the foot of Bow Glacier Falls. It is open year-round and serves meals to passing travelers. **Saskatchewan River Crossing Resort** is at the 77-KM (47.8-mile) mark, with accommodations and meals during the summer season. This is a scenic location, with mounts Wilson and Murchison dominating the scene. **Icefields Lodge** is located across the highway from the Athabasca Glacier at the Columbia Icefield (at the 126.6-KM or 78.7-mile mark). It too is open during the popular summer months. A Jasper National Park campground is located nearby.

The drive ends at the parkway junction with the Yellowhead Highway (Highway 16) at the Jasper townsite. The town has a good selection of motels, and just east of town is the grande dame of the Jasper resorts, **Jasper Park Lodge**. You will find all accommodations in the Jasper area to be expensive, brought about by the short summer season in this northern park. Lodgings are available year-round.

HIGHWAY LOG
Lake Louise to Jasper
230 KM (143 miles)—2 hours, 45 minutes

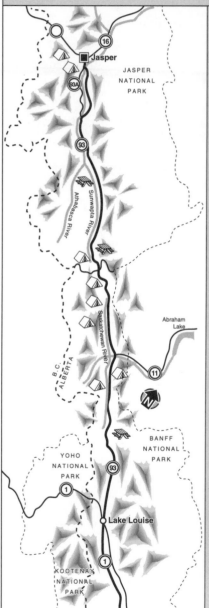

Lake Louise Just off Hwy. 1, with gas, motels, lodges, restaurants, and stores.

Junction–Highway 1 and Highway 93 Hwy. 1 leads east to Banff and west to Golden and Revelstoke. Take Highway 93 north to Jasper.

Parkway Interpretive Exhibit Next to a fine stand of lodgepole pine in an old fire-burn area, the exhibit gives a good preview of the entire parkway trip.

Herbert Lake Picnic Area Beside a beautiful pine-clad lake, with the Bow Range to the south.

Hector Lake Trailhead 1 KM past a viewpoint, this trail offers a short hike down to the Bow River, which can be forded to walk another mile to the lake.

Mosquito Creek Campground 25 KM (15.5 miles) north of Hwy. 1. Year-round camping. Nearby is the first of three youth hostels along the parkway.

Helen Creek Trailhead 6-KM (3.7-mile) hike to alpine meadows. Another 8 KM (5 miles) to Katherine Lake and further to Dolomite Pass.

Crowfoot Glacier Viewpoint at pulloff. Now receding, two of the three original "toes" remain.

Junction–Num-ti-jah Lodge Road
Year-round accommodations and
meals. A 5-KM (3-mile) trail leads
to the foot of Bow Glacier Falls
from the lodge parking lot.
Peyto Lake Trailhead Short
1.6-KM (1-mile) trail to lakeshore.
Rock Slide View of large slide
of orange-colored quartz sandstone.
Waterfowl Lakes Campground
57.5 KM (35.7 miles) from Hwy. 1.
Scenic trail leads from rear of
campground to Chephren and
Cirque Lakes amphitheaters.
Mistaya Canyon Trailhead 71 KM
(41 miles) from Hwy. 1. A short
(300-meter) hike to a limestone
gorge. *Mistaya* is the Cree word for
grizzly bear.
**Saskatchewan River Bridge and
Warden Station** 75 KM (46.5
miles) from Hwy. 1 junction.
**Junction–David Thompson
Highway** North of the Howse
Valley pulloff. Leads east to Rocky
Mountain House (180 KM or
112 miles).
Saskatchewan River Crossing A
summer stop for gas, meals, and
groceries. Excellent views of
mounts Wilson and Murchison
from the lodge.
Rampart Creek Campground
Open June–September. Youth
hostel nearby.

Cirrus Mountain Campground
103 KM (64 miles) from Hwy. 1.
Nigel Creek Canyon View from
pulloff into dolomite gorge.
Saskatchewan Glacier Trailhead
Pulloff on an old road leads to
bridge and trailheads. Walk 400 M
along the old road to waterfalls.
Glacier Trail starts halfway to the
falls.
Panther Falls Trailhead 1-KM trail
to foot of falls.
Wilcox Creek Campground 124
KM (77 miles) from Hwy. 1.
Columbia Icefield Campground
1 mile from glacier.
**Columbia Icefield and Athabasca
Glacier** 126.6 KM (78.7 miles)
from Hwy. 1. The icefield covers
337 square KM (130 square miles).
Lodge, glacier bus trips, short trail
to toe of glacier.
Bubbling Springs Picnic Area
Sunwapta Falls Junction
Honeymoon Lake Campground
Summer camping.
Mount Christie Picnic Area
Goat Picnic Area
Mount Kerkeslin Campground 36
KM (22 miles) south of Jasper.
Junction–Hwy. 93 A scenic route
to waterfall, camping, and Marmot
Basin.
Junction–Highway 16 Jasper
townsite, with motels, resort hotel,
cafes, gas, stores.

Mount Robson Drive

Jasper to Clearwater

The drive from Jasper, Alberta to Clearwater, B.C. connects three of Canada's finest wilderness parks: Jasper, Mount Robson, and Wells Gray.

Starting in a westward direction from the Jasper townsite on the Yellowhead Highway (Hwy. 16), drive 14 KM (9 miles) to the B.C. border and the Yellowhead Pass. The pass was used by early Hudson's Bay Company fur traders as a walking route for exploration of the northern B.C. wilderness.

Mt. Robson Provincial Park has its western entrance at the Alberta/B.C. border, and the highway leads northwest for 61 KM (38 miles) through the park. Although you'll see striking mountain peaks throughout the route, the most famous (and most dominant) peak is Mt. Robson—the highest peak in the Canadian Rockies. The park contains the headwaters of the Fraser River, crossed by the highway 30 miles from its source. This is the world's foremost salmon river. The salmon migrate 1,200 KM (745 miles) up the river, with Rearguard Falls as the final barrier to the northernmost spawning channels.

Most people visit the park during the summer period, from June through September. These are ideal months for hiking and water activity. Yellowhead and Moose Lakes are perfect for canoeing, as they reflect high peaks in their dark green waters. Campsites along the lakes provide excellent places to stay, and hiking trails explore the mountain forests. The most popular and accessible series of trails is located near the information center at the western end of the park. A two-day or three-day hike leads through the Valley of a Thousand Falls, featuring the majestic Emperor Falls, to the shore of Berg Lake. At this point, Mount Robson hovers above Berg Glacier and its lake. The glacier is one of the few advancing glaciers in the Canadian Rockies and frequently calves (drops) icebergs into the lake. The views of the peak, the glacier, and the great floating ice chunks provide an unforgettable experience. The distance from the visitor center to the lake is 22 KM (14 miles). The trail continues through Robson Pass into Jasper National Park and on to the Jasper townsite. Mount Robson Lodge, at the west gate, provides indoor accommodations.

The highway continues past the west gate of the park to the Tete Jaune Cache junction, where Highway 5 (the South Yellowhead) leads south along the west slope of the Rockies with the Cariboo range to the west.

Wells Gray Provincial Park is a huge tract of protected land in the Cariboo Mountains, and it's a short drive west of Clearwater at the end of this drive. Scenic highlights of the park include high mountain meadows resplendent with wildflowers. Trails lead past snowcapped peaks and glaciers and many alpine lakes and waterfalls. Several of the lakes occupy the cones of extinct volcanoes. Here you'll find lava beds and mineral springs.

Four lakes—Clearwater, Azure, Mahood, and Murtle—provide canoeists with an excellent canoe route. Hiking trails provide short nature walks and longer hikes of up to a week's duration. The park hosts 25 wilderness camping areas.

Four car/RV campgrounds are near the main park entrance, which is 69 KM (43 miles) from Clearwater. The main information center for the park is in Clearwater, at the Highway 5 junction with Clearwater Road.

We highly recommend two short hikes. A four-hour, steep walk leads to the base of **Helmcken Falls** (466 feet high and twice as high as Niagara Falls). The falls may also be seen from the end of Helmcken Falls Road. The trailhead for the hike is at this parking lot. The **Battle Mountain/Alpine Meadows Trail** leads hikers on a 25-KM (16 mile) hike, which takes about five hours. This is an ideal place to see the summer wildflowers in profusion on Cariboo Meadows. A further hike of about three hours leads up to the summit of Battle Mountain. The trail begins south of the main park entrance on Clearwater Road. Side trails provide opportunities for a trip taking two or more days.

Clearwater has a full range of visitor services.

HIGHWAY LOG
Jasper to Clearwater
223 KM (138.5 miles)—3 hours

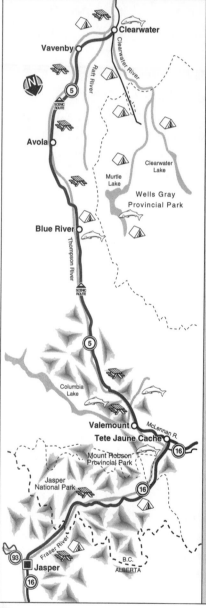

Jasper (townsite) In Jasper National Park. Gas, resort hotel, motels, restaurants, and stores. Hwy. 16 leads west through the park toward the B.C. border.

Yellowhead Pass (el. 1,131 M or 3,710 feet). Used for the Grand Trunk railway route to the Pacific (now CNR). B.C. border (time change). Picnic area beside lake.

Mt. Robson Provincial Park West gate is 75 KM (46.6 miles) from the Tete Jaune Cache Junction. The hwy. runs 61 KM (38 miles) through the park.

Yellowhead Lake Boat launch, picnic area, and viewpoint at east end of lake. Canoeing, view of Yellowhead Mountain.

Lucerne Campground Just west of the lake, north of hwy.

Fraser Crossing Picnic Area The mighty Fraser is little more than a creek at this point. Short trail for view of Mt. Fitzwilliam.

Moose Lake Boat launch. If there ever was a place to put a canoe in the water, this is it!

Roadside Spring North pulloff.

Overlander Falls Viewpoint and Picnic Area The falls are south of the highway.

Mt. Robson Provincial Park Info center 2 KM (1.2 miles) from the west park gate, at the Mt. Robson viewpoint. Cafe, gas, park info center, campgrounds. Mt. Robson (el. 3,954 M or 12,972 feet) is the highest peak in the Canadian Rockies.

Mt. Robson Lodge 3.2 KM (2 miles) west of park gate. Cabins. Finn Creek picnic area on North Thompson River.

Mt. Terry Fox Picnic Area 7 KM (4.3 miles) east of Hwy. 5 junction.

Rearguard Falls Provincial Park Viewpoints, fishing in Fraser River. Trail to 32-foot falls. The falls are close to the limit for salmon migration on the Fraser.

Tete Jaune Cache Picnic Area Just east of the Hwy. 5 junction.

Junction–Highway 5 The South Yellowhead Highway leads south along the west slope of the Rockies to Clearwater and Kamloops.

Tete Jaune Cache Small village at junction. Store and gas on loop road.

Mt. Terry Fox Picnic Area 7.5 KM (4.6 miles) to Valemount.

Valemount Town 30 KM (19 miles) from the Hwy. 16 junction. Gas, motels, cafes, camping, golfing, stores.

Camp Creek Picnic Area 22.5 KM (14 miles) south of Valemount.

Thunder River Rest Area Picnic tables beside a scenic river.

Junction–Road to Myrtle Lake Backroad to portion of Wells Gray Park (24 KM or 15 miles). 2.5-KM (1.5-mile) trail to the lake.

Blue River Logging and tourist town. Gas, motels, store, heli-skiing, camping, swimming, fishing. 105.5 KM (65.5 miles) north of Clearwater.

Finn Creek Picnic Area On North Thompson River

Avola Tiny village with pub (Log Inn) and motel.

Wire Cache Picnic Area

McMurphy Picnic Area 48 KM (30 miles) from Clearwater.

Vavenby Village with gas and store.

Birch Island Village with store and gas. Lost Creek Road leads 22.5 KM (14 miles) across the valley.

Birch Island Picnic Area Views.

Junction–Silence Lake Forest Road 35-KM (22-mile) road to lake.

Clearwater Town and Wells Gray Provincial Park info center at junction.

Junction–Clearwater Valley Road Sidetrip to Wells Gray Provincial Park. This road leads 36 KM (22 miles) to the main entrance of this superb wilderness park.

Spahats Creek Provincial Park 10 KM (6.2 miles) from Clearwater. Camping, canyon, and falls.

Junction–Trophy Mountain Forest Road 11.5 KM (7 miles) to recreation area and Skyline Trail.

Wells Gray Ranch Camping and trail rides, 43.5 KM (27 miles) from Clearwater.

Helmcken Falls Lodge at the park gate. Lodging, camping, hookups.

Alaska Highway Drive

Fort Nelson to Liard River

Celebrated for its first half-century of existence in 1992, the Alaska Highway is a tribute to its military builders during World War II and the present-day people who pioneer the northland along its length. Linking Dawson Creek, B.C. and Fairbanks, Alaska, the 2,395-KM (1,488-mile) highway is a far cry from its original rutted gravel state. Mostly paved, the highway is the primary tourist route to the adventure country of the Yukon and Alaska. We should point out that all of the Alaska Highway and its approaches are included in our companion book, *Alaska–Yukon Adventures.*

It's a common saying that half of the fun of traveling to Alaska is getting there. Part of the "getting there" takes drivers through the most northerly stretch of the Rockies: a wild area filled with wildlife, mountain parks, and rivers that etch the steep mountain valleys. This is the area of British Columbia north of Fort Nelson. It is not the beginning of the Alaska Highway, for the road has its origins 455 KM (283 miles) south in the downtown of Dawson Creek, a town on the northern B.C. prairie. The highway crosses the prairie lands and winds its way across several low ridges before arriving in Fort Nelson, from which the highway quickly ascends into the Rockies, beginning with Steamboat Mountain. Here the mountains are not as high—the Rockies are petering out by this point—but they are Rockies nonetheless. The scenery is no less impressive than in many ranges far to the south.

This stretch of the highway permits excellent opportunities for viewing wildlife: caribou, Stone sheep, mountain goats, moose, and elk. You'll find campgrounds throughout the area, including provincial park campsites in three impressive parks.

Part of the interest in driving this road is in eating and staying in the Alaska Highway lodges spaced at convenient intervals along the route. Several of these were built during the construction period in the 1940s and survive today as rustic but comfortable inns with a homey atmosphere. These include **Toad River**

Lodge, 195 KM (121.6 miles) from Fort Nelson, and **Liard River Lodge** at the end of this drive, located across the highway from Liard Hot Springs, which has my vote for the title of the finest hot springs in North America. Other, newer lodges include **Summit Lake Lodge** in Stone Mountain Provincial Park and **Highland Glen Lodge** in Muncho Lake Provincial Park.

The three provincial parks along this stretch of the Alaska Highway provide the scenic and recreational highlights for visitors to the Northern Rockies. One hundred and fifty KM (93 miles) northwest of Fort Nelson is **Stone Mountain Provincial Park**. This is an area for adventurous hiking or just relaxing in a public campground or at a mountain lodge. **Muncho Lake Provincial Park** has as its centerpiece the beautiful blue-green, 12-mile-long Muncho Lake. This is prime fishing country, with lake trout and Arctic char in the spring through early July. At the east end of the park, an animal lick provides views of caribou, moose, sheep, and goats. Alpine meadows are ablaze with wildflowers during July. Campsites are located at Strawberry Flats and MacDonald campgrounds.

The great river of this trip is the Liard. It picks up steam as it travels down the **Liard Valley**—beside the highway—and flows into the Mackenzie River as it reaches the Northwest Territories. Across the highway from the river is one of the truly unique ecosystems in North America. **Liard Hot Springs**, pouring out of the earth in the provincial park of the same name, creates a steamy northern oasis in the forest. The thermal waters spring from the ground at 130°F (54°C), thus raising the ambient temperature so that more than 60 species of plants unusual to the north thrive here. Dragonflies dart over the warm stream that wanders across the park, and small fish (a variety of lake chub) surviving here for at least 10,000 years swim under the boardwalk leading to the two pools (Alpha and Beta). The park administration has maintained a natural ambiance at the pools, which I can't recommend more highly. In the daytime or after dark, in summer and winter, these pools have a magic of their own.

HIGHWAY LOG
Fort Nelson to Liard River
313.3 KM (194.7 miles)—4 hours, 30 minutes

Fort Nelson Town with gas, motels, cafes, stores, golf course. Information center on Hwy. 97 at west end of town.

Junction–Highway 77 18 KM (11 miles) north of town, Liard Highway leads north to Fort Liard, Fort Simpson, the Northwest Territories, and (via the Mackenzie Hwy.) Yellowknife.

Kledo Creek Picnic Area

Steamboat Mountain Cafe and gas at top of winding ascent. Summit at 1,067 M (3,500 feet). West of the cafe are several scenic viewpoints.

Indian Head Mountain Viewpoint View with head in profile.

Teetering Rock Viewpoint The balancing rock is on the horizon. Trails lead from this viewpoint.

Tetsa River Provincial Park 63.5 KM (39.5 miles) from Fort Nelson. Road leads 1.9 KM (1.2 miles) to a campground and picnic tables.

Tetsa River Services Gas, store, camping, B Y B lodgings.

Picnic Area 4.8 KM (3 miles) from store.

Stone Mountain Provincial Park Stretches 9.2 KM (5.7 miles) along the highway.

Summit Lake Lodge Store, gas, and cafe. Open year-round. Mt. St.

George, el. 1,689 M (7,419 feet) is seen beyond the lake.

Summit Lake Campground Scenic campsites beside lake, picnic tables, boat launch, hiking trail to Summit Peak.

Alaska Highway Summit el. 1,295 M (4,250 feet).

Rocky Crest Lake Picnic Area 3.7 KM (2.3 miles) west of campground.

Erosion Pillars Trailhead Short hike (1 KM) to hoodoos.

Rocky Mountain Lodge Gas, store, lodging. Open year-round. 5.3 KM (3.3 miles) west of Summit Lake.

Wokpash Provincial Recreation Area and Trailhead Via old Churchill Mines Road (4-wheel-drive vehicles only).

115 Creek Provincial Campground Beside 115 Creek and MacDonald Creek. Good fishing for Dolly Varden and grayling.

Toad River Village, 195 KM (121.6 miles) from Fort Nelson. Gas, cafe, store. Lodging at Toad River Lodge (rooms and cabins).

The Poplars Campground, just west of Toad River.

Muncho Lake Provincial Park This large park stretches 82 KM (51 miles) along the route. The linear town of Muncho Lake is contained within the park.

Strawberry Flats Campground On the lakeshore with 15 campsites and picnic tables.

Highland Glen Lodge Popular lodge on the lake, with restaurant, cabins, motel rooms, campground, RV hookups, and laundry.

MacDonald Campground On Muncho Lake, with picnic tables and boat launch.

Muncho Lake (town) Gas, cafes, and lodges with housekeeping cabins, motel rooms, RV hookups, and laundry.

Mineral Lick Short loop trail leads to a Trout River Valley overlook and view of mineral lick at bottom of cliff frequented by caribou, Stone sheep, elk, and goats.

Liard River North of the bridge (the only suspension bridge on the Alaska Hwy.) is Liard River Lodge, with gas, cafe, and lodgings.

Liard Hot Springs Provincial Park A *must* for Alaska Hwy. travelers. Two hot spring pools in natural settings within this park. Camping, boardwalk to the pools. The Alaska Hwy. continues north to the Yukon Border and onward (19.3 KM or 12 miles) to the town of **Watson Lake**. For complete details on the Alaska Highway and the Yukon, refer to *Alaska–Yukon Adventures*.

Canada
Destinations

Alaska Highway Rockies (B.C.)

For the convenience of Alaska Highway travelers, the towns and overnight stopping locations along the highway are listed from south to north instead of in the usual alphabetical order. Accommodations are listed at the end of this chapter, starting on page 73.

- **Dawson Creek**

  Mile "0" of the Alaska Highway is a wooden post, located in the middle of the downtown intersection of 10th Street and 102nd Avenue. It's the most photographed spot in town and somewhat of a hazard for drivers, as tourists cross the road to stand beside the milepost. Close by are shops selling the required "I Drove the Alaska Highway" T-shirts. This is a northern prairie town, lying north of the Rockies at the junction of B.C. Highway 97 (Hart Highway), which runs north to the town from Prince George, and Highway 2, which comes from Alberta through Grand Prairie. The economy here is based on farming and forestry as well as tourism.

  Things to see and do in Dawson Creek include the art gallery, located in a former grain elevator, and the museum next door to it. The town's Infocentre (BC's name for tourist information offices) is in the museum building. The Alaska Highway leads north as Highway 97 toward Fort St. John and the Yukon border. At this point, the B.C. Rockies are to the southwest with only foothills in view.

Private and public campsites are in the area as well as several motels in town (see page 73).

- **Fort St. John**

  Founded in 1793 as a fur trading fort, this town is the oil and gas capital of B.C.—another prairie town north of the B.C. Rockies. Now a town of 13,500 people, Fort St. John has good shopping and a range of hotels and motels, some along the Alaska Highway (see page 73). There's an 18-hole golf course on Charlie Lake, north of town. The nearby community of Hudson's Hope (to the east via Highway 29) has a large hydroelectric dam, and the dam museum displays fossils and prehistoric animal bones that were unearthed during dam construction.

- **Pink Mountain**

  An overnight stopping place, Pink Mountain is little more than a fairly modern motel with a restaurant and lounge, whose regular guests include Alaska Highway maintenance workers and travelers, some of whom park at the adjacent campground. There is gas here, at a scenic location with the Rockies in view to the south, about 150 KM (93 miles) northwest of Fort St. John and 226 KM (140 miles) from Dawson Creek.

  To the north of Pink Mountain are even smaller places to obtain gas and food: Sikanni Chief, Trutch, and Prophet River.

- **Fort Nelson**

  Lying just southeast of the Rockies, Fort Nelson is a resource town (lumber, natural gas) that was first a fur trading post. This is the last town before the Alaska Highway reaches Watson Lake, Yukon, and a good place to stay before tackling the drive over the northernmost Rockies range. An Infocentre offers local and highway information at the north end of town, next to the local museum. Fort Nelson has an interesting evening welcome program for tourists, and the Infocentre will tell you when the program is available. Leaving Fort Nelson, the Alaska Highway quickly ascends Steamboat Mountain and is thoroughly into the Rockies with some of the best scenery and wildlife viewing in B.C. (for motels, see page 76).

Northwest of Fort Nelson are several gas stations, cafes, and Alaska Highway lodges. Steamboat, at the top of the mountain, is a cafe with gas. Summit Lake (116 KM or 72 miles from Fort Nelson), inside Stone Mountain Provincial Park, is a small community with gas, store, cafe and lodging. The public campground has a beautiful site at the east end of Summit Lake. Watch for caribou and Stone sheep.

- **Toad River**

  One-hundred sixty-six KM (103 miles) from Fort Nelson, the Toad River Lodge is a traditional Alaska Highway lodge with cafe, gas, rustic cabin, and lodge accommodations. Fishing is good here, and camping is near the lodge. 115 Creek Provincial Campground is southeast of town. Beyond Toad River is Muncho Lake Provincial Park, the second of the spectacular parks in the northern Rockies. The small community of Muncho Lake offers gas, food, supplies, and accommodations at several lodges in the area. The services are located 218 KM (135.5 miles) from Fort Nelson and 702 KM (436.5 miles) from Dawson Creek. To the northwest, Fireside is a cafe (with gas) in a burn area, after the devastation of 400,000 acres in 1982.

- **Liard River**

  One of the best of the highway lodges is located across the highway from Liard Hot Springs Provincial Park. This is a rustic hotel of log construction built during World War II when the highway was constructed. There is a restaurant in the lodge, and gas is available. The hot springs here are among the most scenic natural wonders in all of the Rockies region. Maintained by the government, the hot springs consist of two pools with wooden changing rooms and decks, but aside from these additions the pools have been left in their natural state. It's worth driving the Alaska Highway this far to visit these wonderful hot pools, which you reach by walking over a boardwalk for about a quarter of a mile. The hot springs park has campsites.

Banff National Park (Alberta)

Canada's most popular park was established as a railway resort shortly after the construction of the trans-continental railroad, which linked the new provinces of Canada following the national confederation in 1867. The president of the Canadian Pacific Railway, seeing the great beauty of the Canadian Rockies, realized that if he couldn't take the Rockies to the Canadian people, he could bring them to the Rockies with his railroad. Donald Smith's dream was realized with the building of the Banff Springs Hotel in 1888, and in 1890, a small chalet was built beside Lake Louise to serve the needs of travelers.

The first known crossing of the Canadian Rockies by Europeans was made in 1800 by two North West Company voyageurs named Le Blanc and La Gassie. Surveyor David Thompson crossed the Rockies by Howse Pass in 1807 and established the first fur trading post in the Columbia Valley. Hudson's Bay Company Governor George Simpson crossed a pass that now hears his name near Banff in 1841; and in 1881, after several abortive attempts to find the right route through the mountains for the CPR, Major A. B. Rogers (an American surveyor) began work on plotting the railway route through the Bow Valley and Kicking Horse Pass. The tracks entered the Banff area in 1883; the railway was completed in 1885, and the real story of Banff National Park began.

In 1887, an area of 260 square miles was set aside as a federal reserve. The following year, the great chateau was finished, and visitors flocked to the new park to have a taste of luxury in a pristine setting. Like Yellowstone in the U.S., Banff National Park was the precursor to Canada's excellent national parks system. It was the first and is still the most visited of Canada's parks.

An easy morning's drive from Calgary, the park houses two town sites: Banff and Lake Louise. The bustling town of Banff is clearly a tourist community, filled with motels, lodges, restaurants, and souvenir shops that appeal to its increasingly up-scale visitors, many of whom are from Japan. Lake Louise, 56 KM (34.5 miles) west of Banff, is quieter, retaining the flavor of Banff from thirty years ago before the hordes arrived. Regardless of the overdevelopment of the Banff townsite, this is still a superb wilderness park with something for everyone, particularly the magnificent mountains that attracted Donald Smith to build the original resort hotel in 1888.

The park is actually one of four contiguous national parks (Kootenay, Yoho, Banff, and Jasper) that span the Canadian Rockies from Radium Hot Springs in the Columbia Valley to north of Jasper. Paved highways link the four parks, and these highways are covered in the scenic drives on page 28. Yoho National Park in British Columbia, west of Banff National Park, is a pure wilderness area and includes the immensely important Burgess Shale Fossil Beds. Declared a World Heritage Site in 1981, the Burgess Shale contains the fossilized remains of more than 120 marine animal species dating back 530 million years.

So why do more than 3 million people visit Banff National Park each year? It has to be the mountains, arguably the most beautiful of all of the Rockies peaks. There seems to be just the right combination of forested mountain slopes, snow-clad peaks, beautiful turquoise alpine lakes reflecting the mountains, and glaciers hanging over the landscape below. Banff contains 25 peaks that climb 3,000 feet or more over the baselands. Mineral hot springs and canyons add to the enjoyment.

Major information centers are located in the Banff and Lake Louise townsites. The **Banff Park Museum** is a restored log building with displays of representative animal life in the park.

The **Cave and Basin Centennial Centre** has a year-round interpretation program, along with swimming and soaking at the original hot springs located near the base of Sulphur Mountain. You can drive on Mountain Avenue from the Banff Springs Hotel area to an overlook giving fine views of the townsite and the valley. The **Upper Hot Springs Pool** is at the end of Mountain Avenue. This is the highest (el. 1,600 M or 5,250 feet) and the hottest of the five springs on Sulphur Mountain. A gondola departs from near the hot springs to the top of the mountain, where you'll find a restaurant and even finer views.

Also in the Banff area are the **Vermilion Lakes**, a wetlands area along a scenic drive where wildlife is abundant, including elk (wapiti), deer, and many birds. The **Fenland Trails** lead around the small lakes and marsh. **Moraine Lake**, east of the Fenland area, is a very scenic lake with a shoreline trail to explore. This lake is a favorite of photographers.

The Banff area has several scenic drives that lead visitors to points of interest and scenic viewpoints. The **Tunnel Mountain Drive** begins at Banff Avenue and Buffalo Street in the townsite and leads 9 KM (6 miles) up the side of Tunnel Mountain, past a viewpoint over Bow Falls and the Banff Springs Hotel, and then onto Tunnel Mountain Road to two viewpoints (Mount Rundle and the Bow Valley) and to the Hoodoos Nature Trail. The loop road continues down the mountain into Banff.

To get closer to the Bow Falls, take **Golf Course Drive**, which leads you for about 11 KM (7 miles), past the Banff Springs golf course (18 holes) and to the falls, which lie between Mount Rundle and Tunnel Mountain.

The **Mount Norquay Drive** gives excellent views of Banff, the valley, and surrounding peaks from a viewpoint near the top of the road. Wildlife along the route include bighorn sheep and mule deer. You'll find a restaurant at the top of the mountain, and the gondola that takes you there is beside the ski lodge. The Minnewanka Loop Road leads past several little lakes with good views all along the way. The loop starts at the Trans-Canada Highway interchange, northwest of Banff. It's a winding route, which takes you first to the **Cascade Ponds** and a picnic area, and then to Lower Bankhead, the ghost town site of an old coal mine that allows self-guided tours of the abandoned buildings and exhibits. **Lake Minnewanka**, 17.7 KM (12 miles) long, is the largest lake in the park and a popular area for boating, fishing, swimming, picnicking, and hiking. Rental boats are available. The loop then continues to **Two Jack Lake**, which offers canoe rentals and a picnic area. This secluded lake is a wonderful place for early-morning and evening canoeing. A road branches off to **Johnson Lake**, with a picnic area and lakeside trail. This is another respectable fishing lake.

Sunshine is a high mountain ski and summer resort; you get there by taking a gondola from the end of Sunshine Road, which is 9.9 KM (6 miles) west of Banff off the Trans-Canada Highway. The lodge at the top has a restaurant, and hiking trails fan out from the lodge area.

The **Bow Parkway** is an alternate 2-lane route between Banff and Lake Louise, which allows you to avoid the freeway aspect of the Trans-Canada Highway. The parkway offers fine views of the Bow Range, including Castle Mountain and other peaks to the east of the road.

Many consider **Lake Louise** the scenic gem of the park. Mount Victoria, with its glacier, hangs over the lake. You'll find many trails (hiking and horse) around the lake and across the slopes of the mountains. Canoeing on the lake is popular, and canoes can be rented at lakeside. This is the location of the **Chateau Lake Louise**, another grand old railway hotel. Several other lodging places are available in the Lake Louise townsite, including the historic **Post Hotel**, which has retained its original log building (although recent additions include ultramodern rooms and suites).

Several scenic drives start from the Lake Louise townsite. The most popular is the **Lake Moraine Drive**, which leads from the junction with Lake Louise Drive for 12.5 KM (7.7 miles) with several viewpoints along the way. Moraine is a popular canoeing lake. By hiking the trail to the pile of rocks at the outlet of the lake, you will get a super view of the 10 peaks that give the valley its name. The most prominent mountain (to the north with glacier) is Mount Temple. A lakeside trail will take you to the far end of the lake. A short walk leads to Consolation Lakes.

Where to Eat

For fine dining, head straight to the historic "chateau" railroad hotels, the **Banff Springs Hotel** and the **Chateau Lake Louise**. The **Post Hotel** (Lake Louise) also has an excellent dining room with superior service and ambiance. **Le Beaujolais** at 212 Buffalo Street and **Joshua's** at 204 Caribou serve continental cuisine. The best hamburgers in town are at **Harvey's** fast-food place in downtown Banff.

Calgary (Alberta)

Calgary, a city of 700,000 with a modern high-rise downtown, was not much more than an overgrown cowtown in the 1960s. Then the Canadian oil and gas industry adopted the city as its headquarters, and Calgary became a very rich Canadian counterpart to Houston, Texas.

Best known around the world for hosting the 1988 Winter Olympics, Calgary is the gateway to an incredible range of recreation opportunities in the Rocky Mountains, just west of the city. Not only is Banff National Park less than two hours' drive from town, but the newly developed Kananaskis Country on the eastern slopes of the Rockies offers skiing, summer hiking, and other pleasures even closer than Banff.

Calgary is at the edge of the great Canadian prairie with the foothills of the Rockies almost touching the city. Because of the climactic effect of the mountains, Calgary often has mild winter temperatures caused by the Chinook winds, which blow over this area of southwestern Alberta.

The city's history goes back to 1875, when the Northwest Mounted Police (NWMP), predecessor of the Royal Canadian Mounted Police, arrived to establish law and order in an area where buffalo hunters, whiskey traders, and indigenous peoples had clashed. Typical in Canada, there was never any great conflict, but the NWMP brought an added measure of security, and Calgary became a center for neighboring ranchers and a stopping place for travelers on their way to Banff National Park.

Now a clean, relaxed city, Calgary is a social and cultural center that boasts the finest museum in western Canada (some say in all of Canada), the **Glenbow Museum**. Located at 130 9th Avenue SE, across the street from the **Calgary Tower** (another popular attraction), the Glenbow houses displays documenting the history of western Canada, including Native American history and cultures, the European explorers who mapped the West and the Rockies, the Northwest Mounted Police, and western settlers. The museum also features displays on the building of the Canadian Pacific Railway, which tied Canada together shortly after the nation was founded.

Also on the cultural side, the **Calgary Science Centre** offers interactive displays and traveling exhibits directed at children and adults. It's located at the corner of 11th Street and 7th Avenue SW.

Calgary's big annual blowout is the famed **Calgary Stampede**, a rodeo and exhibition held in July. The site of the rodeo, Stampede Park, is used year-round. The Olympic Saddledome is home to the city's hockey team, the Flames, while the Grandstand has thoroughbred and harness racing. Stampede Park is at 17th Avenue and 2nd Street SE.

Those interested in natural history should drive south of Calgary to visit the **Royal Tyrrell Museum of Paleontology**, situated in the Alberta badlands near the town of Drumheller. The **Dinosaur Trail** is 6 KM (3.7 miles) north of Drumheller. Go 160 KM (100 miles) south of Calgary via Highways 2 and 785 to find **Head Smashed In Buffalo Jump**, a world heritage site and the best preserved buffalo jump in North America. An interpretive center contains displays on prairie life and wildlife. The Buffalo Jump and the badlands can be explored in a one-day trip from Calgary.

The **Bow Valley Ranch** also offers exhibits that cover the past 8,000 years of history in the area. Located in Fish Creek Park, south of town on Bow Bottom Trail, the ranch house was built by William Roper Hull in 1902. Guided tours are available from the visitor center. **Heritage Park** is another historical exhibit, comprising more than 100 buildings and exhibits that re-create a village from early Canada prior to 1915. You'll enjoy a steam train ride, a paddle wheeler that plies the Glenmore Reservoir, and antique fair rides, all of which make this a terrific place to bring kids for a half-day or more of looking at the past and having fun. The park is located at 1900 Heritage Drive SW. It's open weekdays until 10 P.M.

Downtown Calgary holds a 2.5-acre indoor park called the **Devonian Gardens**. Here are 200,000 plants including local and tropical varieties, reflecting pools, waterfalls, and fountains. What is interesting about this garden is that it's on the fourth floor of the Toronto Dominion Square, at 8th Avenue and 3rd Street SW. Also interesting is the admission price: zero.

Canmore (Alberta)

Canmore, located west of Calgary and hard against the eastern boundary of Banff National Park, calls itself "The Place to Look Up." Looking up is a neck-craning exercise, with some of the scenic Rockies peaks visible from this town in the Bow River Valley.

Canmore is often forgotten, as Banff-bound travelers speed by on the divided Trans-Canada Highway. In the past, the town has served as an overflow for Banff, but in recent years it has taken on a personality of its own, as it has developed several attractions that merit attention. One of these is the **Canmore Nordic Centre**, which hosted several of the cross-country ski events in the 1988 Winter Olympics and now offers superb Nordic skiing during the winter as well as summer hiking and mountain biking.

Native American tribes have inhabited the eastern Rockies slopes for more than 11,000 years; the most recent arrivals came here during the 17th century from Sioux country, in what is now the Dakotas. European settlement took place here in 1883, with the building of the CPR. Canmore became a railroad and mining center, and nearby coal mining camps were established, including Mineside, Anthracite, Bankhead, and Georgetown. Only Mineside continued operations into the 1970s; the rest were abandoned in 1922.

Canmore is also the gateway to Kananaskis Country, a vast mountain wilderness area (most of it is **Peter Lougheed Provincial Park**) lying south of town via Highway 40. Covering more than 1,641 square miles, Kananaskis Country is an awesome mixture of rolling foothills, snow-clad peaks, high-altitude lakes, and mountain streams.

One of the best things about Canmore (which illustrates the relaxed nature of the town) is that it doesn't have a single traffic light or parking meter. Anglers should stay in Canmore to sample the Bow River fishing for Rocky Mountain whitefish (flies only) and brown and brook trout. Nearby creeks supply anglers with small trout. The **Spray Lakes Chain** (in a hanging valley 3 miles above Canmore) has large lake trout, thanks to a successful stocking program.

The **Alberta Travel Office** is an information center just off Highway 1, at 1830 Mountain Avenue. The office handles accommodations reservations for motels and B & B inns in the area (see page 79).

Where to Eat

The restaurants here are relaxed places (the high-priced places with stuffy service are in Banff). **Boccalino** serves pasta, veal, and good pizza on 7th Avenue. The **English Tea Cottage** serves "light British fare," including calorific cream desserts, at 733 8th Street. The **Rose and Crown Restaurant and Pub** is just what it sounds like—an English tavern with pub food and entertainment. **Tatranka Lodge** has a restaurant serving a variety of international dishes, and it also has a bar.

Clearwater (B.C.)

This small lumbering and agricultural town is the gateway to Wells Gray Provincial Park in the Cariboo Mountains, just to the west of the Rockies. The town is the final point, and Wells Gray the destination, for the scenic drive on page 40.

Wells Gray Provincial Park is 32 KM (20 miles) north of the town. The city of Kamloops is a 90-minute drive south, and the highway continues from Kamloops to the coast and Vancouver. Clearwater is clearly a child of the forest industry. Most of the towns along this highway have sawmills; Clearwater has two large mills. Evidence of much clear-cutting are the large clear patches on the Rockies foothills to the east of the valley. On your trip from the north to Clearwater, you may wish to visit **Spahats Creek Provincial Park**, which is 15 KM (9 miles) north of the town. A trail leads along the edge of the waterfall and the gorge, cut by the creek. The creek falls over a lip of volcanic material and plunges 61 M (200 feet). You'll find a picnic area at the north end of the park and a lava cavern near the edge of the valley.

Wells Gray Provincial Park is not just a mountain wilderness; it also has a large number of subalpine and alpine lakes accessible by foot (a few are accessible by car). The park hosts four campgrounds with 150 sites in all. Additional wilderness campsites allow walk-in camping. Canoeing is a special treat in this park, with a canoe route that encompasses Clearwater, Murtle, and Azure Lakes. Campsites on the lakes make possible a relaxed trip of several days. You'll find some of the best fishing for rainbow trout in Murtle Lake.

At high levels, marmots and pikas show themselves during the heat of the summer. Larger animals include moose, caribou, mountain goats, mule deer, wolves, and even black and brown bears, which are usually not seen.

Other than staying in Clearwater, you can choose between two interesting places that have overnight accommodations. At the park, **Helmcken Falls Lodge** has a motel, with dining, and a campground. **Wells Gray Guest Ranch** has cabins and a campground.

A short (two-hour) loop drive through the **North Thompson Valley** will show you the lifestyle of the people who live in this fairly isolated area. Drive north on Highway 5 for eight miles, and you'll come to a sideroad leading down the hill to Birch Island, with sheep and cattle farms on the bottom land. The road crosses the river and turns left, crosses railway tracks, and goes on for less than a mile. This is now Lost Creek Road, which leads to the village of **Vavenby**. There's a marsh on the way with good sightings of wildlife during evening hours. The road climbs and rejoins the river, passing several ranches including the large Avery Sheep Ranch. You'll see two sawmills, and then the road descends into Vavenby. Cross the river again and turn right. The road leads back to Highway 5. Turn left to return to Clearwater.

Columbia Valley (B.C.)

The Columbia River moves through the long and sometimes wide valley called the Rocky Mountain Trench. At the southern end of the valley is the B.C. Rockies area, which is fast becoming a summer and winter playground of some size. This area boasts new and planned resorts, some of the best skiing in western Canada (including heli-skiing), and several notable parks including Kootenay National Park, which has its western entrance at the town of Radium Hot Springs.

Cranbrook is the largest of the Columbia Valley towns. It's a major business center near the south end of the valley, a few miles from the U.S. border. With a population of 16,500, Cranbrook came to life when the CPR moved its divisional center here from Fort Steele down the road. Fort Steele became a ghost town but was revived in the 1960s when the B.C. government took it over, restored many of the buildings, and turned it into an historical theme park. It is well worth visiting at any time of year, and activities are at their peak during summer months. The city has a

Railroad Museum, which includes a full set of nine cars from the old Trans-Canada Limited train inaugurated in 1929.

Kimberley is a mining town on the west side of the valley, in the Selkirks. Kimberley is now in a transition stage because it is losing its mine and is in the process of becoming a year-round resort center. It already has a good ski hill, which also offers summer accommodations and activities. Furthermore, about 10 years ago, the town burghers of Kimberley adopted a Bavarian motif for the town center, complete with alpine-style storefront architecture, German restaurants, and what is said to be the world's largest cuckoo clock in the town square (the "Platzl"). The people of Kimberley have a vivid imagination and maybe a good marketing sense.

Radium Hot Springs is a small town (mostly motels) at the west gate to the breathtaking Kootenay National Park (see the scenic drive on page 32). This strip of land through the Kootenay River Valley was made a national park when a highway (actually a rutted gravel road) was carved and laid through the valley to provide a route from the Columbia Valley to Banff. The park includes the Radium Hot Springs, which are just inside the park at Radium. The Aquacourt with two large pools (one fairly hot, and a warm swimming pool) is open daily. A motel-style lodge has a dining room and its own hot pool, plus cabin operations inside the park, adding to the number of places to stay in this area.

Radium Hot Springs is situated south of Golden and north of Cranbrook on Highway 95. The large **Redstreak Campground** is part of the national park but is reached from the south end of the town of Radium (not through the park). You can find one private RV park in town as well as another 11 miles north of Radium on Highway 95. Highway 93 is the modern highway that has replaced the rutted road through Kootenay National Park from Radium to the Trans-Canada Highway just north of Banff.

While dwelling on hot springs, we should point out that the Columbia Valley is host to several other springs that provide wonderful soaking. In this valley at the western foot of the Rockies is another major hot springs resort, **Fairmont Hot Springs,**

25 KM (15.5 miles) south of Radium. This is a private operation, extremely well-maintained, including a resort hotel, golfing with two 18-hole courses, a campground, store, and a fine restaurant. The first small bathhouse, dating from the early 1900s, is still here and can be used. The hotel is divided into three areas, with a large modern pool and a hot pool maintained at 110°F.

South of Fairmont by a series of backroads is Lussier Hot Springs, located in **White Swan Provincial Park**. This is primitive soaking at its best, as the water flows out of the earth and down a short hill to a series of natural pools. To get to the backroad that leads to the park, drive south along Highway 95 from Radium (or north from Cranbrook) to a junction south of Canal Flats, where you'll see a sign for White Swan Provincial Park. This road is best suited for four-wheel-drive cars and high-clearance vehicles. The park is 16 KM (10 miles) from the junction.

Edmonton (Alberta)

The capital city of Alberta lies in the central part of the province, 294 KM (183 miles) north of Calgary and 590 KM (366 miles) southeast of Dawson Creek, B.C. (mile "0" of the Alaska Highway). Jasper National Park lies almost due west of Edmonton, and it is easily accessed by taking the Yellowhead Highway (Highway 16) to the Jasper townsite 362 KM (225 miles) from the capital. Edmonton (unlike Calgary) is not within viewing range of the Rockies, but we include it here because of its location on the main Alberta access route to the Alaska Highway and the Northern Rockies.

To the chagrin of some locals, the prairie city is best known to many as the site of the world's most famous—and the world's largest, until 1992—shopping mall. The **West Edmonton Mall** contains about 800 stores including 11 major department stores, 110 restaurants and cafes, a large amusement park, a hotel with bizarre theme rooms and a water park complete with submarine rides, a large wave pool, and hot tubs. People fly to Edmonton on

"Shop Till You Drop" excursions. For Edmonton accommodations, see page 81.

Not as apt to benefit from warm winter Chinook winds, Edmonton is a northern city with cold winters but a very pleasant summer climate. The North Saskatchewan River flows through the city, past the downtown city center and through the Edmonton suburbs.

The city has an enviable succession of festivals throughout the summer and fall months. The long-running **Klondike Days** in July is cause for dancing, costume parties, raft races, gambling, and more as the city celebrates the 1898 gold rush (which took place far from here in Dawson City). The city was a starting point for adventurous and foolhardy souls who left for the Klondike by the tough (and deadly) overland route. Early July brings the **Jazz City Festival**, and in early August, Edmonton is the site for the large **Folk Music Festival**. The first Saturday and Sunday in August are **Heritage Days**, when the city celebrates its ethnic diversity. A large number of Ukrainian immigrants settled in this area, and if there is a place to eat piroshkis, this is it!

One of the more interesting sights in the city is seen only on holidays when the historic **High Level Bridge** over the North Saskatchewan River becomes the Great Divide Waterfall, installed in 1980 for Alberta's 75th anniversary. The cascade is best seen from downstream, on the south side of the river. The waterfall operates on Sunday evenings and on the Saturday afternoon during Klondike Days.

A stay in Edmonton could include sightseeing, and one of the most fascinating ways to spend a few hours is by visiting **Fort Edmonton Park**. The fort is a full-scale replica of the old fort that was a major fur trading post, constructed by the Hudson's Bay Company in 1846. This is not one but three historical villages, depicting Edmonton as the original fur trading post, as the new capital city in 1905, and as a "modern" prairie community in 1920. You can ride an old streetcar and a steam train. You get to the fort by driving to Whitemud Drive and Fox Drive, at the south end of the Quesnel Bridge. It's open in the summer from 10 A.M. to 6 P.M. and from 11 A.M. to 5 P.M. on Sundays and holidays only during the winter months.

The **Muttart Conservatory**, with displays of arid, tropical, and temperate plants, is a series of four glass pyramids at 9626 - 96A Street. Three of the pyramids hold permanent displays. The fourth is changed every few months. The conservatory is open daily during the summer from 11 A.M. to 9 P.M. and during the winter Sunday to Wednesday from 11 A.M. to 9 P.M. and Thursday to Saturday from 11 A.M. to 6 P.M.

The **Provincial Museum of Alberta** has four large galleries depicting Alberta's history, with displays of artifacts from Native American history and culture, the fur trading era, railroad history, and the settling of the Canadian West. The provincial archives are also located in the building. It's open Tuesday through Sunday.

Edmonton has an excellent theater center, the **Citadel Theatre**, a complex of several theaters offering dramatic productions throughout the year. It's located at 9828-101A Avenue; you can obtain information and reservations by calling (403) 426-4811.

To catch a view of what this part of Canada looked like before European settlers arrived in the mid-1800s, drive a few miles east of Edmonton to **Elk Island National Park**. The park is home to 1,600 elk and 500 plains bison (buffalo) and 400 wood bison, as well as deer and moose. Enjoy 100 KM (60 miles) of hiking and walking trails throughout the park and a boardwalk over part of a lake.

Located within the park, at the Astotin Recreation Area, is a Ukrainian pioneer home with museum displays inside. For camping, Sandy Beach Campground has 80 sites.

Golden and Revelstoke (B.C.)

These two towns in eastern British Columbia are both situated in deep mountain valleys, surrounded by mountain peaks and sitting beside great rivers. The mountains are not the same, by a long shot, but the towns do share the same river—the Columbia. **Golden** is a Columbia Valley town sitting in the Rocky Mountain Trench next to Yoho National Park. To the east are the Rockies with the Selkirk Mountains rising to the west and southwest. North of Golden, the river is dammed and a long thin lake (Kinbasket) flows down the trench. South of Golden is the B.C. Rockies resort area including Radium Hot Springs, Kimberley, and Fairmont Hot Springs. As a way station and service center for travelers, Golden's facilities are limited. The town has a small museum on 14th Street S and a municipal campground in a park beside the river. You'll find several modest motels in the town (see page 83).

Revelstoke, to the east of Golden, is in the next major valley of the Kootenay River. It is on the west side of the Rogers Pass, one of Canada's major highway construction triumphs and an exciting drive featured in the scenic drive on page 28. The highway cuts through **Glacier National Park** as it climbs the Selkirks and descends into the lush forests of the Kootenay Valley where the Illecillewaet River joins the Columbia. Closer to the town is **Revelstoke National Park**, a good recreation area featuring a fine scenic drive to the top of Revelstoke along Summit Road. The road leads 26 KM (16 miles) and includes a dropoff point for unhooking trailers (it's that kind of road). A trail (10 KM or 6 miles) leads to the summit. **Mount Mackenzie**, the local ski hill, is 6 KM (3.7 miles) from town, offering base facilities including a restaurant and lounge.

As it passes through Revelstoke, the Columbia River flows northeast, makes an abrupt change of direction about 85 miles downstream from Revelstoke, and flows south through the Trench. The **Revelstoke Dam** is a popular attraction for visitors, located 8 KM (5 miles) along Highway 23 north, which is the road to Mica Creek. At the dam site, you can check out the exhibits at a visitor center, which is open from mid-March to November. An elevator speeds you to the top of the dam for impressive views of the lake and the surrounding countryside.

Because of the Revelstoke Dam, the Columbia becomes a string of lakes more than 144.8 KM (90 miles) long. Upper and Lower Arrow Lakes offer boating, camping, old gold and silver camps, and several hot springs including a commercial hot springs resort near the town of Nakusp. Highway 23 leads south from Revelstoke, leading along the Upper Lake. South of Nakusp, Highway 6 leads to a ferry that crosses to the west with access to the Okanagan Valley—a resort, agriculture, and wine area. If you continue south along Highway 6, you'll pass several ghost towns, arriving in scenic and historic Nelson, one of the towns in the mountainous region known as "The Kootenays."

Revelstoke has several private campgrounds/RV parks including a large KOA (see page 88). You can choose among plenty of public campgrounds in the national and provincial parks, as well as at nearby Williamson Lake.

Jasper National Park (Alberta)

Sitting in west/central Alberta, Jasper National Park is the northern cousin of Banff National Park, which lies immediately to the south of this fine wilderness park. Jasper is the largest of the national parks in Canada's Rockies, spanning 10,878 square KM (4,200 square miles), filled with glaciers, alpine lakes, high waterfalls, forests, and several deep canyons. It is an immense area of great beauty, especially if you're a backcountry enthusiast. Which isn't to say that less athletic visitors can't find scenic thrills in Jasper. People who visit the Jasper townsite find the mountains in this area to be very impressive—more so because of the less crowded and more relaxed pace than in the Banff area.

The town of Jasper was settled when the Grand Trunk Railway (now the Canadian National Railway, or CNR) laid its tracks through the area in 1911. The railway route was established to open up the northern post at Prince Rupert, B.C. However, 100 years before the railway arrived, explorer David Thompson and his companions established the Jasper House fur trading post, in the eastern end of what is now the national park, during the 50-year period when Athabasca Pass was used by voyageurs. Outside of the Jasper townsite, the park looks much as it did during Thompson's travels.

The park is active during both summer and winter. Marmot Basin is the ski hill near the townsite, and cross-country trails are groomed and maintained throughout the winter months.

Jasper Park Lodge has long been the premier resort hotel in the park, with a golf course, ski trails, and canoeing on Lac Beauvert. The lodge is a 10-minute drive from the townsite, which has several motels. You'll find more accommodations, in cabin resorts, a few minutes' drive from town. For accommodations in and around Jasper, see page 84.

The most popular route for getting to Jasper is Highway 93, the Icefields Parkway. Attractions along the Parkway are covered in the scenic drive on page 36. The major point of interest on this route—at the southern edge of the park—is the Columbia Icefield. This is the largest icefield in the Rockies. The **Athabasca Glacier**, a tongue of the icefield, extends almost to the highway (it used to cover the highway route but is receding), and it is possible to walk to the edge of the glacier. For an unforgettable experience, you can ride on the glacier aboard a large bus with enormous wheels, which lumbers over the ice. A visitor center at the icefield offers food and overnight accommodations during summer months. The icefield is 105 KM (63 miles) south of the Jasper townsite. **Stutfield Glacier** is north of the Athabasca Glacier and is another tongue of the main icefield. This glacier features a pair of ice falls seen from a viewpoint on Highway 93.

Other scenic highlights of the park include the **Athabasca Falls**, 22.8 KM (14.2 miles) south of Jasper. The Athabasca River falls through a deep gorge with high spray and sheets of ice hanging from the rock walls. **Sunwapta Falls**, near the Columbia Icefield, is an interesting natural phenomenon. At this point, the Sunwapta River changes course, from northwest to southwest, and then drops through a canyon.

The full beauty of the Athabasca valley can be seen from the top of the Marmot Basin ski lift. Nearby **Mount Edith Cavell**, 29 KM (18 miles) south of Jasper, features a winding trail from the foot of the west wall of the mountain to Angel Glacier and a small powder-blue lake. A longer trail leads to Cavell Meadows, a wonderful place to view summer wildflowers.

Hot springs fans should visit **Miette Hot Springs**, which are farther along Highway 16. This is the hottest spring in the Canadian Rockies, located in a beautiful valley that also features hiking trails and a picnic area. The water comes out of the earth at 129°F and is cooled for the hot pool to 102°F. Summer accommodations are available (see page 84).

For beach activity, **Lake Edith** and **Lake Annette** are both 6 KM (3.6 miles) from the townsite.These are day-use areas with swimming and picnicking. You can enjoy a trail around these small lakes, with a bicycle trail around Lake Edith. Canoeists will enjoy **Patricia** and **Pyramid Lakes**, five miles from Jasper. Pyramid Lake features ice skating and cross-country skiing, and during summer months this is a popular riding and hiking area. The fishing is good here, as it is almost anywhere there is water in the park.

Five miles south of the townsite is **Whistler's Mountain**. The Jasper Tramway takes you to an elevation of 2,285 M (7,496 feet) with stunning views of the mountain ranges, some of which lie 80 miles away. A hiking trail leads to the mountain summit. If you're there on a sunny day, you should be able to see the snowy peak of Mount Robson to the west. It's the highest peak in the Canadian Rockies.

Mount Robson is the scenic highlight of **Mount Robson Provincial Park**, across the border in British Columbia. The park center is an hour's drive from Jasper and is part of our scenic drive on page 40. Moose Lake is an absolutely wonderful canoeing lake near the source of the magnificent Fraser River, which flows from Mount Robson Provincial Park through British Columbia's central plateau to its mouth at Vancouver. This (with the Salmon River) is the remaining major undammed river in North America and the world's top salmon river. Trails within this park will take you to more thundering waterfalls and high alpine meadows.

Back in Jasper National Park, a drive down Maligne Lake Road (southeast of town) provides several scenic highlights. Leading through the **Maligne Valley**, the road runs 11 KM (6.6 miles) to Maligne Canyon, a spectacular gorge where the limestone walls are 50 M (165 feet) deep. A trail winds from a picnic area across six bridges for a view of the cataract. In winter, the frozen canyon is unforgettable. **Medicine Lake** is 31 KM (19 miles) from Jasper along the same road. Because of underground drainage, this lake varies in height from year to year, sometimes disappearing altogether. Maligne Lake, 29 miles down the road, is the second largest glacier-fed lake in the world, with boat cruises taking you past mountain peaks and the glaciers.

Where to Eat

For deluxe dining, the **Jasper Park Lodge** dining room has carefully prepared food and suitable service, but a welcome surprise is the **Auberge**, serving superb French cuisine with reasonable prices in a rustic setting beside the river, just south of town at Becker's Chalets.

Sparwood and Fernie (B.C.)

The southern B.C. route through the Rockies was long a trail for the Kootenai tribe, who traveled across the mountains to the plains for buffalo hunting, then returned home to the Columbia Valley for the winter. The trail became the Canadian Pacific Railway's southern route to the Pacific Ocean in the early 1900s, and much later the highway was established, linking the cities of Alberta with the mining camps of the Kootenay region and the coastal communities. This is Highway 3 (Crowsnest Highway), the subject of the scenic drive on page 24.

Several small communities are located west of the Alberta/ B.C. border, and several more opened with mining activity and then faded from sight. The present-day mining towns along the highway are Sparwood and Fernie. Both have motels and campgrounds.

Sparwood is 18 KM (11 miles) west of the Alberta border. Tours of the Westar coal mine are available daily during July and August. It's the largest open-pit coal mine in Canada. You'll find a golf course in town; next to it is the community campground, which has unserviced sites.

The community of **Elkford** lies deep in the Rockies, 35 KM (22 miles) north of Sparwood. Elkford offers several opportunities for day trips to park areas in the Rockies, including a backroad drive to the high Rockies. **Josephine Falls** offers a fine piece of scenery at the end of a nature trail and is located off Fording Mine Road.

Fernie is another coal mining town, farther down the Elk Valley in a deep mountain bowl situated 48 KM (30 miles) west of the Alberta border. The **Historical Museum** provides a good look at some of the early mining history of the area. The museum is open weekends during July and August: A heritage tour map is offered by the Fernie Infocentre. The town has a challenging 18-hole golf course. Fernie is situated in a deep mountain hole or bowl, with lakes and rivers nearby. The fishing is renowned, as is the white-water activity. Raft trips are available here with information at the Infocentre, which is next to an old oil derrick at the north end of the town.

To the west of Fernie, 14 KM (8.6 miles), is the local ski hill (Snow Valley), and on the same road is **Mount Fernie Provincial Park**, with camping, hiking trails, a creek with a waterfall, and picnic areas.

The community of **Elko** is at the southwestern end of the valley; it's a sawmill town.

For travelers who drive the Crowsnest Highway from Alberta, the major attraction for visitors east of the Alberta/B.C. border is the **Frank Mountain Slide**. West of the border is natural Rockies wilderness with several provincial parks offering camping possibilities and serving as bases for wandering along the slopes of the southern B.C. Rockies. Right at the border is **Crowsnest Provincial Park**, which has a campground for cars and RVs. **Elk Lakes Provincial Park**, on a forest road, has walk-in campsites and several hiking trails.

Kananaskis Country (Alberta)

Kananaskis Country is the name given to a year-round recreation area 90 KM (56 miles) west of Calgary and 60 KM (37 miles) from Banff. On the eastern slope of the Rockies, this area combines a ski hill built for the Calgary Olympics, cross-country skiing, camping, resort lodges, and mountain hiking. You'll also enjoy good fishing in the area, which is less populated by tourists than Banff National Park and has scenery almost as exciting.

The Kananaskis region includes **Peter Lougheed Provincial Park** (named for a former Alberta premier), which is the province's largest park. It is a setting of high peaks, a beautiful valley, and a number of high lakes including the large Upper and Lower Kananaskis Lakes. There are campgrounds in the park, with hiking trails (ski trails in the winter), picnic areas, a store, and cafeteria. You can get there by taking the Trans-Canada Highway (Highway 1) west from Calgary and turning south onto Highway 40. Farther along Highway 40 is Highwood Pass, the highest driveable pass in Canada, with an elevation of 2,227 M (7,306 feet). The road to the pass is open from about mid-June to the end of November, and there are interpretive trails at the pass. You can continue as a loop trip via High River to Calgary.

Back in Calgary, the city has 20 golf courses, and 17 of them offer public play. As a large city, Calgary has accommodations of every type, from hotels (with good dining rooms) to nearby guest ranches and RV parks (see page 85).

A morning's drive of 264 KM (164 miles) south from Calgary will take you to **Waterton Lakes National Park**, which joins Glacier National Park at the U.S. border as an International Peace Park. Waterton shares with Glacier the wondrously rugged beauty of the Rockies. A resort hotel with an 18-hole golf course is located inside the park, plus camping, alpine riding, good fishing, tennis, and mountain trails. To reach Waterton Lakes, take Highway 2 south from Calgary and turn west onto Highway 6 at Cardston. To continue on to Glacier National Park, stay on Highway 2, crossing the Montana border at Carway. A shorter route goes from Waterton Park via Highway 6 to the border at Chief Mountain.

Canada
Places to Stay

Alaska Highway

DAWSON CREEK *Mile "0" of the Alaska Highway, in north-eastern British Columbia.*

Alaska Highway Campground and RV Park
(604) 843-7464

25.7 KM (16 miles) north of Dawson Creek on the Alaska Highway, with treed and grassy sites, full hookups, tent sites, car wash, laundry, and dump station. Open May to September.

George Dawson Inn
11705 8th Street
Dawson Creek, B.C.
V1G 4N9
(604) 782-9151

The largest and most complete hotel in town, with restaurant, lounge, and pub. Air-conditioned rooms and suites. ($)

Mile 0 City Campground
(604) 782-2590

On Alaska Avenue, 1.6 KM (1 mile) west of Highway 97 junction. No hookups, but treed sites and laundry. Located next to golf course. (seasonal)

Peace Villa Motel
1641 Alaska Avenue
Dawson Creek, B.C.
V1G 1Z9
(604) 782-8175

This is a standard motel with some non-smoking rooms and rooms with queen or king beds. ($)

Tubby's RV Park
Comp. 29
1725 Alaska Avenue
Dawson Creek, B.C.
V1G 1P5
(604) 782-2584

On Highway 97, south of town, with full hookups, laundry, dump station, and car wash (important on the Alaska Highway). Open May through October.

FORT NELSON

Coachhouse Inn
4711 50th Avenue S
P.O. Box 27
Fort Nelson, B.C.
V0C 1R0
(604) 774-3911

A hotel with dining room, lounge, whirlpool, and sauna. (**$ to $$**)

Fort Nelson Motor Hotel
P.O. Box 240
Fort Nelson, B.C.
V0C 1R0
(604) 774-6971

A full-service hotel on the Alaska Highway with shopping arcade, some housekeeping rooms, indoor pool, saunas, dining room, coffee shop. (**$**)

Husky 5th Wheel RV Park
Rural Route 1 Mile 293
Alaska Highway
Fort Nelson, B.C.
V0C 1R0
(604) 774-7270

On the Alaska Highway, 12 KM (8 miles) south of Fort Nelson, with full hookups, laundry, store, propane, and transportation to Fort Nelson's visitor program.

Westend Campground
P.O. Box 398
Fort Nelson, B.C. V0C 1R0
(604) 774-2340

On the Alaska Highway (at the 484-KM or 300.5-mile mark) with full and partial hookups, treed sites, laundry, ice, free car wash, store. (seasonal)

FORT ST. JOHN

Caravan Motel
9711 Alaska Road
Fort St. John, B.C.
V1J 1A4
(604) 787-1191

On the Alaska Highway, this is a standard motel with some housekeeping units and laundry. (**$**)

Edgewood (RV) Park
P.O. Box 36
Baldonnel, B.C. V0C 1C0
(604) 785-1211

Located 8 KM (5 miles) south of Fort St. John, with tent sites, partial and full hookups, and dump station.

Pioneer Inn
9830 100th Avenue
Fort St. John, B.C.
V1J IY5
(604) 787-0521 or
800-663-8312

A large, modern downtown hotel with indoor pool, sauna, whirlpool, dining room, and coffee shop. ($$)

Ron's RV Park
P.O. Box 55
Charlie Lake, B.C.
V0C 1H0
(604) 787-1569

On Charlie Lake, this is a campground and trailer park with full hookups, tent sites, laundry, and boat rentals. It's 10 KM (6 miles) north of town.

LIARD RIVER

Liard River Lodge
P.O. Box 9
Muncho Lake, B.C.
V0C 1Z0
(604) 776-7341

Another of the 1940s-era Alaska Highway lodges, this place is highly recommended for friendly service and good food. The lodge is rustic (log) but comfortable and is across the highway from the wonderful Liard Hot Springs. Bathrooms are shared. ($)

MUNCHO LAKE

191 KM (121 miles) north of Fort Nelson.

Highland Glen Lodge
Mile 462 Alaska Highway
Muncho Lake, B.C.
V0C 1Z0
(604) 776-3481

Motel rooms, log cabins, and a campground on Muncho Lake. Laundry, restaurant, boat rentals, propane, fishing guide. ($)

J & H Wilderness Motel and Fishing Camp
P.O. Box 38
Muncho Lake, B.C.
V0C 1Z0
(604) 776-3453

A motel with campground (full hookups), laundry, restaurant, float plane dock, boats, and guides. ($)

Muncho Lake Lodge
Mile 463 Alaska Highway
Muncho Lake, B.C.
V0C 1Z0
(604) 776-3456

A motel with campground on the highway with standard and housekeeping units, restaurant, laundry, and gas. ($) Fully serviced RV sites are available.

PINK MOUNTAIN

Pink Mountain Motor Inn
P.O. Box 15
Fort Nelson, B.C.
V0C 2B0
(604) 772-3234

This oasis on a long wilderness stretch of the Alaska Highway is 130 KM (81 miles) north of Fort St. John. The motor inn has private rooms with bath, a restaurant, and gas. ($) It also has campsites for tents and RVs.

SUMMIT LAKE

Summit Lake Lodge
Mile 392 Alaska Highway
Summit Lake, B.C.
V1G 4J8
(604) 232-7531

A highway motel in a scenic setting, 148 KM (92 miles) beyond Fort Nelson. Standard and housekeeping units, restaurant, gas, and propane. ($)

TOAD RIVER

Toad River Lodge
P.O. Box 12
Toad River, B.C. V0C 2X0
(604) 232-5401

195 KM (121 miles) northwest of Fort Nelson on the Alaska Highway. This is one of the traditional Alaska Highway lodges and has cabins and lodge rooms, propane, and gas. The restaurant has an astounding collection of baseball caps on the ceiling. ($)

WATSON LAKE (YUKON)

This is as far north as we go on the Alaska Highway. For a continuation of the trip north through the Yukon and Alaska, see Alaska–Yukon Adventures, *another book in the* Road Trip Adventures *series.*

Downtown RV Park
P.O. Box 609
Watson Lake, Y.T.
Y0A 1C0

A mid-size RV park with serviced camp-sites, laundry, dump station, and car wash. Open June to September.

Gateway Motor Inn
P.O. Box 560
Watson Lake, Y.T.
Y0A 1C0
(403) 536-7744

All units include a private bath. There are also summer-only cabins, some house-keeping rooms and suites, restaurant, and lounge. ($$)

Hour Lake Lodge B & B
235 Stubenberg Boulevard
Watson Lake, Y.T.
Y0A 1C0
(403) 536-2765

Rooms in a log home on a small lake. Pancake breakfast, sauna, canoeing, and fishing. ($)

Watson Lake Hotel
P.O. Box 370
Watson Lake, Y.T.
Y0A 1C0
(403) 536-7781

Standard rooms (comfortable) with pri-vate bath, laundry, a good dining room, and a lounge. It's beside the Alaska High-way in town. ($ to $$)

Alberta and British Columbia Accommodations

BANFF NATIONAL PARK (ALBERTA)

Banff Park Lodge
222 Lynx Street
P.O. Box 2200
Banff, Alberta T0L 0C0
(403) 762-4433 or
800-661-9266

A motor hotel in the Banff townsite with swimming pool, steam room, whirlpool, dining room, and lounge. ($$$)

Banff Springs Hotel
P.O. Box 960
Banff, Alberta T0L 0C0
(403) 762-2211 or
800-268-9411

This is the doyenne of the Rocky Mountain resort hotels, a historic place to stay with gracious accommodations and service. Tennis courts, winter skating, golf, and riding stables. Fine dining rooms and lounges. ($$$)

Buffalo Mountain Lodge
P.O. Box 1326
Banff, Alberta T0L 0C0
(403) 762-2400 or
800-661-1367

Bungalows, chalets, and townhouse units (some suites) with kitchenettes or full kitchens. Fireplaces, hot tub, steam room. ($$ to $$$)

Park Campgrounds

Three campgrounds are operated by the Parks Service near Banff: **Castle Mountain** is 2 KM (1.3 miles) north of Castle Junction on Highway 1A. **Johnston Canyon** is 26 KM (16 miles) west of Banff on Highway 1A. **Protection Mountain** is located 11 KM (7 miles) west of Castle Junction on Highway 1A.

CALGARY (ALBERTA)

Best Western Hospitality Inn
135 Southland Drive SE
Calgary, Alberta T2J 5X5
(403) 278-5050 or
800-528-1234

A large motor hotel with rooms and suites, restaurants, and lounges. Family rates, children free. ($$)

Delta Bow Valley Inn
209 4th Avenue SE
Calgary, Alberta T2G 0C6
(403) 266-1980 or
800-268-1133

This is a deluxe hotel with large rooms and recreational facilities including a children's creative activity center. Dining room, lounge, indoor pool, and whirlpool. ($$$)

International Hotel of Calgary
220 4th Avenue SW
Calgary, Alberta T2P 1J2
(403) 265-9600 or
800-661-8627

This all-suite hotel has 1- and 2-bedroom units, indoor pool, health spa, dining room, and lounge. Special weekend rates are available. ($$ to $$$)

KOA Calgary West Kampground
P.O. Box 10, Site 12 SS1
Calgary, Alberta T2M 4N3
(403) 288-0411

A large-size campground with full hookups and tent sites, laundry, barbecues, store, dump station. Off Highway 1 (Trans-Canada) 4 KM (3 miles) west of downtown. Open April 15 to October 15.

Lord Nelson Inn
1020 8th Avenue SW
Calgary, Alberta T2P 1J2
(403) 269-8262 (collect)

This is an inexpensive downtown hotel with rooms and suites, dining room, and lounge. Children free. ($$)

Mountain View Farm Campground
P.O. Box 6, Site 8
Rural Route 6
Calgary, Alberta T0L 0M0
(403) 293-6640

A large-size campground with full hookups and tent sites, store, dump station, fishing, laundry, hayrides. Open year-round. 4 KM (3 miles) east of downtown on Highway 1.

CANMORE (ALBERTA)

Green Gables Inn
P.O. Box 520
Canmore, Alberta T0L 0M0
(403) 678-5488 or
800-661-2133

A mid-size inn with suites and queen beds and whirlpools. Some rooms have fireplaces. Coffee shop, lounge. Children free. Located on Highway 1A. ($$ to $$$)

Restwell Trailer Park and Cabins
P.O. Box 388
Canmore, Alberta T0L 0M0
(403) 678-5111

A large-size campground, laundry, dump station, and fishing. Open year-round.

Rocky Mountain Ski Lodge
P.O. Box 3000
Canmore, Alberta T0L 0M0
(403) 678-5564

At Highway 1A and 17th Street. A mid-size lodge, condo units with kitchenettes and fireplaces. Suites, laundry. Children free. ($$)

Rundle Ridge Chalets
P.O. Box 1847
Canmore, Alberta T0L 0M0
(403) 678-5387 or
800-332-1299 (Alberta only)

In the Harvie Heights area. Cabins with kitchenettes and fireplaces in a wooded site with good views of nearby mountains. Studio, 1- to 3-bedroom units. Children free. ($ to $$)

CLEARWATER (B.C.)

**52 Ridge RV Park
and Campground**
373 Clearwater Valley Road
P.O. Box 1813
Clearwater, B.C. V0E 1N0
(604) 674-3909

Tent and RV sites (with full and partial hookups), pool, laundry, and propane.

Helmcken Falls Lodge
P.O. Box 239
Clearwater, B.C. V0E 1N0
(604) 674-3657

This motel and campground is located at Wells Gray Provincial Park, on a sideroad from Clearwater. Motel rooms ($ to $$), a restaurant, and a campground with tent sites and RV sites with full hookups. The lodge organizes trail rides, hikes and other activities.

Wells Gray Guest Ranch
P.O. Box 1766,
Rural Route 1
Clearwater, B.C. V0E 1N0
(604) 674-2792

Located on Wells Gray Park Road, the ranch (like the Helmcken Falls Lodge) is 26 KM (16 miles) north of Clearwater at the park. There are log cabins here, all with showers and more rustic camping cabins accommodating up to six people. ($ to $$) There are also basic campsites with showers, toilets, picnic tables, and organized activities.

Wells Gray Inn
Highway 5 and
Clearwater Village Road
P.O. Box 280
Clearwater, B.C. V0E 1N0
(604) 674-2214

Near Wells Gray Provincial Park. The motel has a coffee shop, lounge, and rooms with queen and king-size beds. ($ to $$)

CRANBROOK (B.C.)

B & J Overnite Trailer Park
2470 Cranbrook Street
Cranbrook, B.C. V1C 3T1
(604) 426-2516

Many sites with full hookups and shaded tent sites, at east end of city.

Coach House Motor Inn
1417 Cranbrook Street
Cranbrook, B.C. V1C 357
(604) 426-7236

This Best Western motel is in the Columbia Valley town, with standard and housekeeping units, outdoor pool, and hot tub. Restaurants are nearby. ($$)

Inn of the South
803 Cranbrook Street
Cranbrook, B.C. V1C 3S2
(604) 489-4301 or
800-663-2708

A modern motel with standard rooms and suites, indoor pool, sauna, whirlpool, dining room, lounge, and nightclub. ($$)

The Original Fort Steele Campground
P.O. Box 426
Cranbrook, B.C. V1C 4H9
(604) 426-5117

Just south of the Fort Steele Heritage Park, with tent sites and full hookups for RVs and trailers, dump station, pool, hot tub, and restaurant. On Kelly Road, 1 mile south of Fort Steele.

Top of the World Guest Ranch
P.O. Box 29
Fort Steele, B.C. V0B 1N0
(604) 426-6306

6 KM (4 miles) north of Fort Steele on Highway 93/95. Log cabins with log lodge (dining room), whirlpool and hot tub, canoeing, fishing, lake swimming, trails nearby. ($$)

Wild Horse Farm
P.O. Box 7
Fort Steele, B.C. V0B 1N0
(604) 426-6000

Across from Fort Steele on Highway 93/95. Large rooms are a part of this early-1900s lodge on a working farm. Rooms and suites with fireplaces, dining room, and some meals supplied. ($ to $$)

EDMONTON (ALBERTA)

Chateau Louis Motor Inn
11727 Kingsway Avenue
Edmonton, Alberta
T5G 3A1
(403) 452-7770 or
800-661-9843

This downtown hotel is far less expensive than its neighbors, with many rooms and suites, room service, a dining room, and lounge. ($ to $$)

Crown Plaza Chateau Lacombe
1011 Bellamy Hill
Edmonton, Alberta
T5J 1N7
(403) 428-6611 or
800-661-9843

Located in downtown Edmonton, the Lacombe has rooms and suites, dining room, and lounge. Children free. ($$$)

Fantasyland Hotel and Resort
17700 87th Avenue
Edmonton, Alberta
T5T 4V4
(403) 444-3000 or
800-661-6454

This hotel is attached to the huge West Edmonton Mall and includes theme rooms, suites with whirlpool, more stores than you will ever want to visit, and a water park nearby. ($$$)

Half Moon Lake Resort
21524 Township Road 520
Sherwood Park, Alberta
T8E 1E5
(403) 922-3045

A campground and RV park with hookups, tent sites, sandy beach, wading pool, baseball diamonds, store, laundry, riding stables, paddleboat rentals. Located 3.2 KM (2 miles) east of Sherwood Park, 6.4 KM (4 miles) south on Highway 21 and 10.4 KM (6.5 miles) east on Township Road 520.

Journey's End Motel (Comfort Inn)
17610 100 Avenue W
Edmonton, Alberta
T5S 1S9
(403) 484-4415 or
800-668-4200

Large rooms and low prices at this traveler's rest stop. Coffee shop, morning coffee. Children free. ($)

Klondike Valley Tent and Trailer Park
1660 Calgary Trail South
Edmonton, Alberta
T6W 1A1
(403) 988-5067

South of Edmonton, this large-size campground has full hookups, laundry, and store, with hiking trails nearby. Near Highway 2 south, take Ellerslie Road west to Service Road south.

Shaker's Acres
21530 103rd Avenue
Edmonton, Alberta
T5S 2C4
(403) 447-3564

This campground is at the western city limits, off Highway 16 (Yellowhead Highway) at the Winterburn Road exit. Many campsites, hookups, tent sites, snack bar, dump station, store, playground. Open year-round.

Travelodge Edmonton South
10320 45th Avenue
Edmonton, Alberta
T6H 5K3
(403) 436-9770 or
800-578-7878

One of a chain of hotels that give good value for money spent, this hotel is in southwest Edmonton. Pool, whirlpool, dining room. Children free. ($)

FERNIE (B.C.)

Griz Inn
Ski Area Road
Fernie, B.C. V0B 1M1
(604) 423-9221

Hotel at the Snow Valley ski resort base. 1- to 3-bedroom units, some with kitchen, indoor pool, sauna, whirlpool, next to restaurant, store, and laundry. (\$\$ to \$\$\$) The inn has campsites and partial hookups. It's on Ski Area Road, off Highway 3, 5 KM (3 miles) south of Fernie.

Park Place Lodge
742 Highway 3
P.O. Box 2560
Fernie, B.C. V0B 1M1
(604) 423-6871

A motor hotel on the highway, with standard rooms, hot tub, sauna, restaurant and lounge, pool, and beer and wine store. (\$ to \$\$)

GOLDEN (B.C.)

Selkirk Inn
P.O. Box 70
Golden, B.C. V0A 1H0
(604) 344-6315

A motor hotel with campground, west of the Highway 1/Highway 95 junction. Some rooms have fireplaces, and the motel has a restaurant, lounge, pool, sauna, and laundry. ($) The campground has sites including full hookups and tent sites.

Swiss Village Motel and Campground
14th Street North
P.O. Box 765
Golden, B.C. V0A 1H0
(604) 344-2276

The motel is at the west side of Golden, with standard rooms and whirlpool. ($) The campground is equipped with full hookups.

JASPER NATIONAL PARK (ALBERTA)

Becker's Roaring River Chalets
P.O. Box 579
Jasper, Alberta T0E 1E0
(403) 852-3779

South of the townsite on Highway 93 (Icefields Parkway), log bungalows and cabins beside the "roaring" rapids of the Athabasca River. Some chalets have kitchens and fireplaces. The best restaurant in the area is here. (**$ to $$**)

Jasper Park Lodge
P.O. Box 40
Jasper, Alberta T0E 1E0
(403) 852-3301 or
800-441-1414

This is the deluxe, large-size lodge in Jasper National Park with a lovely lakeside setting, some suites with fireplaces, swimming, sauna, whirlpools, dining rooms and lounges, riding stable, fishing. Open year-round. Turn south off Highway 16, just east of the Jasper townsite. (**$$$+**)

Miette Hot Springs Resort
P.O. Box 907
Miette Hot Springs,
Alberta T0E 1E0
(403) 866-3750

A small-size resort with bungalows and motel units, some with fireplaces and kitchenettes. Next to the hot spring pools. Open May 24 to Labor Day. Located 10.5 miles (17 KM) south of Pocahontas, east of Jasper via Highway 16. (**$ to $$**)

Mount Robson Inn
P.O. Box 88
Jasper, Alberta T0E 1E0
(403) 852-3327

A mid-size inn with suites and kitchenettes, dining room, whirlpool. Located on Connaught Drive West, near junction of Hwys. 16 and 93. (**$$ to $$$**)

Campsites near Jasper
Folding Mountain Resort
P.O. Box 6085
Hinton, Alberta T7B 1X5
(403) 866-3737

A private campground and RV park, located 8 KM (5 miles) east of the Jasper National Park east gate on Highway 16 (Yellowhead Highway). Many sites, hookups, dump station, store, and snack bar.

Snaring River Campground is located 11 KM (6.8 miles) east of Jasper townsite on Highway 16 north. Open mid-May to Labor Day. **Wabasso Campground** located 16 KM (10 miles) south of the townsite on Highway 93A. Open May 24 holiday weekend, then closed until summer, opening mid-June. No phone. **Wapiti Campground** is 5 KM (3 miles) south of Jasper on Highway 93, with many sites. Open May 24 weekend and then reopening in mid-June for the summer. No phone. **Whistler's Campground** is 3 KM (2 miles) south of the townsite on Highway 93. Open early-May to mid-October. No phone.

KANANASKIS COUNTRY (ALBERTA)

Kananaskis Inn
P.O. Box 10
Kananaskis Village,
Alberta T0L 2H0
(403) 591-7500 or 800-372-9577 (Alberta only)

This modern, mid-size Best Western motor lodge has some units with fireplaces. Also suites with whirlpools, a steam room, and hot tub. Dining room, lounge, indoor pool, and sauna. The inn is in Kananaskis Village, off Highway 1, approaching Canmore. (**$$ to $$$**)

The Lodge at Kananaskis
P.O. Box 6666
Kananaskis Village,
Alberta T0L 2H0
(403) 591-7711 or
800-441-1414

Located in Kananaskis Village, this is the premier resort hotel for the east slope vacation region. It has some rooms with fireplaces, a dining room, indoor pool, sauna, whirlpool, and lounge. Children free. (**$$$**)

Mount Kidd RV Park
P.O. Box 1000
Kananaskis Village,
Alberta T0L 2H0

This large-size, private RV park has sites with full hookups, cable TV, dump station, store, hiking trails, snack bar, and fishing nearby. It's 28 miles south of Highway 1 on Highway 40.

Provincial Campgrounds

More than 20 campgrounds are operated by the Alberta government in the Kananaskis region. Six of them are located in Peter Lougheed Provincial Park along Highway 40, south from the Trans-Canada Highway (Highway 1).

Rafler Six Ranch Resort
General Delivery
Seebe, Alberta T0L 1X0
(403) 673-3622

Located at Seebe, just off the Trans-Canada Highway (Highway 1) near Banff. The ranch offers hayrides, carriage rides, horseback riding, river rafting, and rooms in a log lodge and cabins. No charge for children under 4. (**$$ to $$$**)

KIMBERLEY (B.C.)

Happy Hans Campground
Gerry Sorenson Way
P.O. Box 465
Kimberly, B.C. V1A 3B9
(604) 427-2929

A campground and RV park, 1 mile north of downtown Kimberley, with full and partial hookups, tent sites, pool, store, and laundry.

North Star Motel
Highway 95A, SS#1
Site 20, P.O. Box 6
Kimberly, B.C. V1A 2Y3
(604) 427-5633

An inexpensive motel in the town of Kimberley, with standard and housekeeping units and morning coffee. On Highway 95A, at the north end of town. (**$**)

**Purcell Resort Hotel &
Rocky Mountain Resort**
Gerry Sorenson Way
P.O. Box 280
Kimberly, B.C. V1A 2Y6
(604) 427-5385

These condo-style hotels are located at the Kimberley Ski and Summer Resort, just west of downtown Kimberley. Standard units, as well as condo accommodations—with dining rooms, lounges, and other resort amenities. (**$ to $$**)

LAKE LOUISE (ALBERTA)

Chateau Lake Louise
(403) 522-3511 or
800-441-1414 (U.S.)

This large, old hotel has the finest site of any hotel—anywhere! Sitting beside beautiful Lake Louise, in Banff National

Park, the hotel has over 500 rooms, several dining rooms, a nightclub, and all the mountain wilderness you could wish for outside your window. Children under 13 free. (**$$ to $$$**)

Num-ti-jah Lodge
P.O. Box 39
Lake Louise, Alberta
T0L 1E0
(403) 522-2167

56.3 KM (35 miles) north of Lake Louise on the Icefields Parkway, this lodge has a scenic setting near Bow Lake. Some rooms have shared bathrooms. It has a dining room and a lounge. Drive north on Highway 93. (**$$**)

Park Camping

All campgrounds in the Lake Louise area are operated by the Parks Service. Two major campgrounds operate at Lake Louise. The first is open year-round and has 189 sites suitable for tents, trailers, and RVs. The second campground is open from mid-May to September and has 220 sites.

Post Hotel
P.O. Box 69
Lake Louise, Alberta
T0L 1E0
(403) 522-3989 or
800-661-1586

This used to be a large log building sitting in a wild setting near Lake Louise. It's not a modern hotel (the log part is still here), surrounded by other hotels and shops in the Lake Louise townsite. Now there are many rooms with fireplaces, and some have kitchenettes. Steam room, indoor pool, whirlpool, a fine dining room, and a pub. (**$$ to $$$**)

RADIUM HOT SPRINGS (B.C.)

Radium Golf Resort
P.O. Box 310
Radium Hot Springs, B.C.
V0A 1M0
(604) 347-9311

A modern resort hotel with a golf course, 1 mile south of town, with indoor pool, dining room, and lounge. (**$$ to $$$**)

Radium Hot Springs Lodge
P.O. Box 310
Radium Hot Springs, B.C.
V0A 1M0
(604) 347-9311

This is a motor hotel in Kootenay National Park, across from the hot pools, with its own small pool and dining room. ($$)

REVELSTOKE (B.C.)

Revelstoke KOA
P.O. Box 160
Revelstoke, B.C. V0E 250
(604) 837-2085

At the west entrance to town on the Trans-Canada Highway (Highway 1), with all facilities.

Three Valley Gap Inn
P.O. Box 860
Revelstoke, B.C. V0E 250
(604) 837-2109

12 miles west of Revelstoke on the Trans-Canada Highway (Highway 1), beside a small lake, with indoor pool, restaurant, lounge, laundry, and ghost town theme park. ($ to $$)

Wayside Inn
1901 Laforme Boulevard
P.O. Box 59
Revelstoke, B.C. V0E 250
(604) 837-6161 or
800-528-1234

A Best Western motel in town, with indoor pool, whirlpool, restaurant, and lounge. ($$)

SPARWOOD (B.C.)

Black Nugget Motor Inn
P.O. Box 38
Sparwood, B.C. V0B 2G0
(604) 425-2236 or
800-663-2706

On Highway 3 at Red Cedar Drive. A motor hotel, with coffee shop, dining room, lounge, and pub, near the downtown area. ($)

Idaho

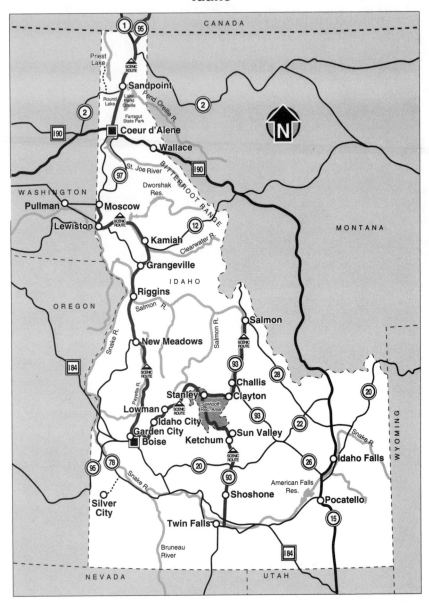

Idaho
Drives

Whon gold was discovered in Orofino Creek on the Panhandle in 1860, the modern history of Idaho began. For 55 years before that, explorers and settlers traveled the region: Lewis and Clark explored the area in 1805, and settlers followed to hunt and trap in the Idaho Rockies. By the time Idaho was declared a state in 1890, the territorial capital had moved from Lewiston to Boise, and the first potatoes had been planted.

Our six drives in Idaho will show you nary a potato patch, because farming occupies only a slight portion of the mostly wild Idaho landscape. The drives do, however, lead through some of the most scenic valleys in the United States, flanked by knife-sharp mountain ranges and carved by primitive rivers.

The northwestern part of the state has routes tracing the Lewis and Clark expedition, providing access to the Snake River and America's deepest gorge, Hell's Canyon. In contrast, the Salmon River, which joins the Snake at Lewiston, provides in this area some of the most relaxed family rafting in North America. Every day during summer and fall, you'll see many small rafts gently floating down the Salmon, starting at Riggins and ending at White Bird, the site of Nez Perce National Historic Park.

The north and central part of the state offers a series of spectacular mountain ranges, including the Sawtooths, Bitterroots, the Beaverhead Range, and the western flank of the Tetons. This is also the area traversed by the Salmon River, probably the best whitewater stream on the continent.

North Idaho Drive

Coeur d'Alene to Eastport

Northern Idaho (the Panhandle) is the state's "lake country," a landscape scooped out by glaciers. It's a land of forests thick with huge cedars, waterfalls, wild huckleberries, lumber towns, and fly-fishing streams. The **Bitterroot Mountains** lie along the Panhandle's east flank, and at the top of the handle, the **Selkirk Range** crosses the Canadian border to fade out in Washington state.

Highway 95 runs north-south up the center of the Panhandle; this route leads from the lake city of **Coeur d'Alene** to **Sandpoint** and north toward two adjacent Canadian border crossings. This route does not lead through the mountains (except for a few miles at the extreme north end) but rather provides access to them through sideroads and a few major highways that run west into the Bitterroot Range. The route is flat, with towns and villages along the way. The location of northern Idaho's major lakes define the recreational attractions of the region. **Coeur d'Alene Lake**, a large reservoir, is a widening of the St. Maries River, which stretches 20 miles south of the city. Coeur d'Alene takes good advantage of its site on the lake, offering large resort hotels, floating boardwalks, and campgrounds with lake access. The city sponsors a variety of lake and lakeside activity, including a chinook salmon derby, sailing regattas, steamboat cruises, and boat parades.

Another major lake, just north of Coeur d'Alene, is **Lake Pend Oreille**, the largest of the state's northern lakes (43 miles long), named for the "ear-ring" tribe. Here, you'll find sternwheeler cruises and several public campgrounds, including Farragut State Park, which provide access to the lake with launch sites. At the north end of Lake Pend Oreille is the tourist town of Sandpoint. This has long been a vacation center for Idahoans; in the past two decades, it has become a growing center for out-of-state vacationers, including those who come for the annual summer music festival.

The third major body of water is **Priest Lake**, accessed via Highways 2 and 37, west of Sandpoint. Priest Lake has some 70 miles of shoreline—much of it untouched—plus spruce and hemlock forests. The Selkirk peaks on the eastern shore are reflected in the lake, and the fishing is good. Year-round resorts offer a perfect rustic ambiance for this natural area. The lodge services, however, are not rustic. Several Forest Service campsites lie along the shore and on Kalispell Island on Priest Lake. A gravel road along the west side of Priest Lake leads to the **Roosevelt Grove of Ancient Cedars** and trees with 12-foot diameters and a height of 150 feet. Nearby Granite Falls provides another scenic thrill. **Round Lake**, much smaller than the others, is 10 miles south of Sandpoint on Highway 95. A state park is situated beside this shallow lake.

The state parks of the Panhandle are worth special mention, and **Farragut State Park** has a fascinating history. During World War II, the site was America's second largest naval training installation, and the deep lake was used for submarine testing. Near the village of Athol, forests and the lake frame the park. You'll find a campground and a picnic area with shelters, a model airplane flying field, and a park museum. It's four miles east of the highway via Road 322. Or, you can get there from Highway 200 at Clark Fork by taking Road 278—a scenic backroad drive.

Priest Lake State Park has a magnificent setting, framed by granite peaks and forested mountainsides. Lake fishing is excellent with kokanee (landlocked salmon) and mackinaw. The park is located 35 miles north of the town of Priest River on a sideroad that meanders around the east side of the beautiful lake.

Round Lake State Park is located on Highway 95, south of Sandpoint. Because this small lake is shallow, the ecology is vastly different from that of Priest Lake. Marsh grasses and water lilies encircle the lake. Wildlife include herons, bullfrogs, hummingbirds, and the occasional lynx. The forest comprises copses of western red cedar, ponderosa pine, hemlock, larch, and Douglas fir. Canoeing here in the evening hours is a real joy.

HIGHWAY LOG
Coeur d'Alene to Eastport
121 miles (195 KM)—2 hours, 20 minutes

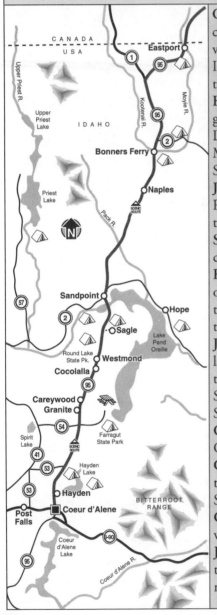

Coeur d'Alene This major tourist center has a full range of visitor services. Post Falls is to the west via I-90. This drive begins at the junction of I-90. Take Hwy. 95 north.

Hayden Town, east of hwy. with gas, cafes, stores, golf club. Hayden Lake offers water recreation. Mokins Bay Campground (Forest Service) is on east side of lake.

Junction–Highway 53 West to Rathdrum. Camping on sideroad, three miles east of hwy.

Silverwood Amusement park, with camping east of hwy.

Farragut State Park Four miles east of hwy. via sideroad. Camping, trailer sites. Gravel road continues to Hwy. 200 at Clark Fork.

Junction–Highway 54 West to village of Athol and Spirit Lake. East to Bayview on Lake Pend Oreille. Stern-wheeler cruises from Bayview. Store and tavern at junction.

Granite Town with gravel road to Granite Lake and Kelso Lake.

Careywood Hamlet with road east to Lake Pend Oreille (Cape Horn). Store, cafe.

Cocolalla Tiny village with lake to west. Cafe.

Junction–Westmond Sideroad East to Lake Pend Oreille. Camping two miles west of hwy. on sportsman access road (a hunting and fishing road).

Round Lake State Park Two miles west of hwy. on sideroad. Camping.

Algoma Village with store and gas. Sagle Road east to Garfield Bay on Lake Pend Oreille. Campgrounds, forest camping, and other visitor facilities.

Lake Pend Oreille Bridge The bridge crosses over a bay of the lake near the eastern outlet.

Sandpoint Resort town 44 miles from Coeur d'Alene, 58 miles from Canada border. Gas, motels, resort hotels, restaurants, stores, golfing, museum. Selkirk range to west.

Junction–Highway 2 West to Priest River. This route leads to several campgrounds provided by the Corps of Engineers, including Priest River Campground, 0.5 mile east of Priest River, and Albeni Cove sites, one mile west of Priest River.

Junction–Highway 200 East along Pend Oreille lakeshore to Hope and Clark Fork.

Samowen Campground (Forest Service) is two miles south of Hope via Hwy. 200.

Junction–Road to Schweitzer Mountain Resort Skiing west of hwy.

Junction–Road to McArthur Lake Wildlife Area To the west.

Naples Village just west of hwy. with store.

Junction–Road to Blue Lake Camping, RV hookups, west of hwy.

Bonners Ferry Town 31 miles from Canada border on the Kootenai River. Gas, motels, cafes, camping, stores, golf course. Forest ranger station on hwy. at south end of town. Downtown at north end of town beside the river.

Junction–Highway 2 (Three Mile Corner) Located 79 miles from Coeur d'Alene. Take Hwy. 2 east to Moyie Springs and Kalispell, Montana. Gas and store at junction.

Junction–Highway 1 Take Hwy. 1 for the Canada border crossing at Porthill. This road continues north for 8 miles to the B.C. city of Creston, the gateway to Canada's Kootenay region.

Junction–County Road 34 Leads south along the Moyie River to the Meadow Creek Campground (Forest Service).

Robinson Creek Campground (Forest Service) Seven miles south of Eastport border crossing.

Moyie River Bridge Over a deep (450-foot) chasm.

Copper Creek Campground (Forest Service) Two miles south of Eastport and border crossing.

Payette River Drive

Garden City to New Meadows

Garden City—the western suburb of Boise—is the starting point for this northward trip, which shows startling contrasts in landscape. Boise and Garden City are located in the midst of a desert landscape near the southwest corner of the state; the Nevada border and even more desert lies 100 miles to the south.

Boise lies in the green, irrigated Boise River Valley, and the river plays an important part in city life. Parks along the river provide recreation, including tubing from Barber Park. The Boise River Festival is a late-June celebration of the city and the river, with a nighttime boat and float parade from Park Center to Julia Davis Park. Across the river from Julia Davis Park is Boise State University. The park is also home to the Boise Zoo and the city's art museum. A short walk away is the Idaho Historic Museum, with early Native American and more recent pioneer artifacts and displays, including a full-scale mock-up of an historic saloon. Other points of interest include the state capitol, Botanical Gardens, and—next door—the old Idaho Penitentiary. The West Idaho Fair is held in late August.

Upon leaving Garden City at the beginning of the drive, the scenery changes as Highway 55 leads into the foothills of the **Sawtooth Mountains**. The Bogus Basin ski area is located off Highway 55, just north of Garden City. Then, you're quickly in Idaho river country, on meeting the Payette River 28 miles north of the metropolitan Boise area. By the time you reach Smiths Ferry—at the 60 mile mark—you're into the **Boise National Forest**, a prime area for outdoor forest and water recreation. The Payette River offers many recreational pursuits; in the summer, river rafting is a popular sport. Several outfitters operate from Horseshoe Bend and Garden Valley.

Cascade Lake and **Payette Lake** are the main bodies of water along the route. The Cascade Lake (actually a reservoir) is an outgrowth of the Payette River, dammed at the town of Cascade.

To the north, Upper and Lower Payette Lakes stretch from the tourist center of McCall, providing scenic parks and forest campgrounds accessed by National Forest roads that lead off Highway 55.

Cascade Lake offers particularly scenic views of mountains and rugged forest lands. Water sports include boating, windsurfing, and fishing. Among the fish species in the lake are coho, cutthroat, rainbow and brown trout, and perch. Ice huts dot the shoreline during winter months.

Another lake region near the route is the **Warm Lake** area, 20 miles east of Cascade. This is a summer and winter recreation center with rustic lodges and cabin resorts, several very good restaurants, and good fishing.

North of the Cascade area is Payette Lake and the town of **McCall**. This resort town is situated on the southern shore of the lake—sailing is a particularly popular pastime. The town has golf courses east of the downtown area; nearby, a championship 18-hole course is in New Meadows at the end of this drive.

Early February is time for the McCall Winter Carnival, an event that attracts visitors from inside and outside the state. Huge ice sculptures dominate the townscape, and the 10 days of celebration include Friday night and Saturday parades and a lot of eating, in addition to outdoor sports.

Ponderosa State Park is a scenic place to fish, sun, camp, and hike, on the east side of Payette Lake just north of McCall. The campgrounds are set in a forest of very old, high pines.

HIGHWAY LOG
Garden City to New Meadows
85 miles (136 KM)—1 hour, 45 minutes

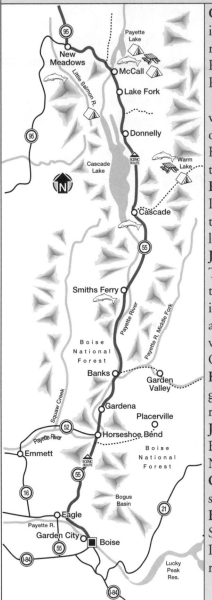

Garden City This suburb of Boise is the starting point for the scenic river route that leads to the Payette River and on to the Little Salmon River.

From Boise, take Route 20/25 west to Garden City and then turn onto Route 44 to the junction of Hwy. 55. Take Hwy. 55 north for the start of this scenic drive.

Eagle Gas, cafe, store. Eagle Island Park is a day-use state park between the channels of the Boise River. It is located west of Eagle, off Hwy. 44.

Junction–Backroad to Placerville This gravel road leads east across the valley to the site of the old mining town. The road also provides access to Centerville and Pioneerville, and beyond Placerville to Garden Valley.

Horseshoe Bend Small town with gas, cafe, store. From here, Hwy. 55 runs beside the Payette River.

Junction–Highway 52 West to Black Canyon Dam, Emmett, and New Plymouth.

Gardena Village with gas, cafe, store.

Banks Small town at junction of South and North Forks of the Payette River. Gas, cafe, store, river rafting.

Junction–Sideroad to Garden Valley and Lowman To the west.

Smiths Ferry Scenic village on Payette River. Gas, cafe, store, lodges.

Cascade Town on Cascade Lake (reservoir), 20 miles south of McCall. Gas, motels, cafes, stores, nine-hole golf course, camping, boat ramps, fishing for trout, perch, bass, coho. Cross-country trails (via Warm Lake Hwy.). National Forest Ranger station.

Junction–Sideroad to Warm Lake Recreation Area Twenty miles east of Cascade on Warm Lake Highway. The lake area features cabins, campgrounds, and cafes.

Donnelly Town with gas, cafe, store.

Junction–Backroad to Roseberry This ghost town is 1.5 miles east of Donnelly. The Valley County Museum is housed in three old buildings.

National Forest Campgrounds Two campgrounds (Rainbow Point and Amanita) on the northwest end of Cascade Lake. Both are south of Rainbow Point, west of Donnelly.

Lake Fork Village.

McCall Town on the southern shore of Payette Lake. Gas, motels, lodges, stores, cafes, golf courses, fishing, beaches. Payette Lake is a prime recreation area for Idahoans and visitors to the state.

Ponderosa State Park Located just north of McCall on Payette Lake, this large state park on a 1,000-acre peninsula has day-use beaches and boat ramps, campgrounds, and trails.

Lake Fork Campground This forest campground is eight miles east of McCall on Lick Creek Road. Trail, picnic tables.

Junction–French Creek Backroad To Upper Payette Lake, Secesh Summit, Burgdorf Hot Springs, Salmon River country, and several forest campgrounds. Take the Warren Wagon Road north from Hwy. 55 near Shore Lodge.

Last Chance Forest Campground Take forest road eight miles east of McCall. Two miles to campground. Tents and trailers.

Packer John's Cabin State Park Primitive campsites at historic site just off hwy.

New Meadows At the junction of Hwys. 55 and 95. Gas, motels, store, cafes.

Salmon/Clearwater Drive

New Meadows to Moscow

Just as the previous drive from Garden City to New Meadows offers startling contrasts in landscape (desert to mountain wilderness), this drive offers an equally impressive flow of scenery, from forested lakes through narrow river canyons, to eastern Idaho prairie lands and the unique rolling fields called the Palouse on the Washington state border. And all of this in a 213-mile drive.

Beginning the drive in New Meadows (the end of the previous drive), Highway 95 soon enters Nez Perce National Forest; by the end of the first hour, you're in Salmon River country. Between New Meadows and Riggins are a number of resorts and other summer recreation areas.

The town of **Riggins** offers wonderful family rafting down the Salmon River. On any summer day you'll see tens (and even hundreds) of small rafts lazily floating down the river, stopping at sandbars for picnics and at riverside campsites. The town is also the takeoff point for jet boat rides on the Salmon, and rafts are available for rent. The town offers a variety of rustic and modern accommodations as well as private and public campgrounds.

Riggins is the gateway to the River of No Return (Salmon River) Wilderness Area east of the town. An excellent backroad drive takes you beside the river past old gold camps. A hiking and riding trail leads across the Salmon into the little-known and much underrated **Gospel Hump Wilderness**, an area of trout-filled lakes and fast-moving mountain streams. The Rapid River Fish Hatchery at Riggins is one of the west's most prolific chinook salmon hatcheries. It's four miles south of town on Rapid River Road.

While in the area of Riggins, we recommend a sidetrip to the **Seven Devils Mountains**. The seven peaks stretch more than 45 miles and climb to 9,000 feet above the town. Around the peaks are 30 alpine lakes and hundreds of miles of walking and hiking trails. A short sideroad leads into the mountains, offering magnificent views. Windy Saddle Camp is a popular place to stay while exploring the Seven Devils area. To get more information on all of these wilderness attractions, stop at the National Forest Service office in Riggins for maps, trail information, and the locations of many campgrounds in the Nez Perce National Forest.

Hells Canyon National Recreation Area, to the west, is a 50-mile-long chasm carved by the Snake River on the Idaho/Oregon boundary. The major access road is from Lewiston, which is north of the area, but for an excellent viewpoint of the canyon—the deepest gorge in North America—take the sideroad north of Riggins near the village of Lucille.

North of Riggins, the highway follows the route of the Salmon River for 40 miles, and then the highway veers northeast, climbing to White Bird Summit in Nez Perce country.

This is the home area of the Nez Perce, and the first major historic site along the route is the **Nez Perce Battlefield**, near White Bird. You'll see a commemorative center beside the highway. This is one of 27 sites that make up the Nez Perce National Historic Park.

After descending from White Bird Summit, the highway enters the Camas Prairie and passes through **Grangeville**, a farming center. From here, motorists have the choice of two routes to Lewiston. Our drive takes the eastern route, along the Clearwater River and through some of the most historic countryside in the American West. This is Lewis and Clark territory, where the explorers spent a winter with the Nez Perce before continuing their journey to the Pacific Coast. It's also the gateway to the Bitterroot Range and Lolo Pass at the Montana border (via Highway 12).

Dworshak Lake, a 53-mile reservoir near the town of Orofino, offers camping and water sports at Dworshak State Park. At Spaulding (just off the highway eight miles east of Lewiston), the Nez Perce National Park Museum has the finest collection of Nez Perce artifacts in the state as well as information on the 26 other park sites. From Lewiston, it's a 28-mile drive north through the Palouse to Moscow, the home of Idaho State University.

HIGHWAY LOG
New Meadows to Moscow
213 miles (344 KM)—4 hours, 30 minutes

New Meadows Town on Little Salmon River. Gas, lodging, cafe, store. Take Hwy. 55 to Hwy. 95 junction.

Junction–Highway 95 Our drive takes Hwy. 95 north toward Grangeville. Hwy. 95 south leads to Council and Weiser.

Riggins Where the "River of No Return" (the Salmon) becomes peaceful and rafting is the popular pastime. A tourist center, Riggins offers jet boat trips on the Salmon. The town has gas, cafes, motels, and stores.

Lucile Small village.

Junction–Slate Creek Backroad (Road 354) To campground on North Fork of Slate Creek, east of hwy.

Skookuschuck Campground On Road 2026, south of White Bird.

White Bird Small village with gas, motel, cafe, store.

Nez Perce Battlefield One of 38 sites comprising the Nez Perce National Historic Park. Views of battlefield from a map/shelter on Hwy. 95. An auto tour map is available from park headquarters.

White Bird Summit (el. 1,593 feet) From the summit, the highway descends to the Camas Prairie, an agricultural area.

Grangeville Farming town at base of Bitterroot Mountain foothills, on the Camas Prairie. Gas, motels, cafes, stores, golf course, Fourth of July weekend rodeo.

Junction–Highway 13 Take Hwy. 13 west to continue this drive.

Junction–Route 14 Leads east to Golden and Elk City.

Harpster Village on Hwy. 13. Gas, cafe, store.

Elk City Wagon Road Look for road marker near milepost 13. This historic dirt road runs 53 miles southeast to the historic village of Elk City (4 to 5 hours). Hot springs near Elk City.

Stites Village on Hwy. 13.

Junction–Highway 12 This road runs east to Syringa, Lowell, the Montana border at Lolo Pass, and on to Missoula. Take Hwy. 12 north to Kamiah and Orofino to continue this drive.

Kooskia Small town on the Clearwater River. Gas, stores, cafe. The town is a staging point for exploring the Selway Bitterroot Wilderness to the east.

Kamiah Town on Hwy. 12 with restored Victorian downtown area. Gas, motels, cafes, stores. East Kamiah has several Nez Perce National Historic Park sites.

Junction–Route 62 West to Nez Perce.

Junction–Route 64 West to Nez Perce and Craigmont (on Hwy. 95).

Junction–Route 11 Leads east to Weippe, Pierce, and Headquarters, along the North Fork of Clearwater River, an interesting backroad drive.

Orofino Town with logging and lumberjack heritage. Gas, motel, cafe, store, museum.

Junction–Sideroad to Dworshak Dam and State Park This 50-mile-long lake has boat-access campsites plus camping at Dworshak State Park.

Lenore Small village.

Myrtle Village. A sideroad leads south to Reubens and Hwy. 95 near Craigmont.

Junction–Highway 95 The unusual geological feature across the river is the Palouse, the unique rolling farmland of southern Washington.

Lewiston River port and industrial city at junction of Clearwater and Snake Rivers and border with Washington state.

Moscow Take Hwy. 95 north. Home of the University of Idaho, 28 miles north of Lewiston.

Sawtooth Mountains Drive

Twin Falls to Stanley

This short, half-day drive could easily be stretched out to a week, or even a month, of exciting vacation time. The Magic Valley lies just north of the Idaho/Nevada border: it's a former desert made green through irrigation. The valley, with Twin Falls in its center, is a miracle of modern technology, and the placid farmland of the area provides a fascinating contrast to several unparalleled natural wonders.

The Twin Falls of the Snake River are impressive enough—yet only a few miles away and just east of the city is **Shoshone Falls**, known as the "Niagara of the West," where the river plunges 212 feet (50 feet farther than Niagara). You reach the falls by taking Blue Lakes Boulevard in Twin Falls to Falls Avenue, then driving three miles east and two miles north.

The other scenic highlight in south-central Idaho is the **Snake River Canyon**, now a wide and sometimes deep chasm that extends west of Twin Falls. This is a prime recreation area with boating, rafting, and waterskiing through the canyon. The river at this point has what are considered among the world's best bass and trout fishing streams. A number of parks and recreation areas are accessible by road along the river's route between Twin Falls and Bliss. An excellent sideroad drive takes you along Highway 30 through the Hagerman Valley along the Snake River, then past the **Hagerman Fossil Beds**, a national landmark. The town of Hagerman is home to the Rose Creek Winery and the State Fossil Museum.

Our drive to Stanley begins at the north end of Twin Falls, via Highway 93. The highway crosses the Snake on the 1,200-foot-long Perrine Bridge, near the site of Evel Knievel's unsuccessful attempt to jump the Snake River Canyon.

It's an uneventful 21-mile desert drive along Highway 93 to the small town of Shoshone. The stark scenery offers an interesting set of views from the Notch Butte fire station, on a hill east of the highway. The area around Shoshone was settled by Basque sheep farmers, and Basque cooking can be sampled at Shoshone cafes.

North of Shoshone, you're now on Highway 75. The **Shoshone Ice Cave** provides a worthwhile family stop. A long underground lava tube preserves a frozen icescape, with a floor of ice 8 to 30 feet deep and 1,000 feet long. Warm dress is required even at the height of summer. The cave is open from the beginning of May through September.

By the time you approach Magic Reservoir and Bellevue, you'll notice the Sawtooth Mountains dominating the scene. Looming ahead of the highway, this impressive range is the setting for a magnificent array of recreational opportunities, many of them spaced along the remainder of our drive. Enter the mountain range to arrive in Hailey and its northern neighbor, Ketchum.

Known around the world as the little town where Ernest Hemingway chose to end his life, **Ketchum** is one of America's foremost resort towns. The **Sun Valley Resort** is located just east of Ketchum, and the town benefits mightily from its association with the resort. As the first major destination ski resort in the United States, Sun Valley has a patina that just can't be matched by the more recently constructed resorts.

North of Ketchum is the **Sawtooth National Recreation Area**, a wilderness preserve of outstanding beauty. Three hundred alpine lakes reflect the peaks and offer excellent trout fishing. The area has several lodges and guest ranches. Campgrounds (with more than 500 campsites) and hiking trails are the primary attractions for summer visitors. Boat ramps and other recreation resources are available on Alturas, Redfish, Petit, and Stanley lakes. You can obtain information on the wilderness at the recreation area headquarters just north of Ketchum. Highway 75 climbs through the Sawtooth range to Galena Summit, and then drops into the Salmon River Valley for the remainder of the drive to Stanley. A ranger station in Stanley will provide Sawtooth Wilderness information should you wish to take this drive from north to south.

HIGHWAY LOG
Twin Falls to Stanley
137 miles (220.5 KM)—2 hours, 45 minutes

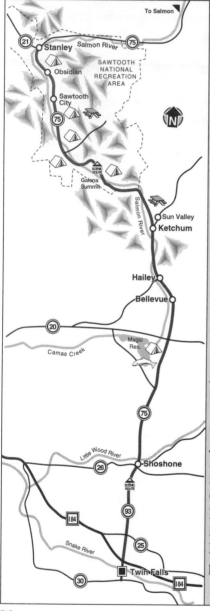

Twin Falls Agricultural city in the Magic Valley. Near the Snake River Canyon (seven miles east).

Shoshone Small town with gas, motel, store, Basque cafes. To continue this drive, take Hwy. 75 north to Ketchum and Stanley.

Junction–Buck Lake Desert Road To Richfield (16 miles).

Shoshone Ice Cave Giant lava tube, open May to October.

Junction–Backroad to Magic Dam A four-mile desert road leads to the dam and reservoir, which is located 0.5 miles north of the Shoshone Ice Cave.

Junction–Road to Reservoir Leads to west side of lake and Lava Point (10 miles).

Lava Beds Volcanic rock beside the hwy.

Junction–Picabo Desert Road To the east, 5.5 miles north of Magic Dam Road. Foxes are often seen along the hwy. here.

Junction–Highway 20 Road to north shore of reservoir (west for five miles). Also west to Fairfield, Corral, and Mountain Home on I-84. Magic Reservoir has good fishing for brown and rainbow trout.

Bellevue Town with cafe, store, RV park, laundry. A backroad from here leads to the Little Wood River and Reservoir.

Hailey Just south of Ketchum with airport, motels, cafes, store.

Junction–Deer Creek Road Forest Access Road to the west of hwy.

Junction–East Fork Road Forest Access Road to the east of hwy.

Junction–Elkhorn Village Road (to east) Resort with hotel, golf course, condo accommodations.

Ketchum Colorful resort town with motels, condo accommodations, cafes, stores. The downtown cemetery is site of Ernest Hemingway's grave.

Sun Valley Just east of downtown Ketchum. Famed winter and summer resort with lodge and inn, golf course, restaurants, shops.

Picnic Area Just north of Ketchum.

Lake Creek Trailhead Two miles north of Ketchum.

Sawtooth National Recreation Area Headquarters and information center 4 miles north of Ketchum.

North Fork Campground West of headquarters building.

Wood River Campground To west of hwy. (2 miles).

Junction–Boulder Creek Road Leads east.

Easley Campground and Hot Springs Half a mile north of Boulder Creek Road.

Boulder View Campground West off hwy., one mile north of Easley Campground.

Prairie Creek Campground Four miles north of Boulder View, west of hwy.

Picnic Area Four miles north of campground. Galena Lodge–Ski Hill Restaurant.

Titus Trailhead North of Galena Lodge 5.5 miles.

Galena Summit (el. 8,201 feet)

Junction–Salmon River Road Leads west from hwy.

Sawtooth City Village with Smiley Creek Lodge, gas, cafe.

Altmas Lake Campground Eleven miles north of Galena Summit.

Junction–Petit Lake Campground Road Three miles north of Altmas Lake Campground, west (two miles) off hwy.

Obsidian Session's Lodge, cafe, Williams Creek Trail, trailer park.

Buckhorn Picnic Area On Salmon River, at bridge.

Junction–Road to Redfish Lake Lodge Three miles north of Obsidian. Sunny Gulch Campground East of hwy.

Stanley Picturesque frontier town at confluence of Stanley River and North Fork of the Salmon River. Motel, cabins, cafes, gas, stores, trail rides, float trips.

Ponderosa Pine Drive

Stanley to Boise

This drive is a logical extension of the previous drive and provides the afternoon part of a one-day tour starting in Twin Falls and ending in Boise. However, this route has so many sights to see and so many things to do that we recommend a slower rate of travel.

Stanley, in the Salmon River Valley, is an outfitting center with one modern motel and several rustic cabin operations. It's a picturesque place to spend a night (or longer). The town is situated at the northern end of the Sawtooth National Recreation Area. Float trips are available from both upper and lower Stanley, and trail rides lead into the mountains. Several campgrounds are located close to town in the Sawtooth Recreation Area.

The Ponderosa Pine Drive is a scenic route designated by the state. The pines are found throughout the **Boise National Forest**, which straddles the Sawtooth Range in this part of Idaho. For most of the first 60 miles, Highway 21 follows the flow of the South Fork of the Payette River. The road climbs after leaving Stanley to Banner Summit at 7,056 feet. Because of the high snowfall on the west slope of the Sawtooths (or is it Sawteeth?), the section southwest of the summit may be closed during parts of the winter. In the summer, the drive through the forested slopes is delightful, leading to the town of **Lowman**.

Now you're entering gold and silver country. Lowman is set in meadowlands, which make the region a prime snowmobiling destination. More than 500 miles of groomed trails through the forest provide superb cross-country skiing as well.

Farther to the south is **Idaho City**, once the largest town in the state. In the 1860s, this community was a booming city with the requisite number of hotels, saloons, dance halls, and brothels. Today, it's a pale shadow of its former bustling self; however, some of it has been restored, and the town is a magnet for history buffs. The "boot hill" cemetery holds the graves of more than 200 of the early gold rush pioneers, most of them dying of unnatural causes. You'll find hot springs near town and enough gold remains in the creeks of the area to provide gold panning opportunities.

The gold rush route continues southward as the highway passes through **Grimes Creek Canyon**, with tailings piles a reminder of the dredges that once worked the creek. The topography changes dramatically once out of the canyon, providing yet another Idaho scenic surprise. Approaching **Lucky Peak Reservoir**, sagebrush and sand appear as the route leads to Boise. This lake—a widening of the Middle Fork of the Boise River—is a favorite recreation area for residents of the Boise area. **Arrow Rock Reservoir** is to the east of Lucky Peak. Both reservoirs are accessible to boats, and boat-in campsites are located on the reservoirs.

The Sawtooth National Recreation Area (administered by Challis National Forest) and Boise National Forest provide superb opportunities for picnicking, camping, and hiking. Many of these locations are listed in the Highway Log that follows; others are accessible via forest backroads. The ranger station in Stanley is the handiest place to obtain detailed forest and recreation area maps and hiking brochures.

Lucky Peak State Park is a popular recreation area less than 10 miles east of Boise on Highway 21. Two day-use areas below the Lucky Peak Dam offer swimming and picnicking. The Spring Shores Marina includes boat launching facilities, and lakeside campsites can be accessed by boat.

Sideroads and Backroads

Many forest roads lead through the recreation area and Boise National Forest (BNF). The color BNF map is a great help in navigating the mountain roads, some of which require four-wheel-drive vehicles. Just north of Stanley, **Forest Road 455** leads west to **Stanley Lake** and several recreation sites. This is a short, well-maintained road, and four-wheel-drive vehicles or pickups may continue through the forest on Road 649 to the base of Elk Mountain.

HIGHWAY LOG
Stanley to Boise
130 miles (209 km)—3 hours

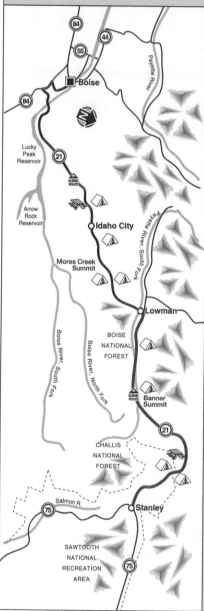

Stanley Motel, cabins, cafes, gas, stores, trail rides, float trips. A thousand miles of groomed snowmobile trails and cross-country ski trails. Sawtooth National Recreation Area ranger station at south end of town on Hwy. 75.

Junction—Highways 75 and 21 Hwy. 75 leads west to Challis, Salmon, and Montana. Take Hwy. 21 toward Boise for this drive.

Viewpoint Located 2.5 miles northwest of Stanley.

Challis National Forest Entrance to national forest with camping and other recreational facilities.

Vader Creek Picnic Area Located 1.5 miles past national forest gate.

Thatcher Creek Campground Located 2 miles past rest area.

Picnic Area At Thatcher Creek Overlook.

Banner Summit (el. 7,056 feet) The road to the southwest of the summit may be closed at times during winter months.

Banner Creek Campground Picnic tables east of hwy. Tent and trailer sites.

Granite Picnic Area East of hwy.

Bench Creek Campground Tent and trailer sites.

Bull Trout Lake Campground Off the highway via a short backroad.

Benoh Creek Picnic Area
Boise National Forest Boundary
Pullouts Three pullouts with scenic views south of the national forest gate.
Junction–Sideroad Leads east from hwy. to Sawtooth Lodge and village of Grandjean.
Bonneville Campground
Warm Springs Trailhead Next to the campground.
Tenmile Trailhead Six miles southwest of Warm Springs Trail.
Cafe, Gas Station
Pulloff Viewpoint to the east, one mile south of cafe and gas station.
Helende Campground RV sites and trailer parking. Located 9.5 miles northeast of Lowman.
Lowman Village with gas, cafe, motel, store. Cross-country skiing and snowmobile center, trail rides. Backroad west to Garden Valley and Banks (on Hwy. 55).
Pullouts with Views For the next 34 miles, between Lowman and Idaho City, you'll see frequent pullouts with scenic views.

Mores Creek Summit (el. 6,118 feet)
Cross-Country Ski Areas Two ski areas with parking south of the summit. Permits are required.
Hayfork Campground, Bad Bear Campground, and Ten Mile Campground Sites for tents and trailers and RVs under 22 feet.
Idaho City Old former mining town with gas, motel, historic Idaho City Hotel, gold panning, saloon, hot springs.
Grayback Gulch Campground Sites for tents and trailers under 16 feet. Picnic tables.
Cafe and Tavern 26 miles from Boise.
Highland Valley Summit (el. 3,782 feet)
Viewpoint Lucky Peak Lake.
Discovery State Park As the hwy. enters Boise, the state park offers water recreation and includes picnic areas.
Boise The largest city in Idaho and the state capital. Gas, hotels, motels, shopping, zoo. Museums include the Boise Art Museum and Idaho Historic Museum.

Salmon River Drive

Stanley to Salmon

The thick-walled log cabins in Stanley are favorite resting places for thousands of tourists annually. The cabins need those thick walls because of the low temperatures of the winter months and an elevation of 6,260 feet. However, winter brings a special cachet to Stanley, much different from its more refined neighbor down the road at Sun Valley. Stanley has to be the world's snowmobile center, with more than 1,000 miles of trails around the town in the **Sawtooth National Recreation Area**. Summer in Stanley is a time for trail rides, float boating on the Stanley River, and hiking on the many recreation area trails.

Our drive beside the river through the Salmon Valley does not match the rude wilderness of the River of No Return Wilderness Area (to the north)—but then, there's no road through the wilderness.

Leaving Stanley, Highway 75 quickly enters the mountains, leading through a narrow canyon and passing several campgrounds and picnic sites in the national recreation area. The Salmon River Mountains come down from the northeast. The White Cloud Peaks lie south of the highway. The village of Sunbeam is a junction point where Yankee Fork joins the Salmon. North of the highway is a fascinating historic area where the old **Yankee Fork Dredge** and a museum commemorate Idaho's early pioneers and the mining history of the region. **Centennial Park** is Idaho's new state park, centered on an old toll road that serviced the gold mining camps of the area. Custer is a ghost town now but was a thriving gold rush town for several years during the 1860s.

Just west of the Yankee Fork junction are the **Sunbeam Hot Springs**, a particularly fine sight in the crisp early morning hours as vapors rise from the springs on both sides of the highway. These springs are not for soaking. The hot pools are farther along the highway, near Challis.

West of Sunbeam, the tiny village of Clayton is the remaining evidence of what was Idaho's largest smelter, which operated from 1880 until the 1950s. Leaving the recreation area, the highway enters a wide valley as it approaches Challis. Challis is a trading center for the Salmon Valley area and is home to the newly opened information center for the Yankee Fork Historic Area. Nearby is **Challis Hot Springs**. This commercial hot spring development includes an RV park and campground and has two pools. The larger (outdoor) pool offers warm water, while the enclosed therapeutic pool has a temperature of around 107°F. The springs are located off our Highway 75 drive, on a short sideroad leading from Highway 93. The pools are open year-round.

Highway 75 leads northeast from Challis for the next 60 miles toward the town of Salmon. This is a prime area for anglers, with frequent fishing access points along the Salmon River (see the Highway Log). Backroads lead east and west from the highway into pristine wilderness. Along the route are small farming communities and several Bureau of Land Management (BLM) campsites.

If Stanley is the snowmobiling headquarters, Salmon is the world's white-water floating capital. Sitting at the junction of the Lemhi and Salmon rivers, the white water offers spectacular trips for kayakers and rafters. Outfitters in Salmon offer a variety of easy and challenging trips. The big blowout of the summer season is Salmon River Days, held during the Fourth of July weekend. The celebration includes a rodeo, parade, auction, staged bank robbery, free breakfast, and a host of hi-jinks.

Yankee Fork Road is a must for history buffs. Leading north from Sunbeam, this old toll road leads to the Yankee Fork Dredge and the mining museum located in **Custer**, the ghost town. This road can be taken through the mountains all the way to Challis, offering a wonderful day of scenery with recreation sites along the way. Campsites are available at Custer and at the Eightmile Campground (east of Custer). The Mill Creek recreation site offers camping and fishing midway between Custer and Challis.

HIGHWAY LOG
Stanley to Salmon
115 miles (185 KM)—2 hours, 30 minutes

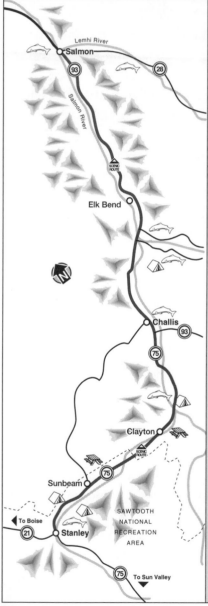

Stanley Log buildings predominate in this frontier town of 140 people. Gas, motel, cabins, cafes, stores, saloon. This drive begins at the junction of Hwys. 75 and 21. Take Hwy. 75 west, toward Challis and Salmon, following the route of the Salmon River.

Viewpoint and Marker Alexander Ross's exploration of area and "ploughed" fields. The road then heads into a canyon; wisps of steam appear at the side of the road.

Sawtooth National Recreation Area The road runs through the recreation area for about 30 miles with frequent recreation sites and backroads leading into the wilderness.

Salmon River Campground Sites by the river and overflow sites across the road.

Junction–Little Casino Creek Road To the east, forest access.

Riverside Campgrounds Both sides of hwy.

Mormon Bend Campground Scenic sites beside the river.

Basin Creek Campground Rough Creek Bridge and road to east with forest access.

Sunbeam Hot Springs Sulphur springs above the road, in the Salmon Mountains.

Junction–Yankee Fork Road North to the Yankee Fork Dredge and an historic gold mine camp from 1879 at Custer, 10 miles north of hwy. (open summer months). The backroad continues to Challis.

Sunbeam Village with cabins.

O'Brien Campground Across bridge on other side of river.

Warm Springs Creek Cascade across the river.

Snyder Springs Picnic Area North side of hwy. Tables hidden in bushes near spring.

Float Boat Launch At parking lot next to Burnt Creek Inn and cafe.

Ranger Station Challis National Forest

RV Park Located 2 miles from ranger station.

Clayton Village with gas, cafe, store, and bar. Historic marker on Clayton Smelter.

East Fork Recreation Area (BLM) Picnic tables and overnight camping, south of bridge.

Junction–Road to Bayhorse Lake To west (eight miles).

Bayhorse Recreation Area (BLM) Beside highway on river. Grassy campsites, toilets.

Viewpoint and Marker Bison Jump site.

Junction–Highway 93 For this drive, take Highway 93 north toward Salmon. Hwy. 93 runs south to Mackay and Arco. **Challis Hot Springs** is an excellent, privately operated hot spring with swimming pool (91°F) and covered hot pool (107°F). A campground with RV hookups beside the pools. Take Hwy. 93 south for one mile and turn to sideroad to springs (4.5 miles).

Challis Town on Hwy. 93, situated 55 miles from Stanley. Gas, motels, RV park, cafes, stores, National Forest Ranger Station. Founded by Hudson's Bay Company trappers in 1878.

Fishing Access Look for signs pointing to several fishing access roads.

Junction–Hat Creek Forest Road Camping at Deer Gulch, west off hwy.

Junction–Cabin Creek Forest Road To west, with national forest access.

Junction–Iron Creek Forest Road

Elk Bend Small village to west of highway. Cafe, bar, RV parking in mobile home park. Twin Falls Guest Ranch north of village, 18 miles south of Salmon. Twelve Mile Road East for national forest access.

Junction—Williams Lake Forest Road This backroad leads to a network of forest roads in the Salmon National Forest.

Salmon Town located in the scenic Salmon Valley. Gas, motels, restaurants, cafes, stores, museum.

Idaho
Destinations

Boise

Idaho's capital city lies at the foot of the Boise Front of the Rockies—a desert town close to the peaks and the treed slopes of the **Boise National Forest**. Lying on both sides of the Boise River, this city is a green space in sagebrush country with parks along the river and an enviable lifestyle. Boise's climate is so benign that one can golf in the city and ski at the nearby ski hill on the same day.

The community was established in 1863 as a staging area and service center for the mining camps, including Idaho City—the largest of the gold and silver mining areas. The area previously had been home to several Native American tribes, and the fur trade exploited the area during the 1820s. From the time of the first mineral discoveries in 1860, the region boomed, giving way to forestry as the gold and silver mines dwindled.

The city has many attractions that make a stay here pleasant and relaxing, including several fine parks and nature preserves. **Kathryn Albertson Park** is located in the heart of the city—a walking park with ponds, fountains, islands, and a wetlands area. The **Boise River Observatory** and its Morris Knudsen Nature Center is a showcase for wildlife on the Boise River, with underwater viewing windows, displays on fish life, and tours taking visitors to ponds, wetland areas, and desert habitats.

South of Boise, near the **Snake River Birds of Prey Natural Area**, is the **World Center for Birds of Prey**. In this nature center, falcons, eagles, and other raptors are studied and reared. It provides an ideal opportunity to see hawks and eagles much closer than you can in the wild. The Tropical Raptor Building displays birds from around the world.

The **Idaho Botanical Garden** is a series of nine theme gardens that include a hillside walking trail, rose and iris gardens, a Basque garden, and the unique Chinese Scholar's Garden. This fine outdoor attraction is on the grounds of the old Idaho State Penitentiary. Boise has the largest Basque community outside of Europe, and the **Basque Museum and Cultural Center** is the nation's only Basque museum. It is a former boarding house, used to house immigrants from 1910 through the 1970s, and it is located at 6th and Grove. More history is exhibited at **Military Reserve Park**, at Fort and Reserve streets. Included are the old Boise Barracks, hiking trails, and the O'Farell Cabin, the city's first permanent home. The city's extensive park system includes **Julia Davis Park** on the Boise River in the downtown area. The park contains the Idaho Historical Museum, the Boise Art Museum, the city zoo, and the Memorial Rose Garden. The 90 acres of parkland include playgrounds, tennis courts, boat rentals, and a band shell featuring entertainment throughout the summer. **The Grove** is Boise's public plaza with nearby shopping and a weekly program of music and other entertainment "Alive after Five."

Where to Eat

The **Chart House** offers riverside dining with steak, seafood, and a children's menu (2288 North Garden Street). **Milford's Fish House** at the 8th Street Marketplace serves fresh fish dinners (open from 5 P.M.). **Garcia's** has two locations for good Mexican food at ParkCenter and Beacon (off Broadway). **TableRock Bar and Grill** (705 Fulton) was Boise's first microbrewery.

Day Trips from Boise

Several jaunts from Boise provide great scenery and a look into the rough and rowdy mining history of the area. An hour's drive northeast of town is **Idaho City**—the region's first town—where gold and silver were discovered in the 1860s. Surrounded by Boise National Forest, Idaho City is on the Ponderosa Pine Drive (see page 108). Many of the original buildings from the 1860s remain today, complete with boardwalks and the Pioneer Cemetery and its tall headboards. You'll find overnight accommodations (see page 138) and a place to eat and drink (in the Miner's Exchange Saloon) in the ambiance of a lusty mining camp. The Idaho City Hotel is one of the originals—completely renovated and retaining the charm of a rustic old inn. Another great place to stay is the Miner's Inn, a former home with three bedrooms and two bathrooms. Warm Springs Resort is 1.5 miles from Idaho City, offering hot pools, cabins, and RV parking.

The ghost town of **Silver City** provides another scenic day trip or overnight jaunt. To get there from the Boise area, drive south until you get to Highway 78 and drive southwest to a backroad five miles south of Murphy. The backroad is unpaved and can be rough in places, leading through desert, foothills, and canyonland on the way to the old 1863 mining camp. You can also get there (from the west) by driving south on Highway 45 to Jordan Valley and then turning west to reach Silver City on a backroad (25 miles). For information on the road and accommodations at the old Idaho Hotel (the only functioning building), call the Idaho Hotel at (208) 495-2520.

Coeur d'Alene

Coeur d'Alene Lake is one of 60 lakes within an hour's drive of the town that bears the lake's name. The other major lakes in the area are Hayden, Pend Oreille, and Spirit, and you can reach them all by traveling along our scenic drive on page 92. The towns of Coeur d'Alene and neighboring Post Falls are the gateways to the forest and lake region of northern Idaho, fast becoming a magnet for vacationers from across the nation.

The longtime home of the Kootenai, mining interests led to opening the area to Europeans in the 1860s. By 1890, almost five million dollars in metals had been taken out of the area, mostly from the towns of Wallace and Kellogg to the east. Idaho's vast timberlands now provide the basis for the regional economy.

With so many lakes in the Idaho Panhandle, it is no wonder that anglers, hunters, canoeists, and other outdoors seekers flock to this area. Coeur d'Alene has also become a sophisticated resort town since the opening in 1986 of the **Coeur d'Alene Resort**, a large, world-class resort operation that occupies a prominent piece of the town's shoreline. The resort boasts large deluxe rooms and penthouse suites and two dining rooms (one for fine dining, the other less formal at dockside). The resort's golf course features the world's first (and only) floating green. A floating boardwalk encircles the hotel and marina. It's a good example of how a single resort operation can put a community into a new tourism league.

You'll find plenty of other things to see and do while visiting Coeur d'Alene. **Post Falls**, west of town and located on the Spokane River, is famous for the Kentucky bluegrass that is grown here for its seed. The whole community of **Wallace**, 60 miles east of Coeur d'Alene, is on the National Historic Register. This was the hub of the mining boom in northern Idaho, and its turn-of-the-century architecture is delightful (see page 147).

Farragut and Heyburn State Parks are north and south of Coeur d'Alene, respectively, offering camping and water sports. Farragut was a naval training (submarine) station during World War II, and it has a park museum and a huge (60,000-seat) amphitheater. Heyburn's chief attraction is wildlife viewing, particularly heron and osprey. This is a wonderful canoeing park with the shadowy St. Joe River winding among several small lakes. **Silverwood**, a theme park, is on Highway 95, located 15 miles north of town. The amusement park is dressed up in a pioneer mining town fashion—to good effect. You can enjoy old-time movies in the theater, old-fashioned carnival rides, and a narrow gauge steam train. A large RV park is located across the highway. Walkers will enjoy the **Tubbs Hill Nature Trail**, a two-mile loop beginning in the parking lot between the Coeur d'Alene Resort and McEuen Park. The two-hour walk contains historic points along with several scenic viewpoints.

Where to Eat

For fine dining, head to the dining room at the **Coeur d'Alene Resort**, which boasts a great wine list and award-winning food. **Dockside** is the less-formal dockside restaurant at the resort. **Chef in the Forest** at 7900 Hauser Lake Road in Post Falls offers a natural ambiance. **Wolf Lodge Inn**, on the lake at I-90, exit 22, serves meals in a prime natural area while eagles fly overhead.

Ketchum and Sun Valley

During the 1930s, railroad magnate Averell Harriman was so impressed by the Winter Olympics at Lake Placid and by European skiing resorts that he commissioned an Austrian count, Felix Schaffgotsch, to find a suitable western site for an American ski resort that would have the ambiance of the European mountain resorts. The result was Sun Valley, America's first destination ski resort, and the first in the world to have chairlifts. The area is covered in our Sawtooth Mountains Drive, starting on page 104.

The resort is set in a side valley just out of the town of Ketchum—a destination in itself for many who wish to "get away from it all." Ernest Hemingway was the most notable of Ketchum's residents. His grave is in the little cemetery in Ketchum, and a memorial to him is near the Sun Valley Golf Course beside Trail Creek.

Sun Valley is a large resort complex that does not reveal its size. Instead, the complex is comfortable, with a 1940s style and ambiance that can't be matched by any of the more modern Rockies resorts. And it's nestled at the foot of the Sawtooth Mountains, which continually provide a jagged scenic backdrop. With its two hostelries (the Lodge and the Inn), Sun Valley can provide accommodations for romantic hideaways or for family vacations. The rink made famous in the Glenn Miller–Sonia Henie 1940s movie *Sun Valley Serenade* is there, winter and summer. Today's top figure skaters provide shows on summer Saturday nights. The rink is part of the Lodge's dining and entertainment area. You can even relax at 5 P.M. in the Lodge to see the movie.

For summer visitors, the Sun Valley resort has two 18-hole golf courses, tennis courts, and swimming pools. In winter months, **Bald Mountain** provides 1,200 acres of downhill skiing with 12 lifts, including three high-speed quad chairs. **Dollar Mountain** is more of a family skiing operation with four lifts. Tickets for the two mountains are interchangeable.

Ketchum and Sun Valley also have two cross-country ski centers, and two more are in the **Sawtooth National Recreation Area** just north of the resort area. In all, you can enjoy 175 miles of groomed trails, including skating lanes. Snowmobile tours are popular as well. In summer, choose among 80 miles of hiking trails in the recreation area.

On winter evenings, horse-drawn sleighs take visitors into the woods for gourmet dinners. Restaurants in the resort complex range from the Konditorei—with outdoor deck dining—to the deluxe dining room in the Lodge.

The other large resort operation is **Elkhorn Village**, located just south of Ketchum off Highway 75. This is a new hotel resort with an 18-hole championship golf course, cross-country trails, and the same skiing arrangements as Sun Valley with ski lifts on Dollar Mountain rising from the Elkhorn base.

In the town of Ketchum, life is more downscale (but not much), compared to the social whirl at the two resorts. Choose among cozy European-style lodgings, bed and breakfast inns, modern accommodations in old, historic buildings, and several larger and modern hotels and motels. In the winter, this is a ski town.

During summer and fall months, the town draws thousands of outdoor types interested in exploring the Sawtooth National Recreation Area and enjoying the rustic environment that the town provides. The recreation area is seven miles north of Ketchum. Over 300 alpine lakes lie in the Sawtooth Range, and a network of hiking trails crisscross the area. You'll find campsites (public and private) throughout the area, including several along Highway 75, the main route. Cabins as well as rustic lodges are available for rent. We recommend stopping at the recreation area's information center, just north of Ketchum, for an overview of the recreational attractions of this vast mountain wilderness. The **Sawtooth National Fish Hatchery** raises more than three million salmon each year—it goes without saying that the area is an angler's paradise. You'll find boat ramps on several of the lakes including Alturas, Redfish Pettit, and Lake Stanley. Highway 75 takes you north through the recreation area to the town of Stanley.

Ketchum, Sun Valley, and Elkhorn Village have a full range of summer and winter festivities. The **Sun Valley Winter Carnival** is held during the third and fourth weeks of January and includes a food fair, dances, and a celebrity ski race. The **Sun Valley Music Festival** is held during July and August, featuring classical music and jazz; the festival is organized by the Sun Valley Center for the Arts and Humanities. **Summerdance at Elkhorn** brings renowned dance stars to the mountains, a counterpart to the summer dance school here. The town of Ketchum celebrates its pioneer mining history at the **Wagon Days Celebration** (end of August) with flapjack breakfasts, band concerts, dancing, and a melodrama. A newer entry is the Sun Valley **Swing 'n Dixie Jazz Jamboree**, held in mid-October at the resort.

Aside from the recreation area camping facilities farther north, several campgrounds in the **Sawtooth National Forest** are closer to Ketchum. You'll see two campgrounds on East Fork Road, southeast of town (Federal Gulch and Sawmill). West of Ketchum, on Warm Springs Road, are two units that offer private camping (with one unit each); Cottonwood is 5.5 miles from town, Penny Lake is 4 miles from the highway. Northeast of town are three campgrounds on Trail Creek Road. Boundary campground has a picnic area with 24-hour camping only. Park Creek and Phi Kappa campgrounds have 36 sites with grills and picnic tables.

Where to Eat

The resorts offer fine dining and relaxed eating in small cafes and delis. **Sun Valley Village**, next to the resort hotels, has several smaller places including the **Deli**, **Konditorei**, **Ore House** (steaks and seafood), and the **Ram** (with Austrian decor). The Lodge serves a buffet before the Saturday ice shows. Elkhorn Village has a full range of restaurants and cafes. In Ketchum, eating places range from fine dining at **A Matter of Taste** and **Chez Michael** to **Desperados** (Mexican) on Main Street and **Christiana's**, a continental restaurant on Walnut Avenue.

McCall and Cascade

Ninety minutes north of Boise is a serene land of forests and lakes that offers white water, mountain adventure, and some of the best fishing in Idaho. The Payette River flows through southwestern Idaho, creating three lakes (one is the Cascade Reservoir) in a sterling vacation region.

Cascade Lake is at the center of an outdoor recreation area that includes secluded Warm Lake 25 miles east of Cascade off Highway 55, which has several resorts with rustic cabins, lodges, and campgrounds.

The town of Cascade, on Highway 55, is a fishing center with boat and shore fishing for rainbow, cutthroat, brown, coho, and perch. During the winter, the Cascade area has over 600 miles of snowmobile trails and many additional miles of cross-country trails in the **Boise National Forest**. During summer months, the trails are open to hikers. Cascade features golfing by the lake and private RV parks as well as forest campgrounds.

North of Cascade are **Payette Lake** and **Little Payette Lake**. The town of McCall is situated on the southern shore of Payette Lake. This is also a rustic resort town with lakeside parks and beaches, sailing on the lake, more golfing, and yet more fishing. A new 18-hole golf course is located in New Meadows, a small town just beyond McCall. All of these attractions are shown in the scenic drive that starts on page 96.

While Cascade's major annual event is **Thunder Mountain Days**, a summer rodeo and celebration, McCall's is the **Winter Carnival**. During the carnival held at the beginning of February, the town is decked out with ice sculptures, created by local and visiting artists, and parades on the opening Friday and Saturday nights. Enjoy dances, pancake breakfasts, and a lot of celebrating. Brundage Mountain is the local ski hill, located seven miles north of McCall. Boise National Forest provides recreation areas, forest campgrounds, and other outdoor attractions.

Three hot springs in the region are worth visiting. The most scenic and rustic location is **Burgdorf Hot Springs**, which can be reached by taking the French Creek backroad drive via Warren Wagon Road or by taking Davis Avenue at the southeast end of McCall and then Lick Creek Road and East Side Road. **Zim's Hot Springs** is located along Highway 55, north of McCall, just beyond the **Kimberland Meadows Resort**. This large resort hotel with 18-hole golf course also has a hot pool. The resort features town-house-style accommodations.

A full-service RV park is in McCall, in addition to numerous Payette National Forest campgrounds. **Ponderosa State Park** occupies a scenic site along the eastern shore of Payette Lake, within a few minutes' drive of McCall. You'll find camping here as well, along with several hiking trails, a boat ramp, and picnic areas. At the northern end of the park is a large hill with fine overviews of the lake and the mountains beyond.

Where to Eat

Kimberland Meadows Restaurant is located in the deluxe golf resort, north of McCall. **Houston's**, at 203 East Lake Street, offers lakeside dining with steak and seafood as staples. For rusticity, try the **Mill**, on Highway 55. It has a fine forest setting and piano music on Fridays and Saturdays, and its menu includes steaks, seafood, and prime rib.

Moscow and Lewiston

Moscow and neighboring Lewiston are about as far away from the Rockies as this book will take you. However, the pleasant college town (Moscow) and industrial Lewiston are good stopover places on your way into the Idaho Rockies (if you're traveling from the west), or if you've just completed a trip up the Payette, Salmon, and Clearwater rivers (as in our scenic drive on page 100).

One of the great pleasures of completing your trip in this region is experiencing the **Palouse**, those wonderful rolling hills along the Snake River in both Idaho and Washington states. The Palouse may not be the Rockies in terms of scenic grandeur, but this range is unique in its own way.

Aside from agriculture, Moscow's main industry is the **University of Idaho**, established here in 1889 largely to show the state flag so the Idaho Panhandle would not be annexed to Washington. The university provides a cultural underpinning for the town, with frequent concerts, drama productions, and art shows of high quality. Jazz is frequently heard; the school of music at the university is named after vibraphonist Lionel Hampton, and the annual jazz festival bears his name.

Moscow and Lewiston are logical places from which to explore the history of the Nez Perce, who occupied most of the surrounding territory. The tragic story of Chief Joseph and the fateful conflict between Joseph and the federal government started in this area, ending after the long circuitous escape toward Canada, which was brought short in northern Montana.

Nez Perce National Historic Park is a dispersed collection of 38 different sites located throughout north central Idaho. The park headquarters is located 11 miles east of Lewiston (south of Moscow). The visitor center contains a museum of the Nez Perce culture. Other major park sites in the region include the **White Bird Battlefield** and **East Kamiah**. The latter site is devoted to showing what the tribe called the "Heart of the Monster," the place where the Nez Perce are thought to have originated. The

White Bird Battlefield commemorates the conflict between the union troops and the Nez Perce.

Many additional park sites are located close to the park headquarters, including the **Mission**, established by Henry and Eliza Spalding; the **Indian Agency**, built to oversee the treaties negotiated with the Nez Perce; and **Fort Lapwai**, which was built by a detachment of volunteer soldiers in 1862.

Across the Panhandle, at the border with Montana, is **Lolo Pass** and two additional park sites. At this pass—used by Lewis and Clark—the Nez Perce crossed into Montana during the war of 1877. You'll find a summer visitor center here as well as the Lochsa Historical Ranger Station.

Private RV parks are located in both Lewiston and Moscow, and a large public campground is in **Hell's Gate State Park** four miles south of Lewiston. This is an excellent park to visit, and the **Hell's Canyon National Recreation Area**, with its deep chasm, is to the south. Jet boats take visitors into the gorge.

Salmon

The town of Salmon calls itself the "White Water Capital of the World." Lying just south of the River of No Return Wilderness Area, which contains 2.5 million acres of mountain wonder, Salmon has more outfitters than any other town or city in the Rockies. The route through Salmon is featured in our Salmon River drive on page 112.

Salmon is also in a prime wild-river fishing region, at the confluence of the Lemhi and Salmon rivers. The salmon run is memorable, and it's a major attraction for anglers who come here during the main spawning season, which runs from June to September. Aside from salmon, the rivers have good stocks of rainbow trout and steelhead (the season runs from October through March).

The Salmon River is one of the few undammed rivers left in North America, and it is a target of activism by environmental groups to keep it that way. The "River of No Return" flows rapidly through the eponymous wilderness area, which is the largest such area in the lower 48 states. Chinook salmon spawn in the gravel beds of the river in tremendous numbers, although in recent years the salmon returns have been off their regular rate. Along the river are prehistoric cave paintings and rock drawings that are estimated to be more than 8,000 years old. The wildlife in the wilderness area and in the Salmon and Challis National Forests include deer, elk, black bear, mountain goats, and more. Pack trips are available to take you into the backcountry, where the mountain lakes and streams attract trout anglers from around the world.

Winter visitors find Salmon to be a snowmobile heaven with forest trails everywhere around town. The **Lost Trail Ski Area** is 42 miles north of town, with three chairlifts and the **Lost Trail Hot Springs** nearby for winter (or summer) soaking. Float boating is an extremely popular vacation activity, and the local outfitters offer raft trips ranging from one to eight days down the River of No Return (these days, returning to Salmon is guaranteed). Fishing for trout and steelhead is also a feature of the float trips.

Salmon has motels, bed and breakfast homes, and several guest ranches at which to stay; more accommodations are available in nearby North Fork, 11 miles north of Salmon (see page 142). Private campgrounds are in Salmon and in North Fork. You'll find plenty of public campsites in the national forests.

Salmon River Days—held over the Fourth of July holiday—offers free breakfasts, a rodeo, auction, and other events including a staged bank robbery, reliving the Wild West days of this early frontier town. Salmon is only 60 miles northwest of Challis, where a hot springs resort (with RV park) provides two hot (one is very hot) pools.

Where to Eat

The **North Fork Cafe** in North Fork offers a scenic setting and reasonable food (with a bar). Gibbonsville is an even tinier village just north of North Fork, and the **Broken Arrow Cafe** there is as rustic as the rest of the town. The food in Salmon is basic without much variety: try **Johnny B's** or the **28 Supper Club**.

Sandpoint and the Panhandle

The Idaho Panhandle, north of Coeur d'Alene, is a vacation area that can only be described with superlatives. The two major lakes that define the area are Lake Pend Oreille and Priest Lake. The resort town of Sandpoint lies at the north end of Lake Pend Oreille, with the **Cabinet Mountain Wilderness** to the east and the Selkirk foothills coming down from the north over the Canadian border. The two lakes are joined by the Priest River. Now attracting a growing number of senior citizens, the town has become a retirement haven for Los Angeles police officers.

Sandpoint is a city that takes its visitors seriously. For instance, the Cedar Street Bridge is a unique shopping galleria that spans a 350-foot creek. Included is the Vintage Wheel Museum, which has a large collection of antique vehicles.

The cultural highlight of the summer season in the area is the **Festival at Sandpoint**, founded by composer and conductor Gunther Schuller in 1983; this festival takes place in early August and features symphony, pop rock, and everything in between. The festival is part of a musical training center that joins young musicians with the greats of classical and jazz music. **Schweitzer Mountain Resort** is a year-round resort complex just north of Sandpoint. It's the area's ski hill in winter months and a Selkirk mountain lodge in the summer, offering stunning views from the top of the chairlift. Some of the summer festival events are held here. Ten miles south of Sandpoint, **Round Lake State Park** features campsites in a mixed forest of red cedar, ponderosa pine, Douglas fir, and larch. Sandpoint has a full range of accommodations, including cozy resorts, motels, B & Bs, and RV parks.

North of Sandpoint in Boundary County is the logging town of **Bonners Ferry**. A bridge hanging 450 feet over the Moyie

River has replaced the ferry. This is also a resort town, although the notable lodges are a few miles out of town (and as far away as Moyie Springs, where the Moyie and Kootenai rivers meet). The home of the Lower Kootenai tribe, the area was settled when gold was found across the British Columbia border, and Edwin Bonner established the ferry to aid gold prospectors and tradesmen flocking to the gold region. Steamer service was inaugurated on the Kootenai in 1883. The town, like Sandpoint, is a summer and fall destination for anglers, hunters, and hikers.

The Priest Lake recreation region lies west of Bonners Ferry. Priest River is the small town at the southern foot of the river of the same name. The centerpiece of the area is **Priest Lake State Park**, containing kokanee salmon and mackinaw, with sandy beaches and campsites in the forests of giant cedar. In winter, the area is open to snowmobiles, and cross-country ski trails lie in the Kaniksu National Forest.

All of this area is accessible from the scenic drive that begins on page 92. The major north-south road is Highway 95.

Where to Eat

In Sandpoint, the food is varied and ranges from standard fare at the **Beach House** at the Edgewater Resort, which offers a great view of the lake from inside or on the terrace, to Northwest cuisine at the **Floating Restaurant** on Highway 200. The **Longhorn Barbecue**, on Highway 95 beside the long bridge, is a large, scenic barbecue place. The **Garden Restaurant** serves lunch, dinner, and Sunday brunch at 15 East Lake.

Stanley

The clean, rarefied air of Stanley (el. 6,200 feet) is matched by the great beauty of the White Cloud Peaks of the Sawtooth Mountains, which rise another 4,500 feet above the town. Stanley is the most rustic and pioneer-flavored of any of the towns in the Rockies region, situated in the middle of the Stanley Basin (what Montanans would call a "hole"), part of the valley of the Salmon River. With the **Sawtooth National Recreation Area** only a few minutes away and fabulous fishing at Stanley's doorstep, this is a town to remember.

Three national forests surround the town (Boise, Challis, and Sawtooth), thus the camping and hiking possibilities are beyond description.

The basin is named for Captain John Stanley, a prospector and Civil War survivor who happened on the area on July 4, 1863, while leading a party of 75 prospectors to find new gold fields. They passed through the basin on their way to Idaho City. Stanley didn't return, but one member of the party, A. P. Challis, did, and he mined around Stanley for many summers. A permanent settlement was established in the 1890s. Today, the town comprises two settlements: upper and lower Stanley. They are headquarters for float trip operators who take rafters down the Salmon River. The rustic cabin motels (see page 145) play host to hundreds of visitors who fish for salmon, trout, and steelhead and—in winter—come to snowmobile and cross-country ski in the nearby recreation areas and national forests.

West of Stanley is Idaho's new state park, **Land of the Yankee Fork**. Three prime attractions here, besides the camping and fishing, are the **Yankee Fork Dredge** (near the village of Sunbeam), and two ghost towns. The dredge is a symbol of the gold rush of the 1870s when prospectors came to pan gold from the fork. Later, the dredge was built on the fork by the Snake River Mining Company. From 1940 until 1951, it floated on its own shifting pond, sifting gold out of the valley gravel. **Custer and Bonanza** were the two gold camps established during the 1870s. They are now ghost towns and on display in the state park, which has its headquarters and information center in the town of Challis, 55 miles west of Salmon. A fascinating backroad route will take you through the historic area from Sunbeam to Challis (see the **Yankee Fork Drive** on page 113). An historical museum in Custer tells the story of the gold era.

The **Stanley Museum** focuses on the pioneer history of the town and the Stanley Basin. Several accessible lakes are close to Stanley. Little Redfish and Redfish Lakes are just south of town in the national recreation area. A visitor center between the two lakes is open from the beginning of June to mid-September. **Nip and Tuck Road** offers a scenic sidetrip into the Stanley Basin, passing through mountain meadows filled with wildflowers and offering great views of the Sawtooth range.

Where to Eat

For the size of the town, Stanley has a good share of eating spots; all are on the rustic side, but that's to be expected. Breakfasts and evening meals are served in the old lodge at **Idaho Rocky Mountain Ranch** (reservations needed). The **Kasino Club** serves beef, lamb, seafood, and pasta. The **Victoria Inn** is right on the river with an outside deck.

Twin Falls

Some people (especially the Salt Lake types who travel the freeway) know Twin Falls as "that place just north of Jackpot, Nevada." The people who live in Twin Falls know it as the center of the Magic Valley, a fertile agricultural area—which used to be a sagebrush desert—in south-central Idaho, and as the gateway to the Sawtooth Mountains vacation area, which is a two-hour drive north of the city. A feature of the valley is the collection of lava flows and spatter cones, which provide a sharp contrast to the farmlands.

Twin Falls' greatest tourist asset is the **Snake River Canyon**, a deep and open canyon that provides parks and recreation areas along the river, west from Twin Falls to Bliss. The **Perrine Bridge** north of town crosses the canyon (486 feet deep). There are two sets of waterfalls in the canyon. Of the two falls, the **Shoshone Falls** waterfalls are closer to the city and are the more dramatic—they're higher than Niagara, with a fall of 212 feet.

The best time to see the falls is October through April, for much of the water that would go over the precipice is diverted during the growing season. The parks in the Shoshone Falls area are fine places to visit any time of year. To get there, drive along Blue Lakes Boulevard to Falls Avenue and go three miles east and two miles north to Shoshone Falls/Dierkes Lake Park. The Twin Falls waterfalls are located two miles to the east of Shoshone Falls via Falls Boulevard. Here, too, water is diverted for agricultural purposes.

For a scenic day trip, we highly recommend the Thousand Springs route through the **Hagerman Valley**. This drive takes Highway 30 beginning just south of Twin Falls (or at the Interstate 84 exit near Bliss). The route leads through the canyon valley of the Snake River past farmland, old houses, and barns, and then it passes the **Thousand Springs** area, where the Snake River Plain Aquifer flows out in hundreds of torrents through the black cliffs of the canyon. Near the river are picnic areas, RV parks, hot spring pools, and lodges. You can enjoy fine fishing in the five Oster Lakes (with an early start to the season in March) and in the nearby Anderson West Ponds (rainbow, bluegill, and bass after the first of July). Near the west end of the valley are the **Hagerman Fossil Beds**, a national landmark where more than 125 skeletons of zebra-like horses have been uncovered. To see a full-size replica of the prehistoric horse, visit the Hagerman **Horse Fossil Museum** on State Street in Hagerman.

Where to Eat

Fast food is alive and well in Twin Falls, and aside from strip development eating places, try the **Sandpiper** at 1309 Blue Lakes Boulevard or **H.R. Weston's Restaurant** in the Weston Plaza Hotel at 1350 Blue Lakes Boulevard.

Wallace and the Silver Valley

Wallace is one of the few towns in America where the whole community is on the National Historic Register. Lying alongside

Interstate 90, east of Coeur d'Alene, the town is a living testament to the early silver mining days in the state. The **Coeur d'Alene District Mining Museum** provides a good overview of the town's history with a slide show, mining relics, photos, and displays of old mining techniques.

The downtown area features many original buildings, including the **Northern Pacific Railroad Depot** (now a museum) built of bricks imported from China, the former courthouse (the Smokehouse Building) built in 1890, the Queen Anne-style Rossi Building, and the old White and Bender grocery store building now occupied by Silver Capital Arts. These buildings and more were designed by some of the leading architects of the day. The **Sierra Silver Mine Tour** leaves hourly from downtown Wallace, taking visitors on a surrey ride and then into the mine that extends deep into the ground. You're allowed to pick up and take core samples from the mine floor.

The beautiful mountain region called the Silver Valley is home to many artists and craftspeople. One of the best places to sample local works of art is in an old 1900 log home that has been converted into the **Cottage Creations** gallery. It's located just west of Wallace on old Highway 10 (Osburn Frontage Road).

North of Wallace are several old mining camps. The best preserved of these is **Murray**, where a former bar is now a museum.

Between Coeur d'Alene and Wallace are several points of interest. Idaho's oldest building, the **Cataldo Mission**, was constructed by the Coeur d'Alene people in 1850 for Father Ravalli, a Jesuit missionary. With foot-thick walls, built without nails, the mission is perfectly situated in a mountain pine forest. It has a domed altar, elaborately carved statues, and a large wooden cross. The **Coming of the Black Robes Pageant** is held annually, in mid-August. **Enaville** is a resort area near the mission. Another of the little historic towns of the valley, Enaville has camping nearby in private and forest campgrounds and the old Snake Pit Hotel, which serves food and drink to visitors.

Day Trips from Wallace

A scenic way to travel between Enaville and Wallace is by taking the backroad tour along the North Fork of the Coeur d'Alene River to Pritchard, another old mining camp. The tour continues to Murray and across King's Pass and Dobson Pass to Wallace. At Pritchard, another backroad leads north past the **Avery Creek Picnic Area**. The road forks to the right, beside Shoshone Creek to the Berlin Flats (forest) Campground; to the left, the road leads to several more forest recreation sites and a trail to **Shadow Falls** and **Fern Falls**.

Where to Eat

The **Historic Jamieson** is not only a fine place to stay with a wonderful 1900s ambiance but also a good place to eat, in the old Dining Room and Saloon. The dinner menu ranges from chicken-fried steak to seafood fettucine and sautéed red snapper. The **Wallace Inn** (a Best Western) has a pleasant dining room with much the same fare.

Idaho
Places to Stay

BOISE

Boise KOA
7300 Federal Way
Boise, ID 83706
(208) 345-7673

At I-84, Gowen Road exit (exit 57), six miles from downtown. With all the usual amenities including pool, cabin rentals, store.

Fiesta RV Park
11101 Fairview Avenue
Boise, ID 83713
(208) 375-8207

A few blocks from I-84, exit 50, near shopping mall, with full hookups, dump station, and laundry.

Flying J Motel
8002 Overland Road
Boise, ID 83709
(208) 322-4404

A mid-size motel with pool, sauna, whirlpool, and laundry. It's near restaurants and has in-room VCRs and satellite TV. ($)

Idaho Heritage Inn
109 West Idaho Street
Boise, ID 83702
(208) 342-8066

This is the former Governor's Mansion, a B & B home near downtown. Breakfast served in-room; evening wine. ($$)

Owyee Plaza Hotel
1109 Main Street
Boise, ID 83702
(208) 343-4611 or
800-223-4611
(inside Idaho)

Located downtown, this is probably Boise's finest hotel, with fine dining plus luxurious rooms and a swimming pool. ($$$)

Pioneer Inn at Bogus Basin
2405 Bogus Basin Road
Boise, ID 83702
(208) 332-5100 or
800-367-4397
(outside Idaho)

Out of town at the ski hill base, this mid-size hotel has a dining room and coffee shop, a lounge, sauna, whirlpool, laundry, and some units with kitchenettes. ($$ to $$$)

Victoria's White House
10325 West Victory Street
Boise, ID 83709
(208) 362-0507

Another large B & B, this Victorian-style house is placed on an estate near the freeway in a rural setting. ($ to $$)

BONNERS FERRY

Deep Creek Resort
Route 4, Box 628
Bonners Ferry, ID 83805
Highway 95 (south)
(208) 267-2729

Two miles south of town. Units on the creek, some with kitchenettes; play area, swimming pool, restaurant, golf nearby. ($)

Kootenai River Inn
Kootenai River Plaza
Bonners Ferry, ID 83805
Highway 95
(208) 267-8511

This Best Western motel has riverfront units with restaurant, lounge, pool, whirlpool, sauna, and fitness area. ($$)

Twin Rivers Canyon Resort
HCR 62, Box 25
Moyie Springs, ID 83845
(208) 267-5932

Located in nearby Moyie Springs, at the junction of the Kootenai and Moyie Rivers, with riverside sites, hookups, tent sites, laundry, raft and boat rentals, picnic area. Take Highway 95 north to Three Mile Junction, drive east on Highway 2, and turn onto Road 62 for two miles.

Valley Motel
Highway 95 (south)
Bonners Ferry, ID 83805
(208) 267-7567

This modest motel has some units with kitchenettes; a whirlpool; near shopping and golf facilities. ($)

CASCADE

Arrowhead RV Park
P.O. Box 337
Cascade, ID 83611
(208) 382-4534

On the river, one mile south of town on Highway 55, with full hookups, dump station, store, propane, and boating.

Clear Creek Inn
10694 Highway 55 South
Cascade, ID 83611
(208) 382-4616

A more standard motel in the town of Cascade, close to shopping and cafes, golf course, and Cascade Lake. ($)

North Shore Lodge
175 North Shoreline Drive
Cascade, ID 83611
800-933-3193

In the Warm Lake area in Boise National Forest with rustic but comfortable accommodations, plus campsites. ($ to $$)

Warm Lake Lodge
P.O. Box 450
Cascade, ID 83611
(208) 257-2221 (summer)
or (208) 382-3553 (winter)

Located on Warm Lake east of Cascade in a recreation area that includes restaurants, stores, and forest trails. The lodge also has campsites. ($ to $$)

CHALLIS

Challis Hot Springs Campground
HC63 Box 1779
Challis, ID 83226
(208) 879-4442

Two pools (warm and hot) beside the campground. Hookups, fishing nearby, play area. Drive three miles south from Challis on Highway 93 and then onto Hot Springs Road and drive four miles north.

Valley RV Park
P.O. Box 928
Challis, ID 83226
(208) 879-2393

Hookups, dump station, and propane.

COEUR D'ALENE
AND POST FALLS

Coeur d'Alene Resort
Second and Front streets
Coeur d'Alene, ID 83814
(208) 765-4000 or
800-826-2390 (U.S. only)

This is the North Idaho lake region's premiere resort operation, with restaurants, lounges, penthouse suites as well as rooms and suites, a boardwalk over the lake, fitness center, indoor pool, golf course, and more. (**$$$**)

Coeur d'Alene North KOA
4850 East Garwood Road
Hayden Lake, ID 83835
(208) 772-4557

Located on Hayden Lake, north of town with full hookups, tent sites, boating, dump station, and laundry. Three miles east of Highway 95 on Garwood Road.

Comfort Inn
280 West Appleway
(208) 228-5500 or
800-228-5150

Rooms and suites, sauna and whirlpool, continental breakfast. (**$$**)

Riverbend Inn
4105 Riverbend Avenue
Post Falls, ID 83854
(208) 773-3583 or
800-243-7666

This motor hotel is located in Post Falls just west of Coeur d'Alene. Spa, exercise room, continental breakfast. (**$ to $$**)

Silverwood RV Park and Theme Park
(208) 683-4400

Across Highway 95 from the family amusement park of the same name. Restaurant nearby, full hookups. Fifteen miles north of Coeur d'Alene.

Wolf Lodge Campground
12425 East I-90
Coeur d'Alene, ID 83814
(208) 664-2812

Hookups and tent sites east of town on I-90 (exit 22).

IDAHO CITY

This historic gold mining town offers three places to stay, with reservations made by phoning the same number.

Idaho City Hotel	This tiny, renovated 1900s hotel has rustic and charming accommodations with private baths. ($)
P.O. Box 70	
Idaho City, ID 83631	
208-392-4290	

The Miner's Inn
P.O. Box 70
Idaho City, ID 83631
208-392-4290

Accommodations for six adults or two families with children and a full kitchen. This is another original building. ($)

Prospector Motel
P.O. Box 70
Idaho City, ID 83631
208-392-4290

Rooms and suites with private bath, cable TV, and kitchen units available. ($)

Warm Springs Resort
P.O. Box 28
Idaho City, ID 83631
(208) 392-4437

Located 1.5 miles southwest of Idaho City, at milepost 37 on Highway 21, this is a campground, with cabin accommodations, swimming pool, full hookups, tent sites, picnic areas, hiking trails.

KETCHUM AND SUN VALLEY

Elkhorn Resort
P.O. Box 6009
Sun Valley, ID 83354
(208) 622-4511 or
800-355-4676

This newer and modern resort has several restaurants, deluxe rooms and suites, golfing, and a ski base. It's just south of Ketchum. (\$\$ to \$\$\$)

River Street Inn
100 River Street
Ketchum, ID 83340
P.O. Box 82
Sun Valley, ID 83353
(208) 726-3611

This cozy B & B inn has suites with Japanese soaking tubs and a noted breakfast. It's close to downtown, shopping, and fine cafes. (\$\$)

Sun Valley Resort
Sun Valley Road
Sun Valley, ID 83353
(208) 622-4111 or
800-635-1076 (area
reservations) or
800-786-8259
(Sun Valley Resort only)

Located just east of Ketchum, this is the oldest (and many say the finest) of the ski and summer destination resorts. The Inn and the Lodge provide varied accommodations, the dining in the lodge is superb, and there are more restaurants and lounges, along with golf courses, ice skating, swimming pools, and all the expected resort amenities. ($$ to $$$)

Sun Valley RV Resort
P.O. Box 548
Ketchum, ID 83340
(208) 726-3429

Full hookups, whirlpool, pool, miniature golf, and more. South of Ketchum.

LEWISTON

Carriage House Bed and Breakfast
504 6th Street
Lewiston, ID 83501
(208) 746-4506

A guest house, separate from the main home, with two suites, each with private bath and a shared sitting room. Whirlpool in private courtyard. ($$)

Hells Gate State Park
3620 Snake River Avenue
Lewiston, ID 83501
(208) 799-5015

A public campground located four miles south of town. The park has sites with hookups, showers, and playground.

Sacajawea Motor Inn
1824 Main Street
Lewiston, ID 83501
(208) 746-1393

A large motel with large units (some with kitchens) and some suites, a heated pool, laundry, large beds, restaurant, and lounge. ($$)

Tapadera Motor Inn
1325 Main Street
Lewiston, ID 83501
(208) 746-3311 or
800-722-8277

A motel (with good rates), swimming pool, lounge, and continental breakfast. ($)

MCCALL

Hotel McCall
P.O. Box 1778
McCall, ID 83638
(208) 634-8105

This older hotel in downtown McCall has a warm atmosphere, aided with complimentary tea and wine and free breakfast for guests. All rooms have private bath. ($ to $$)

Kimberland Meadows Resort
(208) 347-2162

Located north of McCall, this is the area's prime resort operation. Take Highway 95 1.5 miles north of McCall. Townhouse accommodations, a fine dining room with lounge, 18-hole golf course; hot spring pools and downhill skiing nearby. ($$ to $$$)

McCall Campground
190 Krahn Lane
McCall, ID 83638
(208) 634-5165

Just south of town on Payette Lake. Campsites with good views, hookups, dump station, laundry, store.

Shore Lodge
501 West Lake
P.O. Box 1006
McCall, ID 83638
(208) 634-2244 or
800-657-6464

This large lodge is on the shore of Payette Lake, just west of downtown McCall. To get there, take Lake Street west along the south shore of the lake to the lodge. Heated pools, a dock, and dining room and informal cafe. ($$ to $$$)

MOSCOW

Mark IV Motor Inn
414 North Main Street
Moscow, ID 83843
(208) 882-7557

This is a large motel with standard rooms and suites, a restaurant, lounge, outdoor beer garden, and a few RV hookups. Indoor pool, whirlpool. ($$)

University Inn
1516 Pullman Road
Moscow, ID 83843
(208) 882-0550 or
800-325-8765

This is a large Best Western motel offering standard rooms and suites, with two restaurants, barbecue in the courtyard, a putting green, and lounges. ($$)

SALMON

Heritage Inn
Bed and Breakfast
510 Lena Street
Salmon, ID 83467
(208) 756-3174

This B & B home evokes the aura of the late 1800s. (**$ to $$**)

Lost Trail Hot Springs Resort
P.O. Box 37
Sula, MT 59871
(406) 821-3574 or
800-825-3574

In the historic area explored by Lewis and Clark, this inn is just north of the Idaho/Montana border on Highway 93. It's not far from the Big Hole National Battlefield. Restaurant, RV hookups and campsites, hot springs pool and sauna. (**$ to $$**)

Motel Deluxe
112 South Church Street
P.O. Box 863
Salmon, ID 83467
(208) 756-2231

A standard motel in town with rooms, kitchenette facilities, large beds, and a barbecue pit. (**$**)

North Fork Motel
P.O. Box 100
North Fork, ID 83466
(208) 865-2412

A small, new two-story motel in a scenic setting beside the river and next to a decent restaurant, a few miles north of Salmon in the village of North Fork. (**$ to $$**)

Salmon Meadows
Campground
P.O. Box 705
Salmon, ID 83467
(208) 756-2640

Full hookups, tent sites, and dump station. On St. Charles Street, two blocks north of the junction of Highway 93 and St. Charles. Campgrounds with RV hookups at both the Williams Lake Resort and the North Fork Motel (see above). Several forest campgrounds within a few miles of Salmon.

Smith House
Bed and Breakfast
49 Salmon River Road
Shoup, ID 83469
(208) 394-2121

Located in Shoup, Idaho, near Salmon, this B & B is in a superb setting on the Salmon River. Hot tub and restaurants are nearby. A "country inn" that's really in the country. (**$ to $$**)

Twin Peaks Guest Ranch
P.O. Box 951
Salmon, ID 83467
(208) 894-2290 or
800-659-4899

In the mountains with a large rustic lodge and offering trail rides, evening barbecues, and fishing adventures. Cabins, pool, and whirlpool. ($$ to $$$)

Williams Lake Resort
P.O. Box 1150
Salmon, ID 83467
800-396-2628

In rainbow trout fishing paradise, located 17 miles southwest of town off Highway 93 on the lake, it's open from Memorial Day to Labor Day. This resort has cabins, motel units, RV sites with hookups, motor boats, and a store, as well as a restaurant and the Red Dog Saloon. ($ to $$)

SANDPOINT

Bighorn Lodge
710 Bull River Road
Noxon, MT 59853
(406) 847-5597

If you wish to drive an hour past Sandpoint into Montana, you'll find this scenic location and a country inn featuring trail rides, canoe river floating, fishing, and eight hiking trails in the Cabinet Mountains. ($$ to $$$)

Fox Farm RV Resort
3160 Dufort Road
Sagle, ID 83860
(208) 263-8896

Located eight miles west of Highway 95 (six miles beyond Round Lake State Park). This campground has full hookups and tent sites.

Idaho Country Resort
141 Idaho County Road
(and 188 Kamloops Road)
Hope, ID 83836
(208) 264-5505

This is a large RV resort on Lake Pend Oreille, three miles west of Hope, Idaho. Full hookups and tent sites, boat docks, laundry, boat rentals, gas, store, and propane. Housekeeping cottages are also at the resort.

Lakeside Inn
106 Bridge Street
Sandpoint, ID 83864
(208) 263-3717 or
800-543-8126

Next to the city park and located on Lake Pend Oreille, the rooms at the Lakeside have private balconies and water views. Kitchen units and suites with complimentary continental breakfast. Boat docks, indoor and outdoor whirlpools and saunas. ($$ to $$$)

Monarch Westlodge
P.O. Box 3171
Sandpoint, ID 83864
(208) 263-1222 or
800-543-8193

A reasonably priced motor hotel on Highway 95 north, this operation has large rooms, three whirlpools, laundry, and large beds. Next to Bonner Mall. (**$ to $$**)

Red Fir Resort
450 Red Fir Road
Hope, ID 83836
(208) 264-5287

Out in the country about 27 miles from Sandpoint. Drive 17 miles east of Sandpoint on Highway 200 and turn right onto Samowen Road and drive about 10 miles to Red Fir Road. This resort features large housekeeping cottages (10 people can stay in the largest cabin). Boat docks, laundry, swimming, and fishing, restaurants and stores nearby. (**$$ to $$$**)

River Birch Farm
P.O. Box 280
Laclede, ID 83841
(208) 263-3705

Located 13 miles west of Sandpoint on Highway 2, this outstanding B & B home is on the Pend Oreille River. Open year-round with whirlpool and a "full" four-course breakfast. (**$ to $$**)

Sandpoint KOA Kampground
100 Sagle Road
Sandpoint, ID 83864
(208) 263-4824

Five miles south of Sandpoint, this KOA has all the usual features including full hookups, tent sites and pool.

Schweitzer Mountain Resort
P.O. Box 815
Sandpoint, ID 83864
(208) 263-9555 or
800-831-8810

A ski resort in the winter months as well as a summer mountain resort, this is an excellent place to stay with a scenic location. It's a 30 minute drive north of Sandpoint, off Highway 95. You can stay in a condo unit or in the Overnighter Lodge. Restaurants and pubs. (**$$ to $$$**)

Travel America Park
P.O. Box 199
Sagle, ID 83860
(208) 263-7511 or
(208) 263-6522

A large campground, including full hookups, pull-throughs, laundry, store, and propane. Located six miles south of Sandpoint on the west side of Highway 95.

STANLEY

Idaho Rocky Mountain Ranch
HC64, P.O. Box 9934
Stanley, ID 83278
(208) 774-3544

This is a very special place on Highway 75, 10 miles south of Stanley. Rooms in the lodge and cabin rooms. The summer season runs from the beginning of June to mid-September, and cabins are kept open during winter months. Built as a hunting lodge in 1930, the walls are constructed of logs. Continental breakfast is served each morning with gourmet dinners in the evenings. A hot spring pool adds to the wonder of the place. Picnic lunches are available and there's a stocked fishing pond. ($$ to $$$)

McGowan's Resort
P.O. Box 91
Stanley, ID 83278
(208) 774-2290

Log cabins (quite modern) on the Salmon River. The cabins have kitchenettes, fireplaces, and TV. Fishing is the focus of this resort. ($ to $$)

Mountain Village Lodge
P.O. Box 150
Stanley, ID 83278
(208) 774-3661

Units with gas, store, and dance hall, at the foot of the Sawtooth Mountains. Open year-round, unlike some of the other operations in and around Stanley. ($)

Sawtooth Hotel
P.O. Box 52
Stanley, ID 83278
(208) 774-9947 (summer),
(208) 622-7922 (winter)

This is Stanley's first and, as far as I know, the only B & B in town. It's a renovated motel with dining room. ($)

Sessions Lodge
HC64, Box 9696
Stanley, ID 83278
(208) 774-9947

A motel with trailer spaces, a store, gas station, and cafe. ($)

Sunbeam Village and RV Park
HC67, Box 310
Stanley, ID 83278
(208) 838-2211

RV spaces with dump station and propane. West of town, near the Yankee Fork Dredge. Several cabins are also available.

Valley Creek Motel
P.O. Box 302
Stanley, ID 83278
(208) 774-3606

A small motel with modern rooms. ($)

SUN VALLEY   *See Ketchum.*

TWIN FALLS

Anderson's Camp
Route 1
Eden, ID 83325
(208) 733-6756 or
(208) 825-5336

A huge and busy RV park with full hookups and propane, mini golf and waterslide, on Tipperary Road near exit 182 on I-84.

Canyon Springs Inn
1357 Blue Lakes
Boulevard N
Twin Falls, ID 83301
(208) 734-5000 or
800-727-5003

A Best Western motel with reasonable rates and convenient location. ($)

**Nat-Soo-Pah Hot Springs
and RV Park**
2738 East 2400 N
Twin Falls, ID 83301
(208) 655-4337

On Highway 1, off Highway 93, southeast of Hollister, full hookups, tent sites, hot pool.

Twin Falls/Jerome KOA
5431 U.S. Highway 93
Jerome, ID 83338
(208) 324-4169

Near Jerome off I-84, exit 173, and along Highway 93. Full hookups, tent sites, swimming, miniature golf, store.

Weston Plaza Hotel
1350 Blue Lakes
Boulevard N
Twin Falls, ID 83301
(208) 733-0650 or
800-333-7829

A large, modern hotel with dining room and lounge. ($ to $$)

WALLACE

Blue Anchor Trailer Park
P.O. Box 645
Osburn, ID 83849
(208) 752-3443

Sites for RVs and trailers with hookups and propane. It's near exit 57 off I-90.

The Historic Jameson
304 6th Street
Wallace, ID 83873
(208) 556-1554

This old and small hotel is an absolute gem—a vintage 1908 brick building in downtown Wallace, a fine B & B inn with rooms and shared baths. The inn is airy and delightfully decorated. Continental breakfast and a great restaurant downstairs. The Jameson Saloon is also in the building. ($)

Wallace Inn
100 Front Street
Wallace, ID 83873
(208) 752-1252

Best Western rooms and suites, located at the West Wallace Plaza. This is a modern motor hotel. ($$)

Utah

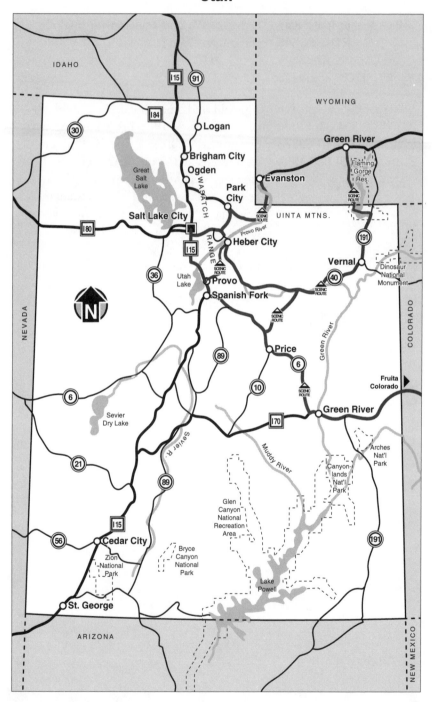

Utah
Drives

The northeast quadrant of Utah is dominated by two mountain ranges: the Wasatch and Uinta. This is the region explored by our four scenic drives.

The Mirror Lake Drive starts with a short but spectacular Wasatch route, northeast on Highway 189 through the Provo Canyon, passing the twin cascades of Bridal Veil Falls. The canyon features lush vegetation, jagged rock formations, frequent viewpoints, and a double waterfall. At the north end of the canyon is Deer Creek Reservoir State Park, a popular recreation site for city dwellers of the region. Passing through Heber City, on the eastern Wasatch slopes, this drive continues along Highways 40 and 150 past the town of Kamas and through the Wasatch National Forest and a host of recreation opportunities. Just to the east is the Uinta High Wilderness region, which offers supreme outdoor treks through this unusual east-to-west mountain range.

The second Utah drive begins at Provo and heads in a southeasterly direction on Highway 6 to the city of Price. Price Canyon and Soldier Summit are the major features of this drive. Several sideroads lead to a network of scenic byways through the forest and to Nine Mile Canyon.

The third Utah scenic route begins in Heber City and leads south of the Uinta Mountains for a half-day trip to Vernal, near the Utah/Colorado border.

Finally, the spectacular beauty of Flaming Gorge is featured on the fourth drive, which leads north from Vernal via Highway 191, and then on Highway 44 through the Flaming Gorge National Recreation Area.

Mirror Lake Drive

Provo to Evanston, Wyoming

Starting in the urban heart of Utah, this route cuts through the southern flank of the Wasatch range north of Provo. Provo is an ideal place for those who wish to explore several of the Utah drives. It's a clean, orderly city, lying between the mountains and Utah Lake. Golf courses and parks surround the city, and the major summer and winter resorts of the Wasatch Mountains are less than an hour away.

For the first 45 minutes of the drive, Highway 189 leads through the short but scenic Provo Canyon. Several recreation sites are accessible from the highway, including the Sundance Resort, campgrounds and trails in the Uinta National Forest, and the Timpanogos Cave National Monument. At the northern end of the canyon is Deer Creek Reservoir, which offers water recreation at Deer Creek Reservoir State Park. **Bridal Veil Falls** cascades to a pool beside the highway; a gondola tramway takes visitors to the top of the falls for views of the Wasatch Range and a close look at the double falls. Private and public campgrounds and RV parks are located along Highway 189.

The drive then takes you through **Heber City**. This town on the eastern slope of the Wasatch offers an unusual train ride on the "Heber Creeper." This historic train operates daily on a run through the Heber Valley and through Provo Canyon. Motels are available in all price ranges, making Heber City another good spot to stay while exploring the joys of the Utah mountain wilderness.

This northeast route then passes by **Park City**, an old mining town from the 1800s and now the state's premier ski resort. Combining the historic Victorian ambiance of its former mining days and the spiffy postmodernist condo look of the 1990s, Park City offers good restaurants, a night in an old hotel, and après-tour hot tub relaxation at several modern lodges. Park City is located four miles west of the Highway 40 junction.

Your drive veers northeast as Highway 150 leaves Highway 40, passing through Kamas into the wilderness of the Wasatch National Forest. You'll pass by high mountain peaks and sub-alpine meadows and along the route of several fast mountain rivers. Much of the trip parallels the Provo River; at Upper Provo Falls, a series of terraces provides a cascade of water, which you can view from walkways near the highway.

This is a high drive providing access to the **Uinta High Wilderness,** which lies to the east. The road climbs to 10,687 feet at Bald Mountain Pass and then descends to Mirror Lake before crossing the Utah/Wyoming border. The drive ends in high desert cattle country at Evanston, Wyoming. Interstate 80 provides a speedy return to the Salt Lake City area.

The route is divided into three separate regions, and each has its attractions: Provo Canyon, Wasatch Mountains and Park City, and Mirror Lake and Uinta Mountains. On the southern portion of the drive, Provo Canyon is the starting point for several side-trips and hiking experiences. **Timpanogos Cave National Monument** on the north slope of Mount Timpanogos features hundreds of colored stalactites and stalagmites.

The monument and several other recreation sites are accessed via Highway 92, which leads west from Highway 189, north of Bridal Veil Falls. This road eventually leads through the mountains to Alpine—passing Robert Redford's **Sundance Resort**—and accessing a network of many backroads throughout the **Timpanogos Wilderness Area.** A six-mile trail from Provo Canyon leads to the top of Mount Timpanogos (el. 11,750 feet). Another interesting hike leads from the Squaw Creek trailhead.

Wasatch Mountain State Park lies west of Highway 40, accessible via a sideroad that passes through Midway. Backroad 224, the Guardian Pass Road, leads through the park and north to Park City. From the park visitor center, the road leads for 22 miles to the resort town. A side route forks west, leading to Big Cottonwood Canyon and the Brighton resort. Exploring these backroads makes for a fascinating summer day (or several days).

HIGHWAY LOG
Provo to Evanston, Wyoming
85 miles (136 KM)—1 hour, 45 minutes

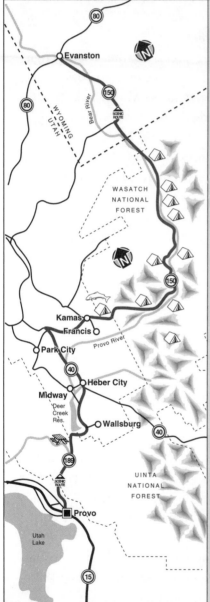

Provo The drive begins at the junction of I-15, exit 266 and Hwy. 189. Head north through downtown Provo, past Brigham Young University.

Junction–Highway 265 Leads west through Provo to link with I-15.

Junction–Highway 52 Leads west through Orem to link with I-15.

Provo Canyon After entering the canyon, the trailhead for Squaw Creek Trail is to the east of the highway. Nunn's Park is to the west.

Bridal Veil Falls A gondola takes you to the top of this scenic double falls, with good views from the lip. Restaurant at the falls. RV parks, store, and cafe located 1.5 miles north of the falls.

Junction–Highway 92 At milepost 14.5. Leads west past Sundance Resort to the Timpanogos Cave National Monument.

Deer Creek Reservoir At milepost 18. State park, marina, RV park to the west of the hwy. Picnic tables next to restaurant.

Junction–Road to Midway Leads north from the hwy. Also to Wasatch Mountain State Park.

Junction–Road to Wallsburg To the east.

Junction–Highway 40 For this drive, go north on Hwy. 40 for Heber City and Park City.

Heber City Tourist center on east slope of the Wasatch Range. Gas, cafes, motels, stores, steam train excursions.

Junction–Highway 248 Leads west four miles to Park City, the ski and summer resort with gas, hotels, motels, restaurants, stores.

Junction–Highway 150 For this drive, go east on Hwy. 150 to Kamas.

Viewpoint Uinta Range, on descent to Kamas.

Kamas Town, 11 miles from junction, with gas, cafe, and store. A one-block jog to Hwy. 150.

Junction–Road to Francis Leads south from Kamas.

Kamas Fish Hatchery At milepost 3.

Wasatch National Forest Entrance at milepost 6. The following are forest campgrounds: Yellow Pine, Beaver Creek, Taylor's Fork, and Shingle Creek.

Junction–Pine Valley Road

North Fork Trailhead

Viewpoint Provo River Overlook on south side of highway.

Junction–Soapstone Road To Soapstone Campground (one mile, at milepost 16).

Shady Dell Campground

Duchesne Tunnel Camping Area

Junction–Spring Canyon Road

Cobblerest Campground

Junction–Murdoch Basin Road

Upper Provo Bridge Campground At milepost 22.5.

Viewpoint Provo River Falls.

Junction–Trial Lake Road Steep climb to west of hwy.

Lily Lake Campground

Lost Creek Campground

Bald Mountain Pass Watershed of the Provo, Weber, Bear, and Duchesne Rivers.

Bald Mountain Trailhead Trail with picnic area.

Moosehorn Campground To west. Trail opposite.

Mirror Lake Camping, trails.

Pass Lake Small fishing lake and trailhead to east.

Butterfly Campground

Hayden's Peak (el. 12,472 feet) Highline trailhead.

Ruth Lake Trail Quarter-mile to east. Sulphur Campground at milepost 39.

Beaver View Campground

Hayden Fork Campground

Gold Hill Trailhead To west.

Stillwater Campground With Ranger Station at milepost 46.

Bear River Campgrounds

Utah/Wyoming Border

Junction–Aspen Drive To the east in high desert at milepost 51.

Evanston I-80 junction. Gas, motels, cafes, and stores.

Soldier Summit Drive

Provo to Fruita, Colorado

If done in one jaunt, this is an all-day drive. This route is a scenic alternative to using only interstate highways from the Salt Lake area to central Colorado.

Like the previous drive, the route from Provo to Fruita is divided into three discrete sections, each of which offers different types of scenery and recreational sidetrips. The first part of the trip leads through the Spanish Fork Canyon between the Provo area and the city of Price. The route then leads through desert country, providing access to the wonderful Nine Mile Canyon, which lies east of the highway, to the float boating center of Green River. Then you join Interstate 70 for the final part of the trip to Fruita, just across the Colorado border. Although for the most part we have eschewed interstate highways in this book, sometimes it's necessary to take one to get to another starting point. And if you look carefully, you'll see that most of the scenic drives are linked to others.

The drive begins at the junction of Interstate 15 and Highway 214, south of Provo. It's a short drive to join Highway 6, which then takes you southwest along the **Spanish Fork River.**

You'll see the Spanish Fork Canyon at its most dramatic when the highway reaches the **Red Narrows.** Here, the Uinta National Forest lies to the north and the Manti–La Sal National Forest is to the south. Both forests provide backroads and hiking trails as well as campsites that may be accessed by several sideroads.

You reach **Soldier Summit** after quite a climb, with a few switchbacks. The summit elevation is 7,477 feet. South of the summit the highway descends, following the route of the **White River** and passing the small communities of Colton and Helper. Helper is an old mining town that still retains memories of its mining heritage through the **Western Mining and Railroad Museum**—it's a worthwhile stop.

Price, the commercial center of this area, is also a college town with a sizable Greek-American population. The Hellenic

Orthodox Church is the oldest Greek church in Utah. The College of Eastern Utah's **Prehistoric Museum** features dinosaur skeletons, eggs, and tracks among many other exhibits. South of Price, via Highway 10, is the **Cleveland-Lloyd Dinosaur Quarry**, operated by the Bureau of Land Management (BLM). More than 12,000 bones have been taken from this quarry, which is open to the public through Labor Day. The **Price Canyon Recreation Area** is just north of town, along the highway.

Upon leaving Price, the geography changes dramatically to the south as the route enters the desert.

This is the land of the Book and Roan Cliffs: large plateaus eroded by wind and rain over the centuries. It's also the ancient homeland of the Fremont peoples who lived along the creeks of the region. A sidetrip to Nine Mile Canyon is a must for those fascinated by Native American history and art.

Sideroads and Backroads

If there ever was an area where it pays to get off the highway and on to backroads, this is it! Off the highway is where the action is and, if you're a history buff, you should depart from Highway 6 as the opportunities arise.

I've mentioned **Nine Mile Canyon** as an archeological and scenic treasure; here's how to get there. Drive two miles east of Wellington (just south of Price) to a backroad and then drive approximately 48 miles west. You'll see remains of old villages along the backroad, and the canyon is decorated with many stunning petroglyphs and pictographs. The region is known as the prime habitat of the prehistoric Fremont culture. Decorated rock panels are found along the road and beside several side canyons. The main canyon is much longer than nine miles, and a spur off the main backroad runs west along the canyon. The road is navigable by ordinary cars but may be difficult after heavy rainfalls. Four-wheel-drive vehicles are recommended for traveling on the several narrow roads that lead off the main backroad.

HIGHWAY LOG
Provo to Fruita, Colorado
419 miles (674 km)—8 hours

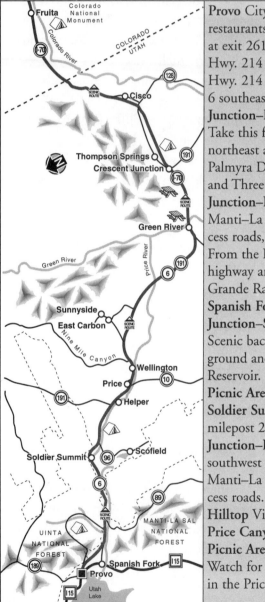

Provo City with hotels, motels, gas, restaurants, stores. This drive starts at exit 261 of I-15, which leads to Hwy. 214 at Spanish Fork. Take Hwy. 214 to Hwy. 6. Go on Hwy. 6 southeast.

Junction–Diamond Fork Road Take this forest road (Road 029) northeast along the river to Palmyra Diamond Campground and Three Forks Campground.

Junction–Highway 89 To Manti–La Sal National Forest access roads, Fairview, and Manti. From the Hwy. 89 junction, the highway and the Denver and Rio Grande Railroad lead through the **Spanish Fork Canyon.**

Junction–Sheep Creek Forest Road Scenic backroad northeast to campground and to the Strawberry Reservoir.

Picnic Area At milepost 204.

Soldier Summit (el. 7,477 feet) At milepost 217. Gas in town.

Junction–Highway 96 Leads southwest to Scofield Reservoir and Manti–La Sal National Forest access roads.

Hilltop Village with gas and store.

Price Canyon Campground and Picnic Area At milepost 223. Watch for unusual rock formations in the Price Canyon.

Castle Gate Coal Mine A historic mine.

Junction–Highway 191 Scenic sideroad to the Bamberger Monument, Ashley National Forest campsites, and the town of Duchesne.

Helper City. This National Historic Site includes the Western Mining and Railroad Museum.

Junction–Road 50 Leads west to ghost towns.

Castellated Ridges Beside the highway, just north of Price.

Price City with gas, motels, cafes, stores, Prehistoric Museum.

Junction–Highway 10 This road leads southwest to Manti–La Sal National Forest access roads and Castledale.

Wellington Small community with gas, cafes.

Junction–Road to Nine Mile Canyon Paved and then gravel road east to Book Cliffs and scenic canyon. Summit on road 7,300 feet.

Junction–Highway 123 Runs east to East Carbon and Sunnyside. Return to highway via Hwy. 124.

Junction–Interstate 70 Take I-70 west toward the Colorado border.

Green River Town with motels, gas, cafes, stores.

Green River State Park is south of town, via a sideroad at exit 162. Camping, picnic tables.

Junction–Highway 19 At Green River exit (exit 162).

Picnic Area With good views, to south of highway.

Junction–Highway 191 Leads south to Moab, Arches National Park, the Colorado River, and recreation areas.

Thompson Springs At exit 185. Gas, cafe, camping.

Junction–Highway 128 At exit 202. Leads south to Cisco and Moab.

Exit 212 To Book Cliffs (north) and Cisco (south).

Exits 220 and 225 To Westwater (south).

Utah/Colorado Border

Exit 1 To Mack, a valley farming community with gas, cafe, store.

Rabbit Valley Dinosaur Trail Quarry via exit 2 in Colorado.

Junction–Highway 139 At exit 15. North to Loma, Baxter Pass (el. 8,422), and Rangely. An alternative route to Vernal, Flaming Gorge National Recreation Area, and the Dinosaur National Monument.

Fruita At exit 19. Town with Colorado Welcome Center (south of interstate), gas, motels, RV parks, cafes, stores. Fruita is eight miles east of Grand Junction.

Colorado National Monument is an outstanding historic site and scenic attraction and is a short drive from Fruita.

Dinosaurland Drive

Heber City to Vernal

This 2.5-hour trip along Highway 40 has probably the least mountain driving of any of our scenic routes and—aside from the first half hour—is basically a flat desert drive through north-central Utah. However, the mountains are always in view, mainly to the north as the highway parallels the east-west course of the Uinta Range. This route avoids interstate driving and provides access to Vernal and the Flaming Gorge National Recreation Area; if you continue west through northern Colorado, you'll find yourself in Steamboat Springs with more Rockies to explore.

A lack of mountain driving does not mean that there aren't interesting things to see and do along the drive. The flatness of the desert is broken with high hills, cliffs, rivers, and reservoirs. Highway 40 is the access route for entering the Uintah and Ouray Reservation, which is in several separate parts north and south of the highway. North of the highway and the reservation is Ashley National Forest and the Uinta High Wilderness Area. The forest has numerous recreation sites with car-accessible campgrounds. From these sites, trails fan north into the High Uintas.

The drive begins in the **Heber Valley**, as Highway 40 quickly enters the Uinta National Forest. The picnic area at Whisky Springs and a short trail leading through Clegg Canyon are just inside the forest boundary. The highway climbs to its summit and then descends to pass **Strawberry Reservoir**, a popular boating lake. The information center located off the highway has a full series of forest maps and other materials. Camping is available at Strawberry Reservoir.

Several viewpoints beyond the reservoir provide good panoramas of the lake and Strawberry River Valley. **Starvation Reservoir** is a widening of the Strawberry River, just west of the town of Duchesne. Several recreation sites are along the shore of the reservoir.

Now you're into the badlands, as the high desert stretches south of Duchesne and the Bad Land Cliffs march across the landscape. Nine Mile Canyon (see previous drive) is accessible via a backroad, which also leads to Pleasant Valley and eventually to the Price area.

Roosevelt, a medium-size town with visitor services, was named for Theodore Roosevelt and has adopted the slogan "A Bully Good Town." It's an access point for roads leading north into the Ashley National Forest. West of Roosevelt, Utah Road 86 leads south to the town of Ouray and the Green River.

Just before the highway reaches Vernal, you'll see a high turnoff with good views of Vernal and Dinosaur country to the west. All along the route, the snowcapped Uintas dominate the skyline. This is an easy drive with a wide variety of scenic changes.

Indian Canyon Scenic Byway is a forest route that joins Highway 40 and Highway 6. Take Utah Highway 191 southwest from Duchesne. It leads 47 miles through the Indian Reservation and the Ashley National Forest and then across the Band Land Cliffs, coming out to join Highway 6 north of Helper. The road follows Indian Canyon through the forest to the summit at Indian Creek Pass, at an elevation of 9,100 feet. The forest species include pinyon (pine), aspen, and juniper. The final part of the drive runs through the lower sections of the Roan and Book cliff formations and along Willow Creek.

Providing access to the many recreation sites of the Ashley National Forest north of Highway 40 are several sideroads that lead through small villages and the Uintah and Ouray Reservation.

One of these is **Utah Road 87**, a loop road which joins the highway at Duchesne and returns to the highway north of Myton. It leads through the community of Mountain Home, then a dirt backroad continues north, entering the national forest with access to Moon Lake and a forest campground. From this point, views of the High Uintas are spectacular and trails lead into the wilderness area.

HIGHWAY LOG
Heber City to Vernal
128 miles (206 km)—2 hours, 30 minutes

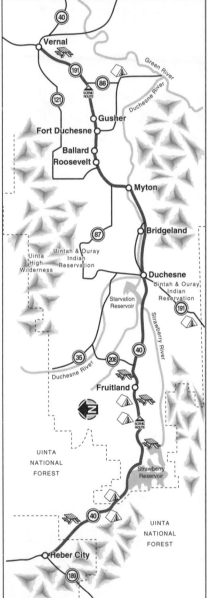

Heber City Town with motels, gas, cafes, stores, steam train excursions. Gateway to Uinta Mountains and recreation areas. For this drive, take Hwy. 40 west to Roosevelt and Vernal.

Whisky Springs Picnic Area Just inside Uinta National Forest boundary.

Clegg Canyon Trailhead To the east of the highway.

Center Canyon The hwy. passes through this short and scenic cut.

Lodgepole Campground To the south.

Summit (el. 8,000 feet)

Junction–Mair Canyon Road To the south.

Strawberry Reservoir This large reservoir is located to the south, 23 miles from Heber City. A recreation area with a forest. Information center located just off the highway.

Day-use park On the reservoir, to the west of the highway.

Soldier Creek Campground To the west with boat ramp. Located 32 miles from Heber City.

Soldier Creek Dam Via sideroad to the west. Leads to Aspen Creek Campground.

Current Creek Campground Via road leading north.

Viewpoint To the south with views of Strawberry River Valley. Picnic tables.

Fruitland Village with gas, store. Uinta foothills to the east.

Viewpoint–Strawberry Pinnacles Red Creek Bridge and red sandstone hills.

Picnic Area Roadside tables with a good view of the Uinta Range.

Starvation Viewpoint Dam and 3,300-acre reservoir with picnic tables at the viewpoint pulloff.

Junction–Highway 87 North to Talmage and Mountain Home rejoining Hwy. 40 near Myton.

Junction–Highway 191 This scenic hwy. leads southwest through the Uintah and Ouray Reservation and the Ashley National Forest to Helper and Price. Campsites.

Duchesne Town with cafes, gas, stores, motels.

Badlands Hwy. 40 leads past high desert badlands between Duschene and Bridgeland, with a narrow green valley below the highway.

Junction–Road to Bridgeland Village just off the highway.

Junction–Backroad to Pleasant Valley Leads over the Bad Land Cliffs for views of Nine Mile Canyon.

Myton Village off the highway to the south. Cafe, gas, store.

Junction–Road 87 Leads north to Ioca and Altamont. Junction is 93 miles from Heber City.

Picnic Area At southwest end of Roosevelt.

Roosevelt Motels, gas, cafes, stores. Our route becomes Hwy. 191.

Junction–Highway 121 Heads north, providing access to Uintah and Ouray Reservation and running west to Vernal.

Ballard Village just west of Roosevelt.

Junction–Road to Whiterocks Leads north to several access roads to Ashley National Forest recreation sites (camping).

Fort Duchesne In Uintah and Ouray Reservation. Motel.

Gusher Village with cafe, gas, store. Seven miles from Roosevelt.

Junction–Road 88 Leads south to Uintah and Ouray Reservation and town of Ouray.

Viewpoint Panoramic views of Dinosaur country. Picnic tables to the south of the hwy., two miles from downtown Vernal.

Vernal City near the Utah/Colorado border. Gateway to Flaming Gorge National Recreation Area (north via Hwy. 191; see next drive). The city has a full range of services.

Dinosaur National Monument Located 18 miles southwest of Vernal via Hwy. 40 and Road 149. The monument operates a visitor center and tours.

Flaming Gorge Drive

Vernal to Green River, Wyoming

This drive is the last of our Utah routes, and it is one of the most impressive drives in the West and stands out in my memory with the great national park experiences. This route doesn't have high mountains; you'll see the core of the Uinta Range instead of the peaks. A day or more in the Flaming Gorge area shows how the land developed—the magnificence of a billion years of nature.

It's 63 miles from Vernal to the village of Manila, a northward route that takes you past the **Red Canyon of the Green River**— the "Flaming Gorge." Running north from Vernal on Highway 191, this drive passes through striking geologic formations including the **Red Fleet** buttes. The route also climbs through the Uinta foothills to reach the plateau from which you can gaze down into the stratified gorge that is filled with the rich, red color of the rock of the area.

The drive begins in Vernal, a city with a full range of visitor services, including an Ashley National Forest Ranger Station. For the first 35 miles, the route passes across flat land to the Red Fleet Reservoir. A series of geology markers point out the unique formations along the route.

Just before reaching Red Fleet, the highway passes the **Steinaker Reservoir**, part of the Colorado River Storage Project. Beside the road at this point is a hillside where the Morrison Formation displays dinosaur bones and gizzard stones.

At the 10-mile point, a turn to the east takes you to the **Red Fleet** recreation area. The landscape is covered with sage and juniper trees, providing a winter range for deer and elk. Here, you can see the huge red sandstone buttes (the Red Fleet) resembling tall ships—hence the reservoir's name. You'll find a boat ramp, and campsites are being constructed. As Highway 191 climbs through the foothills on a series of 10 switchbacks, you get good views of the buttes "sailing" through the reservoir. A turnoff at the 15-mile point leads to the Red Fleet Dam, which holds back

Big Brush Creek. A foot trail (at mile 21) leads to the top of the ridge, with views of the dam, reservoir, and the dramatic terrain that is at once forlorn and awesome.

You won't find any services along this route, but several picnic areas provide places for lunch. The drive continues across the high plateau with the summit at 8,428 feet. At the 35-mile point, the junction of Highways 191 and 44 provides two choices: continue on 191 to visit the **Flaming Gorge Dam** and recreation sites on the eastern shore of Flaming Gorge Reservoir, or take Highway 44 to the Red Canyon.

However, the main attractions of the recreation area lie just off Highway 44, between the Highway 191 junction and Manila. Highway 44 features several campgrounds, including the Red Canyon Campground located next to the major canyon overlook; a second information center is located at the overlook. Accommodations are available at Red Canyon Lodge, also located on Red Canyon Road. The quiet waters of the Green River are seen 1,500 feet below the rim. The visitor center there (open during summer months) includes displays of local plant and animal life.

The drive passes two picnic areas at Dowd Spring. One is located on the highway. A hilltop sideroad leads to a stunning overlook with more picnic tables.

Red Canyon provides one scenic highlight; the **Sheep Creek Canyon Geological Area** provides another. This area, on a loop sideroad, presents an impressive array of twisted rock, tall hoodoos, and upturned formations. You'll find picnic areas beside the loop road, and a marker commemorates an early homesteader, Cleophus Dowd, who farmed near the canyon in the late 1800s and was killed in a violent argument with his partner. A small cabin stands near the marker. Emerging from the canyon, the loop road joins Highway 44 for a short drive north to Manila.

The route continues north through the desert, with frequent sideroads leading to the shore of Flaming Gorge Lake. You'll find a car campground at Buckboard Crossing, near the north end of the lake via Buckboard Road.

HIGHWAY LOG
Vernal to Green River, Wyoming
112 miles (180 KM)—3 hours

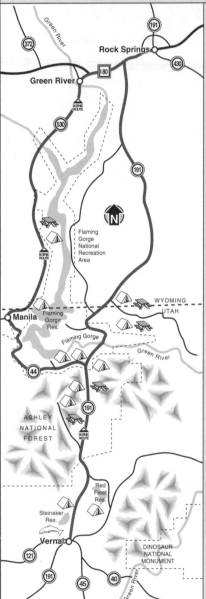

Vernal City with motels, gas, restaurants, stores. Information center in museum building. The drive begins at the junction of Hwy. 40 and Hwy. 191. Take Hwy. 191 north.

Red Fleet State Park To east with camping, RV parking, swimming, boat ramp on reservoir.

Steinaker State Park Recreation area on reservoir to west.

Switchbacks The road ascends with a series of 10 switchbacks. You'll enjoy several viewpoints along the ascent with good views of the Red Fleet buttes, the reservoir, and the High Uintas (to the west).

Sheep Trailhead Access road to the east to top of climb.

Junction–Little Brush Creek Road At milepost 223. Wildlife viewing.

Junction–Road to Diamond Mountain Crosses hills to the east (at milepost 225). Summit (el. 8,428 feet).

Burn Area A fire destroyed the roadside stand of trees in 1988. Marker beside the highway.

Junction–Road 253 Historic site to east.

Lodgepole Campground To east (at milepost 231). Red Springs Campground to west.

Junction–Highway 44 For this drive, take Hwy. 44 for Red Canyon. You could also take Hwy. 191 to Flaming Gorge Dam and campgrounds and as an alternate route to Rock Springs.
Picnic Area and Overlook
Skull Creek Campground At milepost 3 on Hwy. 44.
Junction–Red Canyon Road To Green's Lake Campground and trailhead (200 yards from hwy.), Red Canyon Lodge, visitor center, canyon overlook, and Red Canyon Campground.
Junction–Burnt Creek Road To the south at milepost 10.
Deep Creek Campground and trail.
Picnic Areas Dowd Mountain, hilltop site, and **Dowd Spring**, roadside site.
Junction–Road 221 Leads west to Deep Creek (camping), and on to Spirit Lake, Brownie Lake, Sheep Creek Lake (six miles).
Sheep Creek Canyon Geological Area Sidetrip: Turn on to loop road for viewing of unusual geological formations. The **Palisades Picnic Area** is located along this road. Viewpoints include **Big Spring Creek** with a cascade to Sheep Creek near the Madison Formation sign. You'll see hundreds of erosion pillars along the road including **Tower Rock**, a large hoodoo at the top of the canyon's ridge.

Carmel Picnic Area To north.
Navaho Cliffs Picnic Area
Back on Highway 44:
Bighorn Sheep Range Sheep are often seen at milepost 23.
Manila Village with gas, cafe, store, and Ashley National Forest Ranger Station. Take Hwy. 530 to Green River.
Wyoming/Utah Border
Viewpoint Wildlife views.
Lucerne Recreation complex and Lucerne Valley Marina Road to east for tent and RV camping, gas, store, picnic areas.
Junction–Anvil Draw Road To the east at milepost 39. Boat ramp, toilets.
Junction–Squaw Hollow Road (**Road 4**) To the east. Picnic tables, toilets.
Junction–South Buckboard Road
Junction–Buckboard Road Recreation site on Flaming Gorge Lake—east with camping, RV parking, picnic area, boat ramp, gas.
Flaming Gorge National Recreation Area North Entrance.
Black Fork River Bridge
Ashley National Forest and Rock Springs Information Center Information and ranger station on Flaming Gorge and the Ashley National Forest.
Green River (el. 6,100 feet) Gas, motels, cafes, stores.

Dinosaur National Monument

Dinosaur National Monument straddles the Utah/Colorado border near the city of Vernal. The park headquarters and visitor center are just across the border in Colorado, on Highway 40. Four entrances lead to the monument, although the two most popular sites are in the south off Highway 40. This is a vast arid country of high cliffs, rolling uplands, deep gorges, and whirlpools.

What is now the national monument was a river in ancient times. In the sands of this former river are the fossilized remains of creatures far older than the dinosaur. In this area, the prehistoric Fremont people lived and carved their rock pictures on the cliffs some 3,000 years ago. Paleontologist Earl Douglass came to the area in 1908, searching for dinosaur remains. He wasn't disappointed, for in 1909 he saw tail bones from a brontosaurus. Thousands of bones and several almost-complete skeletons have been taken from the sands of the area.

The **Quarry Site**, near Vernal, was declared a national monument in 1915. A tour bus takes visitors to the Quarry, where the quarry building is a gallery displaying the sandstone face of the cliff, with its bone-bearing layer. During summer months, paleontologists continue to work on uncovering dinosaur bones and are on hand to interpret the Quarry exhibit.

The monument also includes the canyons of the Yampa and Green Rivers. You reach this area by driving into Colorado and turning off Highway 40 and heading north along the **Harper's Corner Scenic Drive** to the canyon overlook and beyond to the

Island Park and Iron Springs overlooks. At the end of the scenic drive is Harriers Corner, where you follow a trail to catch dramatic views of the canyons below.

The **Deerlodge Park** access gate is farther east in Colorado, north of Highway 40. This is a summer-only route. The northern viewpoint, **Gates of Lodore**, is reached via Highway 318 from either Utah or Colorado.

Those with four-wheel-drive vehicles and high-clearance cars may wish to drive the 13 miles of **Echo Park Road**, which leads west from the Harper's Corner Drive. This spectacular backcountry drive leads to yet more canyon views. Beware: This backroad is not driveable when wet.

You'll find developed campsites within the monument. Split Mountain Campground, open year-round, is near the Quarry at the Utah end of the monument. The Green River Campground—a summer operation—is also in this area. Primitive campgrounds are located at Echo Park, Gates of Lodore, and Deerlodge Park.

Flaming Gorge
National Recreation Area

This superb national landmark also straddles a state border—most of **Flaming Gorge Lake** is to the north in Wyoming, while the Flaming Gorge itself lies within the Utah border. This is a truly outstanding place to visit and remains one of my major memories months after completing my tour of the Rockies.

The gorge is the Red Canyon of the Green River, which carved this deep chasm through brilliantly colored rock layers. The lake stretches north from the gorge for 91 miles and is one of the nation's largest reservoirs. The lake was created from the river, as part of the huge Upper Colorado Project, by a dam across this Colorado tributary.

The highway route from Green River, Wyoming, through the recreation area to Vernal, Utah, is described in the Flaming Gorge

Drive on page 162. This drive leads along Highway 530, which runs near the western shore of the lake. Another route, via Highway 191, leads south from Interstate 80 near Rock Springs, skirting the lake but providing access to Firehole Canyon. You can do the complete circle route within a day, but we advise a more gentle exploration of the recreation area. You'll find campsites and even a lodge at Flaming Gorge. This is one natural wonder that shouldn't be rushed through.

The recreation area comprises several separate attractions linked by Highway 44, which runs along the south rim of the gorge, Highway 530, which runs north from Manila near the west shore of the lake, and Highway 191, which leads north from Vernal past the Flaming Gorge Dam to Firehole Canyon. To get to the recreation area from Vernal, take Highway 191. The Highway 44 junction (with access to the central part of the gorge) is 35 miles north of Vernal.

The gorge, seen from the dam and several rim viewpoints, is truly magnificent. **Red Canyon** has vistas with parking areas, summer information center, campground, and the Lodge (see page 181). You can walk along the rim for wonderful views of the red rock walls and the dark green river below. The flooding of the canyon has obviously slowed the river down and raised the water level, but your imagination takes hold when you peer down the steep walls.

The section of Highway 44 running through the recreation area provides several additional viewpoints of the Uinta Mountains and the forests that cover the slopes. Early September is a perfect time to visit Flaming Gorge: large aspen groves show their yellow fall colors in portions of the forest that were harvested in years past. This is one part of the Rockies where clear-cutting has quickly generated early forest development. You can find picnic spots throughout the area. The **Dowd Mountain Overlook** is a particularly scenic picnic area toward the western end of the gorge.

A second feature of the recreation area is the **Sheep Creek Canyon Geological Area**, off Highway 44 on a loop drive. Here, craggy rocks shove their way into the sky, with pinnacles, oddly shaped hoodoos, and tumbled rocks. Signs along the loop road point out the geological formations. Here, too, are picnic sites.

To the north of the small village of Manila are several lake access roads. The Lucerne Valley Road takes you to a marina, camping, boat launch, picnic areas, and a store. Squaw Hollow Road leads to the central part of the lake and a boat ramp. Buckboard Crossing at the northern end of the lake has a campground, boat ramp, dump station, and gas. On the eastern side of the recreation area, via Highway 191, **Firehole Canyon** is another scenic spot with a campground, picnic tables, boat ramp, and dump station. Anglers should be aware that some of the largest mackinaw caught in the West have come out of Flaming Gorge Lake.

Visitors to the **Flaming Gorge Dam** may take a self-guided tour of the facility. The main information center for the recreation area is located at this site, near the small Forest Service community of Dutch John.

Below the dam is one of the finest river-recreation areas in the country. The first 12 miles below the dam is a blue ribbon trout stream of wide renown. Motors are not allowed on the stretch between the dam and Red Creek. Rubber rafts can be rented locally and guided raft trips are available. You'll also find a riverside trail in this area. Below this area, **Brown's Park** is a long valley where the Green River winds through hills and wide, flat stretches. Farther west, the river enters the canyons in the Dinosaur National Monument. This section of the river offers river rafters an exhilarating experience through turbulent rapids and swift-moving stretches. This part of the river is best rafted with tour guides.

Visitors to the recreation area should consider visiting the historic **Swett Ranch**, located north of the dam on Highway 191. This early homestead was settled by Oscar Swett and his family in 1909. The family built cabins and cleared the fields; Oscar ran a sawmill and built a blacksmith shop. The family prospered for many years. Then, the dam was built in the late 1950s, and Oscar, growing old, sold the property in 1968 and died a few months later. His widow continued to live on the ranch, which belonged to a developer until 1970. The ranch was purchased by the Forest Service in 1972, and it was placed on the state and national lists of historic sites. It's a fine example of the western homestead; thousands of tourists visit each year.

The highway route from the Highway 191/44 junction to Manila was named the first National Forest Scenic Byway in 1988. Passing by the red gorge and the Sheep Creek Canyon, it's an unforgettable journey through geological time.

Ogden and Logan

North of Salt Lake City, Interstate 15 leads through Ogden, the historic location of the pounding of the last (gold) spike commemorating the completion of the transcontinental railroad in 1869. The first place to visit in the city is Ogden's grand old **Union Station** and its museum of railroad history. The station also has the Browning Arms Museum, the Browning Kimball Classic Auto Museum, and the Utah Gem Collection. The station building also holds a restaurant and an information center for Ogden and northern Utah. An art gallery features changing exhibits.

Another historical highlight of the area is **Fort Buenaventura**, the re-creation of an original fort constructed in 1846 by Miles Goodyear, one of the most famous of the explorers of the West. With the fur trade coming to an end, Goodyear decided to build this fort as a stopping place along the trail to California. The fort was not successful and was later purchased by Mormons who settled the Weber River Valley. The site became the community of Brownsville, later named Ogden. The state purchased the property and restored the fort, which now operates as an historical interpretation center, complete with authentic artifacts of the period and guides in period dress. You reach the riverside site by driving along 24th Street and then turning down A Avenue.

Another worthwhile outdoor activity is walking the five-mile **Indian Trail** from a parking lot on 22nd Street or from Ogden

Canyon on Highway 39. The old pathway leads along the Ogden River on the south side of the canyon, passing through Warmwater and Coldwater canyons.

You'll find two ski hills in the area: **Powder Mountain** is 19 miles northeast of Ogden, via 12th Street; **Snowbasin** is 17 miles east of town, also in the Wasatch Cache National Forest via 12th Street.

While visiting Ogden, you may want to venture farther northwest to the **Golden Spike National Historic Site**, where the last spike was pounded into the railway track. Within the site is a nine-mile drive on the old railway grade. A visitor center offers films and museum exhibits, and a 1.5-mile trail leads you to the "Big Fill" area and "Big Trestle" site. To get there, take Interstate 15 north past Brigham City and drive west along Highway 83. It is 32 miles west of Brigham City.

Logan is the gateway to the Bear Lake recreation district, via a very scenic drive of 40 miles through **Logan Canyon** in the Wasatch Cache National Forest. The Logan River and Blacksmith Fork are renowned, year-round flyfishing streams for trout and whitefish. **Beaver Mountain Ski Resort** is 27 miles northeast of town on the Logan Canyon scenic drive. This is a thrilling mountain region with the Wellsville Mountains dominating the sky. Several trails along the canyon lead to the spring at Spring Hollow and to the wind caves, which are a series of eroded arches.

Park City and Heber City

Park City and Heber City were named during the gold and silver mining period, when it was fashionable to name even the most humble village a "city"; on the other hand, many of these cities had upwards of 10,000 people during the boom period. Park City and Heber City lie on the eastern slope of the Wasatch Range, just across the mountaintops from Salt Lake City.

Park City was founded as a mining camp in the late 1860s when soldiers stationed in the area discovered silver in the mountains. In 1872, prospectors made a rich silver strike in Ontario Canyon, the main rush was on, and Park City was incorporated in 1884.

Silver mining continued for 50 years until the 1930s and falling prices. This was when skiing took over the town's economy. Snow Park, the area's first ski hill, opened in 1946, followed by two additional resorts. It is now one of the premiere ski areas in the nation, blessed with 350 inches of snow each year, and it still maintains the ambiance of an old mining town with a picturesque main street and wonderful original buildings.

Park City has the state's largest ski operation with a gondola and 11 chairlifts. It is the ski hill closest to town. Park West, four miles south of town, has seven chairlifts. Deer Valley is the toniest of all the ski resorts in the area, with eight chairlifts and deluxe base facilities located one mile east of Park City on Highway 224.

Summers in Park City offer the usual programs featured by ski areas, including gondola rides to the mountaintop and golfing. A mountain slide and six championship courses are within 20 miles of the town. Tennis is also popular; and mountain trails in the nearby Wasatch Mountain State Park (and mountain backroads) offer more outdoor recreation by foot or by car. You can enjoy a healthy cultural season in the old mining town: an outdoor Shakespeare festival, weekly concerts at Deer Valley featuring the Salt Lake Symphony, and the annual Chamber Music Festival. Park City has a full range of hotels, motels, lodges, and condo-type accommodations (see page 182).

Heber City is located 12 miles southeast of the ski town and is a feature of the Mirror Lake Drive (see page 150). Several large reservoirs are close to Heber City, including Strawberry and Deer Creek. Heber City has several modestly priced motels, but Park City offers more sophisticated lodging and dining. For those wanting to explore all of the ski resorts in the area, **Sundance Resort** is in Provo Canyon, a few miles south of Heber City and 15 miles north of Provo.

Where to Eat

For fine dining, head to Park City for a full selection of restaurants. Go high style or casual with **Alex's**, which features contemporary cuisine, or **The Claim Jumper** for steaks and nightly entertainment. **The Tree Room** at Sundance is worth the short trip off the highway.

Price

There are two sides to the town of Price and also to the surrounding countryside. The town is a mining community, originally a rough-and-ready coal mining camp that is now home to the College of Eastern Utah. These two sides of Price—combining many examples of mining history with the social ambiance that a college brings to a community—make for an interesting stay.

To the west of Price lies the **Manti–La Sal National Forest** on the southern part of the Wasatch Range and the Wasatch Plateau. The forest is a wonderful recreation area with backroads leading to ghost towns and a multitude of recreation sites.

However, east and south of Price lies the western portion of the Colorado Plateau. This is high desert country, and the contrasts to the area west of town couldn't be more extreme. Within sight of the Rockies is a scenic desert area featuring two remarkable geological areas: Nine Mile Canyon and the San Raphael Swell.

This area is explored in our Soldier Summit Drive (see page 154), which starts near Provo, crosses the mountains north of Price, and continues through the high plateau to Green River and the Colorado border. Price is the largest town in Castle County, and visitors find good accommodations and restaurants for an overnight stay. The college has the fine **Prehistoric Museum**, on the north side of the Municipal Building, showing the geological features of the area and skeletons from the nearby **Cleveland-Lloyd Dinosaur Quarry**. The quarry, 30 miles south of Price, is also open to visitors. The **Western Mining and Railroad**

Museum is located in the village of Helper, just north of Price on Highway 6. For accommodations details, see page 183.

Nine Mile Canyon (actually 50 miles long) is reached by turning east off Highway 6 just south of Price. The canyon was the main home of the prehistoric Fremont people. It features high cliffs, balancing rocks, panels of rock art, and remains of the Fremont dwellings. Altogether, it provides one of the most satisfying backroad adventures in the West. You won't find any services along the route—a picnic lunch is advised. The entire trip, in and back, takes about six hours.

The **San Raphael Swell**, like Nine Mile Canyon, is managed by the Bureau of Land Management. It is a little-known natural wonder on the high plateau, which includes high mesas, buttes, and pinnacles rising from the desert floor and wide rolling pastures and meadows on which dwell wild antelope. Rivers cut their way through narrow canyons. Major features include the Goblin Valley, the San Raphael Reef, and "Utah's Little Grand Canyon." You'll find a campground in the center of the area, midway between Highway 6 (to the east, north of Green River) and Highway 10, which runs south from Price through Castledale and Ferron.

Two state parks at the edge of the national forest are within a short distance of Price. **Scofield State Park** is on the Scofield Reservoir northwest of town. **Millsite State Park** is on the Millsite Reservoir, four miles west of Ferron off Highway 10.

Provo

This modern city is the home of **Brigham Young University** and is also the gateway to two of the Utah scenic drives: the Mirror Lake Drive (see page 150) and the Soldier Summit Drive from Provo to Price (see page 154). Provo is an ideal overnight point for visiting a number of recreational areas.

Provo Canyon, which you reach by taking Highway 89 north from the city, is a combination of lush vegetation, high rock walls with jagged formations, and the double cataract of

Bridal Veil Falls. At the falls, a tram carries visitors to the top of the cliffs, 1,228 feet above the floor of the canyon. A short drive along **Highway 92** leads past Sundance Resort and into the Uinta National Forest on the slopes of Mount Timpanogos. This road, called the Alpine Loop Drive, provides great vistas of the Wasatch peaks.

Along this road is the **Timpanogos Cave National Monument** at the end of a steep 1.5-mile trail, which takes about three hours for the two-way hike. Guided tours through the three interconnected caverns are given by National Park Service rangers. A picnic area near the visitor center is equipped with grills and water. You'll also find a snack bar at the visitor center at the base of the cave trailhead. The cave is open from mid-May to mid-October; the fee is $3 for adults ($2 for children). Several campgrounds are nearby in the **Uinta National Forest.** You can hike to the summit of the mountain from a trailhead at Aspen Grove in Provo Canyon or from American Fork Canyon. The trail passes beautiful **Emerald Lake**, with wonderful views along the way.

Approaching the north end of Provo Canyon, a fork off Highway 92 leads six miles to **Cascade Springs**, where you take a boardwalk trail over the springs and see views of unusual fish that live in the crystal-clear springwater.

Three miles west of Provo is **Utah Lake State Park**, on the shore of Utah's largest freshwater lake. At the east end of Provo Canyon is **Deer Creek State Park**, located on a large reservoir, providing boating, fishing, and other water sports.

The Provo River, which cuts through the Provo Canyon, is a fine flyfishing stream. One of the best fishing lakes in the area is Strawberry Reservoir, 30 miles east of Heber City (from the top of the canyon drive). Two boat ramps are on this 17,000-acre lake, which holds walleye, perch, largemouth bass, and trout.

The Provo area has a full range of accommodations, including RV parks. The nearest ski hill is at Sundance, a 30-minute drive from downtown Provo. The resort has four chairlifts, a good restaurant, and overnight accommodations.

Enjoy two hot spring pools at **Midway**, north of Heber City and about a one-hour drive from Provo. You can reach the **Saratoga Amusement Park and Resort** via Highway 68 on the northwest side of Utah Lake near the small town of Lehi. The resort has a hot springs pool. The ghost town of Fairfield is beyond Lehi, via Highway 73. It is the site of **Stagecoach State Park**. The town was a stop on the Overland Stage Road.

Salt Lake City and Area

The history and much of the present ambiance of Utah's capital results from the arrival in the Great Salt Lake Valley in July 1847 of 148 Mormon pioneers escaping religious oppression in the eastern states and searching for an area to settle. Within a year, many more Mormons made the arduous trek over the Rocky Mountains to the valley, and Great Salt Lake City became a reality (the "Great" was dropped in 1868). The transcontinental railroad arrived in the valley in 1869, and Utah became the 45th state in 1896. By then, the Mormons had ended their practice of polygamy and with statehood, the modern city took shape.

The Church of Latter Day Saints has put its stamp on Salt Lake City. **Temple Square** is the major attraction in the center of the city; its temple is open only to Mormons, but the square and tabernacle are open to all. Here, the famed Mormon Tabernacle Choir gives its weekly concert. Over the years, the Mormon Church has invested in the city's infrastructure, including $40 million to build the downtown shopping mall.

While summer months bring tourists to the area to visit Temple Square and other city attractions (including the Wasatch Mountains, which provide the dramatic backdrop for the city), winter is when the tourist industry really booms. You'll find 11 ski hills within an hour's drive of the city. They range from the small and cozy Sundance Resort north of Provo to the three big hills at Park City just across the Wasatch Range from Salt Lake City (see page 182). These and other ski operations, such as Alta,

Snowbird, Powder Mountain, and Snowbasin, provide all the action that any dedicated downhill skier could handle in a month.

The best place to begin a stay in Salt Lake City is the Visitor Information Center at 180 South West Temple. It's open daily except Sunday and is in the center of everything in the downtown area. Temple Square is at 50 North West Temple; the spired temple, the tabernacle, and assembly hall are connected by a series of walkways and gardens. The famous choir gives its weekly performance on Sundays at 9:30 A.M. with an open rehearsal on Thursday evenings at 8:00 P.M. **Beehive House**, Mormon founder Brigham Young's first official residence, is a national historic site, open to the public at 67 South East Temple.

Other historical highlights include the **Pioneer Memorial Museum** at 300 North Main, featuring 37 rooms of exhibits focusing on Utah pioneer history, historic vehicles, and farm machinery. The **Hansen Planetarium** is one of the best in the nation, with two floors of astronomical exhibits and the star theater. The **Salt Lake Art Center** at 20 South West Temple has a two-level gallery concentrating on contemporary art. **Symphony Hall**, the home of the Utah Symphony, is renowned for its near-perfect acoustics.

For railroad buffs, two old stations deserve attention. The **Union Pacific Railroad Depot** on South Temple is a grand old station. The **Rio Grande Depot** (300 South Rio Grande) is now occupied by the Utah State Historical Society.

You'll find many places to visit outside of the city, including **Great Salt Lake State Park**, located on the southern edge of the lake, offering boat tours, paddleboats, and a close look at the salt lake. For a reminder of early Mormon history, visit **Pioneer Trail State Park** on East Sunnyside Avenue. The Old Desert Village, a re-created pioneer village, and the "This Is the Place" monument are located here. This is the location of the end of the 1,300-mile trail used by Mormon travelers and others on their route west. **Big Cottonwood Canyon** is a scenic resort area north of the city with two ski hills, Alta and Snowbird.

Day Trips from Salt Lake City

More historical highlights are included on the **Oquirrh Loop Tour**, which provides an excellent day trip from the Salt Lake City. The tour begins just off Interstate 80, 16 miles west of downtown Salt Lake. From this lakeside point, the tour leads to the Old Benson Grist Mill (1860) near Stansbury Park. Continuing on I-80, the loop leads west to exit 99. The mill is 2.5 miles from the exit on Road 1378. Then take Highway 36 to **Tooele**, where the Utah Pioneers Museum is located on Vine Street. The Tooele County Museum contains a mine simulation and railroad displays. It's housed in the former Tooele Valley Railroad depot, built in 1909.

Leaving Tooele on Highway 36 and then Highway 73, the loop leads you to the almost-ghost town of **Ophir** (a common name for mining camps in the West), located off the highway 20 miles southeast of Tooele. The town is located in a beautiful canyon and still has a small population. East of Ophir is **Mercur**, a silver and gold camp that burned to the ground in 1885, was rebuilt, and burned again in 1902. A mining operation still provides a display and video program; it's not possible to see the old town. The loop returns to Salt Lake City by taking Highway 73 south and then west through Cedar Fort and north via Highway 68.

In addition to skiing, other outdoor attractions are available in the area. Enjoy 17 public golf courses (11 with 18 holes) in or close to the city, as well as others in Park City and Provo, which is a short drive south of town.

The Wasatch region around Salt Lake City is especially beautiful during the fall period when colors blaze on the mountains in shades of gold, red, purple, brown, and green. The fall foliage is best seen by driving through Cottonwood Canyons (Big and Little) and Emigrant Canyon.

A loop drive around the eastern slope of the Wasatch also provides views of brilliant fall colors. This side of the range includes **Wasatch Mountain State Park**, the largest in the state with 22,000 acres of wooded mountainside on the east side of the range, near Midway (a half-hour drive from downtown). The park has a 27-hole golf course and campground. During the winter a network of cross-country ski trails is groomed.

Where to Eat

In Emigrant Canyon, the **Santa Fe Restaurant** features Southwest cooking. **Ruth's Diner**, a cozy place with a 1940s setting, is nearby. Downtown, the **Old Salt City Jail** offers an interesting ambiance with steaks, seafood, and prime rib. **La Caille at Quail Run** (9565 Wasatch Boulevard) offers French cuisine in an 18th century-style chateau with a wonderful garden to look at and walk through.

Vernal

This town at the northeastern corner of Utah sits on the high desert just south of the eastern slopes of the Uinta Mountains, North America's only east-west range. It's a staging point for day and overnight trips to Flaming Gorge (to the north) and Dinosaur National Monument just east of town. Vernal is a half-day drive from Salt Lake City and a little more than a half-day's drive from Steamboat Springs, Colorado. The scenic drive that begins on page 162 covers the route through the Flaming Gorge National Recreation Area between Vernal and Green River, Wyoming.

Vernal has a fine little **Dinosaur Museum of Natural History**, at 235 East Main, concentrating on the dinosaur finds in the area with displays of plant and animal life. The Dinosaur Garden features 14 life-size replicas of prehistoric creatures. The town information center is in the museum building. The **Daughters of Utah Pioneer's Museum** features displays of pioneer artifacts and the history of settlement in the area. It's open summers only, from 1 P.M. to 7 P.M., at 5th Street West (at 2nd Street S).

Red Cloud Loop Tour

The nearby mountains provide scenes for a fascinating day trip. The High Uintas northwest of town provide great opportunities for mountain recreation. A day trip through the Uinta region nearest Vernal will take you to the old **Dry Fork Settlement**, which in the early days of eastern Utah was a thriving town in the Ashley Valley. The tour begins by taking Highway 44/191 (the route to Flaming Gorge) north from downtown Vernal. As the road climbs to Windy Point, you get good views of the Ashley Valley and the red rock formations called the "Red Fleet." The highway runs above the line of juniper trees and moves into sage country. Just past the rim of **Hole-in-the-Wall Canyon**, turn left for the Red Cloud route. This is the **Ashley National Forest**, which contains hiking trails, campsites, and other sites. Keep left on the gravel road, past a road to **East Park Reservoir** and past the **Iron Springs Campground**. You'll find a good hiking trail to Brush Creek Cave (0.5 miles off the road). After passing **Kaler Hollow Campground**, you come to a junction. Continue on a straight line to Kaler Hollow, Government Creek, and a park. **Oaks Park Reservoir** (via a backroad) is a good fishing lake with camping and a picnic area.

You'll see a forest ranger station at Trout Creek (a trout stream), and then the loop route turns left, passing the north fork of Ashley Creek with fishing, picnicking, and camping. Leidy Peak (el. 12,020 feet) is in view at this point. At the 43.7-mile mark, continue straight with **Lookout Point**, a viewpoint overlooking Brownie Canyon. The road descends into the canyon and then follows Dry Fork Canyon with more camping and picnic sites along the road. Past the site of the Dry Fork Settlement, the drive continues to the left with a turnoff to **Sadie McConkie Ranch**, where petroglyphs are carved on the sandstone cliffs (you pay a small admission fee). After leaving the ranch, the road enters the Ashley Valley again, passes **Uintah County Park** (with picnicking), and returns to Vernal via the Maeser Highway.

Places to Stay

FLAMING GORGE

Flaming Gorge Lodge
US 191
Dutch John, UT 84023
(801) 889-3783

This is a seasonal operation near the small community of Dutch John, north of Vernal. Located near the lip of the Red Gorge, this lodge has a restaurant, and lounge with moderate rates for rooms as well as more deluxe accommodation. Several public campgrounds are in the area, including a large one near the lodge. (**$ to $$$**)

LOGAN

Bandit's Cove Campground
590 South Main Street
Logan, UT 84321
(801) 753-0508

Sites with full hookups and tent sites, laundry, and dump station.

Center Street Bed & Breakfast
169 East Center Street
Logan, UT 84321
(801) 752-3443

All the rooms in this red-brick Victorian house come with private bath; the suites have a whirlpool. Continental breakfast. Each room has its own theme, including the attic Garden Room and the Arabian Nights Suite. The Victorian Suite has a sunken bathroom. (**$ to $$**)

Weston Inn
250 North Main Street
Logan, UT 84321
(801) 752-5700 or
800-528-1234

This is a mid-size Best Western motel in downtown Logan, with swimming pool and whirlpool. It's near restaurants and shopping. ($)

OGDEN

Century Campground
1399 West 2100 Street S
Ogden, UT 84401
(801) 731-3800

This is a large campground suitable for RVs, trailers, and tent campers. It has full and partial hookups, is open all year, and has laundry, swimming, and dump station.

Motel Orleans
1825 Washington Boulevard
Ogden, UT 84401
(801) 621-8350

If you haven't tried this western region chain of inexpensive motels, you might think of staying here. The rooms are comfortable, and the rates are extremely low. ($)

Ogden Park Hotel
247 24th Street
Ogden, UT 84401
(801) 627-1190 or
800-421-7599

This large hotel has a dining room, lounge, swimming pool and whirlpool, and a wide range in room and suite rates. (**$ to $$$**)

PARK CITY

Park City and nearby Deer Valley have a full range of accommodations from small B & B homes to large national chain hotels. For central reservations, phone Park City at (801) 649-9598 or 800-453-5789 and Deer Valley at (801) 521-3337 or 800-424-3337.

Blue Church Lodge
424 Park Avenue
Park City, UT 84060
(801) 649-8009

This small inn includes rooms in the former church and an annex. All have private bath and kitchen; some have fireplaces. There are whirlpools (indoor and

Blue Church Lodge
(continued)

outdoor) and a laundry. The units range from bedrooms to a four-bedroom suite with three baths. Continental breakfast. All rooms are luxuriously appointed. ($$ to $$$+)

Hidden Haven Campground
2200 Rasmussen Road
Park City, UT 84098
(801) 649-8935

Full hookups, trailer and tent sites, and dump station.

Old Miner's Lodge
615 Woodside Avenue
P.O. Box 2639
Park City, UT 84060
(801) 645-8068 or
800-648-8068

A western-style Victorian, this home was built in 1893 as a boardinghouse for miners. Each room is named and designed for characters in the area's history: for example, the Black Jack Murphy Room is outfitted as a miner's cabin. A full breakfast is served. ($ to $$)

Radisson Hotel
2121 Park Avenue
Park City, UT 84060
(801) 649-5000 or
800-345-5076

This large, deluxe hotel has a restaurant, lounge, pool, whirlpool, and all the services (including room service) that you would expect in a hotel of this type. ($ to $$$+)

Washington School Inn
543 Park Avenue
P.O. Box 536
Park City, UT 84060
(801) 649-3800 or
800-824-1672

Another old original building, this was a school in 1889. It's now a fine B & B inn, with renowned food (including candlelight gourmet dinners on occasion). Whirlpool, hot tub, and sauna. Rooms and suites, all with private bath. ($$ to $$$+)

PRICE

Budget Host Inn
145 North Carbondale
Road
Price, UT 84501
(801) 637-2424

Open year-round, this motel has a campground with RV sites (full hookups) but no tent sites. ($)

Green Well Inn
655 East Main Street
Price, UT 84501
(801) 637-3520 or
800-666-3520

This mid-size motel has a restaurant and lounge, with kitchens available. ($)

PROVO

Cottontree Inn
2230 North University
Parkway
Provo, UT 84601
(801) 373-7044 or
800-528-1234

A Best Western motor inn, located centrally, with swimming pool and whirlpool. ($ to $$$)

Lakeside Campground
4000 West Center Street
Provo, UT 84601
(801) 373-5267

A large operation with full hookups and tent sites, swimming, laundry, and dump station.

Provo Park Hotel
101 West 100 Street N
Provo, UT 84601
(801) 377-4700 or
800-777-7144

This large downtown hotel has a restaurant, lounge, swimming pool, and whirlpool. ($ to $$)

SALT LAKE CITY

Brigham Street Inn
1135 East South
Temple Street
Salt Lake City, UT 84101
(801) 364-4461

Near Temple Square, this B & B inn is a restored 1898 home with sumptuous guest rooms and a wonderful parlor. A large continental breakfast is served. ($$ to $$$)

The Inn at Temple Square
71 West South
Temple Street
Salt Lake City, UT 84101
(801) 531-1000 or
800-843-4668

If you want to be in the center of things and are willing to pay for it, stay in this mid-size hotel. It has a good restaurant. ($$ to $$$+)

Pinecrest Bed and Breakfast Inn
6211 Emigration Canyon Road
Salt Lake City, UT 84108
(801) 583-6663

Situated in six acres of landscaped garden in the scenic Emigration Canyon, this B & B offers a different ambiance to the city homes. The rooms in the inn and guest house all have private bath, two come with a whirlpool. ($$ to $$$)

VERNAL

Campground Dina
930 North Vernal Avenue
Vernal, UT 84078
(801) 789-2148 or
800-245-2148

This campground has full hookups and a large number of tent sites, with laundry and dump station.

Dinosaur Inn
251 East Main Street
Vernal, UT 84078
(801) 789-2660

This motel has a restaurant and lounge, swimming pool, and hot tub. Centrally located. ($ to $$)

Fossil Valley RV Park
(801) 789-6450

Full hookups on West Highway 40, laundry, and dump station.

Weston Plaza Hotel
1684 West Highway 40
P.O. Box 1905
Vernal, UT 84078
(801) 789-9550

This is one of the regional chain of hotels that offers good value, and this one has a restaurant, lounge, and swimming pool with hot tub. ($)

Montana

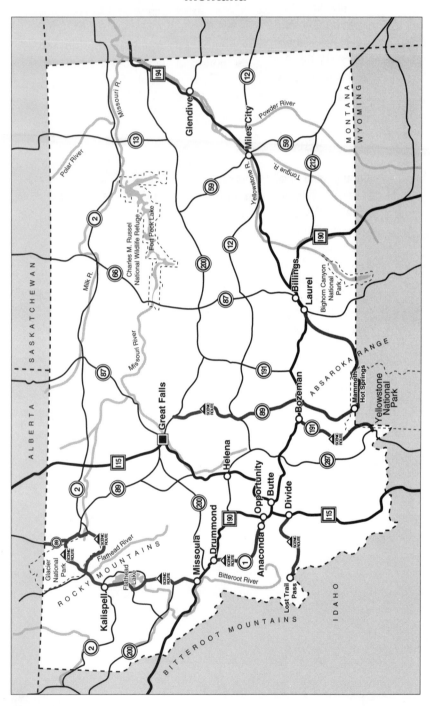

Montana *Drives*

R ising out of the plains of northern Montana, the Front Range of the Rockies presents a dramatic skyline filled with snowcapped peaks and pinnacles reaching to the sky amid the lush forests and rushing streams.

This is the setting for Glacier National Park, a superb wildlife preserve and the foremost hiking area in the nation.

Touching the southern boundary of the state, Yellowstone National Park is another unique natural epic, starring an amazing range of spouting geysers, boiling mud pots, and the equally dramatic silhouettes of the Absaroka Mountains. Bison and elk roam across Yellowstone's meadows; the river bearing the park's name plunges over one of the most scenic falls in the country.

The two parks are the "bookends" for the Montana Rockies experience. The following seven drives in Montana lead to the national parks through wide valleys and across legendary ranges including the Bitterroots, the Beartooths, and the Swan Mountains.

The journey north to Glacier National Park involves the first two drives in this chapter, from Missoula to Kalispell and then from Kalispell to the Canadian border.

On the drive between Missoula and Salmon, Idaho, the Bitterroot Mountains provide another chance to relive the journey of Lewis and Clark as they took shelter near Big Hole, suffering cold and deprivation during the winter of 1804.

The short but scenic Pintler Drive—between Opportunity (near Butte) and Drummond—provides a loop drive through the Anaconda-Pintler Wilderness, Montana's old gold country.

Flathead Lake Drive

Missoula to Kalispell

The wide Flathead Valley provides the focus of this drive north from Missoula, past Flathead Lake and the Mission Mountains and through the Flathead Reservation.

The lake is the largest freshwater lake in Montana, framed by the Mission Range to the east and the Cabinet Mountains to the west. Along the 117 miles of the route are enough scenic and recreational attractions to fill a vacation of several weeks if you wanted to fully explore the area. The fertile valley offers several wildlife preserves, including the **National Bison Range**, where buffalo roam free on a huge tract of land near the community of Moiese.

Flathead Lake is bordered by six state parks with camping and boating access. **Wild Horse Island State Park** fills an island in Big Arm, with more campsites accessible only by boat. On the east side of the lake is the town of Bigfork, a bustling summer tourist center with a network of fine hiking trails.

Highway 93 joins Interstate 90 a few miles west of Missoula. Leading north, it quickly enters the Flathead Reservation. This is the home of the Confederated Salish and Kootenai tribes and a placid rural valley leading to the base of the Mission Range. The Jesuit mission at Saint Ignatius is now a National Historic Site. Within the reservation, **Ninepipe and Pablo National Wildlife Refuges** offer good birding and viewing of other wildlife. You reach the National Bison Range by taking Highway 200 west from Highway 93 or southwest via Road 212 farther north along Highway 93.

The resort town of Polson is situated on the south shore of Flathead Lake. For those who like their creature comforts, Polson is the place to stay; it offers lodges, motels, marina accommodations, and relaxing boat tours of the lake. You'll find local history at the **Miracle of America Museum**, the **Polson Historical Museum**, and the **Polson Feed Mill**. **Big Arm State Recreation Area** and **Elmo State Recreation Area** are both a few minutes' drive north of Polson on Highway 93. Big Arm is the closest boating point for Wild Horse Island State Park.

You'll come across a Montana anomaly in the village of Dayton. Here is the state's only winery, which is set in this northern landscape. (One secret is that most of the grapes are imported from Washington state.) Tours and tastings are available daily during summer months. In spite of the unlikely location, the wines are not only drinkable but have won awards.

Back on Highway 93 on the west side of Flathead Lake, a sideroad leads seven miles west from Dayton to **Lambeth State Recreation Area** on Lake Mary Ronan. This is another superb bird-watching area, which also offers campsites, hiking trails, and boating. **West Shore State Park** and **Somers State Recreation Area** are found along the highway north of Dayton.

The village of **Somers**, another resort center, is located at the top of Flathead Lake. Highway 82 leads west to join Highway 35, just north of Bigfork.

Kalispell, a lumber town, is eight miles north of Somers. Kalispell must be the video poker capital of the world, with casino operations on almost every corner. It offers a wide range of accommodations, including convention hotels, chain motels, and several nearby lodges. Kalispell is the gateway to the outdoor recreation area north of town centered on Whitefish Lake.

Across the lake on Montana Highway 35 is **Bigfork,** often featured on winter weather reports as the coldest spot in the United States. During the other months of the year, Bigfork is a thriving recreation center and resort town, and its summer theater, the Bigfork Summer Playhouse, is open from May through Labor Day. **Wayfarers State Recreation Area**, five miles south of Bigfork on Highway 35, is set in a forest; it's ideal for hikers, picnickers, and campers. Swimming and boating are available here. **Jewel Basin Hiking Area**, east of town, covers more than 15,000 acres and features 38 miles of walking and hiking trails leading to alpine lakes, wildflower meadows, and mountain creeks.

HIGHWAY LOG
Missoula to Kalispell
117 miles (188 KM)—2 hours, 40 minutes

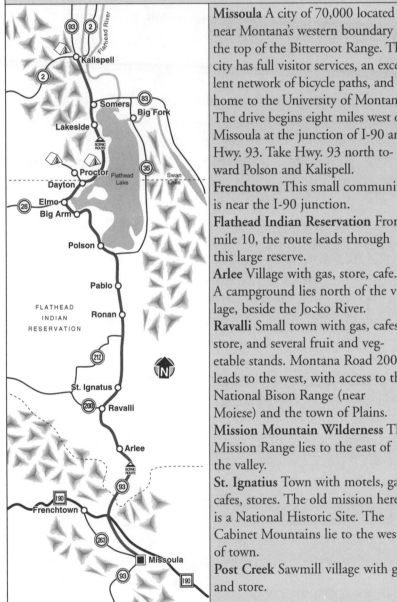

Missoula A city of 70,000 located near Montana's western boundary at the top of the Bitterroot Range. The city has full visitor services, an excellent network of bicycle paths, and is home to the University of Montana. The drive begins eight miles west of Missoula at the junction of I-90 and Hwy. 93. Take Hwy. 93 north toward Polson and Kalispell.

Frenchtown This small community is near the I-90 junction.

Flathead Indian Reservation From mile 10, the route leads through this large reserve.

Arlee Village with gas, store, cafe. A campground lies north of the village, beside the Jocko River.

Ravalli Small town with gas, cafes, store, and several fruit and vegetable stands. Montana Road 200 leads to the west, with access to the National Bison Range (near Moiese) and the town of Plains.

Mission Mountain Wilderness The Mission Range lies to the east of the valley.

St. Ignatius Town with motels, gas, cafes, stores. The old mission here is a National Historic Site. The Cabinet Mountains lie to the west of town.

Post Creek Sawmill village with gas and store.

Ninepipe National Wildlife Refuge This reservoir is surrounded by marshlands providing shelter for many varieties of birds.

Junction–Highway 212 Leads west to wildlife viewing area, and on to Moiese and the National Bison Range.

Picnic Area and Viewpoint One mile north of junction, with views of Mission Range. Tribal Wilderness marker.

Ronan Town with gas, motels, cafes, stores. RV parks (in town and two miles east). Salish Kootenay College at north end of town has interesting architecture.

Pablo Village just off the hwy., with gas, store, cafe. Pablo National Wildlife Refuge is located north of the village.

Junction–Highway 35 Hwy. 35 leads around the east side of Flathead Lake, to the town of Bigfork. This is a scenic alternative route to Kalispell.

Polson Resort town at mile 60 on the south shore of Flathead Lake.

Big Arm A bay and a village with marina and RV park.

Big Arm Recreation Area Located 15 miles north of Polson with campsites and access to the lake.

Elmo Tiny village with store.

Elmo State Recreation Area On north shore of Big Arm, 19 miles north of Polson. Campsites on hill, picnic tables, boat launch.

Dayton Village with winery; tours and tastings are held from May to October. RV resort, cafe, and cabins. **Wild Horse Island** (with state park campsites) lies offshore.

Junction–Sideroad Leads west to village of Proctor and Lambeth State Recreation Area. Camping on Mary Ronan Lake.

West Shore State Park East of highway with campsites.

Lakeside Small town with motels, gas, RV parking, stores, bar, and seafood restaurant.

Somers Town with a picturesque location on the north shore of Flathead Lake. Gas, restaurants, resort hotel.

Junction–Highway 82 Leads east to the town of Bigfork and along the eastern shore of Flathead Lake. The Swan Range lies to the east.

Kalispell City with full visitor services, museum, and golf course. Lone Pine State Park is four miles west of town with camping.

Glacier Park Drive

Kalispell to Alberta Border

Pristine natural setting . . . Stunning panoramas . . . Astonishing
alpine environment . . . A sense of wonder. . . .

The tourist brochures pull out all the stops in promoting Glacier and Waterton Lakes National Parks. And for once, all the hyperbole is correct—it's even understated.

This wilderness area comprising Glacier and Waterton parks is an unsurpassed international preserve. Glacier National Park is Montana's gem, containing several hundred lakes, more than 700 miles of hiking trails, and more peaks and mountain meadows than one can possibly imagine. Wildlife includes bighorn sheep, deer, elk, bear, moose, and mountain goats. And everywhere, you see the panoramic views of mountains over 10,000 feet high accessible by road around the edge of the park areas and (in the case of Going to the Sun Road) through the middle of Glacier National Park.

This drive starts in Kalispell, the lumbering city situated just south of Glacier National Park. Within an hour's drive, you can be inside the park, on a scenic highway drive or a backcountry adventure. For the first 34 miles, Highway 2 leads northwest from Kalispell, past the town of Columbia Falls, and into the Swan Range in Bad Rock Canyon.

The village of **Hungry Horse** is the access point for the loop drive around the Hungry Horse Reservoir, a long, slim lake that backs up from the dam just off the highway. Recreation sites are located around the reservoir, and trails fan out over the ridges on both sides of the lake. This is part of the **Great Bear Wilderness** in the Flathead National Forest. At the southeastern end of the reservoir is the famed **Bob Marshall Wilderness Area**. You can find a visitor center beside the dam and a forest ranger station in Hungry Horse.

West Glacier is the entry point to the southern reaches of Glacier National Park, and it's the beginning of our drive around the southern and western sides of the park. The drive takes the southern route, passing the historic village of **Essex**, climbing to the summit at Marias Pass, into East Glacier with its fine old railroad lodge, then along the boundary of the park to St. Mary and the eastern end of the Going to the Sun Road.

From West Glacier, the road parallels the Flathead River beside thick forested hillsides with pinnacle formations overhead. Several trails lead to scenic viewpoints (including Grant Ridge Trail) and to Stanton Lake. The **Izaak Walton Inn** in Essex—now the state's top cross-country ski resort—was built in 1939 by the Great Northern Railway.

The highway makes a turn to the northwest at the base of Felix Peak, climbing to the Continental Divide at Marias Pass (el. 5,280 feet). A stop at the Divide provides a look at several commemorative markers, one to honor Teddy Roosevelt and another to tell about mountain man and homesteader "Slippery Bill" Morrison, who had squatting rights to the pass property and gave it to the government.

East Glacier Park has a railway station, a motel, several cabins, a store, and the rustic but comfortable **Glacier Park Lodge**. One of the remaining old railway lodges, it's still in operation during summer months. In its early years, railway excursions brought well-heeled tourists to the lodge to explore the edges of Glacier National Park.

HIGHWAY LOG
Kalispell to Alberta Border
148 miles (238 KM)—3 hours

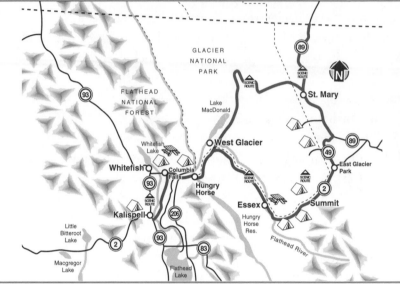

Kalispell City with gas, hotels, motels, restaurants, museums, historic sites, RV parks, and campgrounds. Drive begins in downtown Kalispell, at the junction of Hwys. 93 and 2. Take Hwy. 2 north toward Columbia Falls and West Glacier.

Junction–Highway 40 Leads west to the town of Whitefish and Whitefish State Park (camping).

Columbia Falls Located 18 miles from Kalispell with gas, motels, cafes, stores. Teakettle Park, beside the highway north of town, is a scenic and sheltered picnic spot beside the river.

Junction–Road 206 To Bigfork and the drive along the east shore of Flathead Lake. Gas, motels, cafes, store at Bad Rock junction.

Bad Rock Canyon Historic location (the site of an historic battle), with turnoff and trailhead.

Roadside Spring Pipe sticking out of hill at milepost 141.

Hungry Horse Small town on South Fork of Flathead River, with forest ranger station, gas, RV park, motels, stores, cafes, laundry.

Hungry Horse Reservoir Part of Flathead National Forest, with a scenic loop drive and trails. Several campgrounds in the forest and KOA at milepost 151.

West Glacier Village with services at milepost 153. Turnoff to north for Glacier National Park via Going to the Sun Road.

Our drive continues on Hwy. 2, which skirts the park. East Glacier is 56 miles to the east.

Canyon Middle Fork of the Flathead River flows below the highway.

Moccasin Creek River Access To left at milepost 161.

Trailhead Trail to Stanton Lake at milepost 170. Cafe and cabins beside hwy.

Park Cafe and cabins.

Trailhead Grant Ridge Trail, east of hwy. Half a mile.

Paola Creek Beside the hwy. with river access roads and paths (forest roads).

Junction–Sideroad to Essex Izaak Walton Inn Road. Village with services and renowned mountain lodge.

Walton Picnic Area North of hwy.

Railway Snow Sheds To the south, across river.

Goat Lick Seen from parking area with view of Middle Fork at milepost 183.

Devil Creek Campground South of highway. Cafe, bar, and motel, 0.5 mile east of camp.

Three Forks Campground At milepost 191.5. Open, grassy sites.

Bear Creek Guest Ranch North of hwy. at milepost 192.

Skyline Road and Challenger Creek At milepost 196.

Lewis and Clark National Forest Summit at Marias Pass (el. 5,280 feet) at Continental Divide.

Summit Campground Open summer months, 10 miles from East Glacier.

East Glacier Park Gas, motel, cafes, cabins. Glacier Park Lodge (open summer months) was built by the Great Northern Railway.

Junction–Highway 49 Leads north to St. Mary, Going to the Sun Road, and the Canadian border. Hwy. 2 continues west to Browning. For this drive, take Hwy. 49 for 12 miles to Hwy. 89 junction.

Junction–Two Medicine Road Leads west to campground—7.5 miles.

Junction–Highway 89 For this drive, take Hwy. 89 north to Glacier National Park entrance. Twenty miles to St. Mary, park gate and information center.

Junction–Road to West Cut Bank Campground Ranger station, five miles.

St. Mary Tourist village.

Going to the Sun Road This scenic route runs across the park. Thirteen miles north, Hwy. 17 leads to the Alberta border and Waterton Lakes National Park.

Big Hole River Drive

Divide to Lost Trail Pass

The Big Hole of Montana and the river that bears its name provide the pathway for this drive, through forested lands beside the river and then across grazing fields and sage country in the wide, oval-shaped valley. The drive takes us past the scene of one of the most memorable battles of western history and then leads to Chief Joseph Pass and Lost Trail Pass in the Bitterroot Mountains.

Our drive along Highway 43 provides a convenient route leading from the Butte area to the Bitterroots, where you can drive north along Highway 93 to Missoula or south to Salmon, Idaho.

Although the small town of Wisdom is the only community of any size along this short drive, sideroads lead to villages and towns farther south in the valley, including Jackson. A scenic sidetrip on a byway through the **Beaverhead National Forest** leads through the Pioneer Range to several campgrounds and to the famed **Elkhorn Hot Springs**. So our advice is to disregard the fact that this drive involves only 77 miles of highway and be prepared to spend some time taking side trips to a rich variety of historic sites, ghost towns, hot springs, and forest areas. The legend of the Lewis and Clark expedition comes to life with several locales where the explorers stopped on their return journey to St. Louis in 1805.

The most important historic site in the valley is the **Big Hole National Battlefield**. Located near Chief Joseph Pass, at the western side of Big Hole, the battlefield park commemorates the victory of the Nez Perce over U.S. army soldiers during the flight of the Nez Perce in 1877. Here, Colonel John Gibbon's troops ambushed Chief Joseph's people, with large losses on both sides. An interpretive center provides battlefield tours and displays including remarkable photographic images of the principals of the battle. In the valley below the center is the siege site and the Nez

Perce Campground. Although many other historic sites commemorate the flight of the Nez Perce, particularly in their Idaho homelands, none offers a more poignant retrospective of the injustices that forced the tribe to flee toward safety—a flight that ended in defeat in northern Montana, just a few miles from the promise of safety in Canada.

Another historic site, reached by a sidetrip south of Highway 42, along Montana Highway 278, is **Bannack State Historic Park**. Located near the town of Dillon, this is the site of Montana's first territorial capital and the location of the first major gold strike in 1862. A walking tour of the park includes stops at the old Hotel Meade, the original jailhouse, and Sheriff Henry Plummer's gallows. A visitor center has interpretive exhibits, and the park offers camping, fishing, and picnicking. The Beaverhead County Museum in Dillon provides additional displays and artifacts of this early gold rush period.

In the early stages of the drive, beginning at the junction of Highways Interstate 90 and Highway 41 near Divide, the route parallels the Big Hole River, offering several Bureau of Land Management (BLM) campgrounds, including the excellent **Divide Bridge Recreation Area**. The highway passes through a canyon with evidence of old mine sites above the river. As the river enters the Big Hole, the landscape opens to reveal this large valley, which includes the town of Wisdom in addition to several guest ranches.

The drive ends deep in the Bitterroots, at **Lost Trail Pass**, with a hot springs soaking opportunity. The route explores not only the headwaters region of the Missouri River but one of the most historic areas in Montana where the exploration, mining, and railroad origins of the state's development are highlighted in many ways.

HIGHWAY LOG
Divide to Lost Trail Pass
77 miles (124 KM)—1 hour, 45 minutes

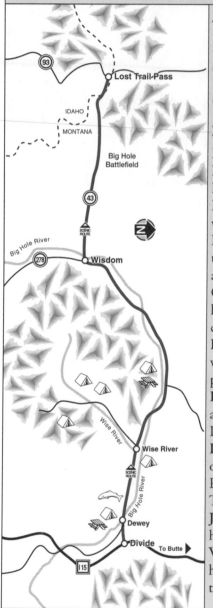

Junction–Interstate 15 and Montana Highway 43 I-90, the major east-west route, is 19 miles north of the Divide junction. The city of Butte is 26 miles from the junction. Our drive begins at the Divide junction via Hwy. 43, which leads west beside the Big Hole River.

Divide Small village just west of I-15 junction. Bar, gas, store.

Divide Bridge Recreation Area BLM area to the south of the highway beside the Big Hole River. Large campground suitable for tents, trailers, and RVs, with water and picnic tables. The Sawmill Gulch Hiking Trail is a short trail leading into the hills from the campground.

Big Hole River Canyon The highway runs through a narrow canyon, passing old mine sites.

Fishing Access To Big Hole River at milepost 71 on east side of Dewey.

Dewey A small village with several old log buildings. The Big Hole River Inn is a bar in the village. There is no gas or store here.

Jerry Creek Bridge To north of the highway with fishing access.

Wise River Village with Beaverhead National Forest ranger station, bar, cafe, gas.

Junction–National Forest Scenic Byway This road leads south along the Wise River with access to three campgrounds and Elkhorn Hot Springs.

Dickie Bridge Recreation Area BLM site to south of road with picnic tables, at milepost 58.

Junction–Bryant Creek Road To south of hwy.

Junction–Forest Road To Johnny Creek at Big River Bridge.

East Bank Recreation Site Very primitive BLM campsites with no water or picnic tables.

Junction–Road to Anaconda Leads north at milepost 54. Passes close to Grassy Mountain (el. 7,900 feet) and crosses the Continental Divide.

Junction–Road to Sundance Lodge To the north with fishing access, at milepost 50.5.

Campground Beside Big Hole River in the Pioneer Range. The road now curves to the west, continuing beside the Big Hole River.

Wisdom Town with gas, motel, cafe, store, forest ranger station.

Junction–Montana Road 278 To Jackson, Bannack State Park

(camping), two hot springs, and town of Dillon (on I-15).

Leading west from Wisdom, Hwy. 43 runs across the prairie grasslands of Big Hole.

Big Hole National Battlefield Quarter-mile off road, at milepost 16. Commemorates the Big Hole battle of August 18, 1877. Information and battlefield interpretive center near the hwy. A road leads down the hill to the siege site and Nez Perce campsite. Picnic tables are located at the siege site parking lot.

Historical Marker Beside the hwy. west of the Battlefield. Commemorates the Lewis and Clark route of 1806 when the explorers camped nearby at Ross's Hole in the Bitterroot Range.

May Creek Campground **Beaverhead National** Forest campsites at milepost 9.

Chief Joseph Pass The Continental Divide, at 7,241 feet.

Lost Trail Pass and Junction–Highway 93 The Montana/Idaho border is just north of the junction.

National Forest Picnic Area Near the junction.

Pintler Scenic Drive

Opportunity to Drummond

The 62 miles of Montana Highway 1 is a loop drive through the heart of the old gold country of west-central Montana. However, Highway 1 is only part of the story. This is backroad country, where forest roads (in Deerlodge and Beaverhead National Forests) lead to lakes, streams, and valleys in the Anaconda-Pintler Wilderness, a spectacular preserve lying south of the highway and accessed from several points along Highway 1.

Georgetown Lake is a popular fishing and boating spot along the highway, which passes by the towns of Anaconda and Philipsburg before reaching its end at Interstate 90 at the town of **Drummond**. The route provides access to old mining sites, ghost towns, and a host of summer and winter recreation areas on or close to the highway.

The loop drive affords an excellent alternative to the mainly prosaic Highway 90 route between Butte and Missoula. The journey begins at the junction of I-90 and Highway 1, at the small town of Opportunity. At once, tailings ponds are seen on both sides of the road, evidence of the giant smelter operations in Anaconda. North of these two communities is the **Warm Springs Wildlife Management Area**, accessed via Sideroad 48. Nearby is **Lost Creek State Park** (on Sideroad 635), which contains campsites and additional wildlife viewing opportunities. A short trail leads to Lost Creek Falls and limestone cliffs that tower 1,200 feet above the floor of the canyon. Mountain goats and bighorn sheep graze in the area and can often be seen from the park.

The town of **Anaconda** was founded in 1833 by Marcus Daly when he built the Washoe Smelting and Reduction Works. The giant facility is seen to the south of Highway 1. **Washoe Park**, in Anaconda, is a popular attraction. The Montana Fish Hatchery—located within this park—features trout display ponds. You'll also enjoy flower gardens and picnic areas here. Since the area is dotted with ghost towns, it's only natural that you'll find the National Ghost Town Hall of Fame in Anaconda. The Copper Village Museum and Arts Center has displays of smelting processes and regional historic artifacts. **Fairmont Hot Springs Resort** is located south of Anaconda, accessible from I-90 or on a sideroad leading south from Highway 1.

The **Anaconda-Pintler Wilderness** covers a 30-mile stretch of the Continental Divide, southwest of Anaconda. You won't find any roads (or even backroads) in the wilderness area, but trails lead into various parts of the region from backroads that snake southward from Georgetown Lake.

Silver and Georgetown Lakes, situated immediately west of Anaconda, offer camping, fishing, and boating. Georgetown Lake, in particular, is in a spectacular setting: the peaks of the Pintler Wilderness provide a backdrop for this reservoir.

The historic mining town of **Philipsburg** is at the halfway point along the drive, with a well-preserved downtown district that is listed on the National Registry of Historic Places. One of the most notable of the region's ghost towns—**Granite**—is located six miles east of Philipsburg. The Miner's Union Hall and the mine superintendent's home are reminders of the silver boom that opened up the area in the 1880s.

The drive ends at Drummond, after the highway passes through a fertile agricultural valley.

Sideroads and Backroads

County Road 348 leads west into the Bitterroots from Philipsburg, past the Granite ghost town to the Crystal Creek and Mud Lake forest campgrounds. As is the case with the previous backroad, this road is open during summer months only.

Garnet, a ghost town, can be reached from the end of this drive at Drummond. Named for the ruby-colored stones found near the mining camp, the site is accessed by driving 10 miles west on Interstate 90, then exiting at the Bearmouth exit, driving six miles east and then 10 miles north on Bear Creek Road. Much of the old 1870s camp remains.

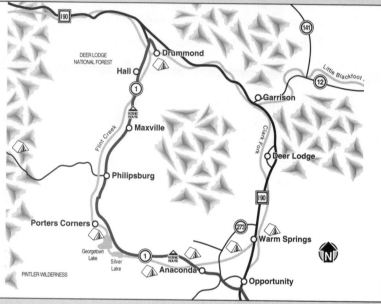

Opportunity Small town off I-90, 15 miles northwest of Butte.

Junction–Interstate 90 and Montana Hwy. 1 Our drive begins at this junction with Hwy. 1 leading west toward Anaconda.

Junction–Sideroad 441 To Fairmont Hot Springs. Leads south from Hwy. 1 at milepost 3.

Junction–Sideroad 274 To Deep Creek Ski Area, Big Hole Valley, and town of Wisdom. Leads south from Hwy. 1, just east of Anaconda.

Lost Creek State Park Via Sideroad 273 to the north of Hwy. 1, 1.5 miles past turnoff to Wisdom at milepost 5.5 with wildlife viewing, campsites. The sideroad also leads to Warm Springs by taking Sideroad 48.

Anaconda Smelter town, 6.5 miles from I-90 junction. Gas, motels, cafes, stores, museum. Two-lane hwy. north of Anaconda.

Warm Springs Campground West of the hwy. at milepost 19, in Deerlodge National Forest.

Spring Hill Campground Quarter-mile past the Warm Springs site.

Historical Marker Atlantic Cable Quartz Lode Gold Discovery. More than $6 million in gold was taken out of these hills.

Junction–Twin Lakes Road To west from the hwy.

Junction–Storm Lake Road To west, one mile past Twin Lakes Road. Trailhead at lake.

Junction–Silver Lake South of highway at milepost 23.

Junction–Denton's Point Road At milepost 24. Gas, cafe, store at south end of Georgetown Lake. The road leads around the shore of this lake, popular for fishing and boating. Several Forest Service campgrounds located on the eastern shore of the lake.

Grassy Point Boat Launch At milepost 25. Campground nearby.

Ski Area Discovery Basin via Sideroad 65. Leads north from hwy.

Lodgepole Campground With boat launch at milepost 27.

Echo Lake Picnic Area Located 100 yards north of the Lodgepole Campground.

Flint Creek Dam At north end of lake. A road leads along the western shore of Georgetown Lake. Hwy. 1 descends into a canyon where an old wooden flume parallels the highway 100 feet above.

There is a pulloff and historical marker at the viewpoint.

Fleet Creek Campground To the east in the valley, past milepost 30.

Junction–Skalkaho Pass Road Road 38 at milepost 31.5. This scenic summer backroad provides a driving adventure, leading west from the junction. It ends at the town of Hamilton on Hwy. 93.

Philipsburg Gas, cafe, store at milepost 36. Forest ranger station in this historic farming community at the north end of the valley.

Junction–Sideroad 348 At the north end of Philipsburg, leading west to the Garnet ghost town, BLM campsites, and on to the Squaw Rock Forest Campground.

Junction–Road to Maxville Leads west to the tiny village.

Historical Marker For Southern Flint Creek Valley, the location of placer mining in the 1800s.

Hall Sawmill village in a rural valley setting. Mrs. Julia Byrne Hall gave her name to the town in 1891.

Drummond Small town on I-90 with Garnet Mountains to left and right. Gas, motels, cafes, store. Campsites in Drummond City Park.

North Route to Yellowstone

Great Falls to Yellowstone National Park

One of the longest drives in this book (at 221 miles), Highway 89 traverses an amazing range of landscapes: from the high desert south of Great Falls near the Highwood Mountains, through cattle and buffalo grazing country near Bozeman, to the west flank of the Absaroka Range and Yankee Jim Canyon, just north of the town of Gardiner and the north gate to Yellowstone National Park.

While Great Falls may be the starting point of this drive, the country surrounding the city is rich in western history and should be fully explored. The city of **Great Falls** is the geographical and spiritual center of "Charlie Russell Country." On canvas and in bronze, the great western artist provided a lasting testament to the Plains people, early cowboy life, and the magnificence of the Missouri River and its valley. The **C. M. Russell Museum** in Great Falls has the world's largest Charlie Russell art collection, along with much memorabilia, his log cabin studio, and the Russell home. Other museums celebrate the Montana cowboy, local traditions, and U.S. Air Force history.

The Upper Missouri, stretching downriver from Fort Benton—a distance of about 150 miles—has been designated a National Wild and Scenic River. Lewis and Clark explored this stretch of the river, camping alongside it in 1805 and 1806. A visitor center for the river park is located in **Fort Benton** (41 miles northeast of Great Falls), and boat tours are available from the town. Visitors to the area should be sure to visit this colorful historic town, which played a significant role in the settling of the Northwest from 1860 to 1887. Farther north via Highway 87—near the town of Chinook—is the **Chief Joseph Bear Paw Battlefield**, the final site on the Nez Perce flight to freedom. This was where Chief Joseph surrendered, in order to save the lives of his few remaining followers. The battlefield marks the end of the 1,700-mile trek of the Nez Perce, on October 5, 1877.

Now, on to our drive heading south from Great Falls across the prairie. After the first half hour, the route slices through the **Lewis and Clark National Forest** with numerous recreation sites, a ski hill, and several creek canyons. **King's Hill Pass**, at an elevation of more than 7,000 feet, offers many options for outdoor activity (including skiing). Farther south, Highway 12 leads east, past more forest campgrounds and to Harlowton with its pioneer museum.

Hot springs fans should plan to reserve some soaking time in the pools at **White Sulphur Springs**, a small town 94 miles south of Great Falls. History buffs will enjoy the Meagher County Museum, housed in a grand stone mansion from the 1890s, and the nearby ghost town of Castle, which was founded in the silver rush of the 1880s. You'll find Castle by taking Highway 194 southeast from the town.

South of White Sulphur Springs, the highway passes through flat, sparse prairie land with the Bridger Range to the west. Highway 86, leading west from our route, provides a scenic shortcut through the Bridger Mountains to Bozeman (for those who wish to take the scenic drive from Bozeman to West Yellowstone on page 212). Fairy Lake is a scenic camping and recreation point along Highway 86.

Arriving at **Livingston**, near the junction of Highway 89 and Interstate 90, this drive leads west for seven miles along the interstate to its junction with Highway 89 south.

Take Highway 89 through the **Gallatin National Forest** and Paradise Valley. This section of the drive is 53 miles long, leading beside the Upper Yellowstone River and a string of fishing access sites that will please every angler. The valley route offers stunning views of the Absaroka Range (to the east). The **Chico Hot Springs** are located a few miles east of the highway. This is an excellent private hot springs complex with a resort hotel and camping facilities. Several forest campgrounds are located along the way.

After passing Mount Cowen and Emigrant Peak, the highway enters the Gallatin Mountains for the final few miles through Yankee Jim Canyon to Gardiner and Yellowstone National Park.

HIGHWAY LOG
Great Falls to Yellowstone National Park
221 miles (356 KM)—5 hours

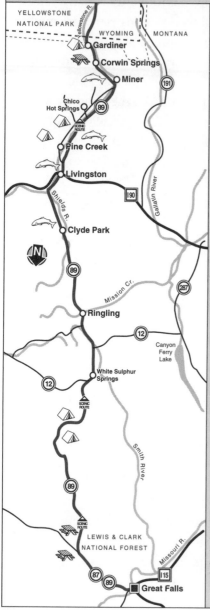

Great Falls A major trading center with a full range of tourist services and the outstanding C. M. Russell Museum complex.

Our drive starts at the junction of I-15 and Hwy. 89. Take Highway 89 south through Great Falls after crossing the Missouri at the north end of town. For the first few miles, the hwy. is labeled 87/89.

Junction–Highway 228 To the east with national forest access roads in the Highwood Mountains.

Junction–Road 331 East to the community of Belt. The road descends through a scenic arroyo for 1.5 miles.

Armington A village with RV park, one mile off the highway.

Junction—Highway 87 Forks southwest to Lewistown.

Picnic Area To the east at the junction. The road now runs beside the Bell River, through the foothills of the Little Belt Mountains.

Picnic Area Izaak Walton Spring, to east of hwy.

Belt Creek Sluice Boxes Historical site beside the road. A trail leads to an old gold mining scene.

Monarch Canyon The hwy. passes through the canyon as it enters the Lewis and Clark National Forest.

Ranger Station Forest information center, beside hwy. at Belt Creek.

Aspen Campground South of ranger station, west of highway.

Many Pines Campground To the east of the highway.

Junction–Highway 12 Leads east to Harlowton, with access to several forest campgrounds.

White Sulphur Springs Town, 94 miles south of Great Falls. Gas, motels, cafes, stores. Hot spring pools are open year-round.

Junction–Highway 294 Leads east to Martindale and ghost town of Castle (silver strikes in the 1880s).

Road to Ringling Just off the hwy. Note: old, weathered church on hill beside hwy.

Viewpoint At milepost 33. Views of snowcapped Bridger Range, to the west. The Absaroka Mountains lie ahead in the distance.

Junction–Road 86 East to Fairy Lake (22 miles), Bridger Ski Bowl (24 miles), Bozeman (37 miles).

Wilsall Farming community with gas station and two bars. Located 22 miles from I-90. The road condition improves at this point.

Clyde Park Village with gas.

Junction–Brackett Creek Road Leads west 16 miles to Battleridge Campground.

Fishing Access At milepost 2.

Yellowstone Bridge Fishing access at milepost 1.5.

Junction–Interstate 90 Take I-90 west to Livingston. Use Livingston west exit to Hwy. 89 south to Yellowstone National Park through Gallatin National Forest. Gas, food, camping, motels in Livingston.

Fishing Access Carter's Creek, off Road 540 at Rock Canyon.

Junction–Pine Creek Road Fishing access and a KOA campground.

Fishing Access Mallard's Rest (Yellowstone River) to east.

Forest Campground East at milepost 37 near village of Pray.

Grey Owl Fishing Access On sideroad at river, at milepost 34 beside Mount Cowen.

Junction–Chico Road Hot springs resort to the east.

Junction–Big Creek Road Road 132, to the west of the hwy.

Picnic Area East beside the river at milepost 124. The hwy. now enters the Gallatin Mountain Range.

Fishing Access Point of Rocks at milepost 21.

Fishing Access Via Rock Creek Road. The road passes through Yankee Jim Canyon with river access from a parking area. Joe Brown Trailhead to the east of hwy.

Corwin Springs Cafe and cabins at milepost 8.

Picnic Area Leduc Spring. Leduc trailhead east of hwy.

Gardiner Tourist town at the north entrance to Yellowstone National Park. Gas, motels, campground, cafes, stores. The Roosevelt Arch marks the park entrance.

Beartooth Mountains Drive

Laurel to Yellowstone National Park

This summer route was described as the "most beautiful drive in America" by none other than CBS's Charles Kurault, and there is some justification for that well-promoted description. Leading southwest from Interstate 90 near Laurel, through the town of Red Lodge, to the northeast corner of Yellowstone National Park, Highway 212 offers unparalleled mountain views from its switch-backs as the route ascends the Beartooth Range to a height of almost 11,000 feet. This is truly a "skyline drive," passing glaciers and pristine little mountain lakes and leading across an alpine plateau at the summit.

The early part of the drive does not forecast the mountains ahead as it crosses the Montana prairie lands between Laurel and Red Lodge. The **Cooney Reservoir** offers recreation sites in Cooney State Park, not too far off the highway via a county road. This loop road leads from Boyd, past the park to meet with Highway 78, which leads south back to Highway 212. This loop provides an alternate route for those who wish to explore or stay in the park.

Forty-five miles from Laurel, the town of **Red Lodge** features a rustic main street with several motels and private campgrounds. The town is a National Historic District, with buildings constructed between 1893 and 1910 during the town's coal mining boom. You may wish to drive four miles east of town to the site of the Smith Mine Disaster, where 74 men died in an underground explosion in 1943. In town, the **Carbon County Museum** displays Red Lodge history with pioneer artifacts and the homestead cabin of John Garrison. South of Red Lodge, **Rock Creek Resort** provides sophisticated accommodations at the foot of the Beartooth Range.

From Red Lodge, the road has been designated a National Forest Scenic Byway, and the highway begins its steep climb toward the summit. You'll encounter frequent switchbacks with fresh views at every turn, and hikers will enjoy the **Gardiner Lake Trail**, which leads to the small, blue alpine lake.

The **Beartooth Summit** lies at an elevation of 10,947 feet. You'll find snow at the summit for much of the year, although summer driving is painless. Those with four-wheel-drive vehicles may want to explore two sideroads leading across the plateau near the summit. The **Morrison Jeep Road** leads south from the highway to the Dollar Lake Trailhead. Fantan Lake Road provides a 2.5-mile drive to this scenic little lake.

Two campgrounds are situated north of the highway just past the summit. The Top of the World store and motel are also located here.

Between the summit and Cooke City—near the park entrance—are several forest campgrounds and two overlooks with splendid views of the Clark Fork River. Clay Butte is a high peak accessed by a short sideroad that leads three miles to another lookout.

Still in high country, **Chief Joseph Scenic Highway** (Road 296) leads southeast, past Sawtooth Mountain to the Sunlight Wildlife Habitat. Past the junction, another overlook pulloff offers views of the high Absarokas. Chief Joseph Highway runs 57 miles to Cody, Wyoming.

Four additional forest campgrounds are past the scenic highway junction. **Goose Creek Jeep Trail** leads five miles to Lulu Pass and more thrilling views.

Cooke City is a small gold town, dating from 1876, lying just east of the **Yellowstone National Park** boundary. Right at the boundary is the village of Silver Gate, with gas, a cafe, and a general store.

From the park gate, the highway leads for 47 miles to the park headquarters at Mammoth Hot Springs.

Tower Junction is a major crossroads in the park. Here is Roosevelt Lodge, open during summer months. From the junction, the highway continues for 18 miles to Mammoth Hot Springs. The junction is on the Yellowstone Park Loop (see the scenic drive on page 256).

HIGHWAY LOG
Laurel to Yellowstone National Park
156 miles (251 KM)—3 hours, 45 minutes

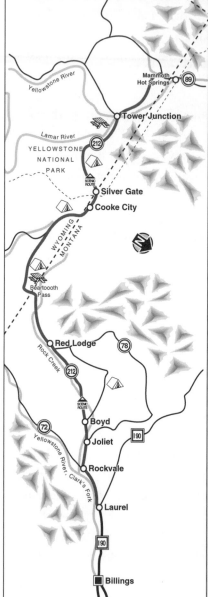

Laurel Located 16 miles west of Billings via I-90. The drive begins at the junction of I-90 and Hwy. 212. Take Hwy. 212 southwest toward Red Lodge.

Rockvale and Junction–Highway 72 For this drive, continue on Hwy. 212.

Joliet Village with gas and store.

Boyd Village with store and Road 78 to Cooney State Park (camping on reservoir).

Red Lodge Town with gas, motels, B & B, cafes, stores, camping 45 miles from Laurel.

Junction–Road to Sundance At milepost 65.

Rock Creek Resort Hotel with restaurant.

Forest Campground At milepost 57. The road crosses the treeline at milepost 47. The road now climbs toward the Beartooth Summit with switchbacks and sharp turns.

Gardiner Lake Trailhead Walk-in campsites.

Picnic Area Near the summit.

Summit Beartooth Pass (el. 10,947 feet).

Junction–Morrison Jeep Road Road 120. South to Dollar Lake Trail (two miles).

Junction–Fantan Lake Road Across the hills to the lake (2.5 miles).

Island Lake Campground To north of hwy.

Beartooth Lake Campground North of highway.

Top of the World Store and motel, 1.5 miles east of the campground.

Clay Butte Lookout Via sideroad (three miles).

Overlook Clark Fork and mountains with spire at west end of range.

Junction–Chief Joseph Scenic Highway Road 296. To Sunlight Wildlife Habitat.

Crazy Creek Campground South of highway beside creek.

Fox Creek Campground and Chief Joseph Campground Access to Clark Fork Trail.

Goose Creek Jeep Trail To Lulu Pass (five miles).

Soda Creek Campground

Cooke City Small 1876 gold mining town, four miles from park. Gas, store, motels, cafes, cabins.

Silver Gate At park entrance with gas, cafes, Grizzly Lodge, store.

In Yellowstone National Park: Northeast Entrance 128 miles from Billings. Entrance fee.

Warm Creek Picnic Area South of hwy.

Wyoming/Montana Border

Icebox Canyon Bridge across Soda Butte Creek. The hwy. continues descending through the canyon.

Pebble Creek Campground To north of highway. Trailhead.

Soda Butte (marker)

Lamar Valley Geology Exhibit To south, near picnic site.

Lamar River Picnic Area South of hwy.

Lamar River Valley Scenic pulloffs, including a view of the Lamar River cataract.

Slough Creek Campground North of highway, with trailhead.

Lamar River Bridge Pulloffs on both sides of bridge.

Yellowstone River Picnic Area South of hwy., at top of hill.

Yellowstone River Bridge

Tower Junction (el. 6,278) Ranger station to south of hwy. before junction. Roosevelt Lodge.

Petrified tree Quarter-mile south of junction.

Wraith Falls Pulloff to south.

Lava Creek Picnic Area

Undine Falls Pulloff to north.

Gardiner River Bridge At east end of Mammoth Hot Springs.

Mammoth Hot Springs National Park Visitor Center, lodge, store, restaurant. Watch for elk on highway and lawn of visitor center.

Gallatin River Drive

Bozeman to West Yellowstone

The short (90-mile) drive from Bozeman to West Yellowstone is not quite the most scenic way to reach America's oldest national park, but the route has its own share of mountains (the Gallatins) and perhaps the best flyfishing in all of the U.S. Almost the full length of the drive leads up the Gallatin River as it runs northward to its encounter with the Missouri. The Gallatin National Forest offers a selection of forest camping areas along the way, including several campgrounds adjacent to the highway.

The route begins in downtown Bozeman. The city is the home of Montana State University and the Museum of the Rockies, which is found on the university campus. The museum covers four billion years of history and prehistory of the northern Rockies. **Missouri Headwaters State Park** is located on Road 286, reached from the Three Forks exit of Interstate 90. The park sits on the site where Lewis and Clark discovered the Jefferson, Madison, and Gallatin rivers meeting to form the Missouri River. You'll find a campground here, along with interpretive displays, hiking trails, and good fishing.

Other Bozeman highlights include the **South Willson Historic District**, which features a walking tour of 48 houses, some dating to 1883, and **Hyalite Canyon**, a park with trails, waterfalls, fishing, and picnicking, on 19th Avenue. The Gallatin Pioneers Museum features local historical displays and artifacts.

The drive begins in downtown Bozeman via Highway 191/84. The route follows city streets past Montana State University until Highway 84 veers off to the west. Continue on Highway 191 toward West Yellowstone.

The first community of any size is **Gallatin Gateway**, 13 miles south of Bozeman. The town was famous as a railway point in the early days of the Chicago, Milwaukee, and St. Paul Railroad. The Gallatin Gateway Inn was built in the mission style by the railway. It served as a rest stop for tourists who were on their way to Yellowstone National Park. From Gallatin Gateway, the highway enters the Gallatin Range and leads beside the Gallatin River. Several forest access roads intersect the highway.

Now to the fishing possibilities! The Gallatin is regarded as one of the best—if not the finest—flyfishing streams in America. On any day, you will pass anglers in hip waders. You'll see signed fishing access points along the route; several forest campgrounds between Castle Rock and Big Sky offer good fishing spots.

There are three such campgrounds in the northern stretch of the canyon, all under the silhouette of Mount Blackmore. Beyond Moose Flat Campground is a historic farm site, homesteaded by the Durnam family in 1936. This was a head lettuce farm until the land was returned to the National Forest in 1978.

You can enjoy several worthwhile hiking trails on the route, including the **Deer Creek Trail**, north of Big Sky. This trail begins by crossing a bridge to the west of the highway.

Big Sky is the famous ski resort that attracts skiers from across America. It's located in the Gallatin Range, just west of Highway 191, and it is also open during summer months.

The highway passes through the corner of the huge burn area, left by one of the fires of 1988.

At the junction with Highway 187, you have the choice of turning north on to 287 to drive a few miles to visit the **Earthquake Visitor Center**. The center overlooks the site of Quake Lake, created by a huge rockslide that dammed the Madison River during the earthquake of 1959, whose epicenter was near the town of West Yellowstone.

Just north of West Yellowstone is **Hebgen Lake**, with a recreation area of more than 12,000 acres offering fishing, boating, camping, and indoor accommodations. The town of West Yellowstone is a tourist mecca, both during summer months when the west gate to Yellowstone is open and during the winter when snowmobilers and Nordic skiers take over the town. You're assured good lodging in West Yellowstone, including the excellent Stage Coach Inn and other less pricey motels.

HIGHWAY LOG
Bozeman to West Yellowstone
90 miles (145 km)—1 hour, 45 minutes

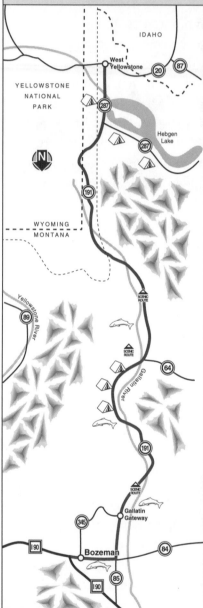

Bozeman This drive begins downtown, via Hwy. 191/84, leading past Montana State University.

Fishing Access Bozeman Ponds to north of hwy.

Junction–Highway 84 Leads west to Norris and Hwy. 287. Our drive continues on Hwy. 191.

Bozeman Hot Springs Campground Beside the hwy. at the hot springs.

Fishing Access Axtell Bridge to west.

Gallatin Gateway Village with lumber mill to west of hwy. Gas, cafe, store, historic hotel.

Little Bear Forest Road Leads east, at milepost 74. The main hwy. now enters the Gallatin Mountains.

Spanish Creek Road Forest access to west of hwy.

Castle Rock Motel (cabins) and RV parking on river to east of hwy. Half a mile south is Squaw Creek Bridge with fishing access. Ranger station and Squaw Creek Road to forest access at milepost 65.

Indian Ridge Trailhead West of hwy.

Hellroaring Creek Trailhead West of hwy. The hwy. continues, leading south into a narrow canyon.

Forest Campground Eight units east of the hwy., another campground just west of hwy. including river sites, at milepost 58.

Swan Creek Campground East of highway.

Moose Flat Campground Beside the Gallatin River with grassy and wooded sites. All of these campgrounds lie at the base of Mt. Blackmore.

Durnam Meadow Historic site west of hwy. Homesteaders (1936–1970) ran head-lettuce farm and cattle operation.

Big Sky Ski and summer resort to west of hwy. via sideroad. Gas at the junction with stores, motels, and restaurant. Saloon and cabins at south end of valley.

Big Doe Road To the west at milepost 44.5.

Red Cliff Campground Beside the river to east of hwy., two miles south of valley. This is the best flyfishing section of the river.

320 Guest Ranch Across the river to east of hwy. with cabin accommodations, at milepost 36.

Sage Creek Trail West of hwy., a popular riding trail.

Teepee Creek Trail To the east at milepost 32.

Daly Creek Trailhead To the east at milepost 30.5.

Black Butte Trailhead To the east at mile 29.

Burn Area Left by the fire that devastated large sections of the Yellowstone forests in 1988.

Junction–Teepee Creek Road The loop road comes out to the hwy. before the hwy. crosses Grayling Creek.

Junction–Highway 287 This route runs northwest from Duck Creek junction past the Earthquake Area Visitor Center. Several Beaverhead National Forest campgrounds along Highway 287 north of the earthquake center. Continuing southward, the town of West Yellowstone is eight miles from the junction.

Cougar Creek Road West of the highway, at milepost 7.

Rainbow Point Campground On Hebgen Lake, with boat launch and picnic area. Take Rainbow Point Road to the campground.

Junction–Madison Arm Road To resort and campground.

Bakershole Campground Just north of West Yellowstone townsite.

West Yellowstone (el. 6,666 feet) Tourist-oriented town at west gate to Yellowstone National Park, with gas, motels, lodge, stores, restaurants.

Montana
Destinations

Bigfork

A hundred miles north of Missoula, Bigfork lies on the eastern side of Flathead Lake, the largest freshwater lake in the American West. The lake is as renowned for its fishing as Bigfork is famous for an annual flood of vacationers who come to this small, cozy village for the unbelievable variety of nearby wilderness and for the town's cultural attractions.

East of Bigfork is the **Bob Marshall Wilderness Area**, a huge untamed area of 950,000 acres—a favorite of backcountry purists. Glacier National Park is an hour's drive to the north. The **Jewel Basin Nature Area** is closer to town and offers 38 miles of nature trails that anyone can navigate.

The lake attracts anglers for its kokanee in the spring and summer months and for mackinaw and Dolly Varden trout in the fall. You can fish in the nearby streams for rainbow, cutthroat, and brook trout, perch, bass, and northern pike. The Swan River flows through the middle of Bigfork; swimming and boating is available right in the village. The river is a frequent scene of float trips and canoeing adventures. Golfing rounds out the recreational scene, and the Eagle Bend course is a beautiful addition to the town.

You'll enjoy the lively arts and crafts ambiance of Bigfork. A live repertory theater in the **Center of Performing Arts** hosts musicals and other productions from June through September. The village park hosts live outdoor performances during summer months as well. Art galleries and craft shops display the work of local craftspeople and visiting artists. The **Bigfork Festival of the Arts** occurs the first weekend of August.

Bigfork is also a popular winter recreation center. The national forest offers miles of cross-country ski trails and forest roads for snowmobilers. **Big Mountain Resort** (with downhill slopes) is less than an hour's drive away, as are the famed cross-country trails at **Essex**. Because of the lake's effect, the winters here are milder than in most northern Montana towns, making Bigfork an excellent place to stay while exploring the recreational opportunities in the area's larger towns, including Whitefish and Kalispell. You'll find a number of motels in the village, as well as a selection of fine B & B homes in and near Bigfork (see page 239).

To get to Bigfork, see the Flathead Lake Drive, which leads from Missoula through the Flathead Lake area (page 188). Bigfork is on Montana Highway 35, which cuts around the eastern shore of Flathead Lake between Polson and Kalispell.

Billings

The largest city in Montana, Billings is the child of the Northern Pacific Railway, which brought settlement to the area in 1882. Lying in the arid Yellowstone River Valley, it is an agricultural and oil refining center.

The Beartooth Mountains are to the southwest and the Big Horns lie to the south; the valley is the traditional home of the Crow or Absarokee people. It's a good place to stay before exploring the attractions of the Beartooth Range (see the Beartooth Mountains Drive, page 208).

To the south, via Interstate 90, is what used to be called the Custer Battlefield Monument, and is now named **Little Big Horn Battlefield National Monument**. It is the site of the defeat of Union troops by Sioux and Cheyenne warriors in June 1876. While the memorial commemorates the death of the unfortunate

Lt. Col. George Armstrong Custer, a movement resulted in the renaming of the monument to recognize the victory rather than the army defeat. The battlefield is 54 miles south of Billings.

The **Bighorn Canyon Recreation Area** is a 1.5-hour drive south of Billings, with striking scenery, lake and stream fishing, and boating. Bighorn Lake, held back by the Yellowtail Dam, is 71 miles long and lies within the limestone walls of the canyon. Below the dam, the Bighorn River is one of the West's most prolific trout streams. You'll find hiking trails and scenic drives within the recreation area as well as campgrounds.

Within Billings are many attractions for visitors, including the **Yellowstone Art Center**, with historical and contemporary art and crafts, and the **Western Heritage Center**, which offers exhibits on Yellowstone Valley history. The **Peter Yegen Museum** located near the airport atop the Rimrocks features Old West history and Native American artifacts.

Western history buffs will also treasure a visit to **Boothill**, the only remaining sign of the former town of Coulson. **Pictograph Cave State Historic Site** preserves the remnants of a prehistoric culture, with rock paintings seen from a short trail. More than 30,000 artifacts have been discovered in the cave. The park, which has picnic sites, is located six miles south of town, via the Lockwood exit of Interstate 90. **Rimrock Drive** leads along a dramatic series of sandstone cliffs from Highway 10 east of town. On a sunny day, you can see five different mountain ranges from atop the ridge at the gravesite of frontier scout Yellowstone Kelly.

The city has a pleasant, modern ambiance, with summertime concerts at **MetraPark**, seven golf courses, and **Riverfront Park**, beside the Yellowstone, offering walks and picnicking (one of 63 municipal parks). The **Moss Mansion**, at 914 Division Street, provides a look into Billings' past; take guided tours through this turn-of-the-century mansion, which is the former home of Preston B. Moss, one of the area's prominent community founders.

Where to Eat

Several good restaurants have a western character, including Jake's on First Avenue North, the **Granary Restaurant** at 1500 Poly Drive, and two **Doc and Eddy's** with casino/dining.

Bozeman

The home of Montana State University, Bozeman is one of the most pleasant towns in the West as well as the gateway to the northwest part of Yellowstone National Park. Bozeman is the starting point of the Gallatin River Drive (page 212). The city is situated at just over 4,700 feet and is surrounded by mountain ranges: the Bridger Range to the east, the Big Belt Mountains to the north (see the scenic drive on page 204), the Tobacco Roots to the west, and the Gallatin Range to the south. The city sits at the northern end of the Gallatin River Canyon, through which the scenic drive to Yellowstone passes.

Montana State University is known for its agricultural programs and research. Its main attraction to visitors is the Museum of the Rockies, which was expanded in 1989 and has exhibits featuring fossils, western art, and Native American artifacts. It also contains a dinosaur exhibit and a new planetarium. Summer in Bozeman offers a walking tour of the historic districts in the downtown area and the adjacent South Willson district of historic homes—48 houses including large mansions and little Victorian homes dating back as far as 1883. This area is particularly beautiful in the winter, when the Christmas Stroll is held.

Bozeman Hot Springs is southeast of town, with a campground and RV park nearby. **Big Sky**, the ski and summer resort, is farther south along our scenic drive on the way to Yellowstone. During summer months, the Big Sky gondola takes visitors to the top of the ski hill with fine views of the Gallatin Mountains. Gallatin River rafting is also available at Big Sky village. You'll find golf courses in Bozeman and at Big Sky.

You'll find skiing as well at **Bridger Bowl**, just northwest of Bozeman. The base lodge has a bar and grill and cross-country skiing with 30 kilometers of trails available at the Bohart Ranch, next to Bridger Bowl.

In summer, Bozeman is the scene of **Shakespeare in the Park** performances and evening concerts by the municipal concert band and the Bozeman Symphony. **Hyalite Canyon** is the site of a scenic park, accessed via South 19th Avenue, with nature trails, waterfalls, fishing, picnicking, and a campground. The **Gallatin Gateway Inn**, in the village south of town on the way to Yellowstone, is a mission-style historic lodge built for railway travelers to the park by the Chicago, Milwaukee, and St. Paul Railroad.

The fishing just south of Bozeman, in the Gallatin, Yellowstone, and Madison rivers is world-renowned. **Missouri Headwaters State Park** is at the confluence of the Madison and Gallatin rivers, offering fine fishing, picnicking, and trails.

Where to Eat

Gallatin Gateway Inn has a fine old dining room, and the food matches the decor. In town, try **Pork Chop John's** (at 1630 West Main) for their famous pork chop sandwiches, and the historic **Sacajawea Inn**, at 1122 West Main (open daily except Tuesdays).

Butte

By 1915, Butte was home to 70,000 people, most of them there because of the huge Anaconda Mining Company. Earlier, in the 1860s, Butte and particularly the nearby foothills were the scene of the great Montana gold rush, with silver and copper strikes to follow. It is said that the mines of Butte have produced more than 20 billion pounds of copper. Millions of ounces of gold and silver have been extracted from the mines, byproducts of the amazingly rich copper ores. The result of all the early mining fervor is two Buttes. Uptown Butte is the original downtown, with elaborate architecture including turreted brick structures and the famous **Copper King Mansion**, the home of copper magnate

William A. Clark. A two-hour walking tour will take you through the historic area, visiting union halls, churches, the courthouse, fire hall, and the original copper mine. You may also tour old Butte on Old Number One, a replica of an early Butte streetcar. The tour begins at the Chamber of Commerce (1950 Harrison). The other Butte is the modern city, a bustling center of commerce servicing the ranch lands that lie around the city.

For outdoor recreation, the **Anaconda-Pintler Wilderness** is less than an hour's drive from Butte (see the scenic drive on page 200). This 62-mile route provides a loop through the heart of the old gold country, taking modern travelers to ghost towns and lake recreation. The wilderness area is a 159,000-acre stretch of forest and lakes, extending more than 30 miles along the Continental Divide. Access to the area is from Georgetown Lake—on the Pintler Scenic Drive—and the East Fork of the Bitterroot River, off Highway 97. No motorized travel is permitted in the wilderness. Closer to Butte, at Anaconda, **Fairmont Hot Springs Resort** features hot pools, an 18-hole golf course, and an RV park as well as deluxe family accommodations.

Railroad fans should not miss the Neversweat and Washoe Railroad at the **World Museum of Mining**. The museum features exhibits on the mining history of the region. The "Neversweat" takes riders on a railway trip past six former mining operations. The Kelly Mine was the last operating underground mine in Butte. Other places to see include the **C. W. Clark Mansion**, now a city arts museum featuring regional artists. **Our Lady of the Rockies** is a 90-foot statue atop the Continental Divide, east of Butte. The **Humbug Spires Primitive Area** is 18 miles south of the city on Interstate 15 (at the Moose Creek exit). The area features rock climbing and hiking around the fascinating limestone formations.

Where to Eat

The **Copper King Restaurant** in the Copper King Mansion serves meals in the Victorian dining room, including breakfast for overnight guests. The restaurant serves classic American cuisine, such as filet mignon and rack of lamb. **Fairmont Resort** has a good dining room. The **Derby** (2016 Harrison) is the place to go for steaks; it's also a casino. The **Red Rooster** is the local supper club. You'll find two **Pork Chop John's** in Butte.

Gardiner

The post office in Gardiner has a display of historical photographs of the town, taken since its founding in 1880. This is as good a place as any to begin an exploration of the area. **Yellowstone National Park** lies across Park Street from Gardiner's downtown district.

In the 1880s and 1890s, Gardiner was a dusty, false-fronted village of no more than 20 buildings in the middle of nowhere, waiting for infrequent stages to come through with supplies and for the next gold rush. The real gold rush came when Yellowstone Park was fully accessible to the public around the turn of the century. With the main (and still the only year-round) park entrance across the street from Gardiner, this town has developed as a tourist town with good and bad consequences. The economy in Gardiner is stable. Some of its "decor" is questionable, although most visitors enjoy the touches that hark back to the tough little frontier village of the 1880s. You'll see what I mean when you see the lineup of false-fronted buildings on Park Street—saloons, bingo halls, cafes, and tourist souvenir shops.

Gardiner lies in the Yellowstone River Valley, at the south end of the Gallatin River Drive to Yellowstone Park from Livingston (see page 212). The drive passes near **Chico Hot Springs** and the base of several magnificent Absaroka peaks. Gardiner is a town of motels and campgrounds, a place for travelers waiting to enter Yellowstone. Some stay here to fish in the Yellowstone and other nearby streams. The **Absaroka-Beartooth Wilderness** is to the north of town, offering hiking and backcountry camping. Gardiner becomes a haunt of snowmobilers in the winter.

The summer scene across the Park Street fence is enhanced during summer months with wild antelope in the meadow and on the Yellowstone Park hills. You can also see bighorn sheep. Once inside the park, passing beneath the (Teddy) Roosevelt Arch, **Mammoth Hot Springs** and the park headquarters are just a few minutes away. Overnight accommodations in Gardiner include cabin courts, modern motels, and a campground and RV park situated on the hill behind the downtown area (see page 242). River rafting trips on the Yellowstone and Gallatin are available in Gardiner as well as pack trips in Yellowstone National Park and guided flyfishing trips down the Yellowstone River.

Where to Eat

One of the more palatable places to eat in the area is the **Ranch Kitchen** in Corwin Springs, seven miles north of Gardiner. It has a "homey" atmosphere and is open early for breakfast. The Paradise Players stage a summer revue, with a buffet dinner before the show. In town, try the **Yellowstone Mine Restaurant** on Highway 89, open for breakfast and dinner. Steaks are the specialty, but you can also get seafood. This respectable restaurant is in the Best Western Motel downtown.

Glacier National Park

At the top of Montana, hard against the Canadian border, sits what pioneer conservationist George Grinnell called the "Crown of the Continent." Two national parks form this crown: Glacier in Montana and Waterton Lakes in Alberta, Canada. Together, they form the Waterton/Glacier Peace Park. Glacier Park itself was created by an act of Congress in 1910. Four thousand visitors came to the park in 1911; in recent years, visits have been at the two million mark.

This is a region of such beauty that it is hard to describe. Superb and magnificent are only two of the possible adjectives for this corner of the world. You see high mountains, many active glaciers, clear lakes, rushing mountain streams, waterfalls, and abundant wildlife.

Leading through the middle of Glacier National Park, **Going to the Sun Road** provides a spectacular route by which to explore the park. Completed in the 1930s, this road has opened the wilderness to everyone (at least during summer months) and provides 50 miles of nonstop spectacle as you cross the park from west to east or vice versa. For a description of the Going to the Sun Road, see the scenic drive described on page 194. The map also includes the route around the edges of the park from Kalispell to the Canadian border.

Glacier Park covers more than three million acres of mountainous country. It has 700 miles of walking and hiking trails, 11 campgrounds used by car travelers (only one is not suitable for trailers), and six hotels and lodges plus food services within the park. You'll also find a hotel at Waterton, on the Canadian side. A long-standing tradition in Glacier Park is to take the scenic tour on the red 1936 coaches with rollback tops.

As you might imagine, the landscape of Glacier National Park has been much affected by the action of glaciers over several million years. The most spectacular of the mountain peaks have been exposed by continual glacial action and erosion. In many places along the Going to the Sun Road, you can see exposed layers of sedimentary rock. Volcanic action deposited lava fields to form a black band atop the limestone layers, which were then covered with thin layers of more limestone and siltstone. The final adjustment to the topography came several thousand years ago when huge slabs of earth moved as much as 30 miles eastward.

Most of the glaciers in the park are shrinking, causing meltwater to run down the mountain slopes and deposit silt in the lakes, giving them a blue-green color. Glacial erratics, the large rocks carried along by advancing glaciers, have created several hanging valleys in the park that appear as large terraces in the mountains, some of which are connected by waterfalls. The Glacier Natural History Association has published a series of books that not only tell the geological story of the park but provide detailed field guides to the interior of the park, the trails, and plant life. These books, along with detailed topographical maps and other booklets, are available in the main information centers.

The park opens its entrance stations at St. Mary and West Glacier around May 20; the Many Glacier Station opens a week later. Following are a few of the highlights.

- **Wildlife**

  Walking through wildflower meadows, visitors see many species of alpine and subalpine plants. The east side of the park has plants that thrive in the prairie landscape, including geraniums (red and white), asters, Indian paintbrush, and gaillardia. The more mountainous western side has hardier species such as heather, gentian, beargrass, and glacier lily.

  The animals of the park include mountain goats, bighorn sheep, elk, wolves, whitetail and mule deer, and black bears. A bison herd is on display in a paddock in Waterton Lakes National Park. You may see beavers in Waterton Park and on the high rocky slopes are marmots and pikas sunning themselves on warm summer days. The bald eagle lives in both parks, along with ptarmigan, osprey, and the golden eagle.

- **Trails**

  You can enjoy 114 miles of backcountry trails leading through the park interior. All backcountry hikers must register with the park information center at St. Mary or with the park headquarters. However, more than 70 trails are suitable for day-hiking, and they are located throughout the more accessible areas of the park, particularly along the Going to the Sun Road. The St. Mary area on the eastern side of the park has a number of trails that lead along St. Mary Lake to St. Mary Falls and Florence Falls and up the mountain past Siyeh Pass to Piegan Pass.

Two of these hikes, the Red Eagle Lake Trail (7.5 miles) and the Beaver Pond Trail (1.2 miles), begin at the 1913 Ranger Station, near the St. Mary entrance station. The Piegan Pass/Siyeh Pass trailhead is on the Going to the Sun Road, 15 miles west of St. Mary. The trailhead is signed, and there is a pullout. The trail passes through three different ecological zones along subalpine meadows with views of several glaciers. Siyeh Pass has an elevation of 8,240 feet. The Many Glacier area in the northeast corner of Glacier Park has several interesting day-hikes, including the self-guided Swiftcurrent Lake Trail, which leads 2.4 miles from the south end of the Many Glacier Hotel. The same trailhead also has a trail leading to Grinnell Lake and the Grinnell Glacier. The lake trail passes Josephine Lake and then climbs 200 feet to Feather Plume Falls. The Glacier Trail also uses the Josephine Lake Trail and then branches off to the glacier. The hike is 5.4 miles long.

The Lake McDonald Area at the western end of the park features a trail along the northwest side of the lake, from Lake McDonald Lodge to the Fish Creek and the North Fork Road. This walk is 6.7 miles long. The Trail of the Cedars provides a shorter walk (0.8 miles) through a forest with trees more than 500 years old. It is a boardwalk trail with the option of continuing on another trail to Avalanche Lake (another two miles). This trail winds through Avalanche Gorge and climbs 500 feet to the lake.

Where to Stay

Of the seven car-campgrounds, only Sprague Creek Campground is not suitable for trailers. The large campgrounds at Apgar and St. Mary are near the two main park entrances and are open year-round with primitive camping outside of summer months. Many Glacier and Two Medicine Campgrounds have park services during summer months and then are open as primitive campsites until snow closes them. The roads leading to the campgrounds at Bowman Lake, Cut Bank, and Kintla Lake are so rough that RVs and trailer units are not advised to travel to these sites. All campgrounds are operated on a first come, first served basis. Private campgrounds are near the major entrances to the park, including West Glacier and St. Mary.

The park concessionaire, Glacier Park Inc., operates several hotels and motels in (and near) the park. All are seasonal operations.

- **Glacier Park Lodge**
  The historic railway lodge at East Glacier, with rooms and suites.

- **Lake McDonald Lodge**
  A hotel complex beside the lake on the west side of the park, with lodge, motel, and cabins.

- **Many Glacier Hotel**
  On the shore of Swiftcurrent Lake. The park's largest resort with more than 200 rooms and suites.

- **Rising Sun Motor Inn**
  With rustic motel accommodations, near St. Mary's Lake.

- **Swiftcurrent Motor Inn**
  In the center of the park near Swiftcurrent Lake and the Many Glacier Hotel, with motel and cabin accommodations.

- **Prince of Wales Hotel**
  In Waterton Lakes National Park (Alberta), a deluxe hotel overlooking the Waterton Lakes.

For information and reservations, contact Glacier Park Inc. In the U.S.: (602) 248-6000 from October to mid-May; (406) 226-5551 from mid-May through September. In Canada: (403) 236-3400 year-round.

Two rustic high-mountain chalets are accessible only by walking alpine trails. **Granite Park Chalet** and **Sperry Chalet** are historic mountain lodges built by Jim and Louis Hill of the Great

Northern Railway around 1914. Reservations for July and August are taken only in writing to Belton Chalets, P.O. Box 188, West Glacier, MT 59936.

Those traveling to or from Glacier National Park usually find themselves staying overnight in one of the nearby towns. Kalispell and Columbia Falls are an hour's drive south of the West Glacier entrance and offer a selection of motels and hotels for overnight stays. **Kalispell** is a large lumbering and mill town with a full range of visitor services, including modern downtown hotels, many motels, campgrounds, and a variety of restaurants. Kalispell also seems to be the casino capital of Montana.

The resort town of **Whitefish** is nearby, located five miles west of Columbia Falls. This is a ski resort, but during summer months Whitefish is renowned for its fishing and other outdoor pursuits. Bigfork, a delightful little resort village on the eastern shore of Flathead Lake, is also within an hour of the West Glacier entrance to the park (see page 216).

You'll find communities closer to the park, just outside the park boundaries. These towns and villages cater to park visitors with camping supply stores as well as motels and campgrounds for those not staying inside the park. Near the park headquarters, **West Glacier** has a lodge, several small motels, and an RV park with golf course. This is a handy place to stay if you're about to enter the park at the southern entrance and work your way through the park on the Going to the Sun Road. Four campgrounds are located within three miles of the village.

For those driving outside the southern park boundary on Highway 2 (see the scenic drive on page 192), the **Izaak Walton Inn** is a historic inn with a wonderful ambiance. During summer months this hotel caters to travelers, and during the winter it is the center for probably the best cross-country skiing in the nation. The inn is in the small community of **Essex**, which has additional accommodations.

East Glacier is just outside the park border at the southeast corner. Here is the historic **Glacier Park Lodge**, built by the

Great Northern Railway for park tourists and now operating as a summer lodge (see page 227 for reservations information). The East Glacier area has several other places to stay, including the Bear Creek and Bison guest ranches as well as several motels and cabin operations. You'll also find several campgrounds in the area, including one in Browning, which is 10 miles west.

The village of **St. Mary** is at the eastern side of the park, next to the park visitor center and at the eastern end of the Going to the Sun Road. **St. Mary Lodge** is a large, modern motor hotel with a restaurant, lounge, and store. St. Mary has three campgrounds, including a KOA.

Babb is the village at the junction of Highway 89 and Many Glacier Road. This community has three motels. Only the Chief Mountain Motel is open year-round. The road into the park from Babb leads to the Many Glacier Hotel. Babb has three campgrounds.

Great Falls

Now rolling placidly through the middle of Great Falls, the Missouri River was free-spirited when Meriwether Lewis first saw the falls on June 13, 1805. He described the view as the "grandest sight" he had ever seen. He then went on to see four other falls, each with its own character and beauty. The Lewis and Clark canoeing party was required to portage around an 18-mile stretch of the river. On June 18, Lewis came across what is now called Giant Springs at the side of the river.

Although much of the scenic beauty of the river remains, the river has been dammed in five places, raising the water level and capping falls with steel structures. Some of the fountains of water that constituted Giant Springs are now covered by the widened river below the Rainbow Dam. The remainder of the spring is protected within **Giant Springs Heritage State Park**, one of a number of parks and recreation sites along the falls portion of the river.

The city—Montana's second-largest—is a sprawling, modern community of 80,000 in the center of a ranching area. It has full visitor services and offers arts and entertainment programs year-round.

Great Falls was the home of the great cowboy and western artist Charlie Russell. The **C. M. Russell Museum** contains the most complete collection of Russell works in the world. The complex includes Russell's home and his log cabin studio. It houses more than 7,000 works including paintings by several of Russell's contemporaries. Native American artifacts and the Browning Firearms Collection are also displayed. The museum complex is located at 400 13th Street North. Near the museum is the city's first high school, now called Paris Gibson Square, housing the **Center for Contemporary Arts** and the **Cascade County Historical Museum**.

Great Falls is the site of the **Montana State Fair**, held in late July and early August. The fair features a rodeo, lumberjack shows, racing, and entertainment. You'll find overlooks and parks in the city, where walking along the river and looking at the falls is the most popular activity for visitors. You can also enjoy an excellent self-guided tour of the Lewis and Clark portage route; the map is available at the Chamber of Commerce on 926 Central Avenue.

For a day trip, drive 12 miles west of Great Falls via Interstate 15 to **Ulm** and visit the **Ulm Pishkum Buffalo Jump**. Now a state monument, this is where Native Americans stampeded herds of bison off the steep cliffs in order to obtain a winter's supply of food. This jump is 30 feet high and a mile long.

Where to Eat

Eating in Great Falls is largely on the informal side. For those who like their food in great quantities and inexpensive, many casinos in the city run dining facilities, including the **Riverboat** at 1012 9th Street S. Otherwise, **Borrie's** at 1800 Smelter Avenue serves a full range of steaks, chicken, seafood, and Italian-style pasta.

Helena

Halfway between Glacier and Yellowstone National Parks, Helena is nestled in the midst of the Big Belt, Garnet, and Elkhorn mountain ranges. **Mount Helena**, a city park, enables visitors to look down on the city from the 5,460-foot peak. For Helena accommodations, see page 245.

Originally a gold boom town, Helena is the state capital and still a town that produces and refines minerals. The Missouri River flows near the city, and the river and **Canyon Ferry Lake** (above the Hauser Dam) provide a host of recreation sites, including campgrounds. The lake has good fishing and is wide enough for good boating. To the north, the river flows through the scenic **Gates of the Mountains**, a series of 1,200-foot-deep canyons named by Lewis and Clark. Boat tours of the river are available 16 miles north of Helena via Interstate 15.

The **Helena National Forest** lies just outside the city limits, with recreation sites close to town to the west. With probably the finest view in the area, **Frontier Town** is a reproduction of an old western town, atop the Continental Divide, with a dining room that overlooks a landscape stretching 75 miles. The attraction is open daily from April through October; take Highway 12 to McDonald Pass.

For a more serious look at history, the **Montana Historical Society Museum** (225 North Roberts) features displays and artifacts of Montana's heritage, from prehistoric tribes to the current period. The museum was opened in 1865, during the gold rush. Its Mackay Gallery contains C. M. Russell paintings and other western works. The **Holter Museum of Art** features more contemporary art forms, including painting, sculpture, and crafts; it's located at 12 East Lawrence. The **Original Governor's Mansion**, built in 1888, is open as a museum and is furnished in the 1913–1921 period style. The mansion is open Tuesday through Saturday, April through December.

Probably the best way to get acquainted with Helena is to take the **Last Chance Tour Train**, which leaves the Historical Society Museum on an hourly schedule from 8:30 A.M. to 4:30 P.M. from June 1 through Labor Day and from 10:30 A.M. to 2:30 P.M. through the remainder of September. The fee for adults is $3.50, for seniors $3, and for children $2.50. Choose a self-guided tour of the **State Capitol** building or guided tours on the hour during summer months. The tour passes C. M. Russell's famous Lewis and Clark mural. The capitol is located at 1301 6th Avenue.

We recommend a day trip to the town of Deer Lodge and **Grant Kohr's Ranch Historic Site**, once the headquarters of a huge cattle operation that stretched from Canada to Colorado. It opened as a historic site in 1977 and offers self-guided tours of several buildings including the cowboys' bunkhouse, the blacksmith shop, a wagon collection, and the ranch house. The ranch is off Interstate 90 north of Deer Lodge, via Highway 12 driving west from Helena—a one-way trip of 56 miles.

Missoula

Straddling the Clark Fork River, Missoula is a far cry from its origins as Hellgate Village, founded to service the sawmills and flour mills on the river east of the present townsite. It's the largest city in western Montana and a center for the forest industry. The University of Montana there has 9,600 students. Missoula is the take-off point for our scenic drive to Flathead Lake and Kalispell and on to Glacier National Park (see page 188). Lying just east of the long Bitterroot Range, Missoula is a hub for wilderness adventure. The **Bob Marshall Wilderness Area** is to the north, and the **Anaconda-Pintler Wilderness** in the Deerlodge National Forest is to the south. The Mission Mountains begin just north of town (in the Flathead Reservation). Flathead Lake is an hour's drive north of town.

River recreation is available in all directions. The Bitterroot, Clark Fork, Blackfoot, and Flathead Rivers all feature fishing and river rafting expeditions. Within 50 miles of the city are more than 200 miles of prime floating rivers and many more miles of fishing streams. The variety of fish available is staggering: rainbow, cutthroat, brown and brook trout, Dolly Varden, kokanee, whitefish, bass, and northern pike. Many public campgrounds (most of them are managed by the National Forest Service) and private RV parks are available in the city.

Fort Missoula includes an historical museum, a forest service lookout, and 12 historic buildings at the site of the original fort; it's located on South Avenue. The **Missoula Museum of the Arts**, at 335 North Pattee, presents changing art exhibitions along with films, lectures, and concerts. A convenient day trip north from Missoula will take you not only to Flathead Lake but to the **National Bison Range**, the home of up to 500 bison in the Flathead Reservation; take Highway 93 to get there. This 19,000-acre range is also home to other wildlife, including whitetail and mule deer, elk, bighorn sheep, mountain goats, and pronghorn antelope. You'll find a visitor center at the community of Moiese.

The city features four golf courses, two of them (Missoula Country Club and Larchmont Golf Course) with 18 holes. The area also has two ski areas: Snow Bowl and Marshall. Wildlife refuges are located north and south of town. The **Lee Metcalf Refuge** (25 miles south) hosts migratory waterfowl. The **Ninepipe and Pablo National Wildlife Refuges** (north via Highway 93) are on the way to Flathead Lake and the town of Polson. The area is a definite plus for hot springs fans. **Lolo Pass Hot Springs** is west of the city on the Montana/Idaho border. Other hot spring operations include Sleeping Child, Lost Trail, and Medicine Hot Springs.

Where to Eat

Heidelhaus (2620 Brooks) serves German cuisine along with steak and seafood. Missoula is pie heaven, with three pie places that also dish up meals, including **Zimorino's Red Pies Over Montana**.

Polson

This little resort town on the south shore of Flathead Lake is located midway between Missoula and Glacier National Park. It's a likely place to break the trip with an overnight stay. For details of the drive through the Mission and Flathead valleys, see the scenic drive starting on page 188.

Flathead Lake is the largest natural lake in the American West, lying between the Swan Range to the east and the Salish Mountains to the west. Polson is situated just north of the Flathead Reservation through which Highway 93 leads on its route from Missoula. Just south of the town is the **Pablo National Wildlife Refuge**, a stopping place for migratory waterfowl. To the north and east is the **Flathead National Forest**. Several state recreation (campground and day-use) areas are along the lakeshore north of town. Polson is a target for anglers who come to the lake for the giant lake trout. You'll find a marina in town with boat rentals; charter companies will take you out on the lake for a fee.

Polson is a handy center for exploring either the Flathead Reservation towns south of the lake, including **St. Ignatius** (with its historic mission church) and the National Bison Range at Moiese, or the forest and mountain country north and west of town in the Flathead National Forest. **Lake Mary Ronan**, a few miles northwest of town, is a popular day-fishing park and a good campground location.

The **Miracle of America Museum** is an amazing jumble of western and military memorabilia including cars, cycles, snowmobiles, tractors, and military vehicles. There are also displays of doll collections, toys, sleighs, and almost everything else you could think of. The cost is right (one dollar), and the museum is open most of the year.

You can arrange for a raft trip down the Flathead River below the Kerr Dam. The Glacier Raft Company in Polson organizes

half-day trips from early June through Labor Day. For golfers, Polson has an 18-hole course and driving range at the Polson Country Club along the lakeshore. Another golf course, the Mission Country Club, is in nearby Ronan and also has 18 holes. You'll find a KOA campground in Polson and an RV park just north of town on Big Arm (Skipping Rock Resort). The latter has a marina on site. Polson has a good selection of moderately priced motels and cabin resorts. Most are on the lake (see page 248).

Where to Eat

Polson has an advantage over many similarly sized Montana towns in that it has a few good places to eat. **Gautier's Steak and Seafood Restaurant** is located just south of town and serves fresh fish, steak, and prime rib dinners on Fridays and Saturdays. **Orchard's Landing** is a good restaurant and lounge, with an outstanding view of the lake and mountains and a menu that includes seafood, pasta, steaks, and chicken. They have a fair wine list here, which is another unusual occurrence in this part of the state.

Red Lodge

Not a large town—it's more like a large village—Red Lodge is on the scenic Beartooth Highway, which makes up most of our Beartooth Mountains Drive (page 208). Its main virtues lie in the wilderness around: **Yellowstone National Park** to the west of the Beartooth Range, the **Absaroka-Beartooth Wilderness** to the north of Yellowstone, and the wild beauty of the Beartooths and the scenic drives available on its ridges.

This is another of Montana's historic mining towns. Red Lodge was a booming coal mining town between 1893 and 1910. During those years, European miners settled the town, leaving their continental stamp on the community. Today, the ethnic heritage of these miners is felt during the Festival of Nations, held every August. A mining disaster has led to one of the town's most popular tourist attractions. Four miles east of town, at Washoe, 74 men died in an underground explosion at the Smith Mine in 1943. The mine's tipple and several buildings still stand on the site. To get more of the mining perspective, visit the **Carbon County Museum**, which is south of town on Highway 212. The museum features the homestead cabin of John Garrison, the prototype for the movie character "Jeremiah Johnson."

Twenty-one miles north of Red Lodge, via Highway 212 and then west of Boyd on a sideroad, **Cooney State Park** offers camping, boating, and fishing. More campgrounds operated by the U.S. Forest Service are along the scenic byway as it climbs the Beartooth Range (see page 210).

The whole downtown of Red Lodge (it isn't that big) has been declared a National Historic District. Here are buildings that were constructed during the mining boom from 1893. One of the houses (all or in part) may be rented. The **Montana Guest Lodge** has hosted such guests as Buffalo Bill Cody and Calamity Jane. You'll find several motels as well as bed and breakfast homes. The **Rock Creek Resort**, west of Red Lodge and at the base of the Beartooths, is a deluxe vacation resort with all the amenities. For accommodations details, see page 249. A good feature of the Red Lodge accommodation scene is a central reservations office, which handles reservations for all motels and guest houses; call 800-444-8977.

Where to Eat

Rock Creek Resort has a fine dining room that is the best in the area. It's west of Red Lodge on Highway 212. The Old Piney Dell, just south of town, has a scenic location and is open daily from 5 P.M. to 10 P.M. except on Sundays, when it opens for brunch from 8 A.M. to 1 P.M. and dinner from 3 P.M. to 9 P.M. The **Carbon County Coal Company** is a summer-only steak house. **Bear Creek Saloon**, seven miles east of town, serves Mexican food Wednesday to Sunday and has pig racing on weekends. I don't guarantee the quality of the entertainment at this "event."

West Yellowstone and Virginia City

Set at the west entrance to Yellowstone National Park, West Yellowstone is a friendly western town, surrounded by the park and the adjacent Gallatin and Targhee National Forests.

The town is reached from Bozeman by taking Highway 191 through the Gallatin River Canyon. This fine scenic route is detailed in the Gallatin River Drive (page 212). Along the way is some of the best river fishing on the continent. The west gate to the park is northeast of Ashton, Idaho via Highway 20. The town has a good supply of lodges, motels, RV parks (see page 251), and nearby forest campgrounds. **Hebgen Lake Recreational Area** features a 12,000-acre reservoir with good fishing, boating, and sailing. Rafting is available on the nearby rivers: the Yellowstone, Gallatin, and Madison. These three rivers and the North Fork of the Snake provide excellent trout fishing, as does Quake Lake (part of the Madison system), north of town. Anglers will enjoy the **International Fly Fishing Center**, located in the historic Union Pacific Dining Lodge. The **Museum of the Rockies** houses displays on Yellowstone bears, Native American artifacts, and western history. In 1959, a powerful earthquake rocked the West Yellowstone area, tumbling 80 million tons of rock down a mountainside into the Madison River, blocking the river and creating Quake Lake. The U.S. Forest Service operates the **Earthquake Information Center** beside Quake Lake on Highway 287, northwest of town.

This is an ideal place from which to take day trips to several old mining towns, particularly **Virginia City** and **Nevada City**. The two old gold rush towns sit side by side on Highway 287, 85 miles from West Yellowstone. In 1863, six prospectors discovered what would become one of the most productive placer mining districts in the world. In five years, Alder Gulch (in the Tobacco Root Mountains) produced more than $30 million in gold. By 1874, 35,000 people lived in the gulch. The two towns declined until they were ghosts, then in 1940, Charles and Sue Bovey began restoring the communities. Today, the mining camps provide an excellent day visit or an overnight stay during summer months in the B & B homes, a motel, or campground. The Mount Vernon Dredge is part of the River of Gold Mining Museum. It was one of five dredges that scoured the gulch. There's a functional saloon with adjoining cafe in Virginia City. A recent fire in Nevada City did some damage, but work is underway to restore the tiny mining camp. The Virginia City Players stage 19th century melodramas. A narrow gauge railway line connects the two "cities."

Where to Eat

In West Yellowstone, the **Totem Restaurant** serves three meals a day. The **Ranch Restaurant and Lounge** on Canyon Street provides slightly more upscale dining. **Alice's Restaurant**, serving German specialties, is seven miles west of town on Targhee Pass Highway. The **Virginia City Cafe and Pioneer Bar** provides basic meals, as does the **Star Bakery**.

BIGFORK

Flathead Lake Lodge
Rural Route 35,
P.O. Box 248
Bigfork, MT 59911
(406) 837-4391

For all-inclusive, week-long family vacations. Guests come from all over the continent to enjoy the ranch activities and water sports here—from wind surfing to lake cruises to a children's rodeo. ($$$)

Marina Cay Resort
180 Vista Lane
Bigfork, MT 59911
(406) 837-5861

A deluxe facility on Bigfork Bay with some suites and cooking rooms, pool, whirlpool, boat and canoe rentals. ($$ to $$$)

O'Dua'chain Country Inn
675 Ferndale Drive
Bigfork, MT 59911
(406) 837-6851

The owners of this spacious log home go to great lengths to make their guests comfortable and to superbly feed them at breakfast. Kids will enjoy a pond plus a whole menagerie of birds and animals to play with; for adults, a hot tub is accessible at all hours. Both suites and rooms are available. ($ to $$)

BILLINGS

Billings—the largest city in the state—is well-represented by the major hotel and motel chains and several campgrounds in the area. For reservations at B & B homes, call Bed and Breakfast Western Adventure at (406) 259-7993.

Big Sky Campground
5516 Laurel Road
Billings, MT 59101
(406) 259-4110

Open year-round with tenting and RV sites, restaurant, and gift shop. Take I-90 exit 446.

Billings Inn
880 North 29th Street
Billings, MT 59101
(406) 252-6800

Some rooms here have refrigerators and even microwaves. Coin laundry and winter plug-ins. ($)

Homestead Quality Inn
2036 Overland Avenue
Billings, MT 59102
(406) 652-1320

Take exit 446 off I-90. This motel features a heated pool and whirlpool, VCR rentals, refrigerators in some rooms, and a restaurant nearby. ($ to $$)

Radisson Northern Hotel
19 North 28th Street
Billings, MT 59101
(406) 245-5121 or
800-333-3333

In central Billings, near shopping and museums, this hotel also boasts an award-winning restaurant. ($$ to $$$)

Sheraton Billings Hotel
27 North 27th Street
Billings, MT 59101
(406) 252-7400 or
800-325-3535 or
800-588-ROOM

Some rooms in this large hotel are equipped with refrigerators. Heated indoor pool, whirlpool, and exercise room. Dining room, cocktails, and entertainment in the evenings. ($$ to $$$)

BOZEMAN

Bear Canyon Campground
(406) 587-1575

Located about four miles east of town on I-90 (exit 313), this campground features a playground, swimming pool, and all services for tent and RV sites. Open May through October.

Bozeman Hot Springs KOA
133 Lower Rainbow Road
Bozeman, MT 59715
(406) 587-3030

For hot springs enthusiasts, take Highway 84 seven miles west, then Highway 191 three-quarters of a mile south. It's open year-round with full hookups and a playground.

Bozeman Inn
1235 North 7th Avenue
Bozeman, MT 59715
(406) 587-3176 or
800-648-7515

This motel features a heated pool, sauna and whirlpool, restaurant, and lounge. Take I-90, exit 306. (**$ to $$**)

Gallatin Gateway Inn
Highway 191
P.O. Box 376
Gallatin Gateway, MT 59730
(406) 763-4672

A historic inn housed in a restored railroad hotel, featuring a pool, hot tub, and fine dining. Located 12 miles south of town. (**$ to $$**)

Torch and Toes B & B
309 South Third Avenue
Bozeman, MT 59715
(406) 586-7285

A fascinating "mail-order" house built in the early part of the century, this B & B home is filled with an interesting mix of antiques and contemporary art. Full breakfast is included. (**$$**)

Voss Inn
319 South Willson
Bozeman, MT 59715
(406) 587-0982

An elegantly furnished Victorian mansion, restored in 1984, offers rooms, with a bath, plus a cozy parlor with a piano and plenty of reading material. A full breakfast is served. (**$$**)

BUTTE

Butte KOA
(406) 782-0663

Take exit 126 off I-90 for this full-service campground, complete with fishing, swimming, and a deli.

Capri Motel
220 North Wyoming Street
Butte, MT 59701
(406) 723-4391

A smaller, budget-priced motel with some two-bedroom units. (**$**)

Copper King Inn
4665 Harrison Avenue S
Butte, MT 59701
(406) 494-6666 or
800-332-8600

One of the Best Western chain, featuring large rooms, all with king or queen beds, indoor pool and sauna, and a lounge with live music and dancing. (**$$**)

Copper King Mansion
219 West Granite Street
Butte, MT 59701
(406) 782-7580

A few rooms in this spectacular mansion are now available as B & Bs. The house, built in 1884, was the home of "Copper King" William A. Clark and is also open for tours. Although none of the original furnishings remain, the mansion has been filled with a wonderful collection of period antiques. As well, it houses the excellent Copper King Restaurant in the former parlor, a dining room, and a billiard room. (**$ to $$**)

Townhouse Inns of Butte
2777 Harrison Avenue
Butte, MT 59701
(406) 494-8850 or
800-442-4667

Another large motel, part of a statewide chain, featuring a sauna, whirlpool, and exercise room. Weekly rates are available. (**$ to $$**)

GARDINER

Best Western–Mammoth Hot Springs
U.S. Highway 89
Gardiner, MT 59030
(406) 848-7311

Most rooms in this motor inn have river or mountain views; some have kitchens or in-room whirlpools. There's a lounge and the Yellowstone Mine Restaurant with old west mine decor and steak and seafood dinners. (**$$**)

Chico Hot Springs Lodge
P.O. Box 127
Pray, MT 59065
(406) 333-4933

Beautifully set in the Paradise Valley about 25 miles north of Gardiner, this lodge offers rooms in the remodeled old hotel and also has a modern motel addition plus cabins and condo units. The lodge's restaurant, the Chico Inn, attracts diners from all over with its wonderful food. Hiking, trout fishing, riding, and river rafting in summer or cross-country skiing in the winter. And of course there are the hot springs pools to be enjoyed at any time of the year. (**$$ to $$$**)

Rocky Mountain Campground
14 Jardine Road
Gardiner, MT 59030
(406) 848-7251

Open year-round with RV and tent sites (some with full hookups). Also a grocery store, laundry, game room, and showers. Located just east of Gardiner on Jardine Road.

Yellowstone Village North Motel and Campground
1102 Scott Street West
Gardiner, MT 59030
(406) 848-7417

Among the motel units available here are one condo unit and one with two bedrooms. Heated indoor pool and sauna. ($ to $$)

GLACIER NATIONAL PARK

The authorized concessionaire for the park, Glacier Park, Inc., operates several hotels, inns and lodges inside the park (see page 227). Because of the short season here (usually early June to early- to mid-September), accommodations fill up quickly, and reservations are generally required months in advance. Rates vary from under $30 to more than $100. Other accommodations near the park are as follows.

Apgar Village Lodge
P.O. Box 398
Glacier National Park, MT 59936
(406) 888-5484

Located near the west end of Lake McDonald, facilities include motel rooms and cottages. ($ to $$)

Firebrand Pass Campground
P.O. Box 146
East Glacier, MT 59434
(406) 226-5573

Restaurant and playground, plus full hookups. It's located three miles west of East Glacier on U.S. Highway 2.

Glacier Campground
P.O. Box 447
West Glacier, MT 59936
(406) 387-5689

One mile west of West Glacier on U.S. Highway 2, attractions here include volleyball and a barbecue.

Izaak Walton Inn
P.O. Box 653
Essex, MT 59916
(406) 888-5700

One of the most fascinating places to stay in the Rockies, this inn was built in 1939 by the Great Northern Railway to accommodate its service crews. Even today, helper engines stand by to push the trains (15 to 20 freight trains daily, plus Amtrak) over the Continental Divide. Railway buffs understandably love this place, and others may find themselves becoming train enthusiasts. There is even a train caboose that sleeps four. Open year-round, in winter the inn is a renowned cross-country ski center. (\$ to \$\$)

Polebridge Mercantile and Cabins
P.O. Box 146
Polebridge, MT 59928
(406) 888-9926

These rustic cabins, available year-round, are located along the scenic North Fork of the Flathead River and are listed on the National Register of Historic Places. (\$)

GREAT FALLS

The Chalet Bed and Breakfast
1204 Fourth Avenue N
Great Falls, MT 59401
(406) 452-9001

This B & B is a lovely Victorian house built in 1909 and was once the home of a governor of the state. It features the original wood paneling, leaded glass and high-beamed ceilings, and is furnished with period pieces. The location is convenient, across from the C. M. Russell Museum and within walking distance of town. The price includes a delicious, varied breakfast; you can also reserve a fixed-price dinner. (\$ to \$\$)

Dick's Trailer and RV Park
1403 11th Street SW
Great Falls, MT 59404
(406) 452-0333

This park has mostly RV sites but is open year-round. Take exit 278 off I-15.

Great Falls Holiday Inn
400 10th Avenue S
Great Falls, MT 59405
(406) 727-7200 or
800-626-5009 (within
Montana) or 800-257-1998
(outside of Montana)

Amenities at this hotel include a heated indoor pool, sauna, and whirlpool. As well as, a lovely spacious lobby, dining room, and coffee shop. ($$)

Great Falls KOA
1500 51st Street S
Great Falls, MT 59405
(406) 727-3191 or
800-422-1002

Full hookups, a playground, and "kamping kitchens." It's located on the east edge of town at 10th Avenue S and 51st Street.

O'Haire Motor Inn
17 7th Street S
P.O. Box 1667
Great Falls, MT 59401
(406) 454-2141 or
800-332-9819
(within the U.S. only)

A moderately priced inn with heated indoor pool, coffee shop, and cocktail lounge. ($)

HELENA

Best Western Colonial Inn
2301 Colonial Drive
Helena, MT 59601
(406) 443-2100

A full range of services await you here, including two heated pools, whirlpool, sauna, and exercise room. Also a restaurant and a beautifully landscaped courtyard. ($$)

Branding Iron RV Park
1803 Cedar Street
Helena, MT 59601
(406) 443-9703

Full services are available here, including an adult lounge, store, and laundry. It's open year-round with tent and RV sites. Located on the southwest corner of Cedar Street, at Exchange.

Kim's Marina and RV Park
Canyon Ferry Road
Helena, MT 59601
(406) 475-3723

A seasonal operation, with a bar, restaurant, tennis court and boat rentals, plus full hookups. Located 20 miles east of town on Highway 284.

Lamplighter Motel
1006 Madison
Helena, MT 59601
(406) 442-9200

Motel rooms or cottages are available here year-round and at budget rates. ($)

Park Plaza Hotel
22 North Last
Chance Gulch
Helena, MT 59601
(406) 443-2200 or
800-332-2290

Recently redecorated rooms plus a new restaurant, lounge, and nightclub are features of this downtown hotel. (**$ to $$**)

The Sanders
328 North Ewing
Helena, MT 59601
(406) 442-3309

For bed and breakfast accommodations, try this atmospheric Queen Anne-style home that is still filled with some of the Victorian furnishings and personal collections gathered by its builder, U.S. Senator Sanders. The current owners have managed to strike a fine balance between period furnishings and modern conveniences. They are also well known for their creative and delicious breakfasts. There are several double rooms, open year-round, all with private bath, some with fireplaces. (**$ to $$**)

KALISPELL AND COLUMBIA FALLS

Aero Inn
1830 Highway 93 S
Kalispell, MT 59901
(406) 755-3798 or
800-843-6114

Free continental breakfast, pool, whirlpool, and sauna. (**$ to $$**)

Best Western Outlaw Inn
1701 Highway 93 S
Kalispell, MT 59901
(406) 755-6100 or
800-237-7445

This motor inn calls itself a "resort hotel," and with good reason: it sports two heated indoor pools, tennis and racquetball courts, sauna, whirlpool, and playground. Also a dining room and casino. (**$$ to $$$**)

Mountain Timbers Lodge
5385 Rabe Road
Columbia Falls, MT 59912
(387) 387-5830

For an interesting stay, try this lodge built from logs that are over 450 years old. Rooms have private baths, and a full breakfast is included. ($$)

Osprey Inn
5557 Highway 93 S
Somers, MT 59932
(406) 857-2042

This inn is set on an acre of land right on Flathead Lake, about 10 miles south of Kalispell. Two decks allow wonderful views of the lake and mountains, while the lower deck provides rocking chairs and a hot tub. The hosts allow use of their power boat, canoe, and dock, as well as binoculars for osprey viewing. The guest rooms are full of thoughtful extras, such as plates of cookies and baskets of fruit, and a full breakfast is served. Some rooms with private bath; they're open year-round, with reservations. ($ to $$)

Rocky Mountain 'Hi'
Campground
825 Helena Flats Road
Kalispell, MT 59901
(406) 755-9573

Open year-round, five miles east of the Highway 93 junction on U.S. 2, featuring canoeing and fishing as well as full services.

Vacation Farm
566 Creston Road
Kalispell, MT 59901
(406) 756-8217

For a family or group alternative to a motel in the Kalispell area, you may want to try Vacation Farm, a completely furnished farm home with bedrooms, full baths, a kitchen, formal dining room, and family room. Volleyball court and a heated pool are available. Located 10 miles east of Kalispell on Highway 35, it's open year-round.

MISSOULA

Goldsmith's Inn
809 East Front Street
Missoula, MT 59802
(406) 721-6732

This lovely brick home built in 1911 by the University of Montana's second president, Clyde Duniway, was slated for demolition when it was rescued by the

Goldsmith's Inn
(continued)

Goldsmiths and moved to its present location. It has been lovingly restored and furnished. The view of the Clark Fork River and the Sapphire and Bitterroot mountains can be enjoyed while breakfasting on the outdoor deck. ($ to $$)

Holiday Inn–
Missoula Parkside
200 South Pattee Street
Missoula, MT 59802
(406) 721-8550 or
800-399-0408

A beautifully landscaped atrium is a feature here, along with a heated indoor pool, sauna, and whirlpool. ($$)

Missoula El-Mar KOA
3450 Tina Avenue
Missoula, MT 59802
(406) 549-0881

The largest campground in the area (tenting and RV sites) also features a swimming pool, hot tub, and mini-golf. Full hookups. Take exit 101 off I-90 to Reserve Street.

Thunderbird Motel
1009 East Broadway
Missoula, MT 59802
(406) 543-7251

Some rooms here have refrigerators; also a heated indoor pool, sauna, and whirlpool. ($)

POLSON AND AREA

Big Arm Resort and Marina
P.O. Box 99
Big Arm, MT 59910
(406) 849-5622

Located just north of town on the west shore of Flathead Lake, this resort offers lakefront housekeeping cabins and lakeside RV sites. Boat rentals, gas, tackle, and ice. ($ to $$)

Hammond's Bed
and Breakfast
10141 Eastshore Route
Polson, MT 59860
(406) 887-2766

On the east shore of Flathead Lake at milepost 10 is this private, furnished cabin with bath, refrigerator, living room, deck, and dock. ($$)

Polson KOA
Highway 93 and Irvine
Flats Road
P.O. Box 317
Polson, MT 59860
(406) 883-2151

One-half mile northwest of Polson on Highway 93 on the east side of Flathead Lake is this full-service campground, featuring a pool and hot tub.

Port Polson Inn
U.S. Highway 93
P.O. Box 1411
Polson, MT 59860
(406) 883-5385

Among the rooms overlooking Flathead Lake are large balcony suites and a honeymoon suite. Some kitchen units are available too, plus free continental breakfast, a hot tub, and a picnic area with barbecue. (**$ to $$**)

Schiefelbein Haus
6395 Eastshore Route
Polson, MT 59860
(406) 887-2431

This combination motel, RV park, and campground is open year-round and features home cooking and outdoor beer garden. (**$**)

Skipping Rock Resort
Big Arm, MT 59910
(406) 849-5678

Also in Big Arm, this resort has apartments, a campground, and an RV park with full hookups, plus a marina with a dock and boat ramp. There's also a beach with volleyball, horseshoe pit, and evening campfires. (**$$**)

RED LODGE

For central reservations in Red Lodge, call 800-444-8977.

Red Lodge KOA
U.S. Highway 212
Red Lodge, MT 59068
(406) 446-2364

Full hookups, a pool, and playground. Open June 1 to October 1 on U.S. 212, four miles north of town.

Rock Creek Resort
Rural Route 2
P.O. Box 3500
Red Lodge, MT 59608
(406) 446-1111

This deluxe, year-round vacation resort offers fishing, tennis, riding, and bicycle rentals in the summer, plus skiing and snowmobiling in the winter. Also a heated indoor pool, sauna, and whirlpool. On U.S. 212, 5 miles from town. (**$ to $$**)

Willows Inn
224 South Platt Avenue
Red Lodge, MT 59068
(406) 446-3913

For a cozy B & B experience, try this inn, a private home built in 1903 that later became a boarding house for the Finnish workers at a nearby mine. The house is beautifully decorated with the guest rooms done in a variety of styles. A delicious breakfast plus afternoon beverages are included. Open year-round. ($)

THREE FORKS

Broken Spur Motel
124 West Elm Street
P.O. Box 1009
Three Forks, MT 59752
(406) 285-3237

For a motel easy on the budget, take exit 278 off I-90 to the junction of Highways 287 and 2, then 3 miles southeast on SR2. ($)

KOA Three Forks
U.S. Highway 287
Three Forks, MT 59752
(406) 285-3611

Open from May 1 to October 1, this KOA has a playground, swimming, and sauna as well as the usual full hookups. On Highway 287, one mile south of I-90, exit 274.

VIRGINIA AND NEVADA CITIES

Fairweather Inn
315 West Wallace
P.O. Box 338
Virginia City, MT 59755
(406) 843-5377

The address and phone are the same as for the Nevada City Hotel. The rooms here are furnished with "Old West" decor; the parlor is filled with priceless antiques. Thanks to the restoration efforts of the Boveys, the entire town is a Registered Historical Landmark. ($)

Nevada City Hotel and Cabins
Highway 287
P.O. Box 338
Nevada City, MT 59755
(406) 843-5377

An authentic log hotel, once a stagecoach station. Some of the rooms have antique furnishings, and cabins are available too. A Victorian parlor with plush chairs and an antique organ. The hotel is part of a preserved 1860s mining camp and boasts a two-story outhouse said to be the most photographed building in Montana. Open late-May to mid-September. ($)

Stonehouse Inn
306 East Idaho Street
P.O. Box 202
Virginia City, MT 59755
(406) 843-5504

This B & B inn is set in a historic stone house from 1884. Six rooms are available, and families are welcome. ($$)

Virginia City Campground
Virginia City, MT 59755
(406) 843-5493

Located one mile east of town on Highway 287 and open April 1 to December 1, this campground also features horseback riding and gold panning. Tent and RV sites with full hookups.

WEST YELLOWSTONE

Toll-free central reservations number for West Yellowstone: 800-521-5241.

Big Western Pine Motel
234 Firehole Avenue
P.O. Box 67
West Yellowstone, MT 59758
(406) 646-7622

This two-story motel features HBO and some kitchen units. A heated outdoor pool in summer and an indoor whirlpool all year, plus a family restaurant. ($)

Brandin' Iron Motel
201 Canyon Street
P.O. Box 978
West Yellowstone, MT 59758
(406) 646-9411

The spacious rooms here have queen beds, refrigerators, and cable TV. Also indoor hot tubs and a big lobby with a fireplace. Open year-round, near shops and restaurants. ($ to $$)

Lionshead RV and Dance Resort
Highway 20
West Yellowstone, MT
59758
(406) 646-7296

A unique resort that features square and round dancing all summer, with workshops (they even provide the dance apparel!). Shaded tent sites, full hookups, a picnic pavilion with a barbecue, and a restaurant with fresh trout dinners. Open year-round.

Sportsman's High Bed and Breakfast
750 Deer Street
West Yellowstone, MT
59758
(406) 646-7865

This country home has antique-filled rooms and a large wraparound porch. It's surrounded by aspen and pine with a mountain view. Hot tub and a backyard pond. Reservations are required, and children under 12 are not welcome. ($$)

Stage Coach Inn
209 Madison Avenue
P.O. Box 160
West Yellowstone, MT
59758
(406) 646-7381

This full-service hotel has a western ambiance complete with a knotty-pine lobby and fireplace. A spa with hot tubs and sauna, coffee shop, dining room, and two lounges with entertainment. ($$)

Wyoming

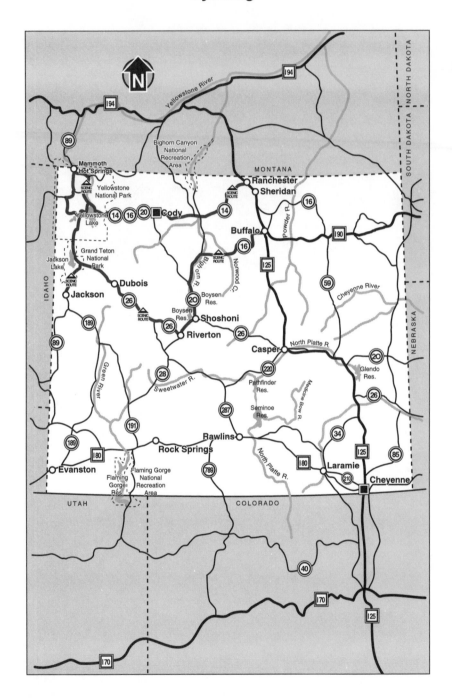

Wyoming *Drives*

This expansive state is the fabled land of Buffalo Bill Cody, Chief Sitting Bull, Calamity Jane, and others of legend, story, and song, all of whom captivated the world at the inception of the twentieth century.

Wyoming sits astride the Rockies like a geological Colossus. A state of geological superlatives, Wyoming has more geothermal activity within its borders than all other parts of the world combined. Its mountain ranges stagger across the state for hundreds of miles, and yet most of the state is open grazing land—home to the country's largest buffalo herds before man decimated the species. It is a state of rivers (Snake, Green, Wind, Big Horn, and Yellowstone), all of which cut their way through canyons, forests, and sageland.

But most of all, there are the mountain ranges: Absaroka, the Big Horns, Tetons, the Wind River Ranges. All of them sculpted over millions of years, each of them with their own craggy personality.

Traveling through Wyoming presents startling changes in landscape, vegetation, and animal life. Within a 100-mile drive, you can pass through high desert, badlands, forested hills, and large open valleys (or "holes") and venture around impenetrable mountain ranges.

Park Loop Drive

Yellowstone National Park

The mountain scenery of Yellowstone is much more subtle than that of Glacier National Park or the northern portion of Colorado. Because the park is situated on a plateau, high above the surrounding regions, the views are gentle—with wide meadows, broad forests, lakes, and sometimes gently flowing rivers.

But all of this bucolic plateau land is hiding one of the globe's great natural wonders: the existence of molten rock very close to the Yellowstone surface, providing the most active geothermal scene in the world. In fact, Yellowstone has more geysers, hot springs, and mud pots than the rest of the world combined. Thus, it's necessary to get out of your vehicle to savor the prime attractions of Yellowstone, which you reach by trails or boardwalks.

The park loop covered here can be driven in a day. But our advice is to take much longer than just one day, especially if you have to drive a fair distance to get to Yellowstone (as most people do). You'll find campgrounds throughout the park in addition to a number of lodges and motels inside and just outside the park. Depending on whether you wish to do some serious hiking along park trails, a visit to Yellowstone should take anywhere from three days to a week or two.

The Park Loop Drive will guide you to most of the attractions available without too much physical exertion, but a number of trails along the way will provide a much more comprehensive view of the park and its ecosystems. You will later treasure those extra hours spent exploring the "nooks and crannies" of the park.

Because a loop drive has to start somewhere, our drive begins at **Mammoth**, the home of the park administration and the site of the park's main information center, which has an excellent supply of books on Yellowstone's geology, wildlife, and trails. Mammoth is located just south of Gardiner, Montana, and is an easy morning's drive from West Yellowstone. Exploring the geothermal area including the **Mammoth Hot Springs** is a fine way to begin a Yellowstone vacation. However, you may wish to begin your driving tour anywhere along the loop by consulting the Highway Log that follows.

During the summer of 1988, eight large fires swept through the park, burning more than 700,000 acres. Part of the interest in visiting the park is seeing the recovery of these areas—some of it is remarkable.

The route east from Mammoth Hot Springs leads to **Undine Falls** and then across meadows around **Blacktail Ponds**, where wildlife (waterfowl, muskrats) is prolific. A sidetrip along **Blacktail Plateau Drive** offers viewing of larger species of wildlife including antelope, mule deer, and elk. This road travels through evergreen forests of Engelmann spruce, lodgepole pine, and Douglas fir. From Tower Junction, our route leads south toward Canyon (the Grand Canyon of the Yellowstone River). **Tower Falls** is a must stop along this section of the drive.

Moving westward and then north, **Old Faithful** is the heart of the **Upper Geyser Basin**. The world's best-known geyser, Old Faithful, blows its stack every 65 minutes, but it's only one of a host of other geysers (more than 70). In addition, more than 600 other hot springs, mud pots, and steam vents have been cataloged in the basin.

Driving north from Old Faithful, the **Midway and Lower Geyser Basins** offer more hot water, steam vents, and boiling mud. Highlights here include the Fountain Paint Pot and two fascinating sideroad drives.

Madison is the junction with the route to the west entrance and West Yellowstone. The loop road leads northeast to Norris (another geyser basin), passing several picnic areas. Turning north to complete the loop drive, you pass **Obsidian Cliff** and the **Bunsen Peak** sideroad before returning to Mammoth and the completion of the tour.

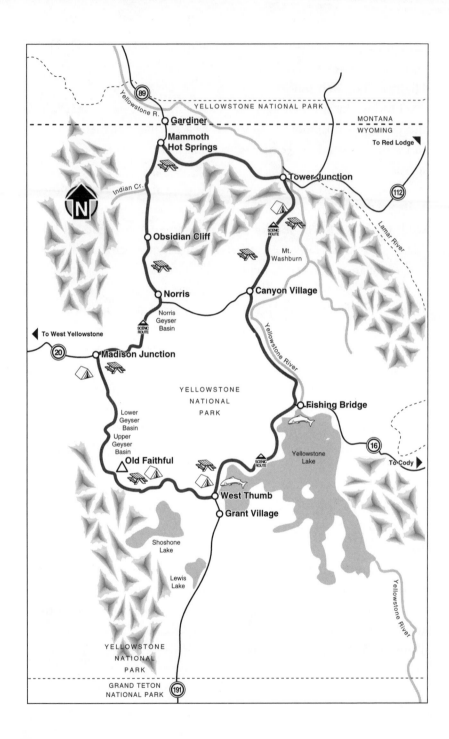

HIGHWAY LOG
Yellowstone National Park
85 miles (136 KM)—2 hours

Mammoth Hot Springs Our drive through the park begins in Mammoth, the site of the park headquarters, main information center, hotel, and extensive geothermal attractions. Upper Terrace Drive is a 1.5-mile road winding among the hot springs and terraces.

Jupiter and Minerva Springs Loop Trails leads past terraces and old (dormant) springs. Our route leads west from Mammoth across the Gardner River Bridge. The Gardner River Canyon is visible from the bridge. Lava Creek Canyon is east of the bridge.

Undine Falls An overlook provides a fine view of the two waterfalls.

Lava Creek Picnic Area

Wraith Falls Trail The 90-foot cascade is seen from a half-mile trail.

Blacktail Lakes Fire burned the meadows here in 1988. View of the Gallatin Mountains to the west.

Blacktail Creek Trail Leads from the highway (seven miles east of Mammoth) for 5.5 miles to the Yellowstone River Trail and Knowles Falls.

Children's Fire Exhibit On short loop to north of hwy.

Junction–Blacktail Plateau Sideroad A seven-mile (one-way) drive along an old trail.

Phantom Lake This pond fills with snow melt and disappears during the summer months.

Hellroaring Mountain Seen to the northeast, a cone-shaped peak named in 1867 for the creek roaring down the mountain. The 1988 fire here burned more than 20,000 acres of parkland. The Yellowstone River Trail leads from the Hellroaring Trailhead, following the river for 18.5 miles to Gardiner, Montana.

Petrified Tree Sideroad A half-mile road to part of a petrified redwood tree.

Tower Junction (el. 6,270 feet) Ranger station and Roosevelt Lodge. Lodge and gas station open during summer months.

Calcite Springs Overlook Loop boardwalk overlooks the Grand Canyon Narrows and gray rock spires.

Overhanging Cliff A lava flow (basalt) hangs over the road.

Tower Fall A short trail leads past the store to the falls.

Tower Campground

Antelope Creek Picnic Area

Mae West Curve This buxom curve in the road overlooks Antelope Creek and sagelands. The Beartooth Mountains are to the northeast.

(continues)

Junction–Old Chittenden Road An old auto road leading to the top of Mount Washburn (el. 10,243 feet). A trail now begins after the first mile.

Dunraven Pass (el. 8,859 feet) Between Dunraven Peak (east) and Mount Washburn (west).

Viewpoint—Washburn Hot Springs Overlook of the Grand Canyon of the Yellowstone.

Dunraven Road Picnic Area

Cascade Lake Picnic Area and Trail The trail leads 2.5 miles across open meadows to the Cascade Creek Trail and the lake.

Lower and Upper Falls Canyon The village offers a lodge, camping, gas, and food services. **North Rim Road** is a 2.5-mile (one-way) road to Inspiration Point and Lookout Point with views of the Grand Canyon and the lower falls (308 feet). Grandview Point provides other great canyon views.

Chittenden Bridge/South Rim Road/Grand Canyon This 2.5-mile road (one way) passes the south rim of the Grand Canyon and ends at Artist Point—another fine overlook.

Otter Creek Picnic Area

Hayden Valley Alum Creek has a sharp astringent taste. Sulphur Spring Creek flows from the Crater Hills (to the west).

Grizzly Overlook Across the Yellowstone River is prime grizzly country. View of Washburn Range.

Mud Volcano Trail This loop trail (two-thirds of a mile) leads to acid hot springs with boiling pots and pools with sulphur odors.

Le Hardy Rapids A boardwalk leads to the river.

Yellowstone River A spot favored by fly anglers and wildlife including pelicans, swans, and moose.

Fishing Bridge/Lake Village Junction of park loop and east entrance road. The Lake Hotel is the park's oldest. Area includes Bridge Bay Marina, campground, and access to Yellowstone Lake with its 110 miles of shoreline and cutthroat trout.

Junction–Sand Point Road To picnic area on the lake.

Pumice Point Views of Mount Sheridan (across lake to the south) and tops of the Tetons.

West Thumb Deepest part of the lake, a crater four miles across. Junction of Road to Grant Village (camping), motel, info center, and south entrance. Our drive continues west toward Old Faithful.

Continental Divide (el. 8,391 feet)

Viewpoint–Shoshone Point The overlook provides a view of Shoshone Lake.

Craig Pass (el. 8,261) Continental Divide. Ida Lake has outlets on each side of the divide.

Upper Geyser Basin/Old Faithful Yellowstone's most popular attraction, Old Faithful, is found here, along with 70 other geysers and more than 600 hot springs and vents. Trails and boardwalks lead through the basin. Lodgings include the Old Faithful Inn, Old Faithful Lodge, and Old Faithful Snow Lodge. Camping, gas, food, picnicking.

Firehole River The valley is named for hot springs and fire of around 1800.

Biscuit Basin Small group of geysers and pools including Sapphire Pool. Mystic Falls Trail leads to 70-foot cascade.

Midway Geyser Basin Boardwalks lead to Excelsior Geyser and Grand Prismatic Spring.

Junction–Firehole Lake Sideroad This loop drive leads to the Great Fountain Geyser and the White Dome Geyser, among many others accessed via boardwalks and short trails.

Fountain Paint Pot A short boardwalk leads to red mud pots and several geysers including Clepsydra.

Junction–Fountain Flat Sideroad Near the picnic area, the road crosses meadows to hot springs, ending at the Goose Lake Picnic Area. A trail leads to Fairy Falls (200 feet).

Junction–Firehole Canyon Sideroad Loop drive beside high lava cliffs to 40-foot Firehole Falls and Cascades of the Firehole. The Firehole is noted for its trout.

Madison Junction of park loop and road to west entrance and West Yellowstone. Camping, museum.

Tuff Cliffs Picnic Area

Gibbon Falls Picnic area and view of falls.

Junction–Artist Paint Pots Sideroad To six groups of geysers and springs. Artist Paint Pots are reached by a half-mile trail.

Gibbon Meadows Picnic Area

Chocolate Pots Mineral mounds formed by springs beside the Gibbon River rapids.

Norris Geyser Basin The most active group of geysers in the park. Two trails lead through the basin.

Norris Junction

SIDETRIP—East-West Road to Canyon

Virginia Cascade A three-mile loop road runs beside the river past the 60-foot falls.

Blanding Hill Climbs to the Solfatara Plateau (gas vent).

Grebe and Wolf Lake Trails From north side of road.

Cascade Creek Meadows Trail To Cascade Lake (one mile) and Yellowstone River (three miles).

BACK ON PARK LOOP At Norris Junction

Beaver Lake Picnic Area Old dams have been abandoned.

Obsidian Cliff Black volcanic glass overlooking road.

Sheepeater Cliffs Picnic Area

Bunsen Peak Sideroad is a loop drive to the east in Gardner's Hole, leading past the Sheepeater Cliffs and Mount Bunsen.

Mammoth Hot Springs Park headquarters and end of loop drive.

Grand Teton Park Drive

Yellowstone National Park to Jackson

Compared with its northern neighbor Yellowstone, Grand Teton National Park appears to be a puny appendage, hanging from the great mass of Yellowstone territory like a little finger.

However, appearances on a map are deceptive. Grand Teton Park is impressive because of its comfortable size, its easy-to-comprehend north-south orientation and because of the closeness of its mountains and lakes. Grand Teton offers an aesthetic and spiritual dimension which, to me, is unparalleled anywhere in the lower forty-eight.

First, let's consider the mountains. The Tetons compare only with the world's most unforgettable mountains, including Fuji and Denali. The range is a magnificent, twisted series of peaks that rise 7,000 feet above the narrow valley. The Snake River winds through the valley. Then a marvelous little necklace of lakes reflect the peaks and clouds, offering some of the most meaningful early mornings and late evenings in my oft-jaded experience. Think of the park as a piece of music. The forests, meadows, and water provide the rhythmic underpinning for the symphony, while the mountains provide the sturdy melody. Maybe I've gone too far, but the Tetons do this to even the most cynical traveler.

Driving from the southern gate of Yellowstone Park to Jackson Hole is easily accomplished in a day—it's only 49 miles from the Yellowstone gate to downtown Jackson—but you'll miss those sunrises and sunsets. Stay a while, and you'll be captivated!

Like Yellowstone, Grand Teton Park has clusters of accommodations and other tourist services along the highway route. The main information points in the park are located at the park headquarters in **Moose** and at the **Colter Bay** visitor center beside Jackson Lake. You'll find marinas with boat rentals, horses for trail rides, and several float trip operators organizing daily float trips down the Snake River. The park maintains a series of campgrounds, RV parks, and picnic areas along the route.

Moving from north to south, our drive begins on the **John D. Rockefeller Memorial Parkway**, a strip of land between the two parks set aside as a protected corridor. **Flagg Ranch**, on the Snake River beside the parkway, offers visitor services including camping, meals, motel accommodations, and gas. Entering the park, the route quickly leads to Jackson Lake. **Lizard Creek Campground**, several picnic sites, and the **Jackson Lake Lookout** take advantage of their positions for first views of the Tetons. Stop here and stop often.

Continuing southbound on Teton Park Road, **Colter Bay Village** provides another cluster of accommodations and services. Just to the south is Jackson Lake Lodge. Both locations are situated to take advantage of lake and mountain views. **Signal Mountain Lodge** (also on the lake) has overnight accommodations, and both Colter Bay and Signal Mountain have campgrounds with RV parking and trailer dump facilities.

Now the small chain of lakes. The newly reconstructed Jenny Lake Loop Road leads to **Jenny Lake Lodge** and the nearby viewpoint. The picture of the peaks above the lake is truly awesome. Trails fan out from the loop road to nearby Leigh and String lakes and beyond to the foot of Mount Moran. Another trail system leads around Jenny Lake and to the flank of the Grand Teton.

South of the lakes are Lupine Meadows and Cottonwood Creek, where more trails head westward toward the mountains, past Bradley and Taggart lakes. Moose has the park information station and the **Menor's Ferry** historical site.

South of Moose is the park boundary. South of the park are several points of interest, including the **National Fish Hatchery** and the **National Elk Refuge**. Anglers will want to fish in Flat Creek (August through October), in water kept warm by springs that feed the creek. At the southern end of the drive, **Jackson** is a colorful resort town famous for skiing. It is filled with good restaurants, resort hotels, and lodges, all in a relaxing, informal ambiance.

HIGHWAY LOG
Yellowstone National Park to Jackson
48.5 miles (78 KM)—1 hour, 15 minutes

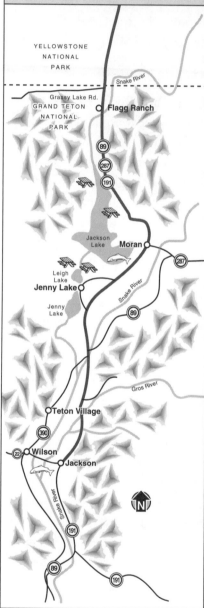

Boundary–Yellowstone and Grand Teton National Parks Our drive starts at the southern gate of Yellowstone Park, leading south along the Rockefeller Memorial Parkway.

Junction–Grassy Lake Road This route leads 45 miles to Ashton, Idaho, winding through forests, meadows, and the Grassy Lake Reservoir. This rough gravel road is not recommended for trailers and RVs but is an excellent backroad drive for nimble cars and pickups.

Flagg Ranch On the Snake River, with RV hookups, cabins, gas, and store.

Lizard Creek Campground Note to the squeamish: the "lizards" here are actually salamanders.

Picnic Area Overlooking the lake.

Jackson Lake Lookout This viewpoint provides the first good look at the Tetons (for southbound travelers). The tilting action during the mountains' formation is evident. The lake, raised by a dam, is 26,000 acres in size.

Picnic Area Beside the lake.

Leek's Marina Boat launch and food. Area pioneer Stephen Leek settled here in the 1800s.

Colter Bay Village One of several clusters of accommodations and park services. Information center, store, gas, camping, motel, cafe.

Jackson Lake Lodge Lodging, gas, restaurant.

Viewpoint–Willow Flats A great view of Jackson Lake, Mount Moran, and the central Tetons. Moose are often seen in the area.

Junction–Road to Jackson Lake Hwy. 26 leads east to the Snake River. Oxbow Bend and Moran (five miles). There is a boat ramp on the river, just past the oxbow bend.

Jackson Lake Dam This is the fourth dam to be placed here since 1910. This one was constructed in 1969. Just downstream of the dam are a boat launch and fishing access.

Junction–Signal Mountain Road/Picnic Area This narrow road leads five miles to the summit of Signal Mountain with a view of Jackson Lake from 1,000 feet higher.

Viewpoint–Potholes On a turnout to the east.

Viewpoint–Mount Moran Turnout to the west with a fine view of the 12,605-foot peak. Hanging Ice Glacier is seen on the east face of the mountain.

SIDETRIP–Jenny Lake Loop Road
This newly reconstructed road winds through meadows to some of the best park views (especially in the early mornings).

Jenny Lake Lodge Overnight accommodations and food.

BACK ON MAIN ROUTE:

Lupine Meadows Crossing Cottonwood Creek, a gravel road leads to the Jenny Lake boat launch and two trailheads.

Viewpoint–Glacier Gulch This turnout provides fine views of the Grand Teton (13,770 feet). Left of the Grand is the Middle Teton. To the north are Mount Owen and Teewinot.

Taggart Lake Trail The trail to Jenny Lake is popular in summer and with winter skiers.

Viewpoint–Windy Point View of the Gros Ventre Slide (1925), seen on Sleeping Indian Mountain across the valley (east).

Snake River/Menor's Ferry The site of William Menor's cable ferry and now the launch point for park float trips.

Moose Park information and ranger station, gas and boat ramp.

Junction–Moose-Wilson Road This road runs south for eight rather rough miles to Teton Village Resort and the town of Jackson.

Junction–Highway 89 Hwy. 89 leads north to Moran junction. Our drive continues south toward the park boundary.

Flat Creek Fed by warm springs, attracting swans, geese and cranes.

Jackson (el. 6,209 feet) Gas, resort hotels, motels, cafes, stores.

Buffalo Bill Drive

Sheridan to Yellowstone National Park

Lying to the west of the sprawling plains of Wyoming, the Big Horn Mountains are the first wave in the series of mountains that define the backbone of America. The first half of the drive to Yellowstone includes a National Forest scenic byway as Highway 14 climbs over the Big Horn range just northwest of the Cloud Peak Wilderness. After descending the western flank of the Big Horns, the route continues across flat landscape to the city of Cody, named after Buffalo Bill, the great showman who staged the great legends of the West (historians say the myths of the West) to admiring audiences throughout America and Europe.

The Big Horn Range provides a wonderful drive, first climbing steeply with signs marking the geologic formations as the road ascends by a series of switchbacks into the mountains. Among the geological treasures is the Fallen City, a jumbled group of rock slabs that have tumbled down a mountainside. After reaching the top, you see impressive views of the Sheridan Valley, including a view of Devil's Tower, more than 100 miles away.

Cutler Hill Summit is at 8,347 feet, and then the road continues to climb to Granite Pass (at 8,950 feet). Between the two high points is **Arrowhead Resort**, a rustic stopping place with a restaurant, motel rooms, and several cabins. Open all year, this is a favorite place for snowmobilers to congregate after the snow falls.

Highway 14 then leads across a plateau with meadows, lodgepole pine forest, and high-country fishing opportunities. Prune Creek Campground offers sites for tents and RVs, and nearby cross-country trails fan out over the high country.

A few miles west of Granite Pass is the Antelope Butte Ski Area. As the highway leads beside Granite Creek, you'll pass through an arid landscape with sagebrush. The highway then moves into Shell Creek Canyon, a recommended stopping point. This is a deep granite and limestone chasm that Shell Creek has carved over the centuries. You'll come across a set of picturesque falls in the canyon, seen from a series of walkways and viewing platforms at an information center.

The highway descends further down the canyon and, at the bottom, cottonwood trees line the creek just before the road leaves the canyon and reaches the village of Shell.

This is the end of the Big Horns (at least on this drive; see the next drive on page 270). The highway crosses a short series of foothills and then a wide, arid valley for another 68 miles until it reaches Cody. The road crosses the Big Horn River—in the town of Greybull.

The city of **Cody** offers a full range of visitor services, but the major attraction here is the magnificent **Buffalo Bill Historical Center**, not one but four museums providing a comprehensive look at the development of the American West through historical displays, art, and artifacts, including a collection devoted to Native American history in the Plains Indian Museum. Another attraction, **Old Trail Town**, is a collection of pioneer buildings and frontier relics, situated at the original location of Old Cody City (for Cody details, see page 282).

From Cody westward, the highway cuts through Shoshone Canyon (Rattlesnake Mountain) and then beside the **Buffalo Bill Reservoir** and state park. By the time the route reaches the village of Wapiti, we're in the Shoshone National Forest. Look for the Holy City, a ridge of pinnacles and other strange formations just north of the highway.

Moving into the Absaroka Range, campgrounds in increasing numbers approach the boundary of Yellowstone National Park. Most of the campsites are beside the North Fork of the Shoshone River. Several rustic lodges are located within the national forest, including the Absaroka Mountain Lodge and Elephant Head Lodge. Shoshone Lodge and Pahaska Teepee Lodge are closer to the Yellowstone Park gate. These lodges and campgrounds are handy stopping places should Yellowstone accommodations be full—as they usually are during summer months—and you don't have a reservation.

HIGHWAY LOG

Sheridan to Yellowstone National Park

178 miles (286 KM)—4 hours

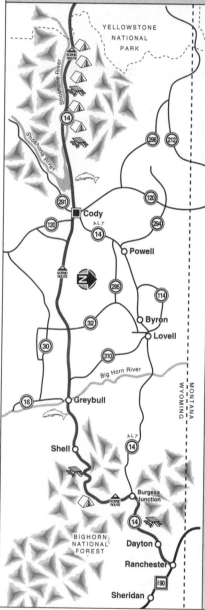

Junction–Interstate 90 and Highway 14 Located 14 miles north of Sheridan. For this drive, take Hwy. 14 west.

Ranchester Small town with gas and motel.

Historical Marker Sawyer Expedition of 1865.

Tongue River Bridge

Dayton Small town with gas, cafe, log cabin motel. The hwy. now climbs into the Big Horn Range with good views of the Tongue River Valley and ridges to the east.

Bighorn National Forest Eastern boundary. A series of geological markers shows an amazing range of rock formations as the hwy. climbs into the mountains.

Scenic Lookout At top of first ridge. Several additional lookout sites are at the top of the climb.

Fallen City Lookout A bank of tumbled rocks. The next quake will loosen more rocks.

Viewpoint At milepost 73. Views of castellated ridge.

Junction–Black Mountain Road To south of hwy., 10 miles to Burgess Junction.

Cutler Hill Summit (8,347 feet) Pulloff to the north, just past the summit.

Pine Island Picnic Area Beside the creek at milepost 60.

Arrowhead Resort Motel, very rustic cabins, and restaurant. The road climbs to a high plateau with grassy landscape, descending through mixed forest.

Burgess Junction Alternate Hwy. 14 leads west to Lovell. For this drive, continue on Hwy. 14 west toward Cody—101 miles.

Blue Spruce Lodge Cafe, one mile west of junction.

Granite Pass (el. 8,950 ft.)

Junction–Paint Rock Road To south with campground and Ranger Creek Guest Ranch. Another forest campground is beside the hwy. The route now enters Shell Creek Canyon; falls with overlook.

Post Creek Picnic Ground To south of highway.

Wagon Wheel Motel Cafe, at end of canyon.

Shell Village (el. 4,210 feet) with gas, store, B & B home, campground.

Greybull Town with motels, gas, camping, stores, ranger station. Cody—53 miles. From here, the hwy. leads across flat, arid countryside.

Junction–Highway 310 North to Lovell and Bighorn Canyon National Recreation Area.

Junction–Highway 32 South to Burlington, north to Lovell.

Cody Large town with gas, motels, stores, restaurants, camping, Buffalo Bill Historical Center, ranger station. Yellowstone National Park—50 miles.

Junction–Highway 120 South to Meeteetse and Thermopolis.

Junction–Alternate Highway 14 Leads east to Powell and Lovell.

Colter's Hell Historical marker beside old geyser area.

Buffalo Bill State Park Day-use area, boat launch, campgrounds.

Wapiti Village with guest ranches nearby. Entering Shoshone National Forest.

Holy City Series of pinnacles to north of highway.

Horse Creek Picnic Area At milepost 24. Ranger station.

Elk Fork Campground

Clearwater Creek Trailhead

Lodge at June Creek At milepost 17.

Rex Hale Campground

Picnic Area Half a mile west.

Newton Creek Campground

Absaroka Mountain Lodge Food, accommodations.

Elephant Head Lodge Food, accommodations.

Eagle Creek Campground

Sleeping Giant Campground

Shoshone Lodge Gas, cafe, accommodations, near park gate.

Ski Area To south of hwy.

Three Mile Campground

Pahaska Teepee Lodge At milepost 2.

Yellowstone National Park East Gate 27 miles to Lake Junction.

Big Horn Mountains Drive

Buffalo to Shoshoni

This is the second of our drives through the Big Horn Mountains, with Highway 16 leading westward toward Worland and Thermopolis and just south of the **Cloud Peak Wilderness**, a spectacularly beautiful area centered on Cloud Peak (el. 13,167 feet) and its glacier. The part of the route that leads through the Bighorn National Forest has been designated a National Scenic Byway and is named the Cloud Peak Skyway.

However, our tour begins in **Buffalo**, a pleasant prairie town at the eastern edge of the Big Horns. Highway 16 leads west from its junction with Interstate 90 passing the site of old **Fort McKinney**, three miles out of Buffalo. A marker commemorates the site of the fort, which was built at the Powder River crossing on the Bozeman Trail. Housing the Ninth Infantry, the fort was used until 1894. The property was then deeded to the state for a soldiers' and sailors' home, which stands nearby.

The forest byway begins seven miles west of Buffalo as the highway starts its Big Horn ascent of about 3,000 feet, with picnic areas and campgrounds along the way. Middle Fork and Circle Park campgrounds have a combined total of 19 sites. An overlook at the top of **Loaf Mountain** provides wonderful views of the Cloud Peak Wilderness and other panoramas to the east and south. The road climbs to an elevation of 9,677 feet at **Powder River Pass**, the highest point on the drive. From here, you get views of the Powder River Valley, the Big Horn Basin, and more stunning Cloud Peak scenery. The pass is high enough for alpine tundra plant life.

The route then descends gently (at first) across the mountain plateau to **Meadowlark National Recreation Area**, with facilities located around Meadowlark Lake. A ski resort here offers lodging and other services. Five campgrounds in the area have sites for all kinds of vehicles. Boating is popular during the summer, and cross-country ski trails are groomed during winter months.

Now the real descent! Ten Sleep Creek cuts through some amazing red and beige limestone cliffs, forming the **Ten Sleep Canyon**; the nearby slopes showcase sage and grasses. The creek is known for its rainbow trout, and you'll find two small campgrounds at the bottom of the canyon (Ten Sleep and Leigh Creek). The fish hatchery has a picnic site. The small community of Ten Sleep is seven miles past the canyon's end.

The highway crosses the Big Horn Basin to the town of Worland. This is the major trading center for the basin, which is largely devoted to farming. Our route turns southward in Worland (via Highway 20) and runs beside the Big Horn River. This is prosperous farmland with many sheep farms. The Owl Creek Mountains are apparent to the southwest. This short range connects the Absarokas to the southern flank of the Big Horn Range.

The highway curves west to avoid running into the Big Horns as the route approaches **Thermopolis**. This hot springs town is famous for its three bath houses—all located in **Hot Springs State Park**. Two commercial pool operations (Teepee and Star Plunge) charge fees; the free state bathhouse is a legacy of Chief Washakie, who gave the hot springs to the state for public enjoyment (he insisted that the facilities be free of charge). The "Big Spring" and walkways around the travertine terrace are an early-morning delight (for Thermopolis details, see page 296).

After leaving Thermopolis and still heading south along Highway 20, the road enters the **Wind River Canyon**, which separates the Owl Creek Range from the Big Horns.

You'll find picnic areas in the canyon and a state park with camping at the south end of the canyon on a large reservoir (Boysen Lake). Passing through the canyon, you will see glacial till, large rocks that have been pushed along the canyon walls and into the river.

From the canyon's south edge to the small, sleepy town of **Shoshoni**, the landscape changes as the highway leads across an arid, high-desert landscape. No self-respecting cow or sheep would graze here, and the land is left to the winds and sparse sage.

HIGHWAY LOG
Buffalo to Shoshoni
153 miles (246 KM)—3 hours

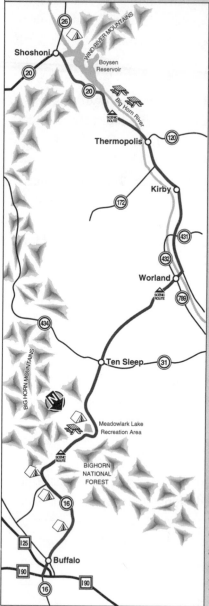

Buffalo Gas, motels, cafes, stores. Town on the east flank of the Big Horn Mountains.

Junction–Interstate 90 and Highway 16 Our drive starts at this junction. Ten Sleep—62 miles; Worland—89 miles. Take Hwy. 16 west and drive two miles through town.

Historical Marker Fort McKinney on the old Bozeman Trail. At milepost 4, the hwy. begins its climb through the Big Horn foothills.

Moose Gulch Picnic Area Partway along ascent. The climb ends with flat grassland on the alpine plateau.

Bighorn National Forest East boundary.

Junction–Cull Watt Park Road Leads west to recreation sites.

North Fork Picnic Area Half a mile off hwy. Guest Ranch, 3.5 miles.

Junction–Schoolhouse Park Road North to recreation sites.

Pines Lodge To south of hwy. with bar, cafe, trail rides. From this point, until the hwy. reaches Ten Sleep, you'll pass numerous forest campgrounds, located mostly on sideroads within a short distance of the hwy. Several picnic areas are situated beside the highway as the route crosses the top of the Big Horns.

Elgin Park Trailhead On loop road to south of hwy. beyond the South Fork Inn.

Poll Creek Road Leads north.

Junction–Caribou Mesa Road To south, leading across ridge tops through mixed forest and ranch lands.

Junction–Hazleton Road Leads south. Doyle Camp—six miles; Dull Knife Reservoir—12 miles.

Lost Cabin Campground One-third mile north of hwy. via sideroad at milepost 62.5.

Junction–Poll Creek Road Mule deer grazing area.

Junction–Powder River Road To south, toward diamond-shaped peaks.

Powder River Pass (el. 9,666 feet) Scenic overlook at milepost 55.

Meadowlark Lake Recreation Area To northeast.

High Park Ski Area South off hwy. Scenic pullout beyond the ski area access road.

Meadowlark Resort On the lake with gas, cabins, store, cafe.

Junction–West Ten Sleep Lake Road To gas, cafe, cabins, camping.

Ten Sleep Canyon The hwy. descends through this glaciated canyon to enter a wide valley.

Junction–Highway 436 Leads south to canyon.

Ten Sleep (el. 4,206 feet) Small town with gas, cafe, motels, store, saloon, museum.

Junction–Road 434 Leads south to Big Trails.

Junction–Lower Norwood Road Leads north to Hyattville.

Badlands Located 26 miles from Worland. The road crosses badlands, which contain a working oil field.

Worland Farming town with gas, motels, cafes, stores.

Junction–Highway 20 Hwy. 16 leads north to Greybull. Our route takes Hwy. 20, leading south beside the Big Horn River through sheep grazing lands. The Owl Creek Range lies to the southwest.

Kirby Village with southern range of Big Horns nearby to the south.

Junction–Highway 172 Black Mountain Road leads east.

Thermopolis This historic town is best known for its hot springs located in Hot Springs State Park. Thermopolis has full visitor services, including a resort hotel within the park.

Wind River Canyon Three miles south of Thermopolis, the highway enters the canyon. There are two picnic areas beside the Big Horn River in the canyon. Two campgrounds are located at the south end of the canyon.

Shoshoni (el. 4,820 feet) Gas, cafe, motels, store. To continue west to Grand Teton National Park, see the Wind River Drive next.

Wind River Drive

Shoshoni to Grand Teton National Park

This drive provides a continuation of the previous drive, which ended in Shoshoni. It also covers the scenic mountain sections of the route between Casper (98 miles to the east of Shoshoni) and the eastern gate of Grand Teton National Park.

The route, over the Wind River and Absaroka ranges, is one of the most thrilling drives in the northern Rockies, offering fine views of high snow-clad peaks in addition to dramatic limestone cliffs and buttes.

The early part of the drive leads through the Wind River foothills, through the **Wind River Reservation** and the modern town of **Riverton**. Between Riverton and Dubois, the road leads along the foothills through the land called "Wind River Country" by the Shoshone and their chief, Washakie. The reservation holds some two million acres of land, the home of the Eastern Shoshone and Northern Arapahoe tribes. Shoshone communities include Crowheart, Wind River, and Washakie. The Arapahoe live in the southeastern part of the reservation—at Arapahoe, St. Stephens, and Ethete, some distance from our route.

Crowheart Butte is a prominent landmark between Riverton and Dubois. An historic battle was fought near here in March 1866 between the Shoshone/Bannock and the Crow tribes. After the battle, largely fought over hunting grounds, victorious Chief Washakie displayed a Crow Indian's heart on his lance. You'll see a battle marker at milepost 89.5.

This region was the focus of the fur trade between 1807 and 1850. John Colter, a mountain man who had been on the Lewis and Clark expedition, was the first to explore the Wind River area—looking for beaver and furs to trade. Fur trapping was big business for almost 40 years, until the beaver and other animals had been trapped to near-extinction.

Northwest of Dubois, the highway passes through the area of the historic **Oregon Trail**, the route of many thousands of pioneers who traveled west to open up the northwest wilderness. **Union Pass** was a preferred route across the Continental Divide on the Oregon Trail. The pass was first explored by Astorians in 1811. These were explorers working for fur trader John Jacob Astor, who wished to set up trading posts on the Pacific coast at the mouth of the Columbia River. The Astorians were a large group, including hunters, guides, and at least 45 French-Canadians who were hired to assist with the expedition.

Dubois is a rustic "Wild West" town, situated at 6,900 feet in the Wind River Range. It is a vacation center, focusing on hunting and fishing, with a good selection of log cabin motels and more standard accommodations. North of town is the Shoshone National Forest as the highway becomes another of the National Forest Scenic Byways. The highway climbs northwest from Dubois, through the Wind River headwaters area, and through mixed ranchland and badlands. Several campgrounds are just inside the national forest boundary, including Falls Campground with 45 sites beside a waterfall. Brooks Lake has another scenic campground.

Then come some of the prime scenic moments of this drive. **Pinnacle Buttes** are seen to the north—a layered array of volcanic rock and ash. Next are the **Breccia Cliffs** with more of the same formations, and then the road climbs to a subalpine wilderness, carpeted with wildflowers during summer months.

Togwotee Pass (el. 9,544 feet) and the nearby Continental Divide mark the boundary of the Bridger Teton National Forest. You can enjoy good views from the pass. Just past Blackrock Creek are the first views of the Tetons. You'll find a trail to Angle Mountain with panoramic views of the Tetons, the mountains in Yellowstone National Park, and the Teton Wilderness. The highway descends slightly into the Buffalo Valley with closer Teton views. Our drive ends after crossing the boundary into Grand Teton National Park and reaching **Grand Teton Drive** at Moran Junction. Because of the frequent opportunities for Teton viewing, you will want to stop along the way for this unforgettable scenery.

HIGHWAY LOG
Shoshoni to Grand Teton National Park
165 miles (265 KM)—3 hours, 30 minutes

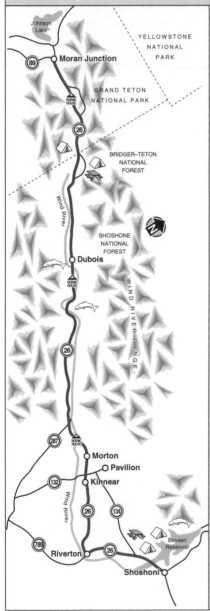

Shoshoni Small town with gas, cafe, motels, store. Located 98 miles from Casper via Hwy. 20/26. Our drive starts south on Hwy. 26.
Boysen Creek Picnic Area To north of hwy.
Wind River Reservation Extends west for more than 50 miles.
Boysen State Park Causeway and bridge over reservoir. Day-use area, camping, boating.
Junction–Bass Lake Road To Boysen Lake west shore and Lake Cameahwait Recreation Site—picnicking, fishing. The hwy. passes through gently rolling farming landscape.
Riverton (el. 4,956 feet) Large, modern prairie town with gas, stores, cafes, motels. Our drive continues via Hwy. 26 leading northwest toward Dubois—78 miles. The Wind River Range lies to the west of the hwy.
Kinnear (el. 5,410 feet) Village with gas and store. Road 131 leads north to Ocean Lake Wildlife Habitat and Pavilion.
Junction–Highway 287 South to Lander and on to South Pass City historic sites.
Crowheart Butte The prominent formation is seen to the northeast.

Bull Lake Creek Bridge Bull Lake Lodge, cabins, fishing, gas, and store (at milepost 85).

Red Rock Lodge Log motel and cafe. River to the east of lodge. Note the red cliffs at this point.

Wind River Bridge Leaving Wind River Reservation. The highway now starts a steep climb with first glimpses of Absarokas—11 miles from Dubois.

Wind River Access Fishing to east of hwy., beginning at milepost 63.5.

Dubois (el. 6,917 feet) Rustic Wild West town with gas, motels, cabins, laundry, stores, ranger station downtown.

Fishing Access To east at milepost 47. Wind River.

Historical Marker–Union Pass At milepost 46.5. Commemorates the route of the Astorians (fur trade expedition).

Junction–Union Pass Road To the south. The historic pass on the Oregon Trail is 17 miles from the junction (Continental Divide). Gas, store at junction (milepost 46). Moran Junction is 46 miles west of the junction.

Shoshone National Forest Boundary at milepost 41. Saloon and store just east of park boundary. Start of designated Forest Byway.

Motel West Wind River Ranch at milepost 39.

Rock Pinnacles To north as the highway climbs into the Absaroka Range.

Junction–Brooks Lake Road Leads north to lodge.

Falls Campground To south of hwy.

Togwotee Pass (el. 9,658 feet) While the pass is slightly higher, the Continental Divide is found 100 yards from the pass (el. 9,544 feet) at milepost 25. The highway skims the top of the mountains for several miles.

Pulloff with Markers Information center for Bridger Teton National Forest (milepost 20.5).

Togwotee Mountain Lodge Cabins, gas at beginning of descent.

Turpin Meadow Recreation Area Picnicking to north—four miles.

Black Rock Campground With ranger station.

Buffalo Valley Road Leads north to Turpin Meadow.

Grand Teton National Park (east boundary)

Moran Junction (el. 6,700 feet) This is the only eastern entrance to Grand Teton National Park. Yellowstone Park lies north of Moran Junction via Hwy. 89 (Rockefeller Memorial Parkway). For Grand Teton Park Drive, see page 262.

Wyoming
Destinations

Buffalo

T he Big Horn Mountains to the west dominate the skyline of this town, which is situated near the junction of Interstate Highways 25 and 90. It was one of the first settlements in northern Wyoming, incorporated in 1884. It's now a good spot to stay when beginning the scenic drive over the Big Horn Mountains. Buffalo is an agricultural community with a selection of motels and campgrounds to choose from (see page 305).

The land around Buffalo saw perhaps more Native American wars than any other part of the United States. Fort Phil Kearney, situated 17 miles north of Buffalo off Highway 87, was built to protect the Bozeman Trail and was constantly in conflict with the Sioux, Arapahoe, and Cheyenne tribes. It was besieged frequently by Chief Red Cloud and his warriors before the trail and the fort were closed in 1868. **Fort McKinney** was originally built near old Fort Reno and was reestablished on a site on Clear Creek, near Buffalo (see the scenic drive on page 270). The property is now the Veterans' Home of Wyoming, a home for senior citizens.

The various conflicts are commemorated in the **Jim Gatchell Museum** in Buffalo. The museum contains more than 10,000 artifacts of that era: of the Union soldiers, Native American culture, and the early pioneers who settled the area.

The area has more than a few guest ranches with mainly cabin accommodations ranging from rustic to deluxe. Riding is the primary recreation. One of the largest is **Paradise Guest Ranch**, 13 miles west of town on Highway 16. Eighteen luxurious log cabins contain fireplaces and kitchens with family meals served in the lodge dining room. The facility is equipped with a hot tub; fishing is nearby, and a children's program is included. A much smaller and more intimate ranch is the **Rafter Y Ranch**, on the slope of the Big Horn Mountains 18 miles northwest of Buffalo. The ranch also features log cabins, and buffet meals are served in the lodge. **V Bar F Cattle Ranch** is a B & B ranch with rooms in the home or in a guest house. Aside from normal summer ranch activity, cross-country skiing is popular here.

Where to Eat

Steve's Restaurant is located in Business Loop 87, one mile south of I-90 at 820 North Main Street. They focus on continental dishes, but this is a family restaurant with children's menu. **Colonel Bozeman's** has a western motif and serves American food. It is also suitable for family dining and is located at 655 East Hart Street, west of I-25.

Casper

Casper is a plains city, the second largest city in Wyoming. Its growth paralleled the development of oil fields in the area following the discovery of oil in 1888. It's now the hub of the oil and gas industry in the Rocky Mountain region.

The city is near the site of **Old Fort Caspar**, which is located on the banks of the North Platte River. The city is named (with a spelling change) for Lieutenant Caspar Collins, an officer from Ohio who died along with most of his volunteer soldiers trying to relieve another cavalry detachment.

While Casper is not on any of the scenic mountain drives (and indeed is many miles east of the Rockies), it may make a handy place to stay before driving through the Wind River Range to Grand Teton National Park (see the scenic drive on page 274).

A particularly scenic day trip from Casper leads south along Highway 220 to **Alcova Lake**. This area, which was once a Native

American campground, is now a state recreation area with a dam widening the North Platte River in Fremont Canyon. You'll find camping here along with water sports. The marina has boat rentals, a restaurant, and a store. The **Gray Reef Reservoir**, 28 miles west of the city on Highway 220, also has a campground with good fishing and boating. Continue on Highway 220 for another six miles, and you'll find the Pathfinder Reservoir with tent and trailer sites and a marina with food and docking. Fifty miles along Highway 220 is **Independence Rock**, a state historic landmark on which are carved more than 5,000 names of early emigrants traveling along the Oregon Trail to the Salt Lake Valley and California. The Rock was named by a party of trappers during a celebration on July 4, 1830.

Sand Creek Ranch is a guest ranch operation, about 70 miles south of Casper on Highway 220. The ranch lies at the foot of the Seminole and Pedro mountains and is next to the **Pathfinder Reservoir**. Three cabins accommodate a total of 18 people. The ranch offers trail rides, mountain photographic junkets, and big game hunting. This is also a working cattle ranch.

Where to Eat

For family dining, **Armor's** should fill the bill. At 3422 South Energy Lane (on State Highway 220, 3.5 miles south of the Poplar Street exit of I-25), Armor's serves continental and American cuisine and has a children's menu. It also features a lounge. **Benham's** is an informal place (as are most Wyoming restaurants), serving American dishes including barbecued ribs (a specialty). A lounge is off the restaurant, which is at 739 Center Street. **El Jarro** is a family-owned Mexican restaurant with food and cocktails at 500 West F Avenue. **Anthony's Italian Restaurant**, 241 South Center Street, offers casual dining in a courtyard setting with pasta as the specialty.

Cheyenne

The name of the state capital recognizes the Cheyenne people who inhabited southeastern Wyoming before European settlement in the mid-1800s. It was founded in 1867 when the Union Pacific laid its tracks in the area. This was the quintessential Wild West town; its residents were a mixture of settlers, soldiers, railroad builders, outlaws, and lawmen. Cowboy history is at its best here, and the city was an early home to cattle barons.

The **State Capitol** has a golden dome, which can be seen for many miles across the plains. It resembles the nation's Capitol in Washington with high columns and a large rotunda. Weekday tours are available from the rotunda, which features the stuffed icons of the state: bison and elk.

The **Governor's Mansion**, used as a home from 1905 to 1976, is now a historic museum that is open year-round. The State Museum is close to the capitol and offers a bewildering collection of western artifacts from the cowboy, trapping, and pioneer eras. An excellent Native American collection includes clothing and archeological items. The museum is located in the Barret Building on Central Avenue. It is open daily, except for state holidays.

Other museums in Cheyenne include the **Frontier Days Museum**, which features rodeo artifacts, including a large collection of horse-drawn vehicles, clothing, and a saloon re-creation. Philatelists enjoy the **National First Day Cover Museum**, which not only contains an authentic 1900 general store but houses the finest collection of first edition stamp covers in the country.

Holliday Park in downtown Cheyenne houses "Big Boy," the world's largest steam locomotive (Old Number 4004), which served the Union Pacific until 1956 and was moved to the park for rail buffs to pore over. The Wyoming Game and Fish Department operates a visitor center beside Interstate 25 at Central Avenue. Besides obtaining information on wildlife and wetlands viewing, you can see displays of many of the state's 600 wildlife species.

If you're traveling between Cheyenne and Laramie, the most scenic way to go is to take the **Happy Jack Road**, which leads for 38 miles through the Medicine Bow National Forest. You'll see high rock towers eroded into fascinating shapes. It joins Interstate

80 at the road's summit (8,400 feet), and from there it's only 12 miles to Laramie. To start along this route, take 19th Street in Cheyenne. **Curt Gowdy State Park** is named after the sportscaster who is a favorite son of the state. It's on the Happy Jack Road and is a great place for fishing and other water sports. You'll find mountain trails for summer hiking and Nordic skiing after the snow falls.

Where to Eat

Poor Richards, at 2333 East Lincolnway, offers an early-American ambiance and all the standard American dishes (steaks, prime rib, seafood), with a Saturday brunch menu. The **Whipple House** (300 East 17th Street) is a dining room in a traditional setting (an older building), with outdoor dining in the summer. This restaurant specializes in continental cuisine.

Cody

Buffalo Bill Cody is the patron saint of this town, which is situated just east of the Absaroka Range. It's the Wyoming gateway to Yellowstone National Park, and the town itself is a fascinating place to visit. The thrilling route to Yellowstone is described in the scenic drive beginning on page 266. It's 50 miles of undiluted mountain splendor through the Wapiti Valley and the Shoshone National Forest, the first designated national forest in the U.S.

The major attraction in town is the **Buffalo Bill Historical Center**, which contains not one but four museums and galleries that began as a modest log building and have now expanded to become one of the nation's preeminent museum complexes. This is the place to experience Americana in all its glory. The Buffalo Bill Museum is a huge collection of Bill Cody's personal memorabilia: photographs of his life as a Civil War soldier, pony express rider, buffalo hunter, and showman. The collection includes a fully restored Deadwood stagecoach and personal items from many of Cody's contemporaries, including Annie Oakley. Buffalo Bill's clothing and show costumes are included.

The **Whitney Gallery of Western Art** contains paintings and sculptures from the likes of Remington, Russell, Bierstadt, Moran, and Wyeth. The Plains Indian Museum houses thousands of cultural artifacts of more than a century of Plains tribal history and a contemporary gallery, plus a re-creation of an 1890 Sioux camp. The **Firearms Museum** presents a full history of the development of firearms in the United States and Europe from the 16th century to today. The Historical Center is open daily from March through November.

Many travelers to Yellowstone Park stay in Cody before making the drive through the Absarokas, past the **Buffalo Bill Reservoir**. You'll find several historic hotels (see page 307) and a good range of modern hotels and motels. **Buffalo Bill State Park**, located along the reservoir just west of town, offers camping facilities and day-use picnic areas. The lake has good trout fishing, as does the North Fork of the Shoshone River. Several private campgrounds and RV parks are in town.

Several guest ranches are in the Cody area, some are in the national forest. These include the Hunter Peak Ranch, 23 miles from the Yellowstone border, with accommodations ranging from rustic cabins to rooms in the main lodge. Castle Rock Ranch is 17 miles southwest of Cody on Highway 291 in the Southfork Valley of the Shoshone River. It is a large lodge with pool and private rooms; activities include the usual riding plus cookouts, river fishing, and llama treks in the mountains.

Where to Eat

The historic **Irma Hotel** with restaurant and saloon is one of the most nostalgic places to eat in Wyoming. The hotel was built by Bill Cody for his daughter, and the ambiance is authentic. The food matches the ambiance. Two of the best places to eat in the area are out of town: **Goff Creek Lodge** has a restaurant and lounge in the Wapiti Valley, via Highway 14/16/20. The meals are Western-style, and they're huge. **Absaroka Mountain Lodge** is farther along the same highway, 12 miles from the Yellowstone gate with a rustic log lodge and excellent food.

Dubois

Sitting beside the upper Wind River, the town of Dubois in the heart of the Wind River Mountains is an unparalleled outdoors recreation center. It's a rustic town with a main street spread along Highway 26/287 containing false-fronted buildings, many made of logs. The town once serviced cattle operations and was the railroad tie capital of Wyoming during the building of the transcontinental lines. Now, Dubois is a hub for guest ranching, fishing, and hunting expeditions to some of the best big game territory in America.

The town is midway between Riverton and Jackson Hole via Grand Teton National Park; it makes a pleasant if somewhat rustic stopover on your way to Yellowstone.

A remarkable sidetrip near Dubois is the **Union Pass Road** tour. The pass was a major mountain crossing during the trek west by thousands of settlers who used the Oregon Trail to get to Utah, California, and the Oregon Territory. This is the land that John Colter discovered in 1807. This mountain man, explorer, and trapper is said to be the first settler to explore what is now Wyoming. He passed through the Dubois area on a trip to Jackson Hole. At the summit of Union Pass, south of Highway 26/287, is a monument marking the role of this road and Union Pass in the settling of the West. The scenery is spectacular. To get to the pass, follow Highway 26/287 west from Dubois (see the scenic drive on page 274). Union Pass Road is on your left and is signed.

You might expect the Dubois area to have plenty of guest ranches, and you're right. A dozen are located within a short drive of town, including the **Absaroka Ranch**, 16 miles northwest of Dubois, located at the foot of Ram's Horn Peak. This secluded ranch offers riding, fishing, and hiking and arranges white-water trips. The ranch is known for its good food, and accommodations include rustic cabins and a sauna. The **CM Ranch** is a relaxed place, with log cabins accommodating up to 50 guests. It's six miles from Dubois on Fish Hatchery Road. The **Washakie Wilderness** is nearby. The ranch has a heated pool and sauna and offers cookouts and fishing in a private stream. For those who like lodge rooms, you can't do better than staying at the Diamond Bar E Ranch, which is 15 miles east of Dubois and a half-mile south of the highway. Meals are provided in the lodge dining room or on dinner rides. Besides riding, the lodge offers fishing and is open for snowmobiling during winter months. For ranch details, see page 309.

Several Forest Service campgrounds are in the Dubois area, including Falls, 23 miles west of town on Highway 287; Horse Creek, 12 miles west of town on a forest road; and Pinnacles, 23 miles west of Dubois via Highway 287 and then north on a forest road. All have tent sites and spaces for trailers under 32 feet.

Where to Eat

The **Double Bar J Ranch**, 23 miles west of Dubois, serves lunch and dinner in the Lodge. This is a scenic location with great views of Pinnacle Buttes and the Shoshone National Forest. The **Cowboy Cafe**, in Dubois, has good soups, pies, and other baking. The **Red Rock Lodge** restaurant is west of town, with views of Red Rock Canyon.

Grand Teton National Park

The unforgettable Teton Range sets the backdrop for the narrow valley in which lies Grand Teton National Park. This long, thin park is ready-made for quiet relaxation beside one of the scenic lakes or for more adventurous hiking and river rafting.

The park was established and dedicated in 1929, but back then it was a tiny portion of what is today's park, containing only the mountains and a thin strip of lakes. In 1950, it grew with the addition of most of the **Jackson Hole National Monument,** which included the 52 square miles of land that John D. Rockefeller Jr. had donated to the public trust. The park extends from its north boundary (with Yellowstone Park via the Rockefeller Parkway) to just north of the town of Jackson.

The small range of mountains called the Tetons rose from the valley floor, beginning about nine million years ago, and they twisted as they rose. At the same time, the valley slipped downward, and now it slopes toward the mountains. This movement continues to this day.

The peaks in the center of the range are said to have been dubbed *Le Trois Tetons* ("the Three Breasts") by lusty French-Canadian trappers when passing through the area. The Idaho side of the range is much more gentle and doubtless led the trappers to fantasize.

The Peaks

As one stands on the east side of the Snake River Valley, the full range is apparent. From south to north (left to right), the peaks appear as follows:

The Wall is the slope of limestone just above the town of Jackson at Jackson Hole. There are many other sedimentary limestone layers in the mountains to the north. **South Teton** (el. 12,514 feet) is the first peak at the south end of the range. **Nez Perce** (el. 11,901 feet) is next, with **Middle Teton** (el. 12,804) to the north. The **Lower Saddle** divides **Middle and Grand Teton** peaks. The Grand is the highest in the range at 13,770 feet, the third highest mountain in Wyoming, and the most spectacular of them all. The first successful climb of the Grand is said to have been made in 1872 by Nathaniel Langford, the first superintendent of Yellowstone National Park, but others have also claimed the distinction. Many routes lead up the Grand, and none of them are easy. The most popular leads from Garnet Canyon and then up via the Upper Saddle.

North of Gunsight Notch, **Mount Owen** rises to a summit at 12,928 feet. It was named after William Owen, an early mountain climber whom the Wyoming legislature has recognized as one of the first party to make the Grand Teton summit in 1898. **Teewinot** (el. 12,325 feet) named by Fritiof Fryxell and Phil Smith, its first climbers, is a Shoshone word meaning "many pinnacles." Then, looking north, you see several less impressive peaks: **Mount St. John** (el. 11,430 feet), **Rockchuck Peak** (el. 11,144 feet), **Mount Woodring** (el. 11,500 feet), and **Thor Peak** (el. 12,028 feet). Anchoring the northern end of the range is **Mount Moran**, at 12,605 feet, named for Thomas Moran, the western artist whose paintings helped to establish Yellowstone as a national park in 1872.

Park Scenes and Facilities

For a detailed listing of the mile-by mile wonders of the park, see the Grand Teton Park Drive on page 262. The Highway Log takes you from the Yellowstone border to the town of Jackson.

Two lakes define the park's valley area. At the north end of the park, **Jackson Lake** is more than 16 miles long and covers about 26,000 acres. Picnic areas, campgrounds, and viewpoints lie along the eastern shore of the lake. It is a natural lake, made larger by the dam near Jackson Lake junction. Anglers will find cutthroat, mackinaw, and brown and brook trout in the lake.

Jenny Lake was named for a Shoshone woman, the wife of an early trapper and local guide, Richard Leigh (for whom Leigh Lake was named). There is no more beautiful lake for awe-inspiring canoeing than Jenny.

You'll find several motels and lodges within the park, providing rustic to deluxe accommodations. **Flagg Ranch** is the most northern place to stay; it has a guest ranch, motel, and cabins with restaurant, saloon, and store. The resort offers riding and river trips. Colter Bay Village on Jackson Lake has moderate rates for its cabins. There is a dining room and lounge but no cooking in the cabins. For details on Park Accommodations, see page 309.

Jackson Lake Lodge is the upscale place to stay if you like lots of people around. The lodge has deluxe rates and a fine dining room with lounge. Just to the south, **Jenny Lake Lodge** is located in a more secluded location on the Jenny Lake Loop Road. Its rates are deluxe, with only 30 units and a dining room with lounge, open during the summer and fall seasons. **Signal Mountain Lodge**, also with deluxe rates, has 22 cooking units among its total of 79 units and it too is a seasonal operation. The lodge has a dining room and cocktail lounge. **Moose Head Ranch** has a horse for each of its 40 guests. It's located on Highway 26/89/191 with cabin accommodations, and it features cookouts with fishing close at hand.

Five campgrounds are inside the park, operated by the Park Service. From north to south, they are: **Lizard Creek**, with 60 sites; **Colter Bay** with 310 sites, laundry, propane, and dump station; **Signal Mountain** with 86 sites and dump station; **Jenny Lake** with 49 sites restricted to tents and small camping vehicles (no trailers) and dump station; and **Gros Ventre**, the largest of the campgrounds with 360 sites and dump station. For information and reservations, see "Places to Stay," page 309.

You'll find service stations and grocery stores along the highway next to the major accommodations areas. Park visitor centers are at **Colter Bay** and **Moose**. The Colter Bay center includes the Indian Arts Museum, where Native American artists demonstrate their work during June, July, and August. The Moose Center features a park orientation video that provides a good overview of park attractions and facilities. Both information centers are open from 8 A.M. to 7 P.M. during summer months and to 5 P.M. the rest of the year. Ranger-led tours and other interpretive activities are available during summer months. Backcountry and boating permits are available at both Moose and Colter Bay centers.

Green River

When the Union Pacific Railway made its way across the West, the Green River was used to float timber from the mountains to be made into railroad ties at the small town of Green River.

By the time the railway arrived, Green River had a population of 2,000.

Earlier, the area was part of the Mexican territory and was annexed to the United States after the Mexican War. This area, dominated by **Flaming Gorge**, has a fascinating geology. The land is made primarily of sedimentary rock formations, piled one on top of the other, made by accumulations of silt on the bottom of a huge freshwater sea during the Tertiary period 40 million years ago. John Wesley Powell mapped the region extensively in 1869 and 1871 as he went down the Green River, naming the Flaming Gorge Canyon and other features of the southern Wyoming landscape.

Two-thirds of the world's supply of soda ash (or trona) comes from Green River, supplying America with an essential ingredient of baking soda, detergents, and glass.

Flaming Gorge is located south of town and is covered in detail in the Utah section of this book (see page 167). It is also covered in the scenic drive that begins on page 162. North of the Utah border, Flaming Gorge Lake is 90 miles long, offering recreation activities and campsites along its 375 miles of shoreline. Closer to Green River is the **Firehole Canyon**, another fascinating piece of scenery that is north of Black's Fork, featuring pinnacles and chimneys.

There are two ways to get to Flaming Gorge from Green River. The Highway 530 route through Manila (Utah) is covered in the Flaming Gorge Drive. Or, you can take the alternative route that leads through the Firehole Canyon region by driving east from Green River on Interstate 80 for eight miles and then turning south onto Highway 191. The road to Firehole is 13 miles south of the Interstate 80 junction and leads 10 miles to the canyon. Highway 191 continues south to Dutch John, the site of the Flaming Gorge Dam. The prime canyon viewpoints are to the west off Highway 44.

The **Seedskadee National Wildlife Refuge** is located 37 miles north of Green River. This outstanding river area is home to more than 170 species of birds during the year and is a breeding ground for Canada geese, ducks, teal, and sage grouse among others. The refuge lies along the Green River, covering more than 14,000 acres. The preserve hosts most of Wyoming's native raptors, including prairie and peregrine falcons, owls, and hawks. The refuge takes its name from the Shoshone word for the Green River: *Seed-kee-dee-Agie*, "River of the Sage Chicken."

The nearest public campground is south of town in the Flaming Gorge National Recreation Area. Buckboard Crossing Campground has 68 sites on the high desert with a marina and store at the crossing. To get there, drive south from town on Highway 530 for 25 miles and then drive two miles east on Road 374. A private RV park with tent sites is in Green River.

Jackson

This all-year resort town is filled with the ambiance of the Old West, combined with the modern frills of one of the top ski resorts in the country. The community lies at the south end of **Jackson Hole**, the valley which was explored by mountain man and guide John Colter in 1807. Originally a member of the Lewis and Clark expedition, Colter came to the area alone and spread the word about this beautiful valley with its distinctive mountain range, which were later named the Tetons.

After Colter, the fur trade dominated Jackson Hole. This was the period of the mountain men, those rugged characters who opened the western frontier during the next 20 years. Among the residents of the hole were Jim Bridger, Jedediah Smith, and David Jackson, after whom the valley and the town were named. Jackson was a hub for the fur trade, where six major fur trails converged. The trappers had disappeared by 1845 and the Tetons were largely left alone for forty years, except for nomadic people who passed through the valley.

The Hayden expeditions of 1871 to 1878 surveyed the valley and its geological features, giving names to the Teton peaks and several of the lakes. By the 1880s, settlers entered the region and homesteads were established.

Today, Jackson is a fine mixture of the old days and modern chic. **Snow King Mountain** provides good powder skiing from mid-December to April. The ski lift operates during the summer, taking tourists to splendid views of the Grand Tetons and the "Hole" below.

The western boundary of the **Teton Wilderness** is less than a mile from the town. This is 585,000 acres of backcountry through which there are no roads. The wilderness is accessible by foot or horse and offers views of waterfalls, evergreen forest, large meadows, and lakes. It is possible to hike to the Continental Divide. The highest point in the wilderness is Yount's Peak (el. 12,165 feet). Another large preserve is the **Gros Ventre Wilderness** with dramatic Rocky Mountain peaks and deep canyons. You'll find a dozen or more fishing lakes in this area and many fishing streams where cutthroat, eastern brook, and rainbow trout are caught. An extensive network of trails run through the Gros Ventre Wilderness. Wildlife species include black bear, moose, bighorn sheep, mule deer, and elk. Large subalpine meadows in the wilderness are surrounded by Engelmann spruce; the lower slopes are populated by lodgepole pine.

Five campgrounds operate in Grand Teton National Park, to the north of town, and you'll find several private operations in or near Jackson. For details, see page 310. Astoria Mineral Springs, 17 miles south of town, offers an RV park along with a hot pool.

Where to Eat

Eating in Jackson provides a choice from burgers to fine dining, including several that serve game, including the **Cadillac Grille** on the Town Square and **JJ's Silver Dollar Bar and Grill** in the Wort Hotel. **Rafferty's**, at the Snow King Resort, serves Northwest cuisine.

Laramie

In May 1868, Laramie was a tent city awaiting the tracks that were to bind the nation together. The tracks were laid through town that month, and the dusty encampment quickly became a permanent community of 3,000 people. Like other western railway towns, Laramie had a few upstanding citizens, a few stockmen who came to town every so often, and a whole lot of rowdies, rustlers, gamblers, thieves, and transient riffraff. However, before the year was out, a group of town leaders organized a vigilante posse and chased most of the bad guys out of the city. Then most of the rest of the population departed for newer railway towns, and Laramie was left with 1,500 residents.

Today, it's Wyoming's third largest city and a university center (the **University of Wyoming** is the state's only four-year college). The number of students today (10,000) far surpasses the original population of the early railway town. Most of the university buildings are constructed of Wyoming sandstone. Amateur and professional geologists should visit the university's **Geological Museum**. Located in the east wing of the geology building, the museum shows the geological history of what is now Wyoming over the past two billion years. The museum contains a skeleton of a giant brontosaurus.

Another historical highlight of the city is **Wyoming Territorial Park**, at the Snowy Lake exit of Interstate 80. The park includes a museum inside the former Wyoming Territorial Prison (built in 1872). The displays commemorate the fur trading and mountain man era, Laramie's railroad days, and the period since statehood. During the summer months, the park stages entertainment and arts and crafts shows.

Day Trips from Laramie

A particularly fine scenic drive leads through the **Medicine Bow Range** southwest of Laramie via Highway 130; the road rejoins Interstate 80 at Walcott, west of Rawlins. The route first passes Centennial, climbing to Snowy Range Pass, at 10,800 feet. Recreation areas throughout the mountain drive include campgrounds, picnic areas, and fishing sites. The road passes several crystal lakes and passes under several 12,000-foot peaks that give the Medicine Bows their nickname—the Snowy Range. The 94-mile loop

 292

makes an extremely scenic alternate route if you're westbound from Laramie, or it can be a superb day drive, returning to Laramie via Interstate 80.

Another scenic route (Highway 210) leads through the **Medicine Bow National Forest**, east of Laramie, to Curt Gowdy State Park and Cheyenne. To get to Highway 210, drive southeast from Laramie on Interstate 80.

You'll find a private campground in Laramie, plus several public campgrounds in the national forest to the east.

Where to Eat

The **Cowboy Bar and Grill**, at 309 South 3rd Street, offers family dining in a western atmosphere. They also have a lounge here. Another western-style restaurant is the **Cavalryman Supper Club**, located 1.75 miles south of I-80 on Highway 287. It features prime rib, seafood, and steaks. A cocktail lounge is here, too.

Riverton, Lander, and South Pass City

The valley of the Big Wind River is a fabled pioneer territory with more history than you can absorb in a short visit. What was once part of the enormous Wind River Reservation is now the town of Riverton. It lies in the center of a half-million acres that were withdrawn from the reservation for homesteading. The town was founded in 1906.

The **Wind River Reservation** is an important player in Wyoming's economy. It's home to the Eastern Shoshone and Northern Arapahoe people. Two million acres of land are owned by these tribes. The Shoshone live in the northern, western, and south-central portions of the reservation, while the Arapahoe occupy the southeast segment. Annual powwows are held at Fort Washakie, Crowheart, Ethete, and Arapahoe. The grave of famed Chief Washakie is found at **Fort Washakie**. He died in 1900 at the age of 102.

Riverton is a modern agricultural community with accommodations for travelers including motels and RV parks. For more information on the area, see the Wind River Drive on page 274.

South Pass City, located southeast of Riverton on Highway 28, is one of the West's most important historic sites. The town was built in 1867 when gold fever struck the region. The outstanding find at the Carissa Mine brought hundreds of prospectors; within a year, the town's population boomed to 2,000. South Pass Avenue was half a mile long, filled with stores, hotels, saloons, banks, and other attractions for miners. More than 30 gold mines were opened. The nation's first female judge, Esther Morris, was appointed by the town; this event was the vanguard of Wyoming's women's suffrage movement. The town boomed, but the bust came in 1872, leaving the region to ranchers. South Pass City is now a remarkable historic site, with 24 old buildings, picnic sites, and a visitor center. The center has demonstrations, lectures, and audio-visual shows during the summer months. The celebration on the Fourth of July draws people from every part of the state and beyond.

To get to South Pass City, drive southwest from Riverton on Highway 789 to Lander and then take Highway 28 south to a sideroad that leads through **Atlantic City** (a semi-ghost town) to the historic site. Atlantic City was a gold mining camp and is now mostly ghost town, although a few rustic homes are occupied. The businesses that are open in the original buildings cater to travelers. A few gold mines still operate in the area. South Pass City is 35 miles southwest of Lander and 59 miles from Riverton. **Sink's Canyon State Park** is six miles southwest of Lander, providing a handy picnicking stop or a campsite when visiting nearby South Pass City. The Riverton RV City Campground is located at 1304 South 8th Street East, one mile south of the city park. This is a small campground with showers and restrooms. Private RV parks are in town.

Where to Eat

Lander has the best eating places in the area and makes a good stop while visiting South Pass City. Try **Judd's Grub** (burgers, seafood, Mexican) at 634 Main, or **The Loft** (upstairs at 351 Main Street) for Thai cuisine.

Sheridan

Sheridan is a historic ranching town nestled beneath the east flank of the Big Horn Mountains in northeastern Wyoming. It played a large part in the terrible wars of the great plains as Crazy Horse and his warriors clashed with army troops. Two of the most ferocious battles were fought near Sheridan: the Wagon Box Fight and the Fetterman Fight.

The community was established when two trappers built a cabin beside Little Goose Creek in 1873. It became a hub for ranchers, miners, and railroad workers. During the latter part of the 1800s, English "remittance men" came to the area and established a flourishing cattle ranching industry and, as a result, the town has a distinct English atmosphere.

The town is situated on Interstate 90, 25 miles south of the Wyoming/Montana border. One of our scenic drives (page 270) begins at Buffalo, 25 miles south of Sheridan. Another drive (page 266) begins just 15 miles north of Sheridan, at the junction of Interstate 90 and Highway 14 west (at Ranchester). Both drives cross the **Big Horn Mountains**, offering superb views of the Cloud Peak Wilderness. All of the Big Horn recreational opportunities can be experienced by taking day trips from Sheridan over either route. In the winter, the Big Horn Mountains offer snowmobiling and cross-country skiing along forest roads.

You can sample the history of the Sheridan area in several ways. The **Trail's End Museum**, finished in superb carved woodwork, is the former home of cattle baron (and Wyoming governor and senator) John B. Kendrick. The **Bradford Brinton Memorial Ranch** is the preserved reminder of the days of the remittance men who settled the area and the ranches they developed. **Fort Phil Kearney**, south of town via Interstate 90 and Highway 87, is the site of the army fort that had the bloodiest times of any army establishment during the settling of the West. It was besieged by Chief Red Cloud on many occasions, in the struggle to protect the Bozeman Trail. The site is open year-round from dawn to dusk. During summer months, the fort's visitor center and State Museum are open to the public. Eleven miles north of Sheridan and just south of Ranchester, the **Connor Battlefield** is a reminder of the famous Tongue River Battle, in which General Patrick Connor and 400 troops of the Powder River Expedition surprised the Cheyenne and Arapahoe villages of Black Bear and Old Devil.

Sheridan has a good selection of motels and B & B homes (see page 312). There is a KOA Kampground and RV park in town, and forest campgrounds are located in Bighorn National Forest to the west (see specific drives for locations). Several guest ranches offer riding in the Big Horn Range and in neighboring cattle country. **Masters Ranch** is located three miles west of Ranchester (north of Sheridan) on Highway 14. There, you'll find lodging plus teepee sleeping and B & B and barbecue dinners. **Eaton's Ranch** is at Wolf, 18 miles west of town, with cabins, a dining room in the lodge, pool, barbecues, and fishing. **Spear-O-Wigwam Ranch** is in the Bighorn National Forest, 30 miles southwest of town; it's a small ranch with modern rooms.

Thermopolis

If you're a hot springs fan, as I am, you must read this section!

One of the preeminent hot springs establishments in America is located in the central Wyoming region where the Owl Creek Mountains meet the Big Horn Range at the Wind River. Thermopolis is the location of **Hot Springs State Park**, containing not one but three bathhouses, all of which are served with hot water from the world's largest single mineral hot spring. **Big Spring** pours out millions of gallons of water each day, at a temperature of 135°F. You can walk to the spring beside steaming mineral terraces. There are two commercial plunge operations and a free state bathhouse. This is a legacy of Chief Washakie, whose tribe originally owned the property but gave it to the state on the understanding that the public would be allowed free access to the waters.

A herd of buffalo roams the hills in the state paddock behind the hot spring pools. The hot springs park has picnic facilities, a hotel (Holiday Inn), and playgrounds. It's a delightful place to spend a day (or more) and it's particularly beautiful early in the morning when the cool air meets the hot water on the travertine terraces, causing ghostly clouds of mist to hover over the park. In town, the **Hot Springs Museum** houses artifacts of the area's history, including the original signed treaty that gave the hot springs to the people of Wyoming.

And there's more to Thermopolis than the hot spring. U.S. Highway 20, east of town, runs through the **Wind River Canyon**, a scenic and geological standout. The water enters the canyon on the south as the Wind River. As it leaves the canyon, it becomes the Big Horn. The brisk waters of the Wind River have carved a 2,000-foot-deep channel. The canyon divides the two mountain ranges. Highway signs point out the formations along the rock walls.

South of the canyon, **Boysen State Park** offers day-use picnicking areas and overnight camping. The park is surrounded by the Wind River Reservation, and Boysen Lake is attractive to anglers because of the plentiful supply of trout and walleye. You'll find a swimming beach and a marina on the lake.

To the north of town, the Gooseberry Formations and Painted Desert show the result of erosion that has sculpted the arid landscape. The skeleton of *eohippus,* a prehistoric horse, was found near here.

Thermopolis has several private RV parks and campgrounds. The motels in town have moderate and budget rates.

Thermopolis is on the Big Horn Mountains Drive (page 270). This route is one of two that lead from Sheridan on Interstate 90 through Thermopolis and Shoshone to Dubois and Grand Teton National Park. If you have time to spend a few days traveling from the east to Grand Teton and Yellowstone, we highly recommend these combined drives—with a stop in Thermopolis for hot springs soaking.

Where to Eat

The **Safari Club** in the Holiday Inn (Hot Springs State Park) provides a good place to eat while relaxing after a long soak. You can enjoy a full range of American dishes and a Sunday buffet.

Yellowstone National Park

The first and still the most popular national park in the United States, Yellowstone sits astride the Continental Divide in northwestern Wyoming, edging over the borders of Montana and Idaho.

This is the world's foremost geothermal region, where molten rock rises close to the surface, providing the heat that results in the hundreds of geysers, fumaroles, and mudpots that dot the park. This is an area where catastrophic volcanic eruptions brought immense changes to the landscape, including the great caldera (a collapsed volcano) that created Yellowstone Lake about 600,000 years ago. Every year, the abundant snowfall melts into the ground and then the water percolates upward, forced back through the ground as steam. **Old Faithful**—the world's most beloved geyser—is the prime example of this geothermal action.

The park is largely situated on a high mountain plateau, with large meadows and subalpine forests. You'll see several large lakes, roaring rivers, and high waterfalls. The area attracted early explorers; the first were fur trappers and mountain men (Jim Bridger, John Colter, and others) who relished the beauty and natural wonder of the region. Prospectors came to the park area but moved farther west. The movement to create a national park and wilderness preserve began when the first Hayden Expedition of 1871 helped to convince Congress to declare the area a national park in 1872. The early developers of the park were more interested in geology than in the abundant wildlife that lived on the mountain slopes and meadows of Yellowstone. The elk, deer, bears, bison, coyotes, antelope, mountain lions, and eagles, among many other species, provide visitors with the thrill of meeting wildlife face to face. Some of the elk are so tame now that they summer on the lawn of the main park visitor center in Mammoth Hot Springs.

In addition to the geysers and colorful geothermal pools, the park contains some of the most dramatic geological scenes in the country, including the **Grand Canyon of the Yellowstone**, the **Upper and Lower Falls**, several examples of petrified forest, the **Cascades of the Firehole River**, and the magnificent **Absaroka Mountains**.

Yellowstone receives 2.5 million visitors each year. Because the great majority see the park during the summer months, the public facilities can become quite crowded. If it is at all possible, we advise you to plan your visit for the spring or fall, when things are a bit calmer. Wilderness such as Yellowstone should be enjoyed with a certain freedom from falling over other people or vice versa. Fall is a particularly enjoyable season at Yellowstone, as the aspens turn into gold and the brisk mountain air wakes your senses. The facilities open during summer months operate until mid-September, making the two weeks after Labor Day a perfect time to visit. The late May and early June period is an equally pleasant time to enjoy the solitude. The park roads closed in winter open for traffic by late April/early May and close around October 31.

The Yellowstone Park Loop Road, which takes you to most of the attractions, is covered in detail in the scenic drive on page 256.

Park Features

Geysers and hot springs are in the western side of the park; many of them are along the 50 miles of road that connects Mammoth Hot Springs (near Gardiner, Montana) and Old Faithful. This area comprises several geothermal basins, which have more than 250 geysers and as many as 10,000 other known features. The **Mammoth Hot Springs Terraces**, near the main visitor center, are best seen from trails and boardwalks. **Upper Terrace Drive** is a 1.5-mile road that winds among large travertine terraces built by active and extinct hot springs. The **Main Terrace Area** features a series of loop trails with boardwalks that take visitors through active terraces and around some old and now-dead springs. The Mammoth area plays host, during the winter, to some of the park's wildlife that come down from their summer range to this warmer climate.

South of Mammoth is the **Norris Geyser Basin**, the hottest of the geyser areas and the oldest. The basin features two major trails: one is around the **Porcelain Basin**, a distance of three-quarters of a mile, and the other is **Back Basin Trail**, which leads 1.5 miles past several notable geysers including Steamboat, Echinus, and Porkchop. A museum is near the parking lot, beside Bathtub Spring.

The **Upper Geyser Basin** is the home of Old Faithful and many other geysers, hot springs, fumaroles, and mudpots. It's located on the loop road just west of Grant Village and West Thumb. Old Faithful erupts more frequently than most of the other large geysers, every 45 to 90 minutes. Its eruptions last two to five minutes, and the spout reaches a height of over 100 feet—as much as 180 feet. Other large geysers in the basin include Castle, Grand, Giant, Beehive, and Daisy. The Upper Geyser Basin is the location for several lodges and eating facilities, centered in the Old Faithful area.

The **Midway Geyser Basin**, north of the Upper Basin, features the Grand Prismatic Spring and Excelsior Geyser. North of here you'll see **Firehole Lake**—a large hot spring—and the **Fountain Paint Pot**, along with several notable geysers including Clepsydra, White Dome, Great Fountain, and Steady. These features are found along a short loop (Firehole Lake Drive) off the main park highway.

The **Grand Canyon of the Yellowstone** extends from Canyon Village—near the center of the park—to Tower Junction on the north park road. The most spectacular section of the canyon is seen from a series of viewpoints along the North Rim and South

Rim, in the Canyon Village area. This area includes the Upper and Lower Falls.

Yellowstone Lake has 110 miles of shoreline and is North America's largest alpine lake. Fishing Bridge, Lake Village, and Bridge Bay are located at the north end of the lake, while West Thumb and Grant Village are on the western bay called West Thumb. Visitor facilities are available in both areas. Scenic picnic areas are spread along the loop road between the two main centers. You'll find a museum devoted to the park's birds at Fishing Bridge. Displays at the Grant Village are centered on the Yellowstone wilderness areas. Backcountry permits are available at the ranger station.

The **Park Headquarters** is at Mammoth Hot Springs. The visitor center here offers advice on "doing" the park and has films and a good selection of booklets about the park and trail guides. Other visitor centers and information desks are at Grant Village, Fishing Bridge, Canyon Village, Old Faithful, and the Norris Geyser Basin.

Park Trails

Many trails throughout the park lead to various features and into the backcountry. Most visitors walk along some of the self-guiding trails that have been laid out in the more popular scenic areas. These include the Mammoth Hot Springs Terraces, Norris Geyser basin, Calcite Springs Overlook and Tower Fall (1.5 miles south of Tower Junction), and the Mud Volcano Trail, which is six miles north of Fishing Bridge, leading to several thermal features including Dragon's Mouth. Walking trails wind along both rims of the Grand Canyon. The South Rim Drive takes you to the trailhead for Uncle Tom's Trail.

For those who want to experience more of the wilderness in the park, many trails lead from the loop road or the entrance roads to the mountains and into the central part of the park, called the Thorofare Area. For long hikes and overnight trips, you must register with one of the park ranger stations. The trailheads for some of the most popular (and moderately easy) hikes are found in the Yellowstone Loop Road logs (pages 258–261). A good guide to the full range of trails in the park is *Yellowstone Trails, A Hiking Guide* by Mark Marschall, published by The Yellowstone Association ($4.95). You can purchase this book in the park visitor centers.

Wildlife

Viewing wildlife is problematic at times. Early morning and late evening are the best times to view the park's wild animals. Elk are seen at Mammoth Hot Springs (sometimes on the lawn) and north and south of Madison. Bison feed in the Lamar Valley, in the northeast corner of the park, in the Hayden Valley north of Fishing Bridge, and north of Old Faithful. Yellowstone has around 300 bighorn sheep, which are seen on the rocky slopes and cliffs, mainly in the Mount Washburn area. Moose are often seen in the Fishing Bridge area, north and south of Madison, and near the south entrance to the park. The grizzly and black bears inhabit the backcountry and are not normally seen by park visitors. Pronghorn antelope live in the northern reaches of the park, above the north road that leads from Mammoth Hot Springs to the northeast entrance.

Boating and Fishing

Permits for all boats and fishing are required. Permits can be obtained at the south entrance, Lewis Lake, Grant Village, Bridge Bay Marina, the Lake Ranger Station, and Mammoth Hot Springs. Yellowstone Lake has the largest supply of cutthroat trout in the world but because of bear problems, parts of the lake have been closed to fishing. Consult the lake ranger station or the Fishing Bridge visitor center for fishing closures.

Where to Stay

There are campgrounds in the major areas of interest in the park, and lodge and motel accommodations are available in major park centers. All campgrounds are operated by the National Parks

Service and all campsites are obtained on a first-come, first-served basis except for the Bridge Bay Campground, which is on a reservation system. You'll find campgrounds at Mammoth Hot Springs, Madison, Norris, Slough Creek, Tower Fall, Fishing Bridge (RV park), Canyon Village (RV park), Grant Village, Indian Creek, Pebble Creek, and Lewis Lake. The two RV parks are for hard-sided vehicles only due to seasonal bear intrusions. The Bridge Bay Campground is on the national Ticketron reservation system, in effect from mid-May through Labor Day. Reservations may be made no more than eight weeks in advance. Phone 800-452-1111 between 8 A.M. and midnight (Central time) or write Ticketron, P.O. Box 617516, Chicago, IL 60661-7516.

The park concessionaire operates several lodges and motels inside the park:

- **Mammoth Hot Springs Hotel**
  Rooms and cabins, open from late May through mid-September.

- **Old Faithful Inn**
  Rooms, open from early May through mid-October.

- **Old Faithful Lodge**
  Cabins, open from late May through mid-September.

- **Old Faithful Snow Lodge**
  Rooms and cabins, open from mid-May through late October.

- **Grant Village**
  Rooms, open from early June through late September.

- **Lake Lodge**
  Cabins, open from mid-June through mid-September.

- **Canyon Lodge**
  Cabins, open from mid-June through Labor Day.

- **Roosevelt Lodge**
  Cabins, open from early June through Labor Day.

For all of these indoor accommodations, you should make reservations (well in advance for summer bookings) through TW Recreational Services at (307) 344-7311.

Accommodations close to the park entrances are available in West Yellowstone and Gardiner, Montana, at Pahaska Indian Village, a large motel near the west gate, and in Cooke City, just outside the northeast gate.

You'll also find cabin and motel accommodations in **Grand Teton National Park** just south of Yellowstone. See pages 287–288 for locations. Unless you're visiting the park for just a day or two or camping, a trip to Yellowstone takes some planning in order to fully enjoy your stay.

Wyoming
Places to Stay

S ome of the most interesting places to stay in Wyoming are the guest ranches, which offer various packages for families and groups. Call ahead for rates and reservations. Some rates are not quoted because of the wide variation. Some wonderful bed and breakfast homes offer special historical flavor and significance. We also include some of the more standard motels.

BUFFALO

Crossroads HoJo Inn
75 North Bypass
Buffalo, WY 82834
(307) 684-2256

60 units with dining room, cocktail lounge, pool. ($$)

Deer Park Campground
Buffalo, WY 82834
(307) 684-5722

This large private facility is located half a mile west of I-80, exit 58, on Highway 16. Sites for RVs, trailers, grassy sites for tents, store, laundry, pool.

H. F. Bar Ranch
Saddlestring, WY 82840
(307) 684-2487

Home to the Horton family since 1902, this ranch located 15 miles northwest of town has rustic cabins with baths and family-style meals in the ranch house. Trout fishing, elk and deer hunting in fall, mountain camp. ($$)

Paradise Guest Ranch
P.O. Box 790
Buffalo, WY 82834
(307) 684-7876

Reservations are required for these luxury log cabins with family-style meals and cocktails in the log dining room. Many activities are available from riding to kids programs. ($$$)

Rafter Y Ranch
P.O. Box 19
Banner, WY 82832
(307) 683-2221

Reservations are also required for this beautifully situated ranch in the Big Horn foothills, 18 miles northwest of Buffalo. Log cabins, fireplaces, meals at main house, and many activities are available. ($$$)

V Bar F Cattle Ranch
1773 Tipperary Road
P.O. Box 121
Buffalo, WY 82834
(307) 758-4382

This B & B ranch has a guest house for up to six people or a room in the ranch house where meals are served. Summer and winter activities are available. ($$$)

CASPER

Bessemer Bend
Bed and Breakfast
5120 Alcova Route
P.O. Box 40
Casper, WY 82604
(307) 265-6819

Ten miles west of Casper, this B & B has two guest rooms, a recreation room, and fishing. ($$)

Casper Hilton Inn
I-25 at North Poplar
Casper, WY 82601
(307) 266-6000

A large deluxe inn with pool, dining room, cocktail lounge, TV. ($$$)

Casper Inn
I-25 at Center Street
Casper, WY 82601
(307) 235-5713

A large motel with dining room, lounge, and pool. ($$)

Sage and Sand
901 West Yellowstone
Casper, WY 82601
(307) 237-2088

Budget rates and kitchens in some rooms are the attractions here. ($)

Sand Creek Ranch Outfitters
Alcova, WY 82620
(307) 234-9597

Open year-round, this working cattle ranch 68 miles southwest of Casper on Highway 220 has three cabins for up to 18 people, and hunting in fall.

CHEYENNE

Big Horn Motel
2004 East Lincoln Way
Cheyenne, WY 82001
(307) 632-3122

A budget motel with some cooking rooms. ($)

Drummond's Bed and Breakfast
399 Happy Jack Road,
Route 210
Cheyenne, WY 82007
(307) 634-6042

A wide range of activities are offered here, from cross-country skiing to rock climbing. It's next to Curt Gowdy State Park, five miles from Medicine Bow National Forest. ($$)

Plains Hotel
1600 Central Avenue
Cheyenne, WY 82001
(307) 638-3311

Moderate to deluxe accommodations with dining room, cocktail lounge, TV, and phones. ($$ to $$$)

Restway Travel Park
4212 Whitney Road
Cheyenne, WY 82001
(307) 634-3811 or
800-443-2751

Located 1.5 miles east of Cheyenne, with tent and trailer sites (full hookups), heated pool, supplies.

CODY

Absaroka Mountain Lodge
P.O. Box 168
Wapiti, WY 82450
(307) 587-3963

Located 12 miles east of Yellowstone National Park and on the route from Cody, the lodge has a warm, log main building with good dining and a rustic saloon. The cabins are also of log construction. Riding, fishing, and hiking. ($$)

Castle Rock Ranch
412 Road 6 NS
Cody, WY 82414
(307) 587-2076

Located 17 miles southwest of Cody in the Southfork Valley, this is an adventure center with many activities including llama treks and kayaking. Full lodge facilities and private rooms. ($ to $$)

Hunter Peak Ranch
P.O. Box 1731
Cody, WY 82414
(307) 587-3711

A guest ranch in the Shoshone National Forest, 65 miles northeast of Cody, with cabins and lodge rooms, private baths, family-style meals, and riding. Open Memorial Day to Labor Day, also for fall hunting. ($$$)

Irma Hotel
1192 Sheridan Avenue
Cody, WY 82414
(307) 587-4221

A Cody original, built by Buffalo Bill for his daughter in 1902—then and now the town's social focal point. The rooms are large and comfortable, all with private bath. The dining room features a carved cherrywood back-bar, sent over as a gift from Queen Victoria, and serves excellent home-cooked meals including prime rib. ($ to $$)

The Lockhart Bed and Breakfast Inn
109 West Yellowstone Avenue
Cody, WY 82414
(307) 587-6074

Another place to stay with a historic focus, this was the home of author and world traveler Caroline Lockhart. Well restored and furnished with antiques, this B & B also features private baths and an all-you-can-eat breakfast. ($$)

DUBOIS

Absaroka Ranch
Dubois, WY 82513
(307) 455-2331

Located 16 miles northwest of town in the Wind River Valley, this ranch offers rustic cabins, sauna, and excellent food and wine. Riding, cookouts, hiking, and fishing.

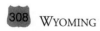

CM Ranch
Dubois, WY 82513
(307) 455-2331

Established in 1927, this ranch is only six miles from town and has accommodations for 50 guests in log cabins with showers. The ranch is near the Fitzpatrick and Washakie Wilderness Areas.

Diamond Bar E Ranch
P.O. Box 1601A
Dubois, WY 82513
(307) 455-3415

Located on Route 60 one-half mile south of Highway 26/287 and 15 miles west of Dubois, this rustic lodge has beautifully decorated rooms plus spectacular scenery with riding, fishing, barn dances, and snowmobiling.

GRAND TETON NATIONAL PARK

The principle concessionaire in the park is the Grand Teton Lodge Company, which operates the following lodges (guests of any of their operations may use facilities at the others). All are seasonal.

Jackson Lake Lodge
P.O. Box 240
Grand Teton National
Park, WY 83013
(307) 543-2855

This large deluxe lodge caters to kids with riding and float trips, but it also features a cocktail lounge, dining room, and pool. ($$ to $$$)

Jenny Lake Lodge
P.O. Box 240
Grand Teton National
Park, WY 83013
(307) 733-4647 or
(307) 543-3100

Cabins in this spectacular location are rustic but luxurious and rates (also luxurious) include two meals a day at the lodge, known for its excellent continental cuisine. Young children are not encouraged here. ($$$)

Moose Head Ranch
P.O. Box 214
Moose, WY 83012
(307) 733-3141

This ranch not only provides a horse for every guest (40), but also provides opportunities for fishing, photography, and cookouts. For reservations before June 1, write the Mettlers at Rural Route 7, P.O. Box 1362, Tallahassee FL 32308, or call (904) 877-1431. ($$$)

Signal Mountain Lodge
P.O. Box 50
Grand Teton National
Park, WY 83013
(307) 543-2831

Located in the park, this resort on the shores of Jackson Lake has motel units and cabins, some with kitchens. Also a dining room and lounge. ($ to $$$)

GREEN RIVER

Mustang Motel
550 East Flaming
Gorge Way
Green River, WY 82935
(307) 875-2468

This moderately priced motel has basic accommodations with pool, TV, and phones. ($ to $$)

Tex's Travel Camp
Jamestown Service Road
Green River, WY 82935
(307) 875-2630

A private campground 30 minutes from the Flaming Gorge Recreation Area on Jamestown Service Road. Take exit 89 west of Green River on Highway 374, three miles west to campground. Or take exit 85, then to one mile east on Highway 374. Open May 1 to October 1, with fishing, rafting, laundry, grassy sites.

JACKSON

Heart Six Ranch
P.O. Box 70
Moran, WY 83013
(307) 543-2477

One of the many guest ranches in the area, this one is 35 miles north of town and at 7500 feet overlooks the Buffalo River and the Tetons. The cabins for 35 to 50 guests have been newly refurbished. The usual activities for children and adults plus float trips. ($$$)

Jackson Hole Campground
(307) 733-2927

With many trailer and tent sites, this facility also features a swimming pool and playground.

310 WYOMING

Painted Porch Bed and Breakfast
P.O. Box 3965
Jackson, WY 83001
(307) 733-1981

This B & B inn is a big old colonial home built in 1900 on seven acres, located six miles from Jackson. Recently renovated, each room has color TV, antique furnishings, and private bath. Two have Japanese soaking tubs. (**$$ to $$$**)

Sundance Inn Bed and Breakfast
135 West Broadway
P.O. Box 1
Jackson, WY 83001
(307) 733-3444

This B & B is centrally located in downtown Jackson within walking distance of shops and restaurants. Breakfast and evening refreshments are served in the lobby. (**$ to $$$+**)

Wort Hotel
50 North Glenwood
P.O. Box 69
Jackson, WY 83001
(307) 733-2190 or
800-322-2727

If you want to be in the thick of things downtown, try the Wort Hotel—it's been in business for more than 50 years. The hotel houses JJ's Silver Dollar Bar and Grill. (**$$$**)

LARAMIE

Annie Moore's Guest House
819 University Avenue
Laramie, WY 82070
(307) 721-4177

Bedrooms sharing baths are to be had in this bright B & B that is close to downtown and the university. (**$$**)

Camelot Motel
I-80 at Snowy Range Exit
Laramie, WY 82070
(307) 721-8860

A budget-priced motel allows pets but has no cooking facilities. Units with TV and phones. (**$**)

Riverside Campground
Off I-80 at Curtis and McCue streets
Laramie, WY 82070
(307) 721-7405

Features tenting near the Laramie River, playground, laundry, store, full hookups.

The Sunset Inn
1104 South 3rd Street
Laramie, WY 82070
(307) 742-3741

This motel features some cooking units, as well as a cocktail lounge, pool, and TV; pets are allowed. (**$ to $$**)

Two Bars Seven Ranch P.O. Box 67-W Tie Siding, WY 82084 (307) 742-6072	Located about 30 miles south and west of town (take U.S. 287), this historic ranch offers many activities in a lovely mountain setting. Open year-round. ($$$)

RIVERTON

Days Inn Riverton 909 West Main Street Riverton, WY 82501 (307) 856-9677	A budget-priced motel, open year-round. ($)
Edna's Bed and Breakfast 53 North Fork Road Lander, WY 82520 (307) 332-3175	Located five miles northwest of Lander, south of Riverton and near the Atlantic City ghost town in the Wind River range. A working cattle ranch with upstairs bedrooms with shared bath. Family-style breakfast. Open year-round. ($$ to $$$)
Miner's Delight Inn Rural Route 62 P.O. Box 205 Atlantic City, WY 82520 (307) 332-3513	A B & B inn right in Atlantic City, a ghost town. This was the historic Carpenter Hotel, built in 1901. Dinners served nightly. ($ to $$)
Rudy's Camper Court 622 East Lincoln Riverton, WY 82501 (307) 856-9764	Open all year, nearby museum, shopping, golf, with full hookups. Located half a block west of U.S. 26.
Sundowner Station 1616 North Federal Street (307) 856-6503 or 800-874-1116	This motel operation has 60 units with dining room, lounge, and pool. TV and phones in rooms. ($ to $$)

SHERIDAN

Arrowhead Lodge P.O. Box 390 Dayton, WY 82836 (307) 655-2388	In the Bighorn National Forest, west of Sheridan and Dayton, this lodge has a dining room and bar and a small store. Accommodations are modest (and inexpensive) motel rooms and some very rus-

tic cabins, mainly used by snowmobilers when the forest trails open after snowfall. ($)

Eaton's Ranch
270 Eaton Ranch Road
Wolf, WY 82844
(307) 655-9285

Located 18 miles west of Sheridan, the cabins here all feature private baths, and some have living rooms. Main lodge has dining room and coffee shop; also a store and pool. ($)

Guest House Motel
2007 North Main Street
Sheridan, WY 82801
(307) 674-7496

A budget motel with pool; pets allowed; two cooking units. ($)

Kilbourne Kastle Bed and Breakfast
320 South Main Street
Sheridan, WY 82801
(307) 674-8716

A downtown location, open year-round, with three bedrooms and two baths; some rooms for up to four people. ($$)

Master's Ranch
Ranchester, WY 82839
(307) 655-2386

This working ranch is open for guests from May to November, with accommodations in the lodge or in teepees. Features riding, hayrides, chuckwagon breakfasts, and barbecued dinners. Located three miles west of Ranchester on U.S. 14, on Bozeman Trail. ($$$)

Mill Inn Motel
2161 Coffeen Avenue
Sheridan, WY 82801
(307) 672-6401

This motel has the distinction of once having been a flour mill! It's open year-round. All rooms have queen beds. ($ to $$)

Spear-O-Wigwam Ranch
P.O. Box 1081
Sheridan, WY 82801
(307) 672-0002 (winter) or
(307) 674-4496
(summer)

Exclusive accommodations set in the Bighorn National Forest, offering excellent food and riding. Ernest Hemingway stayed here to finish *A Farewell to Arms*. ($$$)

THERMOPOLIS

Best Western Moonlighter Motel
600 Broadway
Thermopolis, WY 82443
(307) 864-2321

A pleasant older motel with pool, and movies; pets are allowed. ($)

Holiday Inn of the Waters
Hot Springs State Park
Thermopolis, WY 82443
(307) 864-3131 or
1-800-HOLIDAY

For a deluxe stay (at a moderate price) right inside the Hot Springs State Park, try this inn. Features include hot tubs, hot mineral pool, and exercise room, as well as the usual amenities. ($$)

Latchstring Campground
Star Route 3
P.O. Box 178
Thermopolis, WY 82443
(307) 864-5262

Heated pool, plus the nearby hot pools in the state park. Full hookups and other visitor facilities.

YELLOWSTONE NATIONAL PARK

Reservations Department
Yellowstone National
Park, WY 82190-9989
(307) 344-7311

The authorized concessionaire for the National Park is TW Recreational Services. For a listing of the lodges, see page 303. ($ to $$$)

Colorado

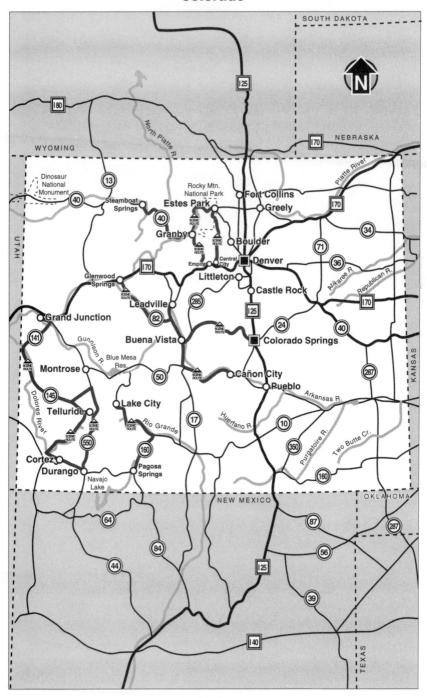

Colorado
Drives

W hat were virtually impenetrable lands to the explorers of the early 1800s had long been occupied by Native American hunters. They first came from the plains, following the huge herds of game through the Rockies, and some remained in the mountains as nomadic hunters and gatherers. Other tribes settled down to farm and to build remarkable cities, including the cliff-dwelling communities of what is now the Four Corners region including southwestern Colorado. It is thought that Native American tribes have lived in the Colorado Rockies for at least 15,000 years.

Spanish explorers came to Colorado in the 1600s searching for gold. Not finding it, they left; fur traders and trappers followed, settling the mountains from the 1830s.

The discovery of gold near the present site of Denver in 1858 brought hordes of prospectors and miners across the great plains to central Colorado, and during the next half century, hundreds of millions of dollars worth of gold and silver were extracted from the mines at Cripple Creek, Central City, Leadville, Creede, and Telluride, among others. The railways came to the territory in the 1870s, and Colorado gained statehood on August 1, 1876.

The following ten scenic drives throughout central and western Colorado have been selected to emphasize the historical perspective. We visit the former mining towns as well as national parks and monuments displaying spectacular scenery. The routes lead to or near Colorado's major ski and summer resorts. If you follow all 10 routes, you'll cross the Continental Divide more than a dozen times, with a different scenic thrill on each occasion.

Middle Park Drive

Empire to Steamboat Springs

The massive Front Range of the Rockies runs north to south, providing a dramatic backdrop for the cities of Boulder and Denver. It is also the range that saw the first of the gold and silver rushes in the state.

This first Colorado drive slices through the west flank of the range, from the old mining village of **Empire**, through some of the most popular skiing country in Colorado at and near the community of Winter Park, and to the lake recreation area at Granby, just south of Rocky Mountain National Park. While visiting Granby, you may wish to explore the **Arapahoe National Recreation Area** and pursue some water activity in Granby and Grand Lakes. This is where the tributaries of the Colorado River come down from the Front Range and Medicine Bow Mountains, with the river itself leading southwest through the valley that makes up most of Grand County. This large valley—called **Middle Park**—is not the same kind of flat valley found in North Park and South Park; it is full of geological points of interest. Middle Park has its southern boundary at the towns of Winter Park and Fraser.

Our route follows the Colorado River as it makes its way through Middle Park, picking up volume and speed, passing by the small communities of White Sulphur Springs and Kremmling. However, our sojourn beside the Colorado is not long-lived. The highway turns north at Kremmling to lead through the arid high desert of the Pinto Valley before climbing again to Muddy Pass and Rabbit Ears Pass, crossing the Continental Divide twice within a distance of 10 miles. From here, it's downhill and only 28 miles to the town of **Steamboat Springs**, a year-round resort area and the home of the U.S. Olympic ski team.

The southern part of the drive—from Interstate 70 to north of Winter Park—leads through the Arapahoe National Forest. Here are many excellent campgrounds and recreation sites, some accessed by taking backroads to the east and west of the highway.

The Arapahoe National Recreation Area is a few miles off the highway near the town of Granby with several additional backroads leading to forest campgrounds and small mountain lakes. A ranger station in Granby has information on forest campsites, trails, and other recreation opportunities.

At Muddy Pass on the Continental Divide, the highway enters Routt National Forest, which has several campgrounds on the descent to Steamboat Springs.

The town of **Winter Park** is the recreation capital of Middle Park. This long, narrow town lies on both sides of Highway 40 with the community of Fraser three miles to the north. The two towns share a full range of lodges, motels, and other services that cater to the large number of skiers who come here throughout the winter months. The **Silver Creek** ski area is 17 miles north of Winter Park. This is a family-oriented operation with the Inn at Silver Creek located at the slopes.

The **Winter Park Resort** is located just south of town. Comprising three separate mountains (Vasquez Ridge, Mary Jane, and Winter Park), this huge area has fine powder skiing on Mary Jane and many easier runs on the other hills. The view from the top of Winter Park Ski Area is magnificent, with panoramic scenes in all directions.

Cross-country skiing is also a highlight of the Winter Park area, with groomed trails at the top of the **Timberline Ski Area** (at Berthoud Pass), including skiing along Sevenmile Trail, an old wagon road from Denver. You'll find more groomed trails at the **Granby/Silver Creek Nordic Center** at the north end of the Middle Park Valley. Just 12 miles north of Winter Park is the **Tabernash/Snow Mountain Ranch Nordic Center** with 30 miles of groomed trails.

There is a hot springs pool in the community of **Hot Sulphur Springs**. Unfortunately, the condition of the pools has deteriorated over the years, but the historic Riverside Hotel and the local historical museum provide an interesting stay.

HIGHWAY LOG
Empire to Steamboat Springs
170 miles (274 KM)—3 hours, 30 minutes

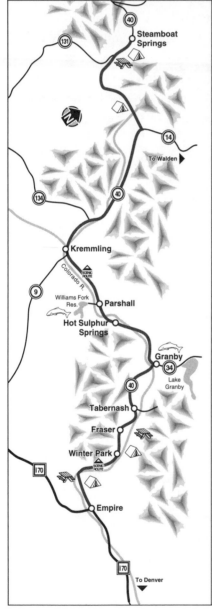

Junction–Interstate 70 and Highway 40 This is the Empire exit, 42 miles west of Denver. Our drive leads north toward Winter Park and Granby. After passing through the small community of Empire, Hwy. 40 follows the path of Wise Fork (Clear Creek), soon entering the Arapaho National Forest.

Clear Creek Picnic Area To the south of the highway.

Mizpah Forest Campground To south of the highway. The road goes through several switchbacks while climbing the Vasquez Mountains.

Berthoud Pass (el. 11,315 feet) Crossing the Continental Divide.

Ski Areas Three ski areas along the hwy. between the pass and Winter Park: Timberline, Mary Jane, and Winter Park.

Robber's Roost Campground Picnic Area

Idlewild Campground

Winter Park This resort community has a range of visitor services, including gas, motels, restaurants, and stores.

Fraser Small community with gas, cafe, motel.

Tabernash Another village, with gas, cafe, store.

Junction–Meadow Creek Forest Road Leads east to the Meadow

Creek Reservoir and Jumbo Lake Trail (beyond the reservoir).

Silver Creek Ski Area To the east.

Granby Town with gas, motels, cafes, stores. Granby is the gateway to the Lake Granby Recreation Area, centered on Lake Granby to the north.

Junction–Highway 34 To Grand Lake and Estes Park. This road leads through Rocky Mountain National Park (see the scenic drive on page 326).

Junction–Highway 125 Leads north, across Willow Creek Pass through the Arapahoe National Wildlife Reserve and on to Walden.

Hot Sulphur Springs (el. 7,647 feet) Gas, motel, cafe, store, museum, hot pool. The road now follows the canyon route of the Colorado River.

Parshall Village with gas, cafe, store.

Junction–Road to Williams Fork Reservoir To the south at milepost 197.

Kremmling Town with gas, cafes, stores, National Forest ranger station.

Junction–Highway 134 To Toponas and Yampa (west), an alternate backcountry route to Steamboat Springs. Hwy. 40 runs through a stretch of badlands as it crosses the Pinto Valley with the Park Range of the Rockies to the east.

Junction–Road 103 Leads east to Chimney Rock, ending at the Continental Divide.

Muddy Pass Lake (el. 8,772 feet) Pulloff at junction of County Road 14, which leads east to Walden. From the junction, the distance to Steamboat Springs is 26 miles.

Parking Area View overlooking valley, to the east.

Rabbit Ears Pass (el. 9,426 feet) Continental Divide.

Junction–Buffalo Park Forest Road Leads south, with access to Red Dirt Reservoir.

Walton Creek Campground To south of highway.

Meadows Campground To the south.

Rabbit Ears Pass West summit

Ferndale Picnic Area To the east, halfway down the long descent.

Steamboat Springs This resort town is one of the nation's premier ski areas and a pleasant summer vacation spot. The community has a full range of resort lodges, motels, and campgrounds along with gas, restaurants, and stores.

Peak to Peak Drive

Central City to Estes Park

This drive includes one of the state's designated scenic byways and begins at the Empire exit of Interstate 70, leading through Clear Creek Canyon on Highway 6. Then, Highway 117 runs northwest to Black Hawk and the sideroad to the historic town of Central City. This is the area where Colorado gold was first discovered, in what was then called Gregory's Gulch (named after Georgia prospector John H. Gregory). Several mining camps were established in the gulch (Hoosier City, Dogtown, Nevadaville, among others) but Central City—named for its position in the middle of the gulch—is the only community that has survived to this day. For a few years, Central City was the largest town in the territory, but it was eclipsed by Denver in the mid-1860s. Just one mile west of Black Hawk, Central City is a must stop on every visitor's itinerary.

The drywall stone buildings in Central City and Black Hawk are the legacy of the Scottish pioneers who flocked to the area during the gold rush. The famed **Central City Opera House** is still in operation as a magnet for opera lovers during its annual summer season. You'll find a wonderful old historic downtown district, charmingly antique restaurants and antique shops, museums, and historic homes to visit. The **Toll Gate Saloon** is more than 100 years old. The Columbine Campground, two miles northwest of town in the Arapaho National Forest, has sites for tenters and RV drivers.

Back on Highway 119, heading toward Meeker and Estes Park, are several recreation sites offering an amazing range of activities. **Golden Gate Canyon State Park** is located seven miles north of Black Hawk and two miles east on Gap Road. You'll find two campgrounds here as well as primitive (walk-in) sites. Other campgrounds are maintained by the Arapaho National Forest, including Pickle Gulch Campground (three miles north of Black Hawk and one mile west). Cold Springs Campground is on the highway, four miles north of Black Hawk.

The highway then enters the **Roosevelt National Forest**, with more campgrounds and recreation sites as the highway leads in a northwest direction. As the highway climbs through the Front Range, the views of the peaks are impressive. The highway passes small mountain communities including Rollinsville and Nederland. At an elevation of 8,236 feet, **Nederland** is in another old mining area with nearby ghost towns and the Eldora Ski Area, which features both downhill and cross-country activity. The **Barker Reservoir**, just to the east, offers fishing and water sports. The **Indian Peaks Wilderness** is located just west of Nederland with hiking trails and camping. This is a large wilderness area, which extends from Nederland to Estes Park and includes Brainard and Rainbow Lakes.

The old ghost town of **Caribou** is located west of Nederland with a working silver mine. Take Eldora Road—west from the highway—to the historic townsite of Eldora and to the Eldora Ski Resort. The route continues to climb. To the west of the highway is the University of Colorado's **Mountain Research Station**. This ecological facility is open to travelers during the summer months and offers guided tours. The Sourdough Trail has an access point here, while a forest road leads west to the Beaver Reservoir and another Sourdough trailhead.

Peaceful Valley has a ski hill and is the center for several trail adventures. A forest recreation area with camp sites is just west of Peaceful Valley. Just north of the village of Raymond, Highway 7 leads east to Lyons with access to the city of Boulder. This is a good alternate route to Estes Park (see below). We continue on Highway 7 northwest to **Meeker Park**. The Meeker Park Lodge (beside the highway) is a favorite stopping place.

Passing Long's Peak, the highway leads briefly through Rocky Mountain National Park and then descends into a valley and the town of **Estes Park**. It's the gateway to Rocky Mountain National Park and Trail Ridge Road, which leads through the park (see the scenic drive on page 326).

HIGHWAY LOG
Central City to Estes Park
85 miles (136 KM)—1 hour, 45 minutes

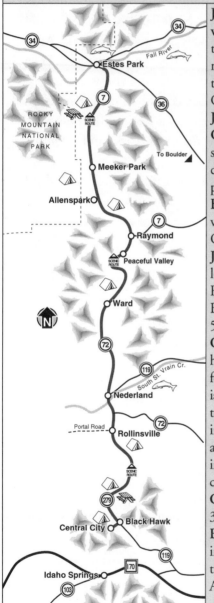

Junction–Interstate 70 and Highway 6 (exit #244) Take Hwy. 6 for two miles to Hwy. 119, through a narrow gorge and tunnel. The distance from I-70 to the town of Central City is 9 miles.

Junction–Road to Golden Gate Canyon State Park Three miles south of Black Hawk. A lodge with cafe is located just north of the park access road.

Black Hawk (el. 8,042 feet) Small village at junction of Hwy. 279. Gas, cafe, store, casino.

Junction–Highway 297 This road leads west to Central City (1 mile). From the junction, the distance to Boulder is 34 miles; to Estes Park, 53 miles.

Central City (el. 8,496 feet) This historic mining town is best known for its superb old opera house, which is a magnet for opera lovers. The town has other picturesque buildings, along with shops, a museum, and a range of visitor services including historic hotels, motels, casinos, cafes, and a ski area to the west.

Columbine Campground West, 3 miles.

Back on Highway 119 After leaving Black Hawk, the road climbs through hills and enters the Arapaho National Forest.

Golden Gate Canyon State Park To the east, at milepost 16. Camping, trails. Within the park are several features including the Panorama Point (viewpoint), Aspen Meadow Campground (tenting), and the Reverend's Ridge Campground (the main campground). All are one mile off the hwy.

Cafe At milepost 17.

Junction–Portal Road To the Moffat Tunnel and (for four-wheel-drive vehicles) on to Hwy. 40 south of Winter Park. At Rollinsville, milepost 21.

Kelly-Dahl Campground To the east of the highway.

Nederland Village with motel and cafe. At milepost 32.

Junction–Highway 119 Our drive continues north via Hwy. 72. Hwy. 119 leads east to Boulder (14 miles).

University of Colorado Mountain Research Station Via sideroad to the west, Sourdough Trail.

Junction–Road to Gold Hill To the east, at milepost 41 via Forest Road 106.

Ward (el. 9,253 feet) Village.

Brainard Lake Recreation Area To the west via Forest Road 119. Camping (trailers), trails, picnic area, swimming.

Junction–Forest Road To the west, to Sourdough Trail and Beaver Reservoir, a scenic backroad drive.

Junction–Forest Road To the east, leading to Ceran St. Vrain Trail and on to Jamestown.

Peaceful Valley Village at milepost 50. Ski area, campground. Forest recreation area to west with recreation sites.

Raymond Small town with services. The drive continues via Hwy. 7, leading northwest to Estes Park. Hwy. 7 also leads east to Lyons.

Overlook–Long's Peak

Junction–Sideroad to Ferncliff and Allenspark Gas, store, and cafe at milepost 9.

Olive Ridge Campground

Meeker Park Lodge and cafe. The village is just east of the highway with forest access (Big Elk Park).

Picnic Area To east of hwy. at milepost 11.

Long's Peak Campground In Rocky Mountain National Park via sideroad to the west.

Twin Sisters Trailhead Leads east from the highway.

Viewpoint To west of highway.

Lilly Lake Visitor Center In Rocky Mountain National Park.

Estes Park (el. 7,522 feet) This resort town is the gateway to Rocky Mountain National Park, with full services including gas, lodges, motels, camping, and golf.

Trail Ridge Drive

Estes Park to Granby

In Montana, mountain valleys are called "holes." Here in Colorado, they're called "parks." Estes Park is one of these mountain-enclosed meadows, named for Joel Estes, who "discovered" the area long after the Ute and Arapahoe people used the area as a hunting route. Because it is so accessible from the east, with no high passes to cross, the valley and the town have been a favorite resort area for many years.

The main attraction here is **Rocky Mountain National Park.** The park attracts more than three million visitors each year, and they come to see the incredible array of craggy peaks, the highest of which is Long's Peak at 14,255 feet. The shortest of the drives in this book (63 miles), this route leads first through the park and quickly ascends the mountains past the tree line to mountain tundra. The alpine valleys were glaciated, and you'll see several of these "parks" along the route of Trail Ridge Road. Other park highlights along the road include the following:

- **Hidden Valley**

  A downhill skiing area at the 9,200 foot level.

- **Many Parks Curve**

  At 9,600 feet, panoramic views of several alpine valleys with glacial moraines standing out as ridges. This is a favorite area for bird-watching; the species include ravens, jays (including Steller's and gray), and Clark's nutcracker with the distinctive white and black coloring.

- **Rainbow Curve**

  The road approaches the tree line and only small shrubs are seen at 10,830 feet.

- **Forest Canyon**

  A viewpoint provides a fine view of this canyon plus Hayden Gorge and Gorge Lakes. A short walk (10 minutes) leads to this overlook—on sunny days you can hear the squeal and maybe see the little pikas that inhabit the area.

- **The Rock Cut**
  At over 12,100 feet, the road crosses the top of the Rockies through alpine tundra. Here, the growing season is less than 10 weeks each year but regardless of the harsh environment, many flowering plants survive.

- **Tundra World Trail**
  Near the Rock Cut, this trail leads across the frozen ground. The return trip takes about 45 minutes.

- **Lava Cliffs**
  At a parking area, dark cliffs display volcanic rock, a reminder that the area was dominated by volcanoes between 26 and 28 million years ago. The cliffs were exposed by passing glaciers.

- **Alpine Visitor Center**
  At Fall River Pass, this is the site of a summer visitor center, which includes a park information desk, restaurant, and gift shop. A short trail leads to a panoramic view.

- **Milner Pass**
  Past Medicine Bow Curve, the highway crosses the Continental Divide. The Crater Trail leads for one mile to a bighorn sheep viewing location.

- **Fairview Curve**
  Views of the Colorado River near its source and the Kawuneeche Valley.

Just before reaching the park boundary, you'll find another visitor center, and by taking a sideroad just south of the boundary (Road 278), you can reach more park trails.

Now you're in Middle Park lake country as the highway passes near Shadow Mountain Lake, Grand Lake, and Lake Granby. The town of **Grand Lake** is a popular recreation town, with excellent fishing prospects.

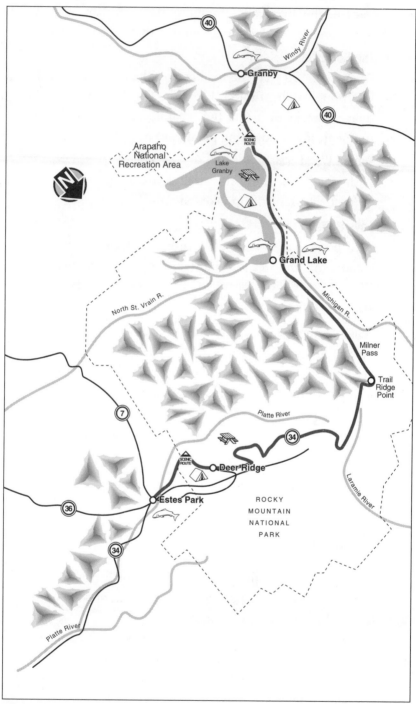

HIGHWAY LOG
Estes Park to Granby
63 miles (101 KM)—2 hours

National Park Entrance At the west edge of Estes Park on Hwy. 34 is the main visitor center for the park. As we head westward, the Beaver Meadows Entrance Station is just past the visitor center.

Junction–Road to Bear Lake Shuttle This road runs south just beyond the entrance station and leads to the Moraine Park Museum, several picnic areas, and the shuttle bus parking area. The bus takes visitors to several trailheads.

Deer Ridge Junction Site of a trailhead. A road leads northwest to Sheep Lakes and camping at Aspenglen. Old Falls River Road leads west (one-way) past Chasm Falls to the Alpine Visitor Center. This is a fine summer adventure drive.

Junction–Trail Ridge Road Our drive continues on Trail Ridge Road toward the alpine region, taking several switchbacks with superb views. The road is closed during winter months.

Overlook–Priest Canyon Tundra Trail This nature trail heads up to an elevation of 12,301 feet, north of the road.

Summit (el. 12,183 feet)

Viewpoint–Gore Ridge Overlook, west of the road.

Alpine Visitor Center At Fall River Pass, this summer operation offers food, ranger advice, and a gift shop, a well as exhibits and trails. The descent from Fall River Pass includes the spectacular Medicine Bow Curve and views of Poudre Lake.

Milner Pass (el. 10,758 feet) Crossing the Continental Divide. After passing through Fairview Curve, the road descends quickly through a series of switchbacks to follow the course of the North Fork of the Colorado River as it flows through the Kawuneeche Valley. You'll find several picnic areas in the valley; the Colorado River Trail and Timber Lake Trail are accessed from trailheads near the Colorado River crossing.

Junction–Road 278 This sideroad leads east to the town of Grand Lake and trails that lead north into the national park. Hwy. 34 now heads south beside Shadow Mountain Lake and Lake Granby to the Arapahoe National Recreation Area. The Stillwater Campground is close to the hwy., and you reach the Arapahoe Bay campsites via Road 6 at the south end of the lake.

Junction–Highway 40 To the town of Granby (one mile south).

Aspen Drive

Glenwood Springs to Leadville

The first of two drives to Leadville (from very different directions), this route begins at the Interstate 70 junction with Highway 82 east, at the town of Glenwood Springs.

The whole region bisected by this route was Ute country. The hot springs in the present town of **Glenwood Springs** were first used by the Ute people, who called the springs *Yampah*, or "Big Medicine." The resort was built here in the 1880s, with high society congregating at the Hotel Colorado. The town lies at the conjunction of the Roaring Fork and Colorado rivers; the hot springs bubble beside the Colorado. Many of the town's original buildings have been preserved, as have the huge hot springs pool and vapor caves (see page 384).

Running for the most part beside the Roaring Fork River, the route is an easy valley drive as far as the resort town of Aspen. With the Elk Mountains to the southwest, views from the first half of the drive are dominated by Mount Sopris, a multipeaked volcano with an elevation of 12,953 feet. The route takes us through several small farming communities, some with a mining history, like Basalt. The first of the major ski areas on the route is **Snowmass**, just a few miles west of Aspen. A sideroad leads to the ski village, located in the Maroon Bells/Snowmass Wilderness. Then there is **Aspen**, Colorado's premier ski and summer resort community.

From Aspen, the terrain changes dramatically as Highway 82 climbs toward Independence Pass. Now you're in the **White River National Forest**, moving up the flank of the Sawatch Range, on a road that is thrilling to drive during the summer but is not driveable during winter months. You'll find three excellent forest campgrounds on the ascent. This is the old toll route between Aspen and Leadville, which was superseded by the construction of railways in 1887. At the top is **Independence Pass**, above the tree line on the Continental Divide—at an elevation of more than 12,000 feet. The air is as thin as the coating of vegetation on the alpine tundra. The pass supposedly received its name from a gold strike on July 4, 1879, near the pass. The town of Independence was founded at the mining site, four miles west of the pass. The town closed before 1900, but you'll see several buildings below the road and the ghost town provides a popular stopping point.

You'll pass more forest campsites along the highway on the descent to the Arkansas River Valley as the route winds along Lake Creek, passing **Twin Lakes Reservoir** and another campground. Highway 82 ends at its junction with Highway 24; the town of Leadville lies 15 miles north of the junction. The route from Aspen to Leadville, through the Sawatch Range, is one of the finest drives in the Rockies, and if you're approaching Leadville from the east, we highly recommend the route across Independence Pass to Aspen. Just read the Highway Log that follows, from bottom to top.

One of the reasons that Aspen has remained the top resort town in the Rockies is its heritage, which has been so well preserved. Many of the old brick buildings from Aspen's early mining days have been carefully restored. As well, Aspen has developed a thriving summer arts program, which maintains its economy year-round. You won't find a week during the summer and winter seasons when something special isn't happening in this picturesque town at the head of the Roaring Fork Valley. So the town tends to be busy; visitors who wish to stay in Aspen in quieter times choose the "shoulder seasons" in the spring and fall when the town is more relaxed. The fall particularly is a splendid time to visit, when the aspen trees are in full blaze.

West of Aspen is **Castle Creek Road**, which meets Highway 82. Twelve miles up Castle Creek Road is the ghost town of Ashcroft. Mining magnate Horace Tabor developed the Tam O'Shanter and Montezuma silver mines here around 1880. In its heyday, the town had two thriving main streets, but only nine buildings remain today, cradled by the Elk Mountains.

HIGHWAY LOG
Glenwood Springs to Leadville
85 miles (136 KM)—1 hour, 45 minutes

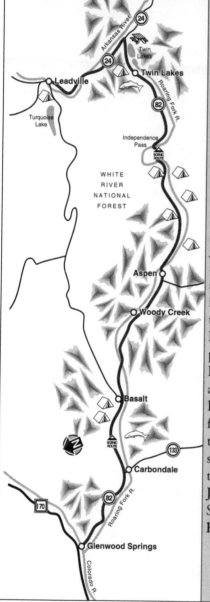

Glenwood Springs Famed for its hot spring pools, this town is a tourist center with full services. From the Interstate 70/Hwy. 82 junction, our drive leads southeast on Hwy. 82, passing through the White River National Forest with a good view of Mt. Sopris (el. 12,953 feet). A volcanic explosion blew the top off the mountain, creating several peaks. Aspen is 41 miles from the I-70 junction.

Carbondale Small community with gas, cafe, and store.

Junction–Highway 133 This scenic sideroad climbs 6,000 feet to Redstone and McClure Pass (el. 8,755 feet). The distance from the junction to Aspen is 30 miles.

Roaring Fork Restaurant at milepost 15.

Eljebel Cafes, gas, store, camping at milepost 19.

Ruedi Reservoir To the north via forest road (Frying Pan Road) from the village of Basalt (gas, cafe, store). Campsites are located along the forest road.

Junction–Edna Road Leads beside Sopris Creek to the south.

Roaring Fork River Bridge

Junction–Village Road At milepost 26.5. Leading south, the road leads eight miles to Snowmass Village and skiing.

Junction–Woody Creek Canyon Road This loop road (to the north) comes out to rejoin the hwy. at milepost 34.

Aspen Airport At milepost 37.

Junction–Maroon Creek Road Heads south to Maroon Hills and Buttermilk Mountain Ski Area.

Aspen (el. 7,908 feet) At milepost 40. This famed resort town has a full range of visitor services and an active summer arts program as well as winter ski activity.

White River National Forest The hwy. reenters the forest just beyond Aspen.

Difficult Campground Three miles east of Aspen (south of hwy. at milepost 45). The road climbs quickly with gates at milepost 47 (winter closure).

Weller Campground To the north with a trailhead south of the hwy. Another trail is one mile beyond the campground, leading to grottos, an ice cave, and picnic area.

Junction–Lincoln Creek Road A short, scenic backroad leading south.

Braille Nature Trailhead At milepost 54.

Lost Man Campground South, at milepost 55.

Lost Man Trailhead North of hwy.

Pulloff–Independence Ghost town (at milepost 57). The log cabins offer an interesting walk down the hill.

Trailhead At milepost 59.

Tree Line At milepost 60, with a good view of the valley.

Alpine Tundra At milepost 61.

Independence Pass (el. 12,095 feet) This famous pass is on the Continental Divide. A viewpoint offers views of the alpine tundra and surrounding peaks.

Viewpoint At milepost 67.5. The highway descends into the valley near the source of the Arkansas River.

Twin Lakes Reservoir A popular fishing spot.

Twin Lakes Tiny village with gas, cabins, and store.

White Star Campground At milepost 80, with fishing, boat ramp.

Mount Elbert Pumping Station Visitor center, picnicking beside reservoir.

Lakeview Campground To the north at milepost 81.

Junction–Highway 24 Our drive continues north to Leadville on Hwy. 24 (11 miles).

Leadville An historic mining town with an elevation of more than 11,000 feet. Gas, motels, saloons, cafes, stores, campgrounds, and RV parks.

Arkansas River Drive

Cañon City to Leadville

A city whose two main features are a penitentiary and a chasm, Cañon City is a quiet town lying in the arid Arkansas River Valley, south of the Tarryall Mountains. The chasm is Royal Gorge, a canyon eight miles long and more than 1,000 feet deep, carved in the rock by the Arkansas. This is the area's most popular tourist attraction: a private enterprise for which there is a fee to enter the property. It's a fine place to take the family for a half-day outing, riding the gondola over the gorge or driving across the chasm in your vehicle. You'll find the requisite pizza stands, souvenir shops, and other tourist traps that may temper your enjoyment of the gorge, but for a natural phenomenon turned into a theme park, the Royal Gorge is hard to beat. Another handy sightseeing route leads along Skyline Drive, a unique short drive along a hogback northwest of the downtown area. The three-mile drive provides great views of the town and the surrounding valley and a few driving thrills as the ridge is negotiated.

For me, the prime attraction of the Cañon City area is the Gold Belt Tour, which loops north of town, leading history buffs to the old mining towns of Cripple Creek and Victor and through the Phantom Canyon (see the "Gold Belt Tour" section later).

This drive heads westward, following the route of the Arkansas River as it winds its way from its source near Leadville. This is a river rafter's paradise, with several places to launch your flat boat or to take one of several commercial river tours. Between Cañon City and Salida, Highway 50 passes several small, quaint villages, including Texas Creek, Cotopaxi, and Coaldale, the latter an old mining town.

Gold Belt Tour

This circle loop, beginning just west of Cañon City, offers practically anything you could want in a scenic drive: history, mountain views, a deep canyon drive, and more! The drive leads north from Highway 50 by taking Highway 9 (or, in reverse order by taking Phantom Canyon Road a few miles east of town). This route has been designated a National Backcountry Scenic Byway by the Bureau of Land Management (BLM), which administers most of the surrounding lands.

Starting to the west of Cañon City on Highway 9, our preferred route leads through ranch lands to the junction with High Park Road. Take Road 11 northward through more rangeland (High Park) and early views of Pike's Peak with cone-shaped Mount Pisgah in the foreground. The High Park region offers views of mule deer. The pavement turns to gravel before reaching the northernmost piece of the drive, before the junction with Road 1, which leads off the Gold Belt Tour to the **Fossil Beds National Monument** in Florissant.

Take Road 1 south to the town of **Cripple Creek**, the subject of an old movie with Robert Mitchum and one of the rowdiest mining towns in Colorado in its day. This region (mainly in nearby Victor) produced more than $600 million in gold, and locals say there's a lot more gold to be found. The town has an original hotel (the Imperial), motels, cafes, saloons, and a museum. You'll find a scenic train trip from the downtown station and much history to explore (see page 371).

An alternate route back to Cañon City is the **Shelf Road**, which leads south from Cripple Creek. So named because part of the road lies on a narrow shelf above a deep canyon, this road is most suitable for four-wheel-drive vehicles but can be driven in cars and pickups with good clearance. Along this road are several historic sites and the **Garden Park Fossil Area**.

The main loop tour continues to the decaying mining town of **Victor**. A storefront museum honors Victor's favorite native son, Lowell Thomas. From Victor, the loop returns to Cañon City on the Phantom Canyon Road, an old railway bed running through granite tunnels and between sheer cliffs. Over its 35 miles, this descending trip from Cripple Creek provides one of the most picturesque drives anywhere.

HIGHWAY LOG
Cañon City to Leadville
150 miles (241 KM)—5 hours

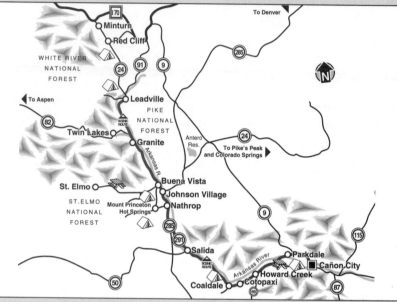

Cañon City (el. 5,332 feet) Gas, motels, RV parks, camping, cafes, stores.

Junction–North Road to Royal Gorge Eight miles west of Cañon City.

Junction–Highway 9 West access to Gold Belt Parkway (Cripple Creek, Victor).

Junction–South Road to Royal Gorge Winding road, no long vehicles. Five Points Recreation Site day-use, rafting, picnicking.

Pinnacle Rock Recreation Area Picnicking, river access.

Junction–Highway 69 To Westcliffe (south), store. The road now twists beside the Arkansas River with shallow rapids and red, diagonally layered rock cliffs.

Howard Farming village with gas, store, cafe, motel, and camping/RV park east of town.

Cotopaxi Store, gas, camping, motel, rock shops. 33 miles from Cañon City.

Coaldale Village. National Forest access road to south (Hayden Creek); two campgrounds in San Isabel National Forest. RV park on hwy. plus motel, cafe, camping.

Swissvale Tiny village beside the river. Camping, RV park.

Salida (el. 7,036 feet) 56 miles from Cañon City. Gas, cafes, motels on hwy. at each end of town.

Junction–Highway 291 Take this route northwest to Hwy. 285, Buena Vista, and Leadville.

Junction–Highway 285 Take this hwy. north to Buena Vista and Leadville.

Junction–Road 162 West to Princeton Hot Springs (five miles) with restaurant, hot pools, and tubs.

Nathrop Gas, store.

Johnson Village Small community with gas, motels, and store. RV park beside river, two miles south of junction.

Junction–Highway 24 East to South Park region, Pike's Peak, Cripple Creek, and Colorado Springs. See the next drive on page 338 which continues north on Hwy. 24.

Viewpoint–Mount Princeton (el. 14,197 feet) To west of hwy.

Buena Vista Town with full services, museum (32 miles from Leadville).

Junction–Road to Cottonwood Pass (el. 12,126 feet) Clear Creek Canyon Road leads west from Buena Vista to the pass on the Continental Divide and on to

many recreation sites in the Gunnison National Forest. This is a fine scenic backroad drive to the town of Gunnison and the Black Canyon of the Gunnison National Monument.

Viewpoint–Mount Yale (el. 14,196 feet) To the west, seen from the north end of Buena Vista.

Viewpoint–Mount Harvard (el. 14,420 feet) Five miles northwest.

Old Stage Road to Leadville Seen on far river bank, historical marker.

Granite Village with gas, store, cafe 17 miles to Leadville.

Junction–Highway 82 To Twin Lakes, Independence Pass, and Aspen (see the drive on page 330).

Junction–Road to Weston Pass East 10 miles to the pass (el. 11,900 feet) and on to meet Hwy. 285.

Junction–Road to Turquoise Lake Halfmoon Campground to west.

Leadville (el. 10,152 feet) Historic mining town with gas, motels, cafes, stores, museum, scenic train ride, ranger station.

At the north end of Leadville, Hwy. 91 leads northeast to Fremont Pass (el. 11,316 feet) and on to join I-70 near Frisco.

Pike's Peak Drive

Colorado Springs to Buena Vista

There's more to this drive than Pike's Peak, but the famous mountain is definitely the chief attraction for visitors who travel Highway 24 west from Colorado Springs. First, Colorado Springs has attractions of its own, including **The Broadmoor Resort** (with three golf courses) and the city's chief natural attraction, the **Garden of the Gods**, a city park filled with unusual red sandstone formations. The **U.S. Air Force Academy** is also in Colorado Springs, attracting millions of visitors each year. Guided tours of the 18,000-acre campus are offered daily. The **Cave of the Winds** offers an underground tour, just west of town. For Colorado Springs highlights, see page 365.

We begin this drive at the junction of Interstate 25 and Highway 24, heading west on a divided highway. The town of **Manitou Springs** lies at the foot of **Pike's Peak**. The cog railway to the summit of Pike's Peak, now more than 100 years old, begins its climb in the downtown area. The bright red train climbs slowly up the side of the mountain with great views across the high desert to the east. The train climbs to the 14,110 foot summit through aspen forest at the start and then above the tree line where passengers can view Denver to the north on a clear day. A more strenuous way to reach the summit is by walking the Barr Trail up the mountain.

The divided highway continues northwest with a turnoff at Green Mountain Falls to the **Pike's Peak Toll Road**. This 19-mile drive offers an alternative way to reach the summit—in the comfort of your car. It's paved for the first seven miles. At the town of Woodland Park, the highway turns east and becomes a two-lane road. At Divide, Highway 67 provides excellent views of Pike's Peak from the back side. This is also the route to **Cripple Creek** and the **Gold Belt Scenic Byway** (see page 334).

Just west of **Divide**, the highway reaches **Ute Pass** at an elevation of 9,165 feet. Eight miles west of Divide is the village of

Florissant and the **Fossil Beds National Monument** (on County Road 1). About 36 million years ago, palm trees and huge redwoods thrived in Colorado, until a nearby range of volcanoes erupted near this lush area, preserving remains of the Oligocene period until today. The Florissant Basin was once a lake that, under the pressure of volcanic debris, became shale. You'll find several trails across the lake bed, the best of which is the Petrified Forest Loop Trail. The monument is open daily during summer months, for which you'll pay a fee. Climbing another 400 feet, you reach **Wilkerson Pass** (at 9,507 feet). A forest information station is located at the pass as well as a short trail. Then the highway descends into South Park, a wide, flat valley lying between the Tarryall Mountains (to the east) and the Sawatch Range to the west. This high grassland basin, 30 miles by 40 miles; it is little known, but it is filled with history and is worthy of attention.

Highway 24 cuts across the middle of the South Park Basin, and most of the interest for visitors is off the highway on sideroads. Our drive intersects Highway 9, the route south to Cañon City; at Antero Junction, it intersects the north-south route from Denver, Highway 285. This road runs beside the South Platte River with fine mountain scenery (see below).

Past Antero Junction, the route leaves South Park, cutting through the hills into the Arkansas River Valley, turning north at Johnson Village to reach Buena Vista two miles on.

Gold Camp Road was once the train route between Colorado Springs and Cripple Creek. It's now a very scenic and quite rough road, which is especially suitable for four-wheel-drive vehicles. The route is open from late spring through late September, when the golden-colored aspens make the drive a special thrill. Most of the thrills, however, come from the narrow track. The road is only 30 miles long and could take more than two hours to negotiate. RV and trailer drivers should not try this road. Cars and pickups with high clearance are normally able to cope with road conditions, and the scenery is quite worth the effort.

HIGHWAY LOG
Colorado Springs to Buena Vista
94 miles (151 KM)—1 hour, 55 minutes

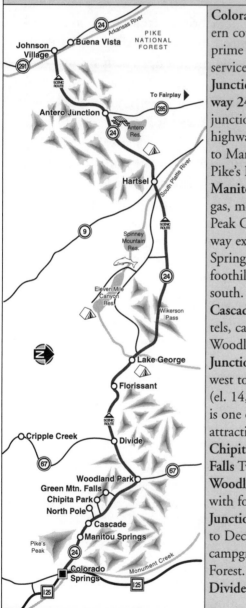

Colorado Springs Denver's southern cousin and one of Colorado's prime resort cities, with full visitor services.

Junction–Interstate 25 and Highway 24 Our drive begins at this junction, taking Hwy. 24, a divided highway that leads north four miles to Manitou Springs and on to Pike's Peak and Wilkerson Pass.

Manitou Springs Resort town with gas, motels, hot spring pools, Pike's Peak Cog Railway (take Cog Railway exit). Leaving Manitou Springs, Hwy. 24 climbs through foothills with Pike's Peak to the south.

Cascade Small town with gas, motels, cafes, stores. Nine miles to Woodland Park.

Junction–Pike's Peak Road Leads west to the summit of Pike's Peak (el. 14,110 feet). This toll road is one of Colorado's top scenic attractions.

Chipita Park, Green Mountain Falls Two exits. Full visitor services.

Woodland Park (el. 8,464) Town with food, motels, stores, gas.

Junction–Highway 67 Leads north to Deckers and recreation sites and campgrounds in Pike National Forest.

Divide Gas, motels, cafes, stores.

Junction–Highway 67 Leads south to Cripple Creek (18 miles) and Victor (Gold Belt Parkway to Cañon City).

Ute Pass Summit (el. 9,165 feet)

Florissant Gas, motel, cafes, store. Fossil Beds National Monument located just south of Florissant via County Road 1, which also leads to the Gold Belt Parkway northwest of Cripple Creek.

Junction–Road to Wagon Tongue Leads south, also to Cedar Creek.

Lake George Village with gas, cafe, ranger station.

Junction–Road 96 Leads south to Eleven Mile Canyon Reservoir.

Junction–Road 77 Leads north to Tarryall Creek and Reservoir. The hwy. now climbs to the pass.

Round Mountain Campground On north side of hwy.

Junction–Road 31 Leads north to Tarryall State Recreation Area (camping beside reservoir).

Wilkerson Pass (el. 9,507) Rest area, infocenter staffed by forest rangers, open seven days. The hwy. now descends to a wide, high valley (South Park) with the Mosquito Range to the west.

Junction–Road 92 Leads south to Spinney Mountain Reservoir and Eleven Mile State Recreation Area (camping).

Hartsel Village with gas, store.

Junction–Highway 9 South Leads southeast to Cañon City (37 miles).

Junction–Highway 9 North Leads 16 miles to Hwy. 285 and historic village of Fairplay.

Antero State Recreation Area To north with camping.

Antero Junction Fairplay is 20 miles north via Hwy. 285. To continue this drive, take Hwy. 24 west to Johnston Village (14 miles) and Buena Vista.

San Isabel National Forest The highway crosses the southern end of the Mosquito Range.

Trout Creek Pass (el. 9,346 feet)

Gulch Road (Road 307) Leads south into mountains, a good scenic backroad drive.

Picnic Area At viewpoint, north of the road.

Johnson Village Small junction town with gas, motels, cafes, stores.

Junction–Highway 24 Take Hwy. 24 north to Buena Vista (two miles).

Buena Vista Town on Arkansas River, with gas, motels, campgrounds/RV parks, cafes, stores, museum. Hwy. 24 leads north to Leadville and Interstate 70 (see the drive on page 336).

Lake City Drive

Pagosa Springs to Lake City

This is perhaps the most varied route of our Colorado drives, beginning beside the San Juan River in southwestern Colorado in a valley almost completely surrounded by the San Juan Range. Highway 160 leads northeast through the eastern flank of the San Juans, across Wolf Creek Pass and the Continental Divide (el. 10,850 feet), and then runs beside the South Fork of the Rio Grande to where it meets the main river at the small town of **South Fork**.

Turning northwest, Highway 149 follows the path of the Rio Grande through a broad valley to the town of Creede, a historic mining town located in a side canyon with a wonderful old main street complete with ancient opera house.

The highway continues to follow the Rio Grande into the main range of the San Juans, providing great views of high peaks as the route approaches another crossing of the Continental Divide at **Spring Creek Pass** (el. 10,901 feet). The highway continues to climb until reaching **Slumgullion Pass** (el. 11,361 feet) and then descends slightly to end at Lake City, a jewel of a mountain town on the shore of Lake San Cristobal.

The drive is only 189 miles long, but the contrasts in scenery along the way are impressive, with continual vistas of the San Juan Range, rushing rivers and creeks, wide river valleys, and a host of recreational opportunities, including some of the most highly regarded fishing spots in America. You may wish to schedule a vacation of several days or a week to take in all of the attractions on this route.

Sideroad and off-road drives along the way and out of Lake City provide additional thrills for both four-wheel-drive owners and drivers of cars and pickups.

The drive begins with a trip through the San Juan National Forest, entering the Rio Grande National Forest at Wolf Creek Pass, and ending the trip in the Gunnison National Forest, which surrounds Lake City. Forest ranger stations are in Pagosa Springs and Creede.

At the beginning of the drive, **Pagosa Springs** offers quiet holidays with golfing or fishing in the San Juan River and nearby lakes. **Echo Lake**, just four miles south of town on Highway 84, is one of the best places in the state to fish for large rainbow trout, yellow perch, and largemouth bass. While the geothermal springs here attracted the Ute in bygone days (*pagosa* is a Ute word meaning "healing waters"), the only commercial hot springs development in Pagosa Springs is at the Spa Motel; however, a wonderful natural spring is accessible by a five-mile walk (see "Sideroads and Backroads"). The **Anasazi Ruins**—17 miles west of town via Highway 160 and Highway 151—is known as the Machu Picchu of North America, with tours of the Chimney Rock habitation of 1,000 years ago. Tours must be reserved at the ranger office in town; tribal tours are available at Lake Capote.

The **Wolf Creek Ski Area**, at the pass, receives more snow than most other Colorado hills and is becoming increasingly popular. More than 450 inches of snow falls in a normal winter.

Creede, located in the remote northern Rio Grande Valley, is an unlikely place for high culture, but that's what you find in this historic mining town. A respected repertory theater company is based in the old **Creede Opera House**, staging plays throughout the summer. You can stay in a motel in town or at one of the many popular guest ranches in the valley.

Just beyond the second Continental Divide crossing, the **Slumgullion Earthflow** is an interesting natural phenomenon. Seven hundred years ago, a mass of volcanic rock and earth slumped down the mountainside, forming a dam that blocked the Lake Fork of the Gunnison River and created **Lake San Cristobal**. For a view of the dam, stop at the lake overlook just before the highway descends to the city. The Slumgullion viewpoint is farther up, on the descent from Slumgullion Pass. **Lake City**, an old mining camp founded in 1874, lies beside the lake and the river, nestled beneath the high peaks of the San Juans. Gunnison is 55 miles northeast of Lake City via Highway 149.

HIGHWAY LOG
Pagosa Springs to Lake City
189 miles (304 KM)—4 hours

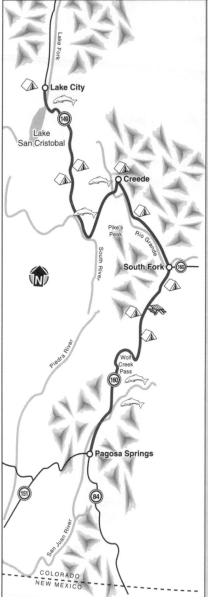

Pagosa Springs Town with full services on Hwy. 160, south of the San Juan Range. Our drive begins in Pagosa Springs, moving northeast via Hwy. 160 beside the San Juan River. The hwy. enters the San Juan National Forest a few miles north of town.

The road climbs steeply, ascending the eastern flank of the San Juan Range.

Wolf Creek Pass (el. 10,857 feet) Continental Divide, trails. Now entering the Rio Grande National Forest.

Viewpoint Scenic overlook to west; sideroad.

Ski Area (Wolf Creek) at milepost 168. The hwy. now descends to the South Fork Valley.

Tucker Ponds Campgrounds To east of hwy.

Junction–Big Meadows Reservoir Road Campground to the west at milepost 175.

National Forest Marker Ice Age architecture (at milepost 176).

Rest Area Picnicking at milepost 176.5. Motel and cafe near picnic area.

Park Creek Campground to the east of the hwy.

Junction–Park Creek Road Forest access, to historic site of Summitville.

Fun Valley Guest ranch with cabins, campground, large RV park, log motel, and store.

Highway Spring Campground At milepost 182.

Riverbend Cabins and RV Park At milepost 183.

South Fork Logging and tourist town with motels, cafes, RV park, camping, and store.

Junction–Highway 149 For this drive, take Hwy. 149 north (76 miles to Lake City). The road crosses Rio Grande River just north of town.

Palisade Campground Riverside sites at milepost 9.

Blue Creek Cabins, cafe.

Cottonwood Cove Cabins and cafe at milepost 13.

Junction–Deep Creek Road To west with river access.

Watson Ranch and Cabins At milepost 18.

Creede (el. 8,800 feet) Historic mining town with motel, gas, store, cafe, old opera house, RV parks. A large campground and RV park is located just north of Creede.

Junction–Miners Creek Road To the east.

Marshall Park Campground On river, west of the hwy. at milepost 28.

Fishing Access Lane to west.

Broken Arrow Ranch Cabins. Fern Creek Road. At milepost 38.

Fern Store, guest ranch.

Viewpoint At milepost 41.

Junction–Rio Grande Reservoir Road Leads west at milepost 41.

Junction–Road to Spring Creek Reservoir Camping, to the west.

Junction–North Clear Creek Road Leads east to Bristol Head Camp (quarter of a mile), Near Creek Campground (two miles) and falls (four miles).

Silver Tread Campground Beside hwy. at milepost 46.

Junction–Rito Hondo Road To Rito Hondo (four miles) and Continental Reservoirs (five miles).

Spring Creek Pass (el. 10,898 feet) Continental Divide.

Slumgullion Pass Summit (el. 11,361 feet)

Windy Point Overlook with a fine view at milepost 64.

Slumgullion Earthflow Viewpoint This geological wonder is worth a stop; you'll see its effect as you descend into Lake City.

Lake Overlook A good view of Lake San Cristobal and Lake City as the hwy. descends.

Lake City Gas, motels, lodges, cafes, stores. This tourist town in the mountains is another historic mining village with one of the most picturesque settings in the state.

San Juan Skyway–Part One

Durango to Telluride

This drive and the following drive cover the famed San Juan Skyway, the premier scenic route through the San Juan Range. Beginning and ending in Durango, the two drives climb to high passes, offer chances to visit unique, historic towns founded during the gold and silver rushes of the mid-19th century, and provide access to dozens of wilderness areas in the San Juan and Uncompahgre National Forests. Skiers use the Skyway highways to drive to several of Colorado's best ski areas, including Purgatory and Telluride. Best of all, this region, tucked into the southwest corner of Colorado, is underutilized by tourists; even during the busier summer months, visitors to the area can enjoy the solitude of the wonderful recreation areas without falling over hundreds of other travelers.

The area is also a mecca for off-road explorers, who must use four-wheel-drive vehicles to negotiate the extremely bumpy and narrow old mining roads that lace the region, connecting the modern highways to ghost town sites and vistas of unparalleled beauty. If you don't own a four-wheel-drive vehicle, you can rent a jeep in several of the towns along the way, including Silverton, Ouray, and Telluride.

The route does not cross the Continental Divide, but the high mountain thrills are still here, as the Skyway crosses numerous mountain passes—some of them higher than the passes on the Divide, which lies to the east.

The first leg of the Skyway drive leads north from Durango to Silverton, a distance of 48 miles, high on the side of the Animas River Valley. **Molas Pass** (at an elevation of 10,910 feet) provides wonderful views of the San Juan peaks near and far. **Durango**, a modern city, reflects three cultures that have left their imprint on the city's architecture and social life: Native American, Spanish, and—more recently—the Anglo-American miners who came to the area by the thousands more than 100 years ago. This delightful city is also the terminus of the restored **Durango** and **Silverton Narrow Gauge Railroad**, which runs daily up the Animas Valley, providing the top scenic railway experience on the continent.

Silverton, at the northern end of the railway line, is a Victorian historic landmark populated by 880 people who live in a high valley at an elevation of 9,303 feet. On the mountains above the town lie a succession of old mining camps, now ghostly reminders of the gold and silver rushes that settled the region.

Then the adventure really begins! The short (23-mile) stretch of road to Ouray is called the **Million Dollar Highway**. Named for the estimated million dollars of gold in the tailings laid to form the roadway, the road climbs over **Red Mountain Pass** (el. 11,008 feet) and nearby **Ophir Pass** (two feet higher). The road drops quickly into the box canyon where lies the town of **Ouray**, another Victorian marvel made even more delightful by the hot springs that offer wonderful soaking (in Ouray and a few miles to the north).

From Ouray to Telluride, the drive is relatively flat as Highway 550 leads north to Ridgway and then the Skyway proceeds west on Highway 62 to the junction at Placerville. You travel southeast for another 15 miles to Telluride and the end of this first leg of the Skyway.

Telluride has been called the "most beautiful town in the United States," and for good reason. It lies in a box canyon along the San Miguel River. It's a Victorian town of 1,300 people, one of the favored ski resorts for the Beautiful People, and a funky summer resort for an amazing mix of people from the very wealthy to the 1990s version of the "hippie" culture. The town features a panoply of summer arts festivals (chamber music, jazz, film, bluegrass, wild mushroom, etc.), offering something for everyone who travels the distance to take in the unique ambiance of this lovely place.

Last Dollar Road connects Telluride to the Dallas Divide on Highway 62, a few miles west of Ridgway. This is an excellent alternate route from Ridgway to Telluride or a day-trip from Telluride.

HIGHWAY LOG
Durango to Telluride
121 miles (195 KM)—3 hours

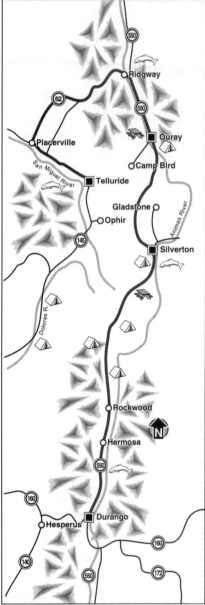

Durango City with full services, historic downtown area, scenic railway line, museums. Our drive starts in the downtown area on Camino Del Rio and then Main Avenue (Hwy. 550).

Junction–Sideroad to Lemon Dam (32nd Street) Take East Animas Road east to the Lemon Dam and Reservoir and several Forest Service recreation sites (in San Juan National Forest).

Trimble Hot Springs To the west, 100 yards off hwy.

Junction–Hermosa Creek Road Forest access to the west.

Viewpoint Scenic railroad line crosses under hwy. bridge.

Junction–Highway 200 To Rockwood (golf).

Purgatory Ski Area West of hwy., with lodge and restaurant.

Forest Campground To the east with trail rides nearby.

Junction–West Hermosa Park Road Forest access, to campground.

Cascade Village, with lodging.

Forest Access Cascade Creek and Animas River recreation sites, from both sides of the hwy.

Picnic Area Just south of the summit (East Lime Creek).

Molas Pass Summit (el. 10,910 feet) Colorado Trail marker.
Junction–Road to Little Molas Lake To west.
Campground and Store At Molas Lake (private campground).
Silverton Gas, cafes, motels, stores, museum. National historic site, terminus of scenic railway, and takeoff point for scenic byway (jeep trails) to Lake City and Ouray. Picnic tables in the town park, at far end of Main Street, beyond the museum. Our drive continues from Silverton on the Million Dollar Hwy., climbing quickly to Red Mountain Pass (el. 11,008 feet).
South Mineral Campground To east of hwy.
Ophir Pass Summit (el. 11,010 feet) The hwy. now descends past old mine workings and tailing piles. Brown Mountain is seen to the east.
Junction–Alpine Loop Jeep trail leading east, just south of Bear Creek Bridge. This scenic byway leads to old mining sites, Engineer Pass, Lake City, and Silverton (four-wheel-drive vehicles only).
Amphitheater Campground Located on hillside overlooking town of Ouray.

Ouray Town with gas, motels, cafes, stores, jeep rentals, hot spring pools, and historic downtown district. Located 23 miles from Silverton. Leaving Ouray, the Ouray Hot Springs are found at the north end of town in Rotary Park (picnic tables).
Bachelor-Syracuse Mine Tours via sideroad leading east.
Junction–Road to Hot Springs To the west.
Junction–Highway 62 Ridgway Junction, 11 miles from Ouray. Hwy. 550 leads northwest to Montrose and Delta. Drive continues west on Hwy. 62 (25 miles to Placerville and 38 miles to Telluride). The route leads through a wide valley with views of high ridges (Sneffels Range).
Junction–Dallas Creek Forest Road To the south, recreation sites.
Junction–West Dallas Road
Junction–Last Dollar Road Backroad to Telluride with forest access leading south near Dallas Divide.
Placerville Small village with gas, store, cafe. Park with picnic tables.
Junction–Highway 145 South to Ophir and Cortez (see next drive).
Telluride Historic resort town, one mile from junction.

San Juan Skyway–Part Two

Telluride to Durango

The second leg of this circle route—the return from Telluride to Durango—is a two-stage trip that begins deep in the San Juan Mountains, climbs shortly to Lizard Head Pass (el. 10,222 feet), and then slowly descends, following the flow of the Dolores River out of the range and emerging into the desert and ranching country around Cortez. Here are several of the most outstanding reminders of the prehistoric Anasazi peoples. The remainder of the drive (46 miles between Cortez and Durango) is flat, with the southern flank of the massive San Juans visible to the north of the highway between the two towns.

The early high driving offers impressive views of the peaks as the highway runs through the **Uncompahgre National Forest** and then the **San Juan National Forest**. West of the highway is a parade of "fourteeners," including Wilson Peak (el. 14,017 feet), Mount Wilson (el. 14,246 feet), and El Diante Peak (el. 14,159 feet).

Before the pass, a short sideroad leads to the village of **Ophir**. This is the second mining camp with that name to be established in this area. The original one was a few miles to the east, closer to Ouray. Ophir Pass Road is a favorite jeep trail.

Communities of any size are scarce as the highway descends with the Dolores. **Rico** has a cafe 18 miles south of Lizard Head Pass; **Priest Gulch** is another tiny village with a cafe, store, and cabins. **Dolores**, a town of 7,000 people, is the largest settlement along the route to Cortez. Dolores is the site of the **Anasazi Heritage Center**, a fine archeological museum opened in 1988. Created when the McPhee Dam and Reservoir were constructed with much damage to the former Anasazi land in the area, the museum was developed to preserve and study Anasazi artifacts found nearby. Construction of the reservoir not only meant the covering of sensitive Anasazi lands but also the loss of the Dolores Canyon.

The cost of the dam included funding of several digs in the area now covered with water as well as construction of the museum. The archeological program began in 1977. The center is open year-round, and admission is free. Next to the center are the **Dominguez/Escalante Ruins**, named for the first Spanish explorers to pass through here, documenting their sighting of Native American ruins. A short trail reaches the ruins from the museum.

Much more to do with the Anasazi people is found in and near the town of Cortez, eight miles southwest of Dolores. The **Cortez Center**, located at 25 Market Street, is an archeological museum operated by the University of Colorado. **Hovenweep National Monument** is one of the most awe-inspiring Anasazi ruins in the Four Corners area. The structures here are quite different from those at Mesa Verde. Stone towers rise up to 20 feet.

Sideroads and Backroads

A loop trip from Cortez provides visits to two Anasazi sites. **Lowry Pueblo**, northwest of Cortez, was discovered in 1928 and has been restored as a National Historic Landmark. This site and Hovenweep National Monument provide reasons to drive a scenic loop from Cortez. Start by heading southwest of town on Highway 666 (for three miles) and turn right onto McElmo Canyon Road. This delightful canyon drive puts you into Utah, with signs pointing to Hovenweep (a trip of about 40 miles). Then drive northeast for 25 miles to Highway 666 northwest of Cortez. Lowry Pueblo is located nine miles west of the town of Pleasant View. A word of warning: these are dirt roads, which suffer after rainstorms. Travelers should contact the Cortez Information Center at (970) 565-3414 or phone Mesa Verde National Park at (970) 529-4465 to check on road conditions.

Mesa Verde National Park is the major Anasazi attraction in the area, which you reach by driving 10 miles east of Cortez on Highway 160 (our return route to Durango). Signs will direct you onto a paved sideroad that leads 21 miles south to the park.

HIGHWAY LOG
Telluride to Durango
85 miles (136 KM)—1 hour, 45 minutes

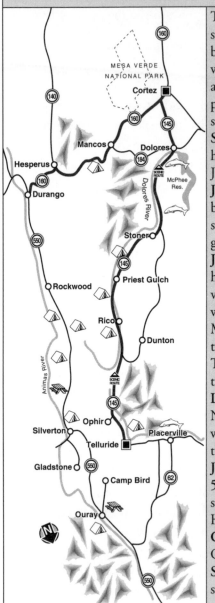

Telluride This ski and summer resort town has one of the most beautiful settings of any town, anywhere. Our drive leaves Telluride and joins Hwy. 145 as it climbs past the upper levels of the ski resort (hotel, lodge).

Sunshine Campground West of the hwy., with fine views of several San Juan peaks.

Junction–Road to Alta Lakes A bad road leading east to beautiful small lakes with a forest campground.

Junction–Road to Ophir This historic mining camp (now a tiny village) is just off the hwy. and is well worth a visit (campgrounds). Matterhorn Campground to the east.

Trout Lake (el. 10,000 feet) Below the hwy. At milepost 61.

Lizard Head Pass (el. 10,250 feet) Named for the nearby peak (to the west); Sheep Mountain is seen to the east.

Junction–Road to Dunton (Road 535) Forest access, camping on scenic backroad. This road rejoins Hwy. 145 south of Stoner.

Cayton Campground On Barlow Creek, to the east.

San Juan National Forest Ranger station.

Rico Small community with gas and cafe. The road leads beside the Dolores River with grassy campsites accessed from Rico village.
Campsites Beside the river; grassy sites at milepost 43.
Priest Gulch Village with camping, cafe, cabins, store, laundry.
Priest Gulch Trailhead West of the hwy.
Bear Creek Trailhead To east of the hwy. at milepost 34.
Stoner Small community with gas, cafe and motel, at milepost 25.
Junction–West Dolores Road Forest access, 13 miles from town of Dolores.
Dolores (el. 6,936 feet) Small town with gas, motels, cafe, RV park, ranger station.
McPhee Reservoir Fifteen miles from Dolores via sideroad.
Junction–Highway 184 Leads 18 miles southeast to meet Hwy. 160 east of Cortez. Also leads west to meet Hwy. 666 northeast of Cortez.
Anasazi Heritage Center Museum of Native American history, south road to McPhee Reservoir.
Cortez (el. 6,200 feet) Farming town located next to San Juan

foothills. Gas, food, shopping, motels. Colorado Welcome Center on Main Street. Cortez is 45 miles from Durango via Hwy. 160.
Junction–Road to Toten Lake Reservoir to the north of Hwy. 160, via sideroad.
Mesa Verde National Park This outstanding national park is located south of Hwy. 160. The park road is eight miles east of Cortez.
Mancos Village with gas, ranger station.
Junction–Highway 184 Leads northwest to meet Hwy. 145, just south of Dolores.
Forest Campground To north of hwy.
Junction–Forest Access Road Leads north beside La Plata River to Mayday, La Plata, and forest campground.
Junction–Highway 140 Leads south to Breen and Highways 170 and 173. Hesperus is a small community just south of our route via Hwy. 140. The Southern Ute Reservation lies to the south.
Durango City with historic downtown area and the end of the San Juan Skyway circle-route drive.

Dolores Canyon Drive

Grand Junction to Telluride

This canyon drive is a largely undiscovered route between the town of Grand Junction and the San Juan Mountains at Telluride. It offers views of the La Sal Mountains to the west and the Grand Mesa to the east. Highway 141 leads beside East Creek and then West Creek and eventually runs through the canyons of the Dolores and San Miguel rivers, all the way to Placerville and Telluride. This is an excellent one-day drive at the western edge of the Rocky Mountain region, passing through some of the most impressive scenery in the state. It provides a gateway to the historic mining country of the San Juans (see the previous two drives) and access to the Anasazi ruins farther to the south, near Cortez.

This route is quite different from the previous Colorado drives—you will not encounter high mountain passes. On the other hand, the drive leads through some of the most beautiful river valleys in the West and offers sideroad and backroad access to wonderful views on the Grand Mesa (the largest flattopped mountain in the country) and to the dry canyonlands of the La Sal Range. Other backroads lead into the Uncompahgre National Forest.

But first, we recommend a thorough exploration of the attractions near Grand Junction, particularly the **Colorado National Monument** and the **Grand Mesa**. Both are accessible by car and RV, and each should take a day to explore.

Our drive begins either in Grand Junction or in the town of Clifton, five miles east of Grand Junction. If you're in downtown Grand Junction, take Highway 50 and drive southeast to the village of Whitewater. If you're driving along Interstate 70, the easiest way to reach Whitewater is by taking Highway 141 south from the Clifton interchange to Highway 50 and Whitewater. From there, we continue southeast on Highway 141.

The **Unaweep Canyon**, through which our drive passes, is 44 miles long and more than 2,000 feet high. Before the **Uncompahgre Plateau** pushed its way into the air about eight million

354 COLORADO

years ago, the canyon was the route of the Colorado and Gunnison rivers, but Unaweep was left dry after the plateau was formed. See "Sideroads and Backroads" for backroad directions.

From the village of Gateway, the highway enters the **Dolores Canyon**, which reveals layers—in many colors—of sandstone, shale, and other sedimentary rock. As the route heads through the canyon, a viewpoint shows the remnants of an old flume hanging on the canyon wall. Built between 1889 and 1891, the six-mile flume carried water to Mesa Creek Flats for the short-lived hydraulic mining operations there. The highway then enters uranium mining country, where uranium was supplied for early atomic bomb research. **Uravan** was the center of mining in the area during the 1950s, but operations ceased in 1962. The town of **Nucla** is another reminder of the uranium period. Several closed uranium mines are located along the ascent of **John Brown Canyon**.

From Uravan, the highway follows the route of the **San Miguel River** through placid countryside until reaching the San Juan Range north of Placerville. The San Miguel, below Norwood, is one of the finest fishing streams in Colorado, although pollution from mine tailings make fishing just south of Telluride risky. Otherwise, anglers often catch large rainbow trout provided by a stocking program.

Sideroads and Backroads

Rim Rock Drive leads across the dramatic Colorado National Monument and is located a few miles west of Grand Junction (via Interstate 70). Deep red canyons and high rock formations populate the monument, which was designated by President William Taft in 1911. It is also a monument to the labors of area pioneer John Otto, who waged a long campaign on behalf of designation and became the first superintendent of the monument. Rim Rock Drive offers great views from the Uncompahgre Plateau with frequent scenic viewpoints along the route. You may access the drive from the main gate to the monument, in Fruita, or from Grand Junction. The route is a favorite cycling course.

HIGHWAY LOG
Grand Junction to Telluride
154 miles (248 KM)—3 hours, 45 minutes

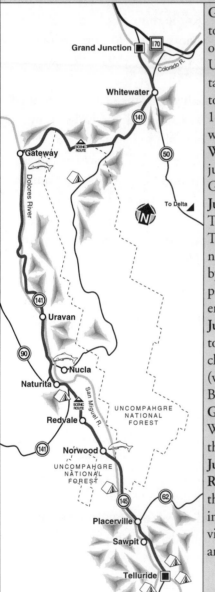

Grand Junction City with full visitor services on I-70, near the Colorado National Monument and the Utah border. To begin this drive, take Hwy. 50 south from downtown Grand Junction, or take Hwy. 141 south from Clifton (five miles west of Grand Junction).

Whitewater Small village at the junction of Hwys. 141 and 50. Gas, store.

Junction–Highways 50 and 141 This is the start of the Unaweep/Tabequache Scenic Byway (designated by the BLM). We follow this byway, which skirts the Uncompahgre National Forest at the north end of the Uncompahgre Plateau.

Junction–Divide Road Forest road to Unaweep Canyon campsites, including Divide Forks Campground (water available) and on to other BLM sites.

Gateway Located 44 miles from Whitewater. Cafe, gas, motel. To the south, Naturita is 52 miles.

Junction–John Brown Canyon Road The backroad leads west through this narrow canyon, climbing to a high plateau with fine views of the surrounding landscape and cliffs below.

Our main route turns southeast at Gateway, following the flow of the Dolores River.

Viewpoint At milepost 81.5. Overlooks Dolores River with a view of an old hanging flume (six miles long) built in the 1890s.

Uravan Mining operation, 37 miles from Gateway and 15 miles to Naturita.

Bridge Road to Nucla The main access to Nucla is from Naturita.

Junction–Highway 90 Leads west to Bedrock and Paradox (29 miles).

Naturita (el. 5,400 feet) Town with gas, cafe, stores, camping, motels.

Junction–Highway 97 To Nucla (four miles). Nucla is an old mining town (uranium) with a pleasant main street (false-fronted buildings), gas, cafe, store.

Junction–Forest Access Road To the east, along the San Miguel River.

Junction–Highways 141 and 145 Hwy. 141 leads southwest to Gypsum Gap Pass (el. 6,100 feet) Our drive continues southward on Hwy. 145.

Redvale Village with RV park and store.

Norwood (el. 7,015 feet) Small town with gas, motel, stores, cafe, and ranger station. Located 17 miles from Placerville, 34 miles to Telluride.

Junction–Road 442 Leads south past Gurlie and Cone Reservoirs and on to Miramonte State Recreation Area (camping).

Norwood Hill Our route descends to a wooded canyon.

Junction–Forest Access Road To Specie Creek.

Placerville Small village at Hwy. 62 junction with gas, store, cafe, county picnic park. Hwy. 62 leads east to Ridgway and to Ouray. Hwy. 141 continues our route toward Telluride and Cortez.

Junction–Fall Creek Forest Road Sawpit Tiny old village with cafe and gas.

Junction–Silver Pick Road National Forest access.

Junction–South Fork Road Forest access.

Telluride Junction Two miles to downtown Telluride and gas, motels, cafes, stores, municipal campground.

Telluride A historic mining town and one of Colorado's unique ski and summer destinations. The town is situated on two levels.

Sunshine Campground (National Forest) is located at the top of the hill via Hwy. 145. The Alta Lakes Backroad provides a rough but scenic drive to two small lakes and more camping.

Colorado
Destinations

Aspen

This historic mining town, situated at the head of the Roaring Valley, is Colorado's top ski resort and summer cultural center. The combination of antique buildings, chic shops, and social activities is hard to resist, and few do. In summer months, the resort busies itself with ballet, drama, music concerts, food and wine festivals, and other kinds of arts and gustatory activity. With wilderness all around, visitors have no reason for neglecting their favorite outdoor interests: fishing, hiking, and water sports. The rainy spring months are fairly quiet, but people flock to Aspen for the annual fall color display in the huge aspen groves that surround the town. Fall is also a particularly good time to drive to Independence Pass, with many fine scenic vistas along the way.

The **Aspen Ski Area**, inaugurated in 1936, brought a very sleepy village back to life, after an up and down period since silver was first sighted in 1879. By 1880, the town had a population of more than 1,000. The Denver and Rio Grande Railroad arrived in 1887. Aspen grew again, and by 1892, the town bulged with 12,000 inhabitants, but like all other mining towns, the ore ran out. By the early 1930s, the town had a population of only 700. The ski boom began after the end of World War II, and the town became a magnet for skiers from around the world. The **Snowmass Ski Area** is a more recent development.

First, let's deal with the skiing possibilities. Downhill skiing is Aspen's life blood, and the mountains that have runs cut into them are the most popular set of hills in the state. Three of the four skiing operations (Aspen Mountain, Buttermilk, and Snowmass) are owned by one company, the Aspen Skiing Company. The fourth ski operation is Aspen Highlands. **Aspen Mountain** (or Ajax Mountain) looms 11,300 feet above the town, and the ski runs here are for expert and senior-intermediate skiers. The Silver Queen Gondola takes skiers to the top.

Buttermilk is two miles west of town and has miles and miles of bunny hills and novice and intermediate runs. Cross-country skiers can receive telemark ski instruction at Buttermilk. **Snowmass** is located 12 miles southwest of Aspen and is a well-rounded family skiing operation. The ski area has four peaks and many runs, a majority of them intermediate. You can dine on the mountain or at the base. For information on the three Aspen Skiing Company hills, call (970) 925-1220; you can also call about Snowmass at (970) 923-2000. **Aspen Highlands** provides a good mix of beginner, intermediate, and advanced skiing. **Highland's Bowl** offers a large powder area for experts only. For information, call (970) 925-5300.

Aspen has groomed and backcountry trails for cross-country skiers. The backcountry trails are mostly in the national forest. Groomed trails are available at the **Ashcroft Ski Touring Center**, in the little town of the same name, 12 miles from Aspen. You'll find 19 miles of groomed trails, warming huts, and food at the Pine Creek Cookhouse. The **Aspen/Snowmass Nordic Trail System** features almost 50 miles of groomed trails between the two towns, coordinated by the nonprofit Nordic Council. Use of the trail is free, and maps are available at the Aspen Visitors Center (downtown), the Wheeler Opera House, or in sports stores.

Summer is a time for sightseeing and for the arts. The **Aspen Music Festival** stages its season from late June through August with music ranging from jazz to symphony and with seating in the famous tent or on the grass. For festival information, call (970) 925-3254. Sightseeing is another favorite summer activity, including trips to view the peaks of the **Maroon Bells**. Fishing is best on the Fryingpan Lakes, the Fryingpan River, and Hunter

Creek. You'll find golf courses in Aspen and at Snowmass. The **Conundrum Hot Springs** are located at the end of a nine-mile hike from Forest Road 128. Enjoy two pools (three- and five-feet deep) in addition to Conundrum Creek, near Triangle Pass. To get there, drive up Castle Creek Road from Aspen for about five miles, and turn right onto Forest Road 128, driving one mile to the trailhead.

Cultural facilities in Aspen include the **Aspen Arts Museum** (on North Mill Street), featuring touring shows as well as exhibits by local artists and craftspeople. It is located in a park beside the Roaring Fork River. The **Wheeler Stallard House Museum**, a large Victorian home on West Bleeker Street, is operated by the Aspen Historical Society; it houses Victorian collections including clothing, children's toys, and room settings.

While Aspen is known for its jet-setters, people on a budget can also enjoy the striking ambience of the resort. Hotel rates are lower in summer, and several low-cost places are available in town during the ski season (see page 411).

Where to Eat

Probably the most expensive (and the best) restaurant is **Chez Grandmere** in Snowmass Village. French cuisine is served in a fine Victorian house, with a fixed-price menu changing nightly. The **Ute City Banque** has a historical atmosphere and good—although expensive—food. Less expensive and more homey places to eat include **Home Plate** on East Durant Avenue and **La Cochina** with Mexican food on East Hopkins.

Away from town, in Carbondale, the **Village Smithy** is well known for its great breakfasts served in a converted black-smith's shop.

Buena Vista and Salida

The Upper Arkansas Valley is found in south-central Colorado, stretching between Salida (at the south), to the historic mining town of Granite at the north end of the valley (see the scenic drive on page 334). The river begins its leisurely route near Leadville (farther north) and runs through Granite, Buena Vista, and Salida, before turning west toward Cañon City. The Sawatch Range, with several magnificent "fourteers," lies to the west of the valley. You'll find many old ghost towns, many off the beaten track and accessible by sideroads and forest backroads. This was Ute country, and the Ute people occupied camps in this valley, while the Comanche inhabited the upper reaches of the river. Very few Native Americans lived in the valley by the time Zebulon Pike explored the area in 1806; the Ute moved on to better hunting grounds.

Gold was discovered near Granite—at Kelly's Bar—in 1860, and miners worked the river for the next 20 years. Later, these modest operations were supplanted by larger mines, in communities such as Vicksburg, St. Elmo, and Winfield. The area was of interest to ranchers who established cattle operations in the river valley. In 1880, the county seat was moved from Granite to Buena Vista—but not peacefully. The people of Granite refused to give up the county records, so the folks from Buena Vista stole into Granite one night to seize them.

Two sizable towns are in the valley, and both offer visitor services. Salida, the larger, has a population of 4,500. The 12 "fourteeners" in the area provide good hiking and sightseeing. The **San Isabel National Forest** has many trails, and information on these trails and forest campgrounds is available from the ranger station in Salida. **Princeton Hot Springs Resort** is close to both towns. The pools at **Salida Hot Springs** offer swimming, plus several smaller pools and private hot tubs. Other recreational opportunities include float boating on the Arkansas. The 47 miles between Granite and Salida offer a wide range of water (calm to roaring white), including the notorious **Numbers Rapids**. From Salida east to Cañon City, the river leads through the Arkansas River Canyon, and outfitters along the river offer float trips. The 9-hole golf course in Buena Vista provides great views of the Sawatch Range. The Salida Golf Club offers more challenging play.

An interesting backroad drive joins two towns on the east side of the Arkansas River. The turnoff from Highway 291 is located one mile past the intersection of 1st and F Streets in Salida. Turn right onto County Road 153, then cross the river, and turn right onto Road 175 (the Ute Trail). After seven miles, turn right onto Road 185. The route passes Calumet ghost town before reaching Bassam Park and a picnic area. The road is suitable only for vehicles with high clearance and is best done by four-wheel-drive vehicles.

Where to Eat

Salida offers the **First Street Cafe**, with steak, seafood, and good breakfasts in an historic building, and the **Windmill** on Highway 50, with Tex-Mex specialties, among other dishes. The **Princeton Club**, at the hot spring resort on Road 162, has a fine setting, with Cajun and Tex-Mex cuisine.

Cañon City

Once the locale for Tom Mix movies, Cañon City sits on the edge of the Great Plains, with the Sangre de Cristo Mountains to the southwest. Red sandstone cliffs punctuate the horizon north of town, while the area's most notable geological feature, the **Royal Gorge**, is located eight miles west of Cañon City.

The great chasm has been cut through solid granite by the Arkansas River, and it's a sight that has amazed travelers for many years. In 1929, the world's highest suspension bridge was constructed across the Royal Gorge—more than 1,000 feet above the fast-flowing river. You can see the gorge for free if you take the north route to the site and stop before entering the commercial attraction. However, the best way to get the full effect of the gorge is to pay a fee and enter the theme park that has developed around the gorge. You may drive over the suspension bridge, then take a ride on the aerial tramway, or pay your way onto the incline railway that descends to river level, stopping meanwhile to have a piece of pizza or to buy a souvenir. A scenic railway provides a 30-minute ride to the lip of the gorge. There are restaurants beside the canyon, and several other attractions outside the immediate gorge area (including the **Buckskin Joe** theme park). These people knew from Day One how to exploit one of the world's natural wonders. The same approach applied to the Grand Canyon would make a gazillion dollars a year.

You may also take a tour of the **Colorado Territorial Prison Museum**, at 1st Street and Macon Avenue. Prisons are the area's chief industry, providing a secure (and growing) economy.

For motoring tourists, however, the chief attraction is the **Gold Belt Tour**, a loop drive that will take you to the old mining towns of Cripple Creek and Victor, with a choice of two dramatic routes through deep canyons. Which road you take depends on what kind of car you drive (four-wheel-drive or not). For details, see the scenic drive on page 334. The **Oak Creek Grade** provides another five scenic drive, with great views of the Wet Mountain Valley and the Sangre de Cristo Range.

The best place to fish (for brown trout) is **Texas Creek**, located 26 miles west of town. Texas Creek Road leads, as well, to other streams and several lakes. It is also possible to pull trout out of the Arkansas River, but the fishing is better near Salida. River floating is a popular pastime. You can raft through the Royal Gorge, but this seven-mile stretch of the river has dangerous rapids and is suitable for only the most intrepid floaters. The rafting is more placid above the gorge, between Salida and Cañon City. You'll find outfitters in both towns.

Where to Eat

The **Robison Mansion**, at 840 First Street, is a historic home built in 1884, serving lunch and dinner daily. **Merlino's Belvedere** is a fine Italian cafe that also serves steak and seafood; it's on Highway 115, two miles south of town. The **Bavarian Inn**, on 1006 Royal Gorge Boulevard, serves good German food and beer, in addition to seafood and American cuisine.

Central City

The famous **Central City Opera House** attracts music buffs from far and wide each summer. The old opera house was built shortly after the gold rush of 1859, which propelled the Colorado territory into modern times. But music isn't the only reason to make the mile-long sidetrip from Black Hawk on Highway 119. The town is very much a living memorial to the rowdy Victorian era that continues to influence the culture and society of this high mountain state. Recent years have brought gambling to the town.

John H. Gregory was responsible for it all. Gregory was a prospector from Georgia who made his way up a gulch from North Clear Creek, and, at a site between Central City and Black Hawk, found gold. Within a year, thousands of miners flocked to Central City and Black Hawk, and to the towns of Missouri City, Nevadaville, Dogtown, and Gregory Point. Quartz Hill was found to hold a huge vein containing gold, silver, copper, and lead. The Central City area was named "The Richest Square Mile On Earth," and more fortunes were made.

A devastating fire destroyed most of Central City in 1874, but the town was quickly rebuilt, using stone instead of wood this time, and these are the buildings that survive today. A notable example is the Central City Opera House, which opened in 1878.

By 1890, most of the miners had left the area, but the opera house remained open until 1927, when it closed for four years. In the summer of 1932, Lillian Gish starred in a production of *Camille*, drawing large audiences from Denver. The hall hasn't looked back from that day.

The whole downtown area has been designated a National Historic Site. It's filled with wonderful old buildings housing stores, cafes, and saloons. The area offers scenic drives to nearby ghost towns—**Nevadaville** and **Apex**—and four-wheel-drive trips to St. Mary's Glacier and over the **Oh My God Road** through the Virginia Canyon.

The summer opera season extends from early July through mid-August. For information, contact the Central City Opera, 621 17th Street, Suite 1625, Denver, CO 80293, or call (303) 292-6700. **Lou Bunch Day**, an annual whoop-up in honor of the town's last madam, is held on the third Saturday in June. The Central City Jazz festival is held on the third weekend of August and includes a Saturday parade through the old winding streets; call (303) 582-5563.

Where to Eat

The **Teller House** is a historic hotel, located next to the Opera House on Eureka Street. The hotel has five dining rooms, serving everything from burgers and pizza at lunch to steak and seafood at dinner time. The **Black Forest Inn**, in Black Hawk, is a favorite of local residents, serving up goulash and schnitzel as well as game and seafood. It's a huge but comfortable place. Originally an ice house, the **Mermaid Cafe** serves Mexican cuisine, plus steak and seafood.

Colorado Springs

Sitting at the edge of the Rockies, Colorado Springs is the state's most popular tourist destination. The attractions are many, both natural and man-made. Undoubtedly the greatest of these is **Pike's Peak**, the mountain that rises alone from the high Colorado Plateau and overshadows everything at its feet.

In addition to visiting the nearby mountain, you can enjoy a rich variety of sights and events in the Colorado Springs area, not the least of which is the **U.S. Air Force Academy**, which attracts more than a million visitors each year. Indeed, this city is a gigantic military installation, with several major enterprises based in or near the urban area. These include **NORAD** (North American Aerospace Defense Command), in an underground fortress within Cheyenne Mountain, nearby **Fort Carson**, and **Peterson**

Air Force Base. Colorado Springs is also home to the **U.S. Space Command;** its complex lies east of town.

The Air Force Academy has a campus of more than 18,000 acres sitting at the foot of the Rampart Mountains. Some of it is open to the public, and a good way to visit the grounds is to obtain a self-guiding tour brochure at the Academy's visitor center. The soaring chapel, with its 17 spires, is a favorite with visitors to the campus. The large square below the chapel is filled with parading cadets at noon, Monday through Friday, during the school year.

If you could only visit one attraction during a stopover in Colorado Springs, then it should be the **Garden of the Gods.** This 1,350-acre city park at the west end of town features hundreds of red sandstone formations, pinnacles, balancing rocks, and other strangely shaped natural sights. This unique area was formed when erosion and other forces brought rocks and other debris from the nearby mountains about 250 million years ago. Then the Rockies began to rise once more, tilting the rock layers in the park. More wind and water laid bare the rocks and pinnacles we see today: Steamboat Rock, Balanced Rock, the Rocking Chair, and the Three Graces, among many others.

The park was dedicated in 1909 and is now a Registered National Landmark. While it is possible to take a short drive through the Garden of the Gods, you really can't get the full effect of the dramatic sandstone shapes unless you park and walk along one of several trails that lead to various scenic viewpoints. The **Hidden Inn** is in the center of the garden, with a lookout tower, cafe, and gift shop. The famous **Trading Post**, which has been here since the 1920s, has Pueblo-style architecture. It's the largest gift shop in the area, selling Southwest arts and crafts; it is located at the west end of the park near Balanced Rock.

Other very popular area attractions include **Seven Falls,** a spectacular series of connected falls that cascade 300 feet down a granite cliff in the South Cheyenne Canyon. On summer nights, the complete canyon is illuminated by thousands of colored lights, adding a surreal beauty to the falls. Two pathways with stairs lead to the viewing locations. You must pay admission for entry to the falls and South Canyon, located at the southwestern edge of Colorado Springs. To get to the entry point, take Cheyenne Boulevard and drive west to the end of the road. It is possible to walk to the rim of the canyon (and see the falls for free) by walking through North Cheyenne Canyon and along the Mount Cutler Trail for two miles. This is an easy walk, and the view of the falls is spectacular.

Another commercialized natural attraction is **Cave of the Winds**, located six miles west of Colorado Springs off Highway 3. A 40-minute guided tour of the underground passages takes you into several huge rooms with stalactites and stalagmites. A recently added feature is a 60-foot-long room (35 feet high) lit by a gigantic lighting system. A windbreaker is advised for the longer (wild) tour of the caverns. This rugged tour takes more than two hours, and it leads through the deepest parts of the cave. An admission fee is charged.

The **Cheyenne Mountain Zoo** is a small but interesting collection of mostly endangered species housed in fascinating habitats. Admission to the zoo also includes entry to the **Will Rogers Shrine of the Sun**, commemorating the great western humorist. The zoo is open year-round. To get there, take Nevada Avenue (which becomes Highway 155), turn right onto Lake Avenue, and drive to The Broadmoor resort. Turn right onto Miranda Road, and drive to the zoo.

The thin mountain air of Colorado Springs is perfect for athletic training, and so the U.S. Olympic Committee established a national training center in the city. Nine teams are housed at the **U.S. Olympic Complex**, and athletes train here regularly. You'll see a visitor center with an Olympic film show and gift shop. A 90-minute tour of the complex is also available. The complex is located at 1776 Boulder Street.

Pike's Peak is located west of Colorado Springs, near the old resort town of Manitou Springs. For those who wish to assault the peak—by one of several ways—turn to the Manitou Springs page (390).

Where to Eat

Of course, there is **The Broadmoor**, that venerable and very posh resort, opened by magnate Spencer Penrose in 1918. The resort has several restaurants, the toniest of which is the **Charles Court**, located in the newer Broadmoor West, with a fine view of the lake. The food is exquisite, the prices are extreme, and people get very excited about dining here. They serve breakfast, Sunday brunch, and dinner (dinner daily from 6 P.M. to 9 P.M.). If you need to ask about prices, go somewhere else! The **Penrose Room** is another restaurant at The Broadmoor, offering European cuisine services in an Edwardian setting, on the ninth floor of Broadmoor South. Both rooms require coat and tie for dinner, and the maitre d' has ties for the uncouth or unprepared. Less high-priced establishments include **Zeb's**, featuring prime rib and very good pork ribs, with fine mountain views at 945 South 8th Street. **Giuseppe's Old Depot** is a restored Denver and Rio Grande Railroad station, with Italian cuisine and a salad bar. If you're a train (or food) fan, the depot is for you. It's at 10 South Sierra Madre Street.

Cortez

This is the nearest Colorado town to the famous Four Corners, that unique spot where you can stand in four states at the same time by carefully positioning your feet (the larger the better). More important, Cortez is the center for exploration of the prehistoric people called the Anasazi, a Navajo word for "Ancient Ones." Once thriving in cliff settlements, the Anasazi disappeared around 1300 A.D. The Anasazi were farmers and grew squash, corn, and beans in the valleys and on the mesas of the region. They lived in caves and were artists, potters, and basket makers. In their later years, they lived under overhanging cliffs;

you'll find excellent examples of these cliff dwellings in **Mesa Verde National Park.**

To learn about the Anasazi culture, visit these places: the fascinating **Anasazi Heritage Center** at Dolores, just north of Cortez; the **Hovenweep National Monument**, east of town at the Utah border; the **Lowry Pueblo**, northeast of Cortez, past the town of Pleasantview; and Mesa Verde. In town, you can see the **Cortez Archeological Center**; call 800-422-8975 or (970) 565-8975. The educational programs include one-week sessions featuring on-site activity at a five-acre dig site.

You can stay within Mesa Verde National Park, at the **Far View Lodge**, which has rooms with a view, a restaurant, and lounge. The lodge is open from June through September. Camping is also available in the park, with 490 sites at the Morefield Campground.

Aside from Anasazi explorations, the **Dolores River**—downstream from the McPhee Reservoir—attracts anglers fishing for rainbow, cutthroat, and brown trout. You'll also find good fishing in the reservoir. Brook, rainbow, and brown trout are found in **Groundhog Reservoir**, located about 32 miles north of Cortez via 11th Street and Forest Road 526.

The popular Navajo Trail leads into the **Lizard Head Wilderness Area**, west of Dolores. The trailhead is two miles north of the village of Dunton, on Forest Road 535. The trail climbs for five miles to Navajo Lake. Three "fourteeners" are there for hardy climbers, but the walk to the lake alone is worth the small effort. The hot springs at Dunton may be open for soaking, but then they may not, as the pool has been closed on and off over the years.

Where to Eat

Mexican food is available at a score of restaurants. Try **Francisca's**, at 125 Main Street, for some of the best. **Stromstead's Restaurant** is an excellent spot for seafood, steaks, and other dishes, served inside and outside on a deck that provides scenic views. The barbecue is also worth trying. It's at 1020 South Broadway. There are lots of fast-food places in Cortez, but for a digestible burger with considerable class, go directly to **Bob's Drive In**, at 610 North Broadway.

Creede

This is one of the least tourist-oriented towns in Colorado, but don't let that deter you from visiting this wonderful little mining town, in a beautiful site in the remote Rio Grande River Valley, north of the town of South Fork. For a description of the drive here, see page 342.

The San Juan Mountains provide a striking setting for Creede, which is situated in a side canyon within the wide valley. The first silver discovery in this area was made by Nicholas Creede in 1889. Within weeks, several mines opened, including the Holy Moses Mine (Creede exclaimed "Holy Moses" when he first spotted silver). The town boomed to a population of 10,000. It was a rowdy, undisciplined place, attracting con men, including the infamous Soapy Smith, who later would be shot to death in Skagway, Alaska, following more dirty tricks. Bat Masterson was the town marshal for a short time. However, like all of the other mining camps of the age, Creede collapsed—in fewer than five years—and then four major fires pretty much wiped out the town.

That didn't stop Creede from rebuilding, and although the last mine (the Homestead) stopped operations, the town continues to exist. It is now a center for artists and writers and for other independent spirits who stay here because of the beautiful scenery and the wilderness recreation that lies at their doorsteps in the **Rio Grande National Forest** and **La Garita Wilderness**. The Rio Grande provides some of the best fishing in this part of the state. A testament to that is the large number of guest ranches that are located along the river, just north of Creede. Other good fishing holes include the **Road Canyon Reservoir**, five miles east of Creede, and **Ute Creek**, west of the Rio Grande Reservoir.

The major summer attraction is the old **Creede Opera House**, which hosts the **Creede Repertory Theater**. Each year, the company stages a series of popular plays—so popular that reservations are required for most evenings. For the playlist and reservations, write to the Creede Opera House, P.O. Box 269, Creede, CO 81130, or call (719) 658-2540.

Those with four-wheel-drive or good clearance should plan to drive the **East Willow Creek Loop**, which leads from the end of the box canyon in Creede through the original settlement (North Creede), past old mining works, to the scenic Willow Park area. The seven-mile loop ends by passing through the old townsite of **Bachelor**, where only a few foundations remain. The road returns to Creede, passing the old pioneer cemetery.

Where to Eat

The **Creede Hotel** has rooms and a small restaurant with excellent food that changes its menu daily. The **Golden Nugget Restaurant** is a homey place with period decor (an old tin ceiling, brick walls) and basic, good food, including stews, steak, local trout, and a salad bar. It's open for breakfast, lunch, and dinner. Another place with character is the **Bristol Inn**, located out of town (18 miles southwest via Highway 149), with wonderful bread and American cuisine including a Sunday buffet. It's open during summer, until the end of September.

Cripple Creek and Victor

The streets of Cripple Creek are literally paved with gold (very low-grade ore), and it's no wonder. This mining region had the most prolific deposit in the world, with more than $600 million in gold taken out of the ground around Cripple Creek and Victor.

Both towns are on the **Gold Belt Tour**, a wonderful circle drive connecting this gold rush region with Cañon City to the south (see scenic drive on page 334). Cripple Creek is also accessible by taking Highway 67, which connects the town with Colorado Springs.

The gold was discovered by "Crazy Bob" Womack in the 1880s, and by 1891, the last great gold rush in the lower 48 states was on. In 1900, 25,000 people lived here. Like many discoverers, Womack died penniless, but the atmosphere and traditions of that era live on today in this town, recently boosted by Colorado's gambling laws.

Cripple Creek became a tourist destination through the fame of a wonderful historic hotel, the **Imperial**, which not only has a good dining room but stages melodramas during the summer months. A narrow-gauge railway takes visitors for a four-mile ride along historic track, past some of the most famous (and now defunct) mining operations.

Mining is still going on in Victor, which saw the bulk of the mining activity. This is a town in decline, and it's sad to see the old hotel with missing windows and the general state of decay. While the town was named after Victor Adams, a town founder, the favorite son was Lowell Thomas, the late and influential radio news broadcaster. The **Lowell Thomas Museum** displays artifacts of the golden age of radio and of Victor.

The **Fossil Beds National Monument** is in Florissant, northwest of Cripple Creek on County Road 1. The fossil bed was created when volcanoes erupted, sending debris into the Florissant Basin and creating a large lake. Shale was formed at the bottom of the lake, trapping an incredible range of plants and animals. Trails lead through the lake bottom, taking visitors to petrified trees, including redwoods that remain from the age when this area was much warmer than it is today.

Eleven Mile Canyon, north of town, is not only a scenic but a fishing wonder. The Eleven Mile Reservoir is stocked with kokanee, pike, and huge mackinaw trout. The area is a fine winter destination, with excellent cross-country skiing in the Crags area on the western slopes of Pike's Peak, only a few miles from Cripple Creek.

Gold Camp Road is an alternate route from Creede to Colorado Springs. Built on an old railway bed, this backroad leads around Cheyenne Mountain, with incredible views all the way. The route is not suitable for RVs and cars with trailers.

Where to Eat

The **Imperial Hotel** has the best restaurant in Cripple Creek: a dining room with all the ambiance of the early 1900s. All meals are served buffet-style, featuring prime rib, roast duck, curries, and seafood. It is open daily from May 15 through October 1 for breakfast, lunch, and dinner. The hotel is located at 123 North 3rd Street, downtown. The **Red Lantern** is a bar and restaurant in a plain setting but with good food, including chicken and barbecue dishes, at 353 Myers Avenue, in the former area of Cripple Creek's "parlor houses."

Denver

The Mile High City: the livable center of commerce in Colorado, and a major transportation hub for the whole western half of the United States.

Denver almost lost it when, in the 1860s, the Union Pacific decided to put its transcontinental railroad line through Cheyenne, about 100 miles north of Denver. However, Denverites wouldn't take this snub lightly and raised more than a quarter of a million dollars to build a railway spur to Cheyenne. **The Denver Pacific Railroad** was inaugurated in 1870 and—thanks to gold and silver strikes and a growing agricultural scene—Denver flourished. Rich cattle barons and millionaire miners built mansions and impressive hotels in the city. After a few years of financial difficulty when mining declined in the 1890s, Denver became a modern diversified city. Today, it has its long-awaited new airport (one of the five busiest in the nation), and it is a major manufacturing and trade center.

Denver occupies a commanding site on the high Colorado plateau. To the west lie foothills, and then the Rockies rise in the distance. Its population is as diversified as its business community.

Because of this great diversity of cultures, the Denver social and cultural scene is impressive, with fine restaurants offering cuisine from around the world, excellent museums, and a steady series of wonderful festivals and celebrations. The downtown area has a mixture of historic hotels and other buildings constructed during the gold rush period and modern high-rise towers.

Denver's daily newspapers include the *Rocky Mountain News*, still publishing more than 130 years after its first edition appeared in April 1859. Its founder, William Byers, brought his printing press here from Omaha, Nebraska, after he heard tales of the impressive gold rushes in the area. The *Denver Post* followed in the 1890s.

Denver is a civilized city with much to attract the visitor. Certainly, it's a fine place to begin or end a tour of the Colorado Rockies.

Parks and Gardens

Denver boasts a marvelous park system, and outside of the city, state parks and national forests provide recreational opportunities of every kind for summer and winter. Here are a few highlights:

- **Denver Botanic Gardens**

  Dominated by a large glass conservatory, the Botanic Gardens offer everything a garden lover could wish for. The park has three major gardens and several other smaller plantings. The alpine garden is a very impressive collection of high-altitude varieties and is perhaps the best alpine display in America. The Japanese garden with its teahouse, lake, and meandering stream is a quiet oasis. You can enjoy rose gardens, peony beds, an herb garden, and more. The conservatory is a modern structure containing the best collection of tropical plants in the West. Woody Allen film fans will recognize the conservatory building, which was used in *Sleeper*. The Botanic Gardens are open daily from dawn to dusk on Wednesdays, Saturdays, and Sundays, from June 1 until Labor Day; and from 9 A.M. to 4:45 P.M. on other days and throughout the year.

- **Washington Park**

  This park is perfect for family enjoyment. Paddleboats are available in the largest of two lakes, as well as fishing, playgrounds, an indoor pool for swimming, tennis courts, and bicycle paths. The park has lots of tall trees and also Rower plantings, including a replica of George Washington's Mount Vernon garden. The park is located between Almeda Avenue and Louisiana Avenue, west of Downing Street.

- **Cheeseman Park**

  Situated north of 8th Avenue and surrounded by residential housing (it was once the city cemetery), this is a favorite place to hear the summer concerts that are held regularly. The western view is quite impressive.

- **Barr Lake State Park**

  A short drive from Denver (20 miles to the west), this reservoir is one of two great bird-watching spots around Denver. Some 300 species have been seen to stop at the lake; the nature center in the park offers information on which birds are currently in residence. Herons and cormorants are permanent nesters on the shoreline. You'll also view eagles, owls, and geese in numbers.

  A trail leads around the lake, with boardwalks and blinds to enhance bird-watching. The trail is nine miles long; in winter months, it is ideal for cross-country skiing. A boat ramp is at the north end of the lake, and sailboats, canoes, rowboats, and boats with electric motors are allowed. The reservoir contains perch, trout, and bass. To get there, take Interstate 76 northeast from Denver.

- **Chatfield State Recreation Area**

  This is the other wonderful bird-watching location, complete with an arboretum, walking trails, hiking trails, and boating. It is another reservoir, part of the South Platte River system, with campsites along the shore. To reach the reservoir, take Interstate 25 to County Road 470 and drive west to Highway 121. Turn south and drive to the recreation area.

Other parks and recreation areas within a short drive of Denver include **Golden Gate Canyon State Park,** north of Black Hawk near Central City. **Devil's Head**, in Pike National Forest, is south of the metropolitan Denver area via Highway 85 past Littleton to Sedali; turn west onto Highway 67 and drive for nine miles. Turn south on Rampart Range Road and drive for another nine miles to Devil's Head Campground. From here, hiking trails lead into the mountains. You may turn this trip into a loop drive, through Colorado Springs by driving south to **Woodland Park** and taking Highway 24 east to Colorado Springs and Interstate 25 north to Denver. You might even plan a trip taking two or three days to fully enjoy the natural sights along this loop drive which cuts across the Rampart Range, passing several forest recreation areas.

Other Things to See and Do

Elitch Gardens is an amusement park built around gardens and it has been here since 1890. This is where Benny Goodman's band first gained its fame, and the place retains the wonderful aura of the early part of the century. The park has myriad flower beds along with rides including a fine roller coaster, The Twister. Many concerts are still held at Elitch Gardens, and a visit here is a summer must during your stay in Denver. It is located at 4620 West 38th Avenue. **Lakeside Amusement Park** is another old amusement park without the massed flowers, but this one has a lake, the Cyclone Coaster, and other wonderful attractions. It's on Sheridan Boulevard, south of Interstate 70.

If beer is important to you, the **Coors Brewery** is a significant cultural icon. The brewery offers a free 30-minute tour of their "unique" brewing process, with beer tasting at the end. It is open

Monday through Saturday from 10 A.M. to 4 P.M. at Ford and 13th Streets in Golden, at the western edge of the metro area.

The **Colorado State Capitol** is a smaller version of the U.S. Capitol, with a gold-plated dome. It sits on a hill with good mountain views. Weekday tours are conducted on the half-hour during summer months from 9 A.M. to 3:30 P.M. You can also get free tours of the **Governor's Mansion**, which is located in a magnificent garden. The house is basically as it was, designed by Walter Cheeseman around 1900; it features the huge Palm Room, which gives a fine view of the garden displays. The free tours are conducted from June through August, from 10 A.M. to 1 P.M.

The museums of Denver reflect the heritage of the community. The **Colorado History Museum** features excellent displays of Colorado's Native American heritage, as well as the rambunctious mining era. This is a fine way to learn about the rich history of this area. A book shop is in the museum, which is located near the State Capitol at 1300 Broadway. It is open daily, Monday to Saturday from 10 A.M. to 4:30 P.M. and Sunday from noon to 4:30 P.M.

The **Black American West Museum** tells the history of the West including the many African-American cowboys who helped to settle it. The museum is located in the Five Points district and offers a fascinating experience. The address is 607 28th Street.

A **children's museum** is across the street from Mile High Stadium, at 2121 Crescent Drive. The museum is filled with interactive displays, a circus tent, and a padded ball room. Puppet shows are often staged, and your children (and you) will have a grand time.

The **Museum of Western Art,** at 1727 Tremont Place, holds probably the best collection of western art in the nation, in one of Denver's original downtown buildings (across the street from the famous **Brown Palace Hotel**). Frederick Remington is only one of the renowned western artists whose works are featured. You'll also find a good selection of works by Georgia O'Keeffe.

And while you're in the area, you must visit "Leadville Johnny" Brown's hotel, even if you're not staying there.

Another popular stop for visitors is the **U.S. Mint.** This is where United States coins are made, and a guided tour takes you through the process. It is also a large repository for gold. The mint is open daily from 8:30 A.M. to 3 P.M. and is located at the corner of Cherokee and Colfax.

Denver nightclubs feature country and western music and jazz in good supply. The **Denver Center for the Performing Arts** is a large complex that offers opera, ballet, drama, and music concerts. It is home to the **Denver Symphony** and the **Stagewest** cabaret theater.

Denver Zoo, in city park on East 23rd Street, features a children's zoo as well as the main displays, which include the "North Shores" exhibit with polar bears and sea lions. There is a miniature zoo trail for children. The zoo is open daily from 10 A.M. to 5 P.M.

Where to Eat

First, the Brown Palace Hotel has several restaurants in an historic setting, including the **Ship Tavern** pub and the more sophisticated **Palace Arms** dining room. Prices in these rooms range from expensive to super-deluxe. Another pricey (but excellent) restaurant complex is **Cliff Young's,** at 638 East 17th Avenue. Portions are large, and the decor is splendid.

The oldest restaurant to have operated continuously in the city is the **Buckhorn Exchange.** Anybody who is anybody has eaten here. Stuffed animal heads are mounted on the walls, and game is served as well as seafood and steaks. A bar is on the upper floor. If you're not allergic to stuffed animals, the Buckhorn should be on your list of atmospheric places in which to dine.

The growth in the number of ethnic restaurants in Denver has been tremendous in recent years. All of the following serve good food at quite reasonable prices. **Pagliacci's** features Italian pasta and other dishes in a homey atmosphere at 1440 West 33rd Avenue. **Las Delicias** is an inexpensive Mexican cafe with modest decor but wonderful food. It's open daily from 9 A.M. at 439 East 19th Ave. **Casa Bonita** is another Mexican experience entirely. The food is excellent, but the decor and ambiance attract diners (including families)—it's a restaurant as theme park. You'll see a pool with caves, as divers leap over a 30-foot cliff and water cascades to the pool. They also have staged gunfights and mariachi bands. This place is an event! It has full bar service and is open each day at 11 A.M. at 6715 Colfax Avenue. Chinese food purists swear that the **House of Hunan** (at 440 South Colorado Boulevard) has the best Chinese food in town, specializing in Hunan and Szechuan cuisine.

The **North Woods Inn** (in Littleton) is a long-time favorite of locals for steak and prime rib dinners. It's a relaxed place with a western ambiance. It is located at 6115 South Santa Fe Drive.

For barbecue, our local tasters recommend **Daddy Bruce's Bar-B-Que** at 1629 Bruce Randolph Boulevard. Ribs, chicken, pork, beef, cornbread, beans—it's all served here with a "patented" sauce. Catfish is a popular alternative to the normal barbecue. Liquor is not served, although some diners bring their own.

Durango

The wonderful old city of Durango is blessed with the history and cultures of its inhabitants and early settlers: the Native Americans, the Spanish, and the Northern European immigrants who came to live in the splendid Animas Valley.

The Spanish called it *El Rio de las Animas Perdidas,* "The River of Lost Souls." Lying at the southern foot of the San Juan Mountains, Durango bears the heritage of the mining boom of the 1880s that happened just to the north of the city, in the area around Silverton and Ouray. The Ute people, who had been granted this large tract of land by the government, were dispossessed, forced to relinquish some 6,000 square miles of territory, and moved to a reservation on the New Mexico border. At the same time, a small town named Durango was becoming an important railway center.

The first settlement in the area was **Animas City**, a few miles north of the present city of Durango. When the residents of this town refused to let the railway build their terminus there, the plum went to Durango. The growing city served the mining interests of the region until the silver and gold ran out. Tourism took over as the primary industry, and Durango remains a charming historic town with a Wild West and Spanish ambiance, combining to make this a wonderful place to visit.

One of the chief attractions is the **Durango and Silverton Narrow Gauge Railroad,** a scenic railroad that runs along the old route to the silver mines, developed by the Denver and Rio Grande Western. This is a spectacular day-long return trip through the beautiful Animas Valley, climbing high above the river with incredible views of the massive San Juan peaks. The round trip takes eight hours, although you can ride the trail one way and stay in Silverton overnight or return to Durango by bus over scenic Molas Pass. People with cars often split up: some take the train ride to Silverton, while the rest drive to Silverton and make the return trip by train. We highly recommend this trip (you'll need reservations). Contact the Durango and Silverton Narrow Gauge Railway, 479 Main Avenue, Durango CO 81301 or phone (970) 247-2733.

The **Animas River** is well known for its white water, offering excellent rafting, canoeing, and kayaking. **Animas River Days** is a celebration held the last weekend in June with river races and other events. **Colorfest** is an ongoing festival held while the trees are turning, from mid-September to mid-October. Special events are staged during these four weeks including an auto show, more raft races, art shows, fishing derbies, and more. **Snowdown,** a slightly crazy event to get rid of cabin fever, is held late in January each year. For information on special events in Durango, call (970) 247-0312.

Hikers enjoy the challenge of the **Colorado Trail,** which begins its 469 mile jaunt over the mountains and across the Continental Divide near Durango. You reach the trailhead by taking

25th Street from North Main Street and then stopping just inside the San Juan National Forest. The **Goulding Creek Trail** provides an interesting day-long hike through aspen groves, 17 miles north of Durango. The trailhead is on the west side of Highway 550. It's a six-mile round trip with quite a climb above the Hermosa Cliffs. Check with the forest ranger station for trail information and maps.

The area has several fine golf clubs, including the **Hillcrest Golf Course**, which offers good views of the mountains. The club is located on the Fort Lewis College mesa at the east end of town. The **Tamarron Resort** has a championship course, and the resort is one of Colorado's finest. If you're staying at the resort, you have your choice of tee times. If you're not, you take your chances when you get there. The resort is located beside Highway 550, 18 miles north of Durango, on the way to Silverton.

Day drives in the La Plata Mountains and along the Animas River provide visits to several ghost towns. Two Durango/Cortez area drives are detailed on page 351.

Anglers don't have to go farther than the Animas River to catch trout. The best locations are south of the city or below Devil's Falls. The **Vallecito Reservoir** has a 22-mile shoreline and boat ramps and is well stocked with rainbow, German brown trout, northern pike, and kokanee. The reservoir is 23 miles to the northeast of town via County Road 240 and then on County Road 501, which runs beside the Los Piños River to the miles north of reservoir.

Skiers are coming increasingly to **Purgatory**, the ski area north of Durango on Highway 550. This is a good downhill area with 35 miles of runs and a vertical drop of 1,750 feet. Although a lodge is located next to the ski hill, accommodations are limited, and many skiers stay in Durango and drive the 28 miles. Purgatory also has a fine series of cross-country ski trails in the San Juan National Forest, across the highway from the ski lifts.

Soakers will want to have a plunge in the **Trimble Hot Springs**, just north of town via Highway 550. The operation was a spa in the 1880s and the current owners, the Bears, renovated the facilities in 1988; it has an Olympic-size pool, a spacious bathhouse, and a small outdoor pool plus private hot tubs. The water in the small therapeutic pool has a temperature of 104°F. The large pool has warm water and is suitable for swimming. A picnic park with barbecue grills is on the site.

Durango boasts a busy nightlife scene in the hotels and clubs, and those interested in local culture can visit the downtown arts and craft shops and the **Animas School Museum** at 2nd Avenue and 31st Street.

Where to Eat

The **Strater Hotel** was built more than 100 years ago and is still in business. Its dining room (**Henry's Restaurant**) and saloon are popular places to eat in a marvelous old-time atmosphere. The Sunday brunch buffet is an experience suited to gourmets and gourmands. Highly regarded **Ariano's Restaurant** delivers northern Italian cuisine and the seafood and steaks that many tourists demand. It has a bar, and the wine list is superb. It opens daily at 5:30 P.M. For steaks and seafood, the **Ore House** is decorated with old mining tools and offers a rustic, barn-like ambiance. The bar opens at 5 P.M. and the dining room at 5:30 P.M. The place to eat Mexican is **Francisco's**, at 619 Main Street, open weekdays from 11 A.M. and for Sunday brunch at 10 A.M.

Estes Park

Surrounding crags dominate this beautiful valley town at the gateway to Rocky Mountain National Park. The highest of the nearby mountains is Long's Peak, which is 14,255 feet high. During the summer months, thousands of people crowd the streets of Estes Park each day. Most come to visit Rocky Mountain Park, staying overnight in one of the town's motels or hotels. In a normal year, more than three million people visit Estes Park. Very few of them come during the spring or fall, and these are the best

times to appreciate the town and the park. My first visit to the park was in mid-September with fall color on the lower slopes and a comfortable number of travelers with whom to share the beauty of the mountains. You can reach Estes Park either by the Peak to Peak route (see the scenic drive on page 322), from the Central City/Black Hawk area west of Denver, or by driving from Denver north on Interstate 25 to Boulder and taking the Boulder Turnpike (Highway 36) through Boulder to Lyons and on to Estes Park.

Although you will have many other things to see and do around the resort town, **Rocky Mountain National Park** is the major attraction. For park attractions, see page 398. Fishing is better outside the park than inside, and local anglers recommend fishing the **Big Thompson River** five to eight miles downstream from Estes Park. You can get there by taking Highway 34, and you'll find fishing access parking spots beside the road. You should find rainbow and brown trout. Lake Estes east of town offers small rainbow trout stocked regularly. **Mary's Lake** is a tiny lake at the west end of Estes Park via Highway 36 and Mary's Lake Road. You'll probably find fish at the inlet to the lake.

Two golf courses are in town. **Estes Park Golf Club,** on Highway 7, has an 18-hole course and is open from April into October. The mountain views are tremendous, and play is challenging. The **Lake Estes Executive Course** has nine holes, is open year-round, and provides an equal challenge. It's on Highway 34 (Big Thompson Avenue).

Hikers may wish to take a walk outside of the national park area, and **Roosevelt National Forest** offers several fine trails leading to spectacular views. One of the best (and easiest to climb) is the **Lily Mountain Trail.** It climbs 1.5 miles to the summit, where you can enjoy great views of Long's Peak—the town lying below and the Mummy Range to the north. The trailhead is located six miles south of Estes Park, via Highway 7. You'll see a turnoff to the west and a parking area.

Where to Eat

Because Estes Park is a resort town, food in local restaurants tends to be expensive, although the quality of food usually matches the prices. **Black Canyon Inn** at 800 MacGregor Avenue, not only has good food (European and American cuisine) but it has mountain atmosphere in high- roofed log dining rooms. The **Fawn Brook Inn** in nearby Allenspark is renowned for its fine food, quiet service and ambiance. Because of changing hours of operation, call (970) 747-2256. Choose **La Casa** for Mexican and Cajun (both are equally good) at 222 East Elkhorn. Open since the 1930s, the **Old Plantation** at 128 East Elkhorn is a local favorite for fish, chicken, duck, and great pies.

Glenwood Springs

The Ute people knew what was good for them, and they congregated, for many years, at the hot springs near the confluence of the Colorado and Roaring Fork rivers. In the 1880s, the springs became a hot spot for high society after wealthy miners "discovered" the springs and made them their own. The scions of America's great families stayed at the famous **Hotel Colorado** where the waters could be taken amidst top-class service and all the luxuries of home.

Now that the ski resort of **Aspen** is just down the road and **Sunlight** is even closer, summer rafters come to try out the Colorado River through the Glenwood Canyon, and the springs continue to attract visitors to Glenwood Springs.

Built more than 100 years ago, the **Glenwood Hot Springs Pool** is touted as the world's largest outdoor mineral hot springs pool. Actually, there are two pools. The small pool is heated to 104°F while the large pool is heated to 90°F. You can rent bathing suits and towels, and you'll also find a restaurant on the site. In summer months, the pools are open daily; from September through May, the facility is closed the second Wednesday of each month. The **Vapor Caves** are located next to the hot pools and provide steam-bathing as well as a spa program. The caves are open daily, year-round except on Thanksgiving and Christmas. The pools and caves are located at 709 East 6th Street.

Other caves near the town offer spelunking adventure. Some of the caves are inside **Iron Mountain**, to the north of town. Across the river is **Hubbard's Cave**. For touring information, contact Timberline Grotto at (970) 945-5053. Glenwood Springs has two golf courses (four if you count the two naturally landscaped mini-golf courses at Johnson Park). The **Glenwood Springs Golf Club** is an excellent 9-hole course with a pro shop, driving range, and restaurant. It's on Highway 6. The **Westbank Ranch Golf Course** (at 1007 Westbank Road) also has nine holes with carts available.

You can enjoy cross-country skiing at the local **Sunlight Ski Area**. Groomed trails are accessible from the ski area base and from at least two of the chairlifts. Lessons and equipment are available. Located 16 miles northwest of town via Interstate 70 and Elk Creek Road, the White River National Forest has an excellent trail system, which leads through the Flat Tops Wilderness. The downhill slopes of Aspen and Snowmass are about 42 miles south of Glenwood Springs via Highway 82 (see the scenic drive on page 330).

Where to Eat

French cuisine is the specialty at **Sopris Restaurant and Lounge**, but the atmosphere is casual. It's seven miles south of town on Highway 82. Seafood and beef dishes are served at **Penelope's**, at 2525 Grand Avenue, which has a wonderful view of the Roaring Fork River from its restaurant and from the outdoor deck. It's open for dinner daily and opens early for Sunday brunch. For tasty and less expensive fare, try **Los Desperados** on Mel-Rey Road, and the **19th Street Diner** on Grand Avenue.

Grand Junction

Located in western Colorado, Grand Junction is a little-known and underrated place to visit. It's the takeoff point for the Dolores

Canyon Drive (to Telluride, starting on page 354) and the gateway to the Grand Mesa, America's largest flattopped mountain. Grand Junction is a trading center for the many cattle ranches and fruit farms in the area. There was a uranium boom in the 1950s, but mining faded quickly. Today, tourism is a slowly growing but steady feature of this unpretentious community.

The major single attraction is the **Colorado National Monument,** located at Fruita a few miles west of Grand Junction. Open year-round, the monument offers superb hiking, biking, and driving with views of the deep red canyons and massive rock pillars. The major road through the Monument is **Rim Rock Drive,** a 23-mile tour of the park built by the Civilian Conservation Corps in the 1930s. From the heights of the drive are wonderful overlooks from the Uncompahgre Plateau over the desert canyons. If you start this drive in Grand Junction instead of Fruita, the drive covers 35 miles. You'll find a visitor center toward the western end of the monument.

Trails down into the canyons provide fine views and eerie experiences. **John Otto's Trail, Window Rock Trail,** and the **Coke Ovens Trail** provide other short walks that can be completed (both ways) in about two hours. The **Monument Canyon Trail** takes longer (about four hours each way) and leads past high cliffs descending more than 600 feet. **Serpent's Trail** is located near the east end of the park, following the winding path of an old road for 2.5 miles.

Grand Mesa is located east of Grand Junction. This flat top rises more than a mile above the level of the town. The lava surface is dotted with lakes and is covered with forest (pine and aspen). The entire mountain top is part of Grand Mesa National Forest; several lodges on the mountain are open during summer months. **Crag Crest Trail** provides a 10-mile loop hike past several lakes. It leads to high spots where there are fine views of the surrounding mesa and distant mountain ranges. For information, go to the **Grand Mesa Visitor Center** at Carp Lake.

You have two ways to get to the mesa. From Grand Junction, drive northeast on Interstate 70 for 20 miles and then take Highway 65 for another 25 miles. Highway 65 is **Skyway Drive**, which traverses the mesa. The other route is Land's End Road, which offers a spectacular drive up the mountain. To get to this route, take Highway 50 south from Grand Junction past Whitewater and turn left onto the access road. The road leads to Highway 65 on the mesa.

Where to Eat

Sweetwaters, on the Main Street Mall, downtown, serves northern Italian cuisine with a good wine and beer selection. A more romantic ambiance is found at the **Winery** at 642 Main Street. Dishes include steak, prime rib, and several seafood entrees. The town has two good Mexican cafes: **Los Reyes** at 811 South 7th Street and **W.W. Peppers** at 759 Horizon Drive.

Lake City

Lake City is another of those amazing Colorado places that first sprang up during the gold and silver rushes of the late-1800s and then metamorphosed into a quaint, historic tourist town. What makes Lake City different from the rest is its remote location in a canyon on the Lake Fork of the Gunnison River, surrounded by the highest peaks of the San Juan Range with a large lake just down the road.

Until the gold rush of 1874, the Ute had fiercely protected this area. Other violent incidents occurred in this area as well. In the winter just before gold was found, a man named Alferd Packer guided a group of prospectors over the mountains from Delta. They had set out with only enough provisions to last the party 10 days. Packer appeared six weeks later, some 76 miles north of the Lake City area—alone but with several wallets containing money, which he used to go on a binge. Later that summer, five partially decomposed bodies were found a few miles south of Lake City, beside Lake San Cristobal. Four of the men had been murdered with an axe, and the fifth had been shot to death. By this time, Packer had disappeared. He was found nine years later in Wyoming and was tried in the Lake City Court House. After two trials (the first was declared unconstitutional), Packer was convicted of manslaughter and sentenced to 45 years in the Cañon City Penitentiary. However, the governor pardoned Packer, who was released after serving only five years. He died in 1907 and is buried in Littleton. You'll find a historic marker at the massacre site; every September, the citizens of Lake City hold their "Alferd Packer Jeep Tour and Barbecue."

Lake San Cristobal is the second largest natural lake in Colorado and was formed more than 800 years ago when the valley was blocked by the Slumgullion Earthflow. The lake has a marvelous setting, with high peaks all around. Rainbow and brown trout and mackinaw are found in the lake. To get to the lake and recreation sites, drive two miles south from town on Highway 149 and turn onto County Road 30.

Backroad fans have one of the best drives in the Rockies starting from Lake City. The **Engineer Pass/Cinnamon Pass Loop** is a National (BLM) Scenic Byway. The 49-mile loop connects this area with Ouray, with an additional spur to Silverton. To get started (and normal cars can do the first part of the drive), depart from the south end of Lake City—a sign points to the byway—and head for Engineer Pass. The road reaches the ghost town of **Capitol City** after nine miles. Cars can drive for another 4.5 miles, to Rose's Cabin. From then on, it's four-wheel-drive all the way to Ouray. The road leads above the tree line to Engineer Pass (el. 13,100 feet), and then descends to Ouray.

Where to Eat

Located in the downtown historic district, **Mountain Harvest Cafe** serves up good breakfasts, large burger plates, chicken fried steak, and more. **Crystal Lodge** (also a good place to stay) is located two miles south of town on Highway 149. It is open for three meals a day, serving American cuisine. **Lake Fork Restaurant** is five miles north of town on Highway 149 amidst fine scenery, serving European and American dishes, including seafood and steaks.

Leadville

Leadville is one of the main reasons for the growth of Denver, and indeed for the development of Colorado in the 1880s and 1890s. By 1880, it was the second largest city in the state. Almost 25,000 people lived there as the result of enormous mineral strikes. By 1880, the area was producing more than $10 million in silver per year. More than a few fortunes were made in this high mountain region (the town has an elevation of 10,152 feet), including that of Henry A. W. Tabor, who became the state's first multimillionaire. Tabor had first settled with his wife in Oroville, 2.5 miles south of Leadville, but moved his general store to Leadville after strikes were made there. He lucked into grub-staking a mining operation, which made his fortune. The town boomed and soon State Street (now Second Avenue) boasted a quarter mile of saloons, gambling halls, brothels, and other entertainment spots. Houses, stores, and banks followed. The **Tabor Opera House** still stands, along with impressive Victorian homes. Tabor was the cause of a notorious scandal when he left his wife to marry Elizabeth "Baby Doe" McCourt. Tabor died penniless in Denver, while Baby Doe lived near Leadville in a cabin at the "Matchless" Mine, until she froze to death in 1935. Tabor's first wife, Augusta, fared better. She enjoyed a wealthy estate for the rest of her life.

Leadville not only produced silver but also gold, zinc, manganese, molybdenum, and turquoise. Many of America's wealthiest families got their start in the area: the Guggenheims, the Marshall Fields, and the fabulous James J. Brown ("Leadville Johnny"), who owned the Little Johnny Mine and plumbed an enormous vein of gold. He built the Brown Palace Hotel in

Denver and his wife was the "unsinkable" Molly Brown, the heroine of the Titanic and of musical comedy fame.

Leadville today reflects all of this history in the old homes and office buildings and two of the original saloons. The town offers several special celebrations, such as the **Leadville Music Festival** (July), **Boom Days** (early August), and a summer mining camp re-creation at Oro City. There are several campgrounds and RV parks including forest camp sites on **Turquoise Lake,** three miles from town. Fishing in the lake is good, as is fishing in the Twin Lakes Reservoir. The **Leadville, Colorado and Southern Railroad** provides an excellent scenic train ride which operates during the summer and fall months.

Where to Eat

The **Delaware Hotel** at 700 Harrison Avenue (the main street) is a cozy, historic hotel with a good dining room, Le Grande Cafe, on the second floor. Three miles north of town on Highway 91, the **Prospector** provides a fine mountain view and a mainly steak and seafood menu. The modest **Garden Cafe,** on West 4th Street, has fine breakfasts and Italian entrees later in the day. The **Grill** (Elm Street) and **La Cantina** (Highway 24) both serve good Mexican food.

Manitou Springs

This long time resort town is located just west of the larger city of Colorado Springs. The springs referred to in both place names are actually in Manitou Springs, at the foot of Pike's Peak. The area has been an attraction for visitors since the day Zebulon Pike spotted his namesake peak in 1806. The real boom happened in 1859 when gold was discovered in Central City (to the north) and the hot springs here generated a spa resort, bringing America's wealthy to "take the waters." Twenty-six springs still bubble and feed pools. The town has a National Historic District and a collection of antique and curio stores, hotels, and restaurants.

Most of the excitement in Manitou Springs is based on Pike's Peak tourism. The **Manitou and Pike's Peak Cog Railway** takes you to the Pike's Peak summit (el. 14,110 feet). Originally powered by steam engines from its founding in 1891, the railroad now operates with diesel power. It offers a painless way to get to the top of Pike's Peak; trains leave regularly from the depot on Ruxton Avenue. Passing through aspen groves at the lower levels, the train passes the timberline with wonderful views of the valley below as the cars complete their climb up the slope. The round trip takes just over three hours. The train runs from mid-May through October. The other way to get to the top of Pike's Peak is by the **Pike's Peak Highway,** a 38-mile round trip that climbs nearly 7,000 feet and offers spectacular views of the Continental Divide and the surrounding countryside. The first seven miles of the road are paved. Opened in 1916, the toll road is open from May through October and is reached by taking Highway 24 northwest from Manitou Springs. Drivers should be reminded that this road is steep and engines can overheat. The road is patrolled in case help is required. You'll find a restaurant as well as a gift shop at the summit.

The **Public Swimming Pool** is an indoor pool open year-round at 202 Manitou Avenue. The **Old Manitou Spa** is a bed and breakfast hotel with a spa program. A popular attraction in Manitou Springs, the **Miramont Castle** is a wild, eccentric, rambling structure built by Father Jean Baptiste Francolon for his mother in 1895. It was later a sanitarium and also an apartment complex. Its architecture is varied to say the least, ranging from Byzantine to Victorian, and the 46 rooms display everything under the sun. The castle is now on the National Register of Historic Places and has been a museum since the late 1970s. Admission is charged.

Where to Eat

The **Stagecoach Inn** at 702 Manitou Avenue is a former home built on the site of the stagecoach stop on the route to Cripple

Creek. Lunch and dinner are served; on Sundays, you can enjoy a champagne brunch. **Iron Springs Chateau** offers dinner and entertainment in the form of a nightly comedy melodrama. The event begins with an all-you-can-eat meal (fried chicken and barbecued beef between 6 P.M. and 7 P.M.), and the melodrama starts at 8:30 P.M. The **Briarhurst Manor Inn** serves European and American dishes in a atmospheric log building at 404 Manitou Avenue.

Mesa Verde National Park

Two thousand years ago, nomadic people settled on the mesas of southern Colorado, establishing farms and developing crafts such as woven baskets. They later made pottery and established crude homes in the recesses of cliffs. The Basket Makers emerged as a Pueblo culture around A.D. 750, and they are called the Anasazi. As their culture advanced, they built homes on top of the mesas—of stone and masonry. Underground rooms (kivas) were used for ceremonial and social occasions. They began to weave cotton cloth and they became proficient in pottery manufacturing.

Over a period of time, the Anasazi sought protection for their homes under overhanging cliffs. By A.D. 1200, some lived in masonry homes built into the cliffs, while others lived on top of the mesas. By the time the Anasazi had completely disappeared (A.D. 1300), their pottery-making had developed to a very sophisticated stage. And then, they disappeared. Some archeologists believe that the Anasazi vanished from the Four Corners area because of a long drought. In any event, the mesas and cliff dwellings were deserted, and it was two more centuries before the Ute moved into this area of the Southwest.

This astounding national park, located southeast of the town of Cortez, provides the most notable display of Anasazi ruins and artifacts in the Four Corners region. Here are the remains of the huge housing developments containing up to 200 rooms, some of them

four stories high. The **Cliff Palace**, one of the largest of the dwellings, was found by ranchers Richard Wetherill and Charlie Mason in 1888 on their search for stray cattle. In the following decade, many people came to the area to collect artifacts. As a result, the U.S. Congress created the national park in 1906 to protect this superb archeological reminder of the Anasazi for all of us to share.

Today, the park is also a UNESCO-designated World Heritage Site with a museum that is open year-round. The park is separated into two major areas: **Far View/Wetherill Mesa**, and **Chapin Mesa**. Each has its own road and its own special ruins and other attractions.

Morefield Village, the name for the group of facilities in the north end of the park, is four miles from the park entrance. It includes a gas station, cafe, and picnic areas. **Morefield Campground** is located here and evening programs are held in the campground amphitheater. The visitor center is open during summer months.

South of Morefield Village, the park road leads through a tunnel before reaching the **Montezuma Valley Overlook** and then **Park Point**, which both provide spectacular views of the valley below. The road then approaches the **Far View Visitor Center** where there is a full range of information on the park, including trail maps and the interpretive activities conducted by park rangers. The Far View area also has a gas station and a cafe. The **Wetherill Mesa** is seen by driving along a road that begins just west of the **Farview Visitor Center**. The road runs across the mesa for 12 miles, taking you to **Step House**, **Long House**, and **Badger House**, the three major ruins in this portion of the park. The **Park Point Nature Trail** provides wonderful views of the Four Corners region from a fire outlook. View the **Far View Ruins** by taking a self-guided tour across the mesa. This part of the park is open during summer months only.

The **Archeological Museum** is located on **Chapin Mesa**, which you get to by driving south along an access road that begins at the Farview Visitor Center. In the museum, dioramas show the living conditions of the Anasazi.

Also on Chapin Mesa, a half-mile self-guided tour will take you around the Cliff Palace ruins. This site is a 10-minute drive from the museum. Other attractions of this area include the **Spruce Tree House** (again with a self-guided tour) and **Balcony House**, which features a guided ranger tour that lasts one hour.

Two hiking trails lead into Spruce Canyon. The **Petroglyph Point Trail** is a three-mile loop taking between two and three hours to complete. The trail will introduce you to mesa plant species and it passes a remarkable panel of petroglyphs (carvings) in the sandstone. The geological makeup of the mesa is also apparent from this trail. The **Spruce Canyon Trail** provides a 2.1-mile round trip, climbing from 6,440 feet to the 7,000 foot level. The walk takes between one and two hours. Both of the canyon trails begin along the Spruce Tree House Trail.

Cyclists may wish to ride on the park roads, except for the Wetherill Mesa Road where bicycles are not permitted.

How to Get There and Where to Stay

The park lies south of Highway 160, 10 miles east of the town of Cortez. The park entrance is 36 miles west of Durango. Good motel and hotel accommodations are in both towns (see Cortez accommodations on page 414 and Durango accommodations on page 417). A signed road leads south from Highway 160 into the park, and the **Morefield Campground** is four miles south of the park entrance. This is the only campground in the park and it is open from mid-April through October. The campground is suitable for trailers and RVs, with some partial hookups and a dump station.

The **Far View Motor Lodge** is open from May through October. For information and reservations, phone (970) 529-4421 or write ARA Mesa Verde Company, P.O. Box 277, Mancos, CO 81328. The Far View area is 15 miles from the park entrance.

Ouray

Best known for its hot springs, this quiet little Victorian town is a haven for lovers of outdoor recreation. In the summer, the things to do here are camping, hiking, and—most popular of all—jeeping. The area to the south, east, and west of Ouray is laced with old mining roads and rail beds that attract thousands of four-wheel-drivers every summer. Rocky drives to Engineer, Cinnamon, Black Bear, and Imogene passes provide memorable experiences for those who own their own four-wheel-drive vehicles and for those who arrive in Ouray to rent the necessary wheels.

Winter in Ouray provides excellent cross-country skiing, attracting backcountry skiers who head for the **Mount Sneffels Wilderness Area** (also great summer adventure country). You'll find excellent skiing near Red Mountain Pass, which you reach by driving the Million Dollar Highway between Silverton and Ouray. Trail guides are available in town during the cross-country season. Winter in Ouray is a special pleasure, as the little town situated in a box canyon glows with twinkling lights reflecting the Victorian architecture on the snow. The hot springs bubble at the edge of town providing wonderful winter soaking.

Not that the soaking isn't fine in the summer too! You can enjoy two hot springs places. **The Ouray Hot Springs** are located at the north end of town in the civic park. It has two pools; the smaller pool is heated to 104°F. Admission is good for the whole day. **Orvis Hot Springs,** nine miles north of Ouray, features a large outdoor pool and four smaller indoor pools. You'll find overnight rooms at the hot springs site. The view of the Sneffels Range from the outdoor pool is splendid. Bathing suits are optional, and the pools are open to the public from 10 A.M. to 10 P.M.

The former St. Joseph's Hospital is now the **Ouray Historical Museum**, which displays artifacts from the town's Victorian era in a succession of rooms. Included are displays of mining equipment, re-created hospital rooms, and a general store. Outside are two restored cabins from Ouray's pioneer period. The museum is located at the corner of 5th Street and 6th Avenue. The **Bachelor-Syracuse Mine** provides an excellent mine tour; it mined gold and silver until the 1980s when it closed with the slump in silver prices. Tours leading through more than 3,000 feet of rock take an hour during which the whole hard rock mining process is explained. It's open daily from 10 A.M. from mid-May to mid-September. Drive north on Highway 550 and turn right onto County Road 14.

Jeep touring is at its best here, on the network of old mining roads that lead above the tree line. To rent a jeep or to take a guided tour, contact Switzerland of America Jeep Rentals at (970) 325-4484 or San Juan Scenic Jeep Tours/Jeeps Ouray at (970) 325-4444.

Where to Eat

The **Outlaw** on Main Street is a popular steak and seafood place that also operates a barbecue cookout in the mountains during summer months. The **Bon Ton Restaurant** (on Main) serves fine northern Italian cuisine and specialties like Beef Wellington. The **Adobe Inn** serves great Mexican food (in the summer on an outdoor patio) 10 miles north of Ouray in the town of Ridgway.

Pagosa Springs

This town off the southeastern slopes of the San Juan Mountains is not a noted tourist center. Yet you will find excellent opportunities for sightseeing and outdoor recreation in the area, particularly north of town where the San Juans rise and the San Juan National Forest provides recreational opportunities including some of the best skiing in the state. The town is also a gateway to the Rio Grande River and lake country beyond the San Juan Range. This area is covered on the Lake City Drive (Pagosa Springs to Lake City, page 342).

The hot springs are not a great attraction today, although the Spa Motel has a small pool and indoor bathhouses. The wonderfully natural **Rainbow Hot Spring** is northeast of town, which you reach after a hike of five miles along the West Fork of the San Juan River. To get there, drive along Highway 160 toward Wolf Creek Pass for 13 miles, and then turn west on Born's Lake Road. The trailhead is about three miles down the road. The trail leads through the **Weminuche Wilderness Area** to the spring. The hot water comes out of a rock wall into a pool beside the river. This spring is a little-known treasure, which offers one of the best hot pool experiences anywhere.

If you've explored Anasazi ruins near Cortez and haven't yet had enough of this fascinating culture, you should head for **Chimney Rock** southwest of Pagosa Springs. This Anasazi town has been compared to Machu Picchu and was occupied by at least 2,000 Anasazi who farmed along the Piedra River and on the nearby mesas. The archeological area was set aside for preservation in 1970 and is managed by the U.S. Forest Service. The site is open daily, and forest rangers provide tours. Tour reservations are necessary, and you can make them through the Pagosa Springs Ranger Station at (970) 264-2268. You get to the entrance to Chimney Rock by driving west for 17 miles on Highway 160 and then turning south on Highway 151 for three miles. You can also take guided tours of the site arranged by the Southern Ute Reservation. For information on these tours, call (970) 731-5256.

A range of cross-country skiing areas are available near Pagosa Springs, including the **Pagosa Pines Touring Center**, which uses the golf course for a network of 7.5 miles of groomed trails. Ski rentals are available at the clubhouse. Downhill skiing is at its best at the **Wolf Creek Ski Area** on Highway 160 (at Wolf Creek Pass). You'll always find powder at Wolf Creek, as it receives more snowfall than any other ski area in the state—a whopping average of 450 inches a year.

Where to Eat

The **Old Miner's Steakhouse** is your typical Colorado steak and seafood place, with a cozy rustic atmosphere. The restaurant is not licensed. It's open for lunch and dinner and is located three miles northeast of town on Highway 160. The **Rocky Mountain Pie Company** serves good breakfasts and lunches and pie (of course). The **Elkhorn** is a small cafe on Main Street serving Mexican food.

Rocky Mountain National Park

Words can't properly describe the awesome effect of this wilderness area, and even pictures can't tell the story. You have to go there to get the full impact of this magnificent natural area, which straddles the Continental Divide northwest of Denver and Boulder. This is the foremost outdoor attraction in Colorado and it justly deserves the raves it gets from the more than three million visitors who see the park each year.

A movement began, after the turn of the century, to protect and preserve this unique mountain area. It took until 1915 for the federal government and President Woodrow Wilson to dedicate the area as a national park. **Fall River Road**, the first access road through the park, was opened to the public five years later. Through the first half of the century, the park became increasingly popular, drawing visitors from around the world—to the point that damage was done to the mountain environment. New regulations restricting access to the alpine tundra were put into effect and much of the damaged areas have recovered.

It is still possible to reach the high mountain areas, and a relatively new route—**Trail Ridge Road**—runs between **Estes Park** and **Grand Lake**, offering visitors an unparalleled view of the park's 40 miles of Continental Divide and the surrounding alpine region, at a height of more than 12,000 feet in some places. The park headquarters and information center are located at the east boundary of the park, off Highway 36 near the town of Estes Park. Another visitor center is at the west (Grand Lake) entrance.

Elk live within the park and may be seen in the meadows. The park also serves as a home for deer, bears, bighorn sheep, and mountain lions. You'll see eagles and hawks circling overhead.

Camping

Four campgrounds are located within the park, accommodating cars, trailers, and RVs. **Aspen Campground** is located five miles into the park, off Highway 34 near the Fall River entrance and Estes Park. This campground is open year-round. **Glacier Basin Campground** is nine miles west of Estes Park, on Bear Lake Road. This large campground is closed during winter months. **Moraine Park Campground** is another summer operation, located on Moraine Park Road (via Bear Lake Road) three miles from the east park entrance. At the far end of the park, **Timber Creek Campground** is located seven miles inside the west entrance (Grand Lake entrance).

A camping area devoted solely to tent camping is **Long's Peak Campground**, which you reach from Highway 7, south from Estes Park. Drive on Highway 7 for nine miles and turn west to the ranger station. The road leads one mile to the campground.

You can make advance reservations for campsites in the Aspenglen and Glacier Basin Campgrounds year-round by phoning Ticketron at 800-452-1111. You can also write to Ticketron at P.O. Box 617516, Chicago, IL 60661-7516. The other campgrounds are on a first come, first served basis.

Touring the Park

Trail Ridge Road is the primary route through the middle of the park. It begins at the east entrance (at Estes Park) and climbs to 12,000 feet to the Continental Divide and the Alpine Visitor Center. It descends to the Colorado River Valley and ends at the western boundary, near Grand Lake. For details and a Highway Log, see the scenic drive on page 326.

Fall River Road was the original road into the park. To reach it, drive west from Estes Park through the east entrance to the park, continue for another two miles, and turn right. This road is not suitable for trailers and RVs, which are prohibited because of the steep hills and narrow switchback curves. The road is paved for its first two miles from the junction at Highway 34 and then it becomes a gravel, one-way route that climbs for another 11 miles before joining Trail Ridge Road. This junction is at Fall River Pass with an elevation of 11,796 feet. It is possible to pull off the road to view the subalpine and alpine tundra scenery. The road is closed during the winter, around October 15th.

Bear Lake Road provides access to the high lake after a 10-mile drive. You can also take a shuttle bus from the Glacier Basin Campground halfway up the road. At the end of the drive, a short trail leads to the lakeshore. This is a particularly scenic location, the subject of many photographs.

Aspen is a predominant species on the lower reaches of the mountains within the park. Aspen viewing is most popular during the fall, when the groves blaze in yellow hues. Some of the most impressive colors are seen in the **Kawuneeche Valley**, where Trail Ridge Road passes through a 10-mile stretch of aspens between the Timber Lake trailhead and the Grand Lake entrance. Another fine aspen viewing spot is along Bear Lake Road. Take the trail to **Alberta Falls**, a wonderful 1.2-mile round trip filled with scenes of quaking aspen. The eastern slope of **Long's Peak** offers another fine aspen view, via Highway 7 south of Estes Park.

Those who wish to receive a thorough indoctrination to the park and its ecology may wish to enroll with Rocky Mountain Seminars, which calls itself The University Without Walls. The centers for the day-long, weekend, or week-long classes are the Hidden Valley Ski Lodge, 10 miles from Estes Park on Trail Ridge Drive, and Camp Kawuheeche on the west side of the park. Most of the sessions include hiking, and continuing education credit is given for most seminars. Topics of the various seminars include bird-watching, Estes Valley history, wildlife and landscape drawing, photography, and geological studies. For a brochure, write to Rocky Mountain Nature Association, Rocky Mountain National Park, Estes Park, CO 80517 or phone (970) 586-2371, ext. 258 or 294.

Winter visitors will want to check out the park's cross-country skiing possibilities. An easy trail departs from Glacier Basin Campground and leads to Sprague Lake. A number of other trails are close to this camping area. The Alberta Falls trail (from the Glacier Gorge parking area, 11 miles up Bear Lake Road) is part of a longer ski route to three lakes. The trail follows Glacier Creek to its end at Black Lake where you'll get a fine view of Long's Peak and other park scenery.

Silverton

The whole town, high in the San Juan Range, is designated a National Historic Landmark. With a permanent population of 800, this living example of a Victorian mining town is complete with a fine old hotel (the **Grand Imperial**), a courthouse with a gold dome, a nostalgic main street complete with false fronts, old brick buildings, and a passenger train station that still operates as the terminus for the **Durango and Silverton Narrow Gauge Railway**, bringing travelers from Durango each day.

The town is busiest during summer days when the train is in and visitors have about two hours to eat, shop, look at the town, and then return to their train cars. The wise ones stay overnight to fully sample the delights of this unique place. You may choose to drive one way and take the train one way. Many groups of people do this by sharing the driving chores. Put this together with an overnight stay in one of Silverton's hotels or motels and you've got it made! For railway information and reservations, call (970) 387-5416 (Silverton), or (970) 247-2733 (Durango).

In the late 1800s, gold and silver mines were developed, thus opening up several towns in this alpine area, among them Ouray and Lake City. Silverton, in those days, was a bustling, brawling town, with 32 gambling halls and saloons and a street of brothels (Blair Street). Even now, the town is isolated by its location surrounded by the high San Juan Mountains, including **Storm Peak** (the highest, with an elevation of 13,487 feet). The town itself is over 9,000 feet above sea level. The winters are exceedingly long in San Juan County, and agriculture is nonexistent because of the very short growing season.

The town is located 43 miles north of Durango, on the scenic byway known as the San Juan Skyway. North of town is the short but challenging Million Dollar Highway to Ouray. Telluride is about four hours away. The route is featured on the scenic drive on page 346.

Fishing in the area is pretty much restricted to several small lakes that do have good trout fishing. **Molas, Little Molas**, and **Andrews Lakes** are located a few miles south of Silverton, just off Highway 550. Several forest lakes are off the same highway north of Silverton along Forest Road 585. A trail heads from the South Mineral Campground along the South Fork of the creek to four little lakes where cutthroat trout are in good number.

A popular summer activity is jeep touring, using the network of old mining roads and trails through the high alpine area. These roads include the **Black Bear Pass Road** (west of Highway 550, near the Red Mountain summit) and the **Scenic Byway**, which loops from Silverton to Ouray and Lake City. You reach the byway, suited only for four-wheel-drive vehicles, by driving to the north end of Silverton and continuing past the mine operations along the creek. **Ophir Pass**, west of Silverton, is a relatively easy four-wheel-drive experience and connects the area with Telluride. The road is five miles north of town via Highway 550. It passes the townsite of Old Ophir, which is 3.5 miles from the pass. A few people still live here, although the new Ophir townsite was developed to the west near Telluride. For jeep rentals, call (970) 387-5721 or (970) 387-9990. For jeep tours, phone (970) 387-5372.

South Fork

Situated in the Rio Grande River Valley on Highway 160, South Fork lies at a point between Pagosa Springs (to the south), Creede and Lake City (to the west), and Alamosa (to the southeast). Not much of a town of interest for its own sake, this lumbering and logging center is nevertheless the place where many people stay and eat while traveling through this remote area of the San Juan Mountains, or where they stay when skiing the Wolf Creek slopes a few miles south of town. The most attractive thing about South Fork is the fishing to the north. It's a highway town with motels, restaurants, and other businesses spread along Highway 160 and on Highway 149, which leads west along the Rio Grande to Creede.

The Rio Grande National Forest lies around the town, offering a raft of recreation sites. In the high mountain lakes near South Fork and Creede, fishing is excellent. The **Weminuche Wilderness Area** is west of the two towns. A trail leads to three fine fishing lakes: **Little Ruby Lake**, **Ruby Lake**, and **Fuch's Reservoir**. You can fish for rainbow and brook trout in all three. Higher up the mountainside is Trout Lake, where you'll find cutthroat trout.

Fishing is at its most accessible in the Rio Grande River. The guest ranches between South Fork and Creede are a testament to the Rio Grande's attraction for outdoors lovers. Six miles west of South Fork is a stretch of river that runs for about 15 miles (Gold Medal water), which is perfect for wading. Large trout are regularly caught here. You'll also find good fishing for trout farther west along the Rio Grande system, at and above the Rio Grande Reservoir (30 miles west of Creede). Many anglers who fish this area stay in South Fork and make early morning runs to their favorite fishing holes. Several smaller streams feed the Rio Grande between South Fork and Creede. These include Ute Creek, which runs through the Weminuche Wilderness. Little Squaw Creek flows into the Rio Grande at River Hill (a large campground is here). A hike on Fern Creek Trail from the Thirtymile Campground leads to the upper reaches of Little Squaw Creek. For trail information, visit the forest ranger station in Creede.

The **Wolf Creek Ski Area** is noted for its abundant snow (the most snow pack of any ski operation in the state) and its short lineups and low ticket prices. The base sits on the Continental Divide and the mountain goes up from there to an elevation of 11,775 feet.

Where to Eat

The **Hungry Logger** is a large family restaurant at the junction in South Fork. It's open early for breakfast (all those anglers need an early start) and serves lunch and dinner with a standard assortment of chicken fried steak, burgers, and salad bar. **Brown's Sandwich Shop** is a basic pizza and burger place with draft beer. It's next to the Spruce Ski Lodge on east Highway 160. Those who hanker for more than the basics should drive a few miles to Creede (see page 342).

Steamboat Springs

With its ski mountains rising out of cattle country in northern Colorado, the town of Steamboat Springs is a pleasing blend of the old (the mining and ranching roots of the town) and the new (the ultramodern ski developments just outside of the older downtown and residential areas). This separation of the new from the old is what gives the town its special cachet; it is not only a thriving ski resort in winter months but an active summer destination for outdoor adventurers. Six thousand people live here in the place named for the site discovered by French trappers, who were traveling up the Yampa River and heard a chugging sound like that of a steamboat. It turned out to be a hot spring burbling through a small cave beside the river. That spring is no longer chugging, but hot springs feed the large pool downtown, which is now enjoyed by townsfolk and visitors alike. The **Strawberry Hot Springs** offer a more natural alternative.

Skiing is definitely the winter priority here. The U.S. Olympic ski team trains here, and many of America's top skiers have grown up in the town. You'll find two major ski operations in the area. **Steamboat** offers 2,500 acres of skiing spread out over four neighboring mountains. Snow is plentiful here, and the runs offer an amazing range of difficulty. The Storm Peak runs are almost all expert runs, often with powder skiing. Sunshine Peak offers more gentle runs through aspen groves. Thunderhead Mountain offers thrills of a different kind. Daily ski clinics and individual lessons are available. For Steamboat information, call (970) 879-6111. **Howelsen Hill** is the second ski operation, and it was the first ski operation in the area. It is a shorter hill, suitable for family skiing. This is also the hill with ski jumps used for Olympic training. The hill is located near town, across the 5th Street Bridge.

Cross-country skiing is available at the **Steamboat Ski Touring Center**, which turns the Sheraton Golf Course into an excellent series of groomed ski trails leading for more than 17 miles. Ski rentals are available; for information, phone (970) 879-8180. You'll also find an impressive backcountry ski trail system at Rabbit Ears Pass. At the 10,000 foot level, trails fan out through aspen and pine forest. The trail center is located 10 miles south of Steamboat Springs.

A number of guest ranches are open year-round, offering trail rides in the summer and ski trails or sleigh rides when the snow is on the ground. These include the **Home Ranch**, the **Vista Verde Ranch**, and the **All Seasons' Ranch**. For details, see page 423.

Where to Eat

As a resort town, Steamboat Springs offers a wide range of places to eat, from very fancy to western/homestyle. **Mattie Silks** is named in tribute to the notorious madam from Denver who engaged in a pistol duel, killing another woman. This fine Victorian restaurant features French cuisine and a superbly decorated bar area. It's located at Ski Time Square. The **Old West Steak House** is just that, and a fine one too. In addition to beef, this place serves buffalo and elk steaks. It's at 11th and Lincoln. **Old Town Pub** at 8th and Lincoln is a fun place, with draft beer and basic dishes from burger plates to pot roast.

Telluride

Prominent locals, including *Megatrends* author John Naisbitt, claim that Telluride is the most beautiful place on earth. That may be a bit extreme, although Telluride is quite likely the most beautiful place in Colorado.

Nestled in a box canyon along the San Miguel River in the midst of the San Juan Mountains, Telluride is a special town with a special aura in both summer and winter. Part of it comes from its preserved 1875 mining artifacts including historic buildings, a fine old main street, and a large town park near the end of the box canyon. Part of it comes from the fact that Telluride is now the center for great skiing, marvelous outdoor adventure in the **Uncompahgre National Forest,** a thriving and diversified summer arts festival season, and thrills for four-wheel-drive aficionados.

The historic downtown area has a good supply of cafes, most in historic buildings. A stay in the **New Sheridan Hotel** (opened in 1895) will put you back in the gold rush era.

Telluride skiing offers challenging runs for the expert on the mountain's front side and novice runs on the back (south) side. The ski area has some very long and mogul-strewn runs with soft powder most of the time on the front side. It also has, from the summit, the finest scenery of any ski area—anywhere. Several "fourteeners" tower in the San Miguel Range; from 14,000 feet at the top of the lifts, you can see the La Sal Mountains in Utah. The ski area is accessible from downtown and from Telluride Mountain Village, a new and growing hotel and condo development partway up the mountain. For general resort information, phone (970) 728-3041, or write the **Telluride Chamber of Commerce** at 666 West Colorado Avenue, Telluride, CO 81435.

In summer and fall months, Telluride turns into a cultural center with a series of short (weekend or week-long) festivals devoted to a full range of arts activity. Festival themes include jazz, bluegrass, chamber music, film, and much more. The **Jazz Festival** is held in July; the respected **Film Festival** is in early September. Fall brings the **Hang Gliding Festival.**

Anglers fish in the San Miguel and Dolores rivers, in Trout Lake (12 miles south of town), or in Woods Lake, set in a beautiful remote location reached by driving to Sawpit (10 miles north), then driving south on Forest Road 618 for another nine miles to the lake. Fish for rainbow and brook trout and the occasional cutthroat. From the end of the canyon, in town, a short hike will take you to Bridal Veil Falls and Ingram Falls. Walk up the jeep road to the falls and you'll also see the old hydroelectric plant hanging from the top of the ridge. For a short scenic drive, take the Alta Lakes Road south of Telluride via Highway 145. Forest Road 632 leads four miles to the old mining camp of Alta and lakes with fishing and camping. You get great views of Lizard Head Peak, Mount Wilson, and El Diente Peak.

Where to Eat

Most restaurants in Telluride are on the casual side. The oldest eating establishment in town is the **Floradora Saloon**, where you will find food ranging from excellent burgers to Mexican food. **Julian's Restaurant** in the New Sheridan Hotel has cuisine with a northern Italian theme and an extensive wine list. The growing number of ritzy resort hotels, on the resort town's upper level, have their own deluxe restaurants and coffee shops.

Vail

The ski operation in Vail is the largest in North America. Add to this the nearby Beaver Creek and Arrowhead ski areas, and you have more downhill opportunities than any skier could ever ask for. The town of Vail is unlike most of the other resort towns, lacking the historic underpinnings of the older towns. Vail is new, glitzy, and stylish—and it's only 30 years old. It is the vacation home of an ever-growing number of celebrities, and people watching is a prime après-ski activity here. The wealth attached to its sometime-residents means a collection of fine restaurants and some very good hotels and lodges. The town is located 100 miles west of Denver on Interstate 70. For information, write the

Vail Resort Association at P.O. Box 7, Vail, CO 81658 or phone 800-525-9132 (national).

The **Vail Ski Area** combines the best back bowls in America with four base areas and enough lifts to move more than 30,000 skiers each hour. Adults are not permitted on Golden Peak—it's for children only. The Vail Ski School is also America's largest. **Beaver Creek** is located 10 miles west of Vail with a square mile of runs. Lift tickets can be used here or at Vail. In operation since 1980, this is a classy operation where the easiest runs are at the top of the mountain and the expert runs challenge the most experienced skier. **Arrowhead Ski Area** is a much smaller independent operation, two miles from Beaver Creek. Log buildings provide a rustic atmosphere at the base and the whole operation is designed for family skiing. Cross-country skiing is popular in the Vail Valley with backcountry trails in White River National Forest. The Tenth Mountain Trail Association operates a series of ski huts with the intention to connect Vail and Aspen.

Summer recreation centers around hiking, tennis, golf, and summer chairlift rides. Golf clubs are located beside the three ski areas, and you'll find more golfing at the **Singletree Golf Course** at the west end of the valley seven miles from Beaver Creek and the **Eagle-Vail Golf Course** midway between Vail and Beaver Creek. The national forest and the Eagle's Nest Wilderness Area provide fine hiking and backpacking opportunities.

The **Booth Falls Trail** offers a short (two-mile) hike in the Eagle's Nest area. You'll pass a whole series of waterfalls on this walk with wonderful mountain and valley views. To reach the trailhead, take the East Vail exit off Interstate 70 and drive along the frontage road north of the interstate. Drive one mile west, turn onto Booth Falls Road, and drive to its end. For a superb backroad drive, take the Vail Pass Road; just east of the summit, turn onto Shrine Pass Road. The summit (at 11,000 feet) offers fine views of the Sawatch and Tenmile ranges and the Flat Tops in the distance. Continue along the road to Redcliff and Highway 24, which leads to Leadville.

Where to Eat

Mirabelle's, at Beaver Creek, is a renowned French restaurant in an old farmhouse with wonderful decor, superb cuisine, and an impressive wine list. The **Ore House** in Vail has a barn atmosphere and features steaks, seafood, and a huge salad bar. **Alfie Packers** "celebrates" the infamous cannibal of the gold rush period with a similar but less expensive selection of dishes.

Winter Park

Located northwest of Denver, Winter Park and its neighbor, Fraser, provide ski facilities and accommodations in a recreation area that is much more relaxed than the tonier ski resorts of Aspen and Vail. However, rusticity has not hampered the Fraser Valley area in developing its tourist industry. Winter Park is now one of the most popular ski areas in the state. Rio Grande ski trains bring hundreds of skiers from Denver; when the snow disappears in the spring, the area throngs with golfers, anglers, and others who enjoy the recreational opportunities around Winter Park and the Middle Park valley just to the north.

Located on Highway 40, north of Berthoud Pass, Winter Park and the Middle Park area were favorite hunting grounds for the Ute and Arapahoe tribes. Trappers came to the area in the early 1800s and after the turn of the century, nearby Hot Sulphur Springs attracted many tourists to its pools. Skiers have been coming here since the Moffatt Tunnel was opened in 1927 and trails brought skiers from Denver.

The **Winter Park Ski Resort** comprises three interconnected mountains: Winter Park, Mary Jane, and Vasquez Ridge. Mary Jane (with much powder) is for experts, while the other hills attract skiers at all levels. A more recent development is the **SilverCreek Ski Area,** established in 1982 and located 17 miles north of Winter Park on Highway 40. This small area is perfect for family skiing with a separate novice area and good intermediate runs. SilverCreek has an excellent Nordic Center with miles of groomed trails. The **Timberline Ski Area** at Berthoud Pass has both downhill and cross-country skiing. The Sevenmile Trail follows an old wagon road.

During summer months, Winter Park is a way station on the route to Rocky Mountain National Park and provides its own attractions, among them camping in the Arapaho National Forest. There are guest ranches in the area such as the **YMCA Snow Mountain Ranch**, 14 miles north of Winter Park, offering family accommodations including cabins, dorms, and campsites. The Alpine Slide is a long snowy slide (somewhat like a bobsled course) that curves down the Winter Park ski mountain. It has plastic sleds and a lot of family fun. The slide is open from June through Labor Day, seven days a week. For information on Winter Park recreation and accommodations, contact the Fraser Valley Chamber of Commerce at P.O. Box 3236, Winter Park, CO 80482, or phone (970) 726-4118.

Where to Eat

The historic **Riverside Hotel**, in Hot Sulphur Springs, features a unique old dining room, the River Room. The setting and service are excellent with a good view of the Colorado River that runs alongside. The menu changes daily and leans toward seafood, chicken, and chops. The hotel is 26 miles north of Winter Park. In town, **Gasthouse Eichler** has earned an enviable reputation for its German cuisine (schnitzel, sauerbraten, etc.) and seafood. The restaurant is open year-round, except during late April and May. The **Crooked Creek Saloon**, in Fraser, is a raucous place serving breakfast, lunch, and dinner, with burgers, pasta, and steaks. They play music at night.

Colorado
Places to Stay

The following listings are for suggested hotels, motels, and private campgrounds in the Rocky Mountain destination communities. National Forest and National Park campgrounds are listed in the Highway Log pages and in the park (destination) pages. We have tried to include as wide a range of hotel and motel styles and prices as possible for each destination.

ASPEN

Heatherbed Mountain Lodge
1679 Maroon Creek Road
Aspen, CO 81611
(970) 925-7077

Facilities include standard rooms and suites, with a cozy antique ambiance, a pool, hot tub, sauna, and laundry. Some rooms have kitchens. ($ to $$)

Hotel Jerome
330 East Main Street
Aspen, CO 81611
(970) 920-1000 or
800-331-7213

An Aspen original from 1889, this restored wonder includes suites, and the new addition offers many more rooms. Superior accommodations and service. ($$$)

Hotel Lenado
200 South Aspen Street
Aspen, CO 81611
(970) 925-6246

This inn is cozy and romantic, with a multistory lobby, comfortable rooms, and a filling breakfast. Amenities include a hot tub, terrace, and library. ($$$)

Mountain House
Bed and Breakfast
905 East Hopkins Street
Aspen, CO 81611
(970) 920-2550

Rooms and suites, large beds, hot tub, bar, four blocks from ski hill. ($$ to $$$)

**Newcastle/Glenwood
Springs KOA**
581 County Road 241
Newcastle, CO 81647
(970) 984-2240

Full hookups, pool, up to usual KOA standards.

BUENA VISTA

Adobe Inn
303 North Highway 24
P.O. Box 1560
Buena Vista, CO 81211
(719) 395-6340

A very old (more than 100 years) structure, with a few comfortable rooms in two buildings. A Mexican restaurant is located next door. (\$\$ to \$\$\$)

**Buena Vista Family
Campground and RV Park**
27700 County Road 303
Buena Vista, CO 81211
(719) 395-8318

Full trailer and RV hookups, tenting sites, recreation room, and more. Located 2.5 miles south of Buena Vista.

**Mount Princeton
Hot Springs Resort**
15870 County Road 162
Nathrop, CO 81236
(719) 395-2447

The resort is south of Buena Vista. This long time resort has rooms in the main lodge, plus motel units. There are three large hot spring pools, plus rock pools, and hot tubs, a restaurant and lounge. (\$ to \$\$)

CAÑON CITY

Best Western Royal Gorge
1925 Fremont Drive
Cañon City, CO 81212
(719) 275-3377

This is a modern, mid-size motel, with heated pool, whirlpool, trout pond, a restaurant, and lounge. (\$ to \$\$)

Royal View Campground
Highway 50
Cañon City, CO 81212
(719) 275-1900

A conveniently located campground and RV park, with full hookups for trailers, and tent sites, some secluded. Located 1.5 miles west of the Royal Gorge attraction.

CENTRAL CITY

Columbine Campground
On County Road 279

This is the closest campground to Central City, with 47 sites, located 2.1 miles northwest of town. No phone.

Golden Gate Canyon State Park

The park is located seven miles northeast of Black Hawk, via Highway 119, and two miles east on Gap Road. There are sites in the developed campground, plus several primitive campsites. No phone.

Shamrock Inn
351 Gregory Street
Black Hawk, CO 80422
(303) 582-5513

This bed and breakfast home was built about 130 years ago by a Cornish miner. It is well decorated with the three bedrooms on the ground floor. Breakfast is served in the dining room. ($ to $$)

COLORADO SPRINGS

Antlers Hotel
4 South Cascade Avenue
Colorado Springs, CO
80903
(719) 473-5600 or
800-232-2323

The successor to two previous Antlers hotels, this downtown hotel has comfortable rooms, a pool, and offers tennis and golfing at the Broadmoor resort. ($$ to $$$)

The Broadmoor
1 Lake Avenue
Colorado Springs, CO
80906
(719) 634-7711 or
800-634-7711

This is Colorado's (and some say the nation's) top resort hotel complex, a superdeluxe operation containing three hotels. There are hot spring pools, three golf courses, chic shops, tennis courts, restaurants, and lounges. ($$$+)

Cheyenne Mountain Inn
3225 Broadmoor
Valley Road
Colorado Springs, CO
80906
(719) 576-4600 or
800-428-8886

This is another fine, large resort with several modern condo-type buildings. The resort has a golf course, pools, lake with fishing and sailing, restaurants, and lounges. ($$$+)

Hearthstone Inn
506 North Cascade
Avenue
Colorado Springs, CO
80903
(719) 473-4413

A fine B & B operation, the Hearthstone is two Victorian homes near the downtown area. Monument Valley Park is next door. ($$ to $$$)

**Garden of the
Gods Campground**
3704 West
Colorado Avenue
Colorado Springs, CO
80904
(719) 475-9450

This large campground is next to the south entrance to the wonderful city park. Facilities include full hookups, a heated pool, whirlpool, store, and jeep rentals for driving the Pike's Peak backroads.

CORTEZ

Arrow Motor Inn
440 South Broadway
Cortez, CO 81321
(970) 565-3755

A standard motel with large beds, refrigerators, laundry and picnic area. ($ to $$)

Cortez KOA Kampground
27432 East Highway 160
Cortez, CO 81321
(970) 565-9301

Full hookups, laundry, and other KOA features. Located east of town on Hwy. 160.

Holiday Inn Express
2121 East Main Street
Cortez, CO 81321
(970) 565-6000 or
800-626-5652

A modern motel with indoor pool, whirlpool and sauna, large rooms and suites. Restaurants nearby. ($$ to $$$)

Priest Gulch Campground
27646 Highway 145
Dolores, CO 81323
(970) 562-3810

Full hookups, tent sites, drive-through sites, and store. Riverside sites, 23 miles north of Dolores on Highway 145.

Stoner Lodge
25134 Highway 145
Dolores, CO 81323
(970) 882-7825

North of town, this lodge is at the now closed Stoner ski area. There are fine views, a restaurant and bar, with breakfast included. Prices are extremely reasonable. ($)

CREEDE

Broadacres Travelin' Teepee
P.O. Box 39
Creede, CO 81130
(719) 658-2291

This is a ranch and RV park with full hookups beside the Rio Grande. Located five miles west of Creede on Hwy. 149.

Creede Hotel
P.O. Box 284
Creede, CO 81130
(719) 658-2608

This rustic B & B operation is just about the only place to stay in Creede proper. Five rooms with restaurant. ($)

Wason Ranch
P.O. Box 220
Creede, CO 81130
(719) 658-2413

Two miles south of Creede, on the Rio Grande, with modern cabins and great fishing. Cabins have kitchens or kitchenettes. ($$-$$$)

Wetherill Ranch
P.O. Box 370
Creede, CO 81130
(719) 658-2253

A choice of modern and rustic cabins near the Rio Grande, 17 miles southwest of Creede via Hwy. 149. Private fishing spots, ranch restaurant. ($$-$$$)

CRIPPLE CREEK

Imperial Hotel
123 North 3rd Street
Cripple Creek, CO 80813
(719) 689-7777

This historic hotel is an absolute gem. Its dining room is famed for buffet meals, and the hotel stages melodramas during the summer months. Red Rooster Bar. ($ to $$)

Independence Hotel and Casino
P.O. Box 460
Cripple Creek, CO 80813
(719) 689-2744

Now featuring a casino, this hotel still has cheap rates, large beds, laundry. ($)

Lost Burro Campground
4023 County Road 1
P.O. Box 614
Cripple Creek, CO 80813
(719) 689-2345

This campground has RV and tent sites in the woods, four miles north of Cripple Creek.

DENVER

Brown Palace Hotel
321 17th Street
Denver, CO 80202
(303) 297-3111 or
800-321-2599

This is Leadville Johnny's famed hostelry in downtown Denver. Opened in 1892, this hotel has a lobby six stories high, and the whole place is steeped in history. It's a magnificent place to stay or to visit, with rooms and suites, restaurants, and bars. ($$$)

**Holiday Chalet
Bed and Breakfast**
1820 East Colfax Avenue
Denver, CO 80218
(303) 321-9975

A cozy former home, built in 1896, each room has a kitchenette, and the home is beautifully preserved. ($ to $$)

Loew's Giorgio Hotel
4150 East Mississippi
Avenue
Denver, CO 80222
(303) 782-9300 or
800-345-9172
(outside Colorado)

A startling contrast to the Brown Palace, this ultramodern hotel has fine decor that matches the northern Italian food served in the excellent dining room. A complimentary continental breakfast is served. ($$$)

Queen Anne Inn
2147 Tremont Place
Denver, CO 80205
(303) 296-6666 or
800-432-4667

This is Denver's best bed and breakfast, an 1879 home near downtown. It's a perfect place for honeymooning or for anyone visiting Denver for other reasons. Continental breakfast is served. ($$ to $$$)

DURANGO

General Palmer Hotel
567 Main Avenue
Durango, CO 81301
(970) 247-4747 or
800-523-3358
or800-824-2173
(in Colorado)

This historic hotel was built in 1898 and has a wonderful Victorian ambiance and fine service. Complimentary continental breakfast is available. (**$$ to $$$**)

Jarvis Suite Hotel
125 West 10th Street
Durango, CO 81301
(970) 259-6190 or
800-824-1024
(outside Colorado) or
800-228-9836
(in Colorado)

This is a former theater, converted into modern suites. The hotel offers summer railway packages for three nights including a night in Silverton. (**$$ to $$$**)

KOA Kampground
30090 Highway 160
Durango, CO 81301
(970) 247-0783

Full hookups and tent sites, pool, and other KOA amenities. Located east of town.

Strater Hotel
699 Main Avenue
Durango, CO 81301
(970) 247-4431 or
800-247-4431

Another historic hostelry in downtown Durango. Restaurant, saloon, and theater in hotel. (**$$ to $$$**)

ESTES PARK

Glacier Lodge
2166 Highway 66
P.O. Box 2656
Estes Park, CO 80517
(970) 586-4401

This cabin resort is located beside the Big Thompson River. There are cabins—many with fireplaces—rooms in the lodge, a heated pool, facilities for kids, and good food including a cookout on Mondays. (**$$ to $$$**)

Spruce Lake RV Park
1050 Mary's Lake Road
P.O. Box 2497
Estes Park, CO 80517
(970) 586-2889

This is a large RV park with full hook-ups, laundry, and store beside Mary's Lake.

Stanley Hotel
333 Wonderview Street
P.O. Box 1767
Estes Park, CO 80517
(970) 586-3371

Since 1909, this venerable restored hotel has been the "Grand Hotel" of the Colorado Rockies and is on the National Register of Historic Places. The rooms are sumptuous and many have original furniture. The dining room is a delight. ($$$)

YMCA of the Rockies
2515 Tunnel Road
Estes Park, CO 80511-2800
(970) 586-3341

A unique resort with more than 200 cabins and additional lodge rooms set in nearly 1,500 acres of forest. Programs for young people, swimming, riding. ($$ to $$$)

GLENWOOD SPRINGS

The Hideout Campground
1293 County Road 117
Glenwood Springs, CO 81601
(970) 945-5621

A superior RV park, with tent sites and cabins. The Hideout is open year-round with winter sites and cabins available.

Hotel Colorado
526 Pine Street
Glenwood Springs, CO 81601
(970) 945-6511 or 800-544-3998

Opened in 1893, the hotel offers one of the finest historic stays in America. Rooms or deluxe rooms and suites. Dining room and cafe in this Italian Renaissance-style building, which served as the Western White House during the days of Teddy Roosevelt. ($$$)

Hotel Denver
402 7th Street
Glenwood Springs, CO 81601
(970) 945-6565 or 800-826-8820
(in Colorado)

Built in 1906, this historic hotel has been refurbished with a high atrium, lounge, and restaurant. Decorated in Art Deco style, the hotel offers a fine place to stay, across the street from the Amtrak station. ($$ to $$$)

GRAND JUNCTION

Grand Mesa Lodge
Star Route 205
Cedaredge, CO 81413
(970) 856-3211

One of several lodges on the mesa, this one has large cabins that can accommodate families or several couples. Store and restaurant at the resort. (**$$ to $$$**)

LAKE CITY

Crystal Lodge
Lake City, CO 81235
(970) 944-2201

Two miles south of Lake City, the lodge has 14 rooms and a few cabins just above the Lake Fork of the Gunnison River. It has a fine restaurant and a wonderful ambiance. (**$$ to $$$**)

Woodlake Park Campground
Highway 149
Lake City, CO 81235
(970) 944-2283

On a riverbank, this campground is 2.5 miles south of the town on Highway 149. There are RV hookups and tent sites.

LEADVILLE

Delaware Hotel
700 Harrison Avenue
Leadville, CO 80461
(719) 486-1418 or
800-748-2004

The only remaining historic hotel in Leadville, the place exudes the atmosphere of 1888 when the Delaware Block was built. There are rooms and several suites—all with antique furniture. A full breakfast is served to guests. (**$$**)

Hilltop House
100 West 9th Street
Leadville, CO 80461
(719) 486-2362

This small Queen Anne-style home has a few guest rooms with a full breakfast served plus romantic dinners (by reservation). (**$$**)

Sugar Loafin' Campground
303 Highway 300
Leadville, CO 80461
(719) 486-1031

This campground near Turquoise Lake, on County Road 4, has full hookups, tent sites in the woods, showers, laundry, and an ice cream social for guests each evening. It's located 3.5 miles northwest of town.

MANITOU SPRINGS

Gray's Avenue Hotel
711 Manitou Avenue
Manitou Springs, CO
80829
(719) 685-1277 or
800-294-1277

This Victorian-style hotel is in the center of the historic downtown district and was one of the town's original hotels, built in 1885. There are 10 rooms and breakfast is served to guests. (\$\$ to \$\$\$)

Outlook Lodge
Green Mountain Falls, CO
80819
(719) 684-2303

Located 15 miles west of Colorado Springs, off Highway 24, this Victorian B & B operation is in Green Mountain Falls, at the foot of Pike's Peak. The lobby has a large fireplace and the breakfasts are famous. (\$\$)

MESA VERDE NATIONAL PARK

Far View Lodge
P.O. Box 277
Mancos, CO 81328
(970) 529-4421

Inside the national park, the lodge offers good motel-type accommodations and has a restaurant and lounge. Good views of the mesa from the guest rooms. (\$\$ to \$\$\$)

OURAY

The Adobe Inn
651 Liddell Drive
Ridgway, CO 81432
(970) 626-5959

This lodge is located in Ridgway, 10 miles north of Ouray. It lives up to its name with a southwestern ambiance. It's a small hotel with three rooms plus a dorm. Continental breakfast is served to guests. (\$ to \$\$)

KOA Ouray
County Road 4
Ouray, CO 81427
(970) 325-4736

Located four miles north of Ouray, this large campground is open during summer months, with full hookups, tent sites, store, and jeep rentals.

St. Elmo Hotel
426 Main Street
P.O. Box 667
Ouray, CO 81427
(970) 325-4951

This fine B & B was originally a miners' boarding house. Its Victorian character has been preserved and some rooms have parlors. Breakfast is served to guests. (**$$ to $$$**)

Wiesbaden Hot Springs Spa
P.O. Box 349
Ouray, CO 81427
(970) 325-4347

Guests at this downtown hotel have the use of the vapor cave and the hot mineral pool. There's also a sauna and the hotel offers spa services. Free coffee and tea are available. A rustic cabin is set on the hill above the hotel. (**$$**)

PAGOSA SPRINGS

Davidson's Country Inn
Highway 160
Pagosa Springs, CO 81147
(970) 264-5863

Located two miles northeast of town, this is an excellent B & B with 10 rooms, all different, plus a game room and savory breakfasts. (**$ to $$**)

Echo Manor Inn
3366 Highway 84
Pagosa Springs, CO 81147
(970) 264-5646

A sprawling hotel with wonderful views of the San Juans, it has a number of themed rooms and suites and is located three miles south of town on Hwy. 84 across the road from Echo Lake. It's a comfortable and somewhat eccentric (fun) place to stay. (**$$ to $$$**)

The Spa Motel
317 Light Plant Road
Pagosa Springs, CO 81147
(970) 264-5910

An extremely modest (and inexpensive) motel, with the only hot springs pool in Pagosa Springs. Large outdoor pool and indoor bath houses. The yard has picnic tables. (**$**)

SILVERTON

Silverton Lakes Campground
Silverton, CO 81433
(970) 387-5721

With RV hookups and tent sites, this campground is located northeast of Silverton with only a short walk to the Animas River. Store and laundry. Jeeps can be rented here.

Teller House
1250 Greene Street
P.O. Box 2
Silverton, CO 81433
(970) 387-5423

This small hotel is located on top of the French Bakery Restaurant, and that is where guests have a full breakfast as part of the room fare. There are well-furnished private rooms as well as dorms for men and women. Hostelers are welcome. (**$ to $$**)

Wingate House
1045 Snowdon Street
Silverton, CO 81433
(970) 387-5713

This B & B home is an authentic restored Victorian, built in 1886. While the beds are in the home, the full breakfast is served at the adjacent French Bakery Restaurant. The kitchen in the house is available to guests. (**$$**)

Wyman Hotel
1371 Greene Street
Silverton, CO 81433
(970) 387-5372

This is the most comfortable and satisfying of the regular hotels in Silverton. Each room has a private bath. Video movies are available to guests. No smoking. (**$ to $$**)

SOUTH FORK

Riverbend Resort RV Park
P.O. Box 129
South Fork, CO 81154
(719) 873-5344

This campground is located three miles southwest of town and has a scenic site beside the South Fork of the Rio Grande River. Full hookups, tent sites, and cabins.

South Fork Campground
26359 West Highway 160
South Fork, CO 81154
(719) 873-5500

This is a large, typical KOA operation by the Rio Grande. Full hookups, tent sites, store, laundry, and recreation room. It's located east of town.

STEAMBOAT SPRINGS

Harbor Hotel
703 Lincoln Avenue
P.O. Box 774109
Steamboat Springs, CO
80477
(970) 879-1522 or
800-543-8888
(in the United States)

This is a long time Steamboat hotel operation, and the rooms are furnished with antiques. A separate motel next to the old hotel has regular motel rooms and condo units. Hot tubs and a sauna. (**$$ to $$$**)

Home Ranch
(970) 879-1780 and
Vista Verde Ranch
(970) 879-3858 or
800-526-RIDE

Two guest ranches located north of Steamboat at the edge of Routt National Forest offer fine vacation experiences. The ranches have summer accommodations and activities, as well as cross-country skiing during the snowy months. They offer weekly packages during summers and the Home Ranch has a three-day package. The food at both ranches is of gourmet quality. (**$$$**)

TELLURIDE

New Sheridan Hotel
231 West Colorado
Avenue
Telluride, CO 81435
(970) 728-4351

This historic landmark, dating back to 1895, has a variety of rooms and a few have private baths. Don't let that deter you from staying in this wonderful place. All rooms have TV and are comfortable. The ambiance is superb and the food in the dining room (Julian's) is fine. (**$$ to $$$**)

Town Park Campground
(970) 728-3071

This civic campground is in the center of things in the townsite. It's busy during summer months when the festivals are happening in the park. No hookups for RVs.

Victorian Inn
401 West Pacific Avenue
P.O. Box 217
Telluride, CO 81435
(970) 728-6601

This modern (1976) hotel has rooms with private and shared baths. Sauna and hot tub. Continental breakfast is served to guests. ($$)

VAIL

Comfort Inn
161 West Beaver Creek
Boulevard
P.O. Box 5510
Avon, CO 81620
(970) 949-5511 or
800-423-4374

This chain motel in nearby Avon offers reasonable prices and accommodations. It has a swimming pool and whirlpool and offers free continental breakfast. ($$)

The Lodge at Vail
174 East Gore Creek Drive
Vail, CO 81657
(970) 476-5011 or
800-331-LODG

This was Vail's original inn, a large alpine chalet-type hotel. It has a European ambiance with rooms and suites of various sizes. Heated pool, whirlpool, saunas, and an exercise room. ($$$)

WINTER PARK

Riverside Hotel
P.O. Box 22
Hot Sulphur Springs, CO
80451
(970) 725-3589

This historic hotel in Hot Sulphur Springs (26 miles north of Winter Park) has 21 rooms furnished with antiques and shared baths. It has a wonderful bar, and its Riverside Restaurant is outstanding. ($)

Index

The listings in this index cover the drives, cities, towns, and significant attractions that are found in the Destinations pages for this book. When information on attractions is included in the Drives section for each state, these attractions are also included in the index with page numbers shown in bold type. Parks (camping and day-use) along the scenic routes are listed in the highway logs which accompany maps in the Drives pages.

425